MATERIALIEN ZUM AUSLÄNDISCHEN UND INTERNATIONALEN PRIVATRECHT

HERAUSGEGEBEN VOM MAX-PLANCK-INSTITUT FÜR
AUSLÄNDISCHES UND INTERNATIONALES PRIVATRECHT

Direktor: Professor Dr. Konrad Zweigert

23

European Private International Law
of Obligations

Acts and Documents of an International Colloquium
on the European Preliminary Draft Convention on the
Law Applicable to Contractual and Non-Contractual Obligations

held in Copenhagen on April 29 and 30, 1974

Edited

by

OLE LANDO
Copenhagen

BERND VON HOFFMANN
Hamburg

KURT SIEHR
Hamburg

1975

J. C. B. MOHR (PAUL SIEBECK) TÜBINGEN

CIP-Kurztitelaufnahme der Deutschen Bibliothek

European private international law of obligations: acts and documents of an Internat. Colloquium on the Europ. Preliminary Draft Convention on the Law Applicable to Contractual and Non-Contractual Obligations, held in Copenhagen on April 29 and 30, 1974 / ed. by Ole Lando [u. a.].

(Materialien zum ausländischen und internationalen Privatrecht; 23)

ISBN 3-16-636822-1

NE: Lando, Ole [Hrsg.], International

Colloquium on the European Preliminary Draft Convention on the Law Applicable to Contractual and Non-Contractual Obligations ⟨1974, København⟩

Satz und Druck: Buchdruckerei Eugen Göbel, Tübingen

Einband: Großbuchbinderei Heinr. Koch, Tübingen

PREFACE

In private international law one of the most controversial subjects is which law is applicable to contractual and non-contractual obligations.

It has been disputed in both the schools and the courts. The legislators of the world have in general done little about it and international conventions covering the subject are relatively few.

In many countries the courts have not brought about the necessary predictability in the national law. Furthermore, in so far as it is ascertainable, the conflict of laws of torts and contracts of the various countries differs considerably. The consequence of this state of affairs has been uncertainty. It is understandable that many lawyers try to stay away from this subject which they regard with fear and suspicion.

There is a need for predictability and for rules. World trade and world communication have been growing rapidly over the last 30 years. Goods, money and people cross frontiers to an extent never seen before, and with them come the legal disputes and the conflict of law issues.

Therefore, one must greet the initiative of the Commission of the European Communities for having made an effort to create European uniformity of law in this field, and one must greet the Group of Experts which in 1972 has provided a Draft Convention on the Law Applicable to Contractual and Non-Contractual Obligations.

One of the purposes of the Colloquium held in Copenhagen on April 29 and 30, 1974, the acts and documents of which are published in the present volume, was to discuss the Draft Convention with experts from countries which, though belonging to the nations of Western Europe, are not members of the EC. Austria and Switzerland are countries of high and influential legal culture having intensive commercial contacts with the rest of Western Europe. We were, therefore, happy to see representatives from these countries at the meeting and to receive reports from them commenting on the Draft Convention.

Danish lawyers have had for more than a hundred years very close ties to their Scandinavian colleagues. In a division of the world into families of law Denmark, Finland, Iceland, Norway and Sweden belong to one family, the Nordic one. Their cooperation in legislation is well-known. Trade between the five countries has always been considerable, and the creation of the European Free Trade Area intensified it very much. Though Denmark now belongs to the EC, she cannot and will not break the Nordic cooperation. Being tied at the same time to the EC countries and to the Nordic countries may create a problem for her. One way of trying to solve this problem is to invite representatives from the Nordic countries to discuss the rules being drafted in the EC. We were, therefore, happy to greet the representatives from Finland, Norway and Sweden at the meeting and to receive reports from them.

Most members of the Working Group of Experts who made the Preliminary Draft and who all belong to the six old EC countries were present and took part in the discussions after the general reports had been given. These discussions are now summarized and integrated in the general reports with a few exceptions due to most regrettable interruptions in the tape recording.

The Draft Convention was published in 1972 before the entry of Denmark, Ireland and the United Kingdom into the European Communities. Representatives from these countries did not have an opportunity to influence the present Draft. But most of the newly appointed members of the Group of Experts from these countries were present at the meeting.

Monsieur *Jenard,* the Chairman of the Group, had the excellent idea that we should solicit some of the commercial and industrial organisations to send representatives, and several took part in the meeting including a representative of the International Chamber of Commerce.

Several persons and organisations have made it possible to arrange the meeting and to publish the reports and the discussions. We are indebted to the Commission of the European Communities, to "Foreningen til Unge Handelsmænds Uddannelse" and to "Otto Mønsteds Fond" for having financially supported the Colloquium. We thank the Rector of the Copenhagen School of Economics and Business Administration, Professor *Jan Kobbernagel,* for his interest and help in the arrangement of the meeting. We are also obliged to Mr. *Richard Cox,* Stockholm, for checking the English of the general reports and to Monsieur *Marc Fallon,* Louvain, for preparing the French version of *Lando's* report and the résumés of the general reports.

Finally we thank the board of editors of the „Materialien zum ausländischen und internationalen Privatrecht" who kindly consented to the publication of the acts and documents of the Colloquium in that series.

Hamburg and Copenhagen, August 1975

                Bernd von Hoffmann   Ole Lando   Kurt Siehr

CONTENTS

GENERAL REPORTS

SPECIAL REPORTS

DRAFT CONVENTION AND RAPPORT

TABLES

GENERAL REPORT ON CONTRACTUAL OBLIGATIONS

By

BERND VON HOFFMANN

Hamburg *

A. The Determination of the Proper Law of Contract

I. Party Autonomy

1. The Choice of Law by the Parties of the Contract: Art. 2 (1)

Art. 2, para. 1, of the Draft contains a full recognition of the principle of party autonomy: the contract is governed by the law that is chosen by the parties. In principle, that law will govern the contract as a whole to the exclusion of every other law, even to the extent that mandatory provisions of other laws are excluded from application. There are some exceptions to this principle, however, and these will be treated later (*sub* III).

The principle of party autonomy, as such, is universally accepted. The parties' choice of law has proved to be superior to any system which attempts to determine the applicable law by objective connecting factors. This principle ensures the foreseeability of the applicable law at the beginning of the contractual obligation. Moreover, the parties know best the relevant connecting factors of the particular agreement.

---

* *Abbreviated literature:* The Law Commission and the Scottish Law Commission, Private International Law, E.E.C. Preliminary Draft Convention on the Law Applicable to Contractual and Non-contractual Obligations, Consultative Document (August 1974); *D. Mayer,* Information (Comité français de d. i. p., Colloque du 24 mars 1973 sur l'Avant-projet ...): Rev. crit. 62 (1973) p. 373 to 380; *Siehr,* Zum Vorentwurf eines EWG-Übereinkommens über das Internationale Schuldrecht: AWD 1973, p. 569–587; *Zweigert/Kropholler,* Sources of International Uniform Law I (1971) and II (1972).

There is less consensus, however, as to the conditions and limits of party autonomy.

2. *Is the Choice of Law Restricted to International Contracts: Art. 1 (1)?*

The Draft does not contain a particular provision as to the conditions of a choice of law. Art. 1, para. 1, which delimits the scope of the Convention provides that the rules of this Convention shall apply in situations of an international character.

a) The Scope of the Convention. – Lando[1] emphasizes that there are two distinct problems. The first of these problems is whether the scope of the Convention as a whole should be confined to situations of an international character or whether it should also be extended to foreign situations not of an international character. The General Reporter will give you an example: in a contract for the sale of a house both parties have their residence in France. The house is situated in that country and the payments are effectuated there. Afterwards the vendor moves to England. The purchaser brings an action for rescission of the contract to the English courts, stating that the house has hidden defects. According to art. 19 the burden of proof is to be determined not by the *lex fori*, but by the law which governs the contract. There is no reason why this provision should be restricted to international cases and why it should not be applied to foreign cases as well.

In the discussion, *Batiffol*, referring to *Wengler*, stated that an originally domestic situation may become an international one through circumstances arising later[2]. Therefore the subsequent change of residence may be regarded as an element which will establish the international character of the relation. This would have the effect of making the Convention applicable; even a subsequent choice of law, for instance the choice of the law of the forum, will be admitted.

The General Reporter is convinced by this argument. He would not admit, however, that a domestic contract would acquire an international character through the mere fact that it was taken to a foreign court. For those cases, the question of including foreign situations in the scope of the Convention would subsist.

Therefore, *Lando, Siehr* and *Hoyer* suggest the deletion of art. 1, para. 1, of the Draft[3].

---

[1] *Lando, infra* p. 125 s., and RabelsZ 38 (1974) p. 8 s.

[2] *Wengler*, The General Principles of Private International Law: Rec. des Cours 104 (1961-III) p. 273, 417 ss.

[3] *Lando, infra* p. 126, and RabelsZ 38 (1973) p. 9; *Siehr* p. 571 s.; *Hoyer, infra* p. 115.

The second problem is whether or not party autonomy should be restricted to contracts containing an international element. *Lando* and *Lipstein*[4] support this position.

In the discussion, *Schultsz* pleaded for the admission of choice-of-law agreements even in those situations which do not contain an international element. The EC Convention on Jurisdiction and Enforcement of Judgments allows the parties to choose a foreign tribunal even if the issue does not contain an international element[5]. It would be difficult to adopt a completely different attitude in this Convention. To *Lando's* objection that parties should not be permitted to contract out of mandatory provisions in domestic situations, *Schultsz* replied that these would come into play by means of art. 7.

The Draft, in its present form, avoids taking up a clear position on this second question, leaving it outside the scope of application of the Convention. According to the Draft, the problem is to be left to non-unified conflict rules of the *lex fori*[6]. This does not seem to be a good solution, as it will open the door to "forum shopping".

b) The Definition of "International" Contracts. – A primary question raised by the Draft is: "What constitutes a contract having an international character?" Neither the Convention itself nor the Report gives further explanations on this point. *Lando* approves of this attitude, as it would be impossible to give an exact definition of the international contract[7]. *Siesby*, on the other hand, holds that the term "international" should be defined[8].

In the discussion, *van Hoogstraten* referred to the deliberations of the Hague Conference of Private International Law. The same question had been exhaustively discussed when preparing the Convention on the Law Applicable to International Sales of Goods[9]. The scope of that convention was limited to international sales of goods (art. 1, para. 1). The draftsmen preferred not to give a positive definition of what constitutes an "international" sale[10]. Art. 1, para. 4, however, gave a negative definition, providing: "The mere declaration of the parties, relative to the application of a law or the competence of a judge or arbitrator, shall not be sufficient to confer upon a sale the international character provided for in the first paragraph of this article."

Gothot introduced an alternative approach to the determination of what constitutes an international contract. It is commonly held that in order to

---

[4] *Lando, infra* p. 126, and RabelsZ 38 (1974) p. 9; *Lipstein, infra* p. 156.

[5] *Droz*, Compétence judiciaire et effets des jugements dans le Marché Commun (1972) nos. 207 s. (p. 129 s.); *von Hoffmann*, Das Europäische Übereinkommen über die gerichtliche Zuständigkeit . . .: AWD 1973, p. 57, 63, both with reference to the Report on that Convention.

[6] Rapport, *infra* p. 251.

[7] *Lando, infra* p. 126, and RabelsZ 38 (1974) p. 9.

[8] *Siesby, infra* p. 213.

[9] U.N.T.S. vol. 510, p. 149, no. 7411 (1964).

[10] *Cf.* Act. La Haye 7: 1951 (1952) p. 18 ss.

define the international character of a contract, it is necessary to take the contract as the starting point. An alternative approach would be to start from the legal systems involved. Thus a contract is an international one if more than one legal system has a claim for application. Following this second approach, when only one legal system has a claim for application, there would not be a place for any conflict-of-law rule, not even for party autonomy. *Batiffol* considered it would be difficult to introduce *Gothot's* approach into the Draft. In international contracts there is no predetermined law applicable to the issue; that is the reason for giving the choice to the parties. Moreover the present tendency is to regard as international contracts all those contracts which involve international commerce, even if there is no immediate contact with more than one country.

The classical approach to the determining of what constitutes an international contract is the geographical one: a contract is international when the parties each maintain their residence in different countries, or when the transaction involves the movement of goods, services or payments across the frontiers of a country[11]. In the actual practice of international business this approach sometimes seems to be too narrow. In some fields of international commerce, the difference between international and internal markets disappears. In reality, businessmen deal with foreign firms just as they do with domestic firms.

The corn trade[12] is a typical example of what is called by French writers[13] the *"société internationale des commerçants"*. In international corn trade it is customary to use the standard forms of the London Corn Trade Association. Disputes are submitted to arbitration in London, even if the particular transaction has no connection with England. There is, as will be seen, an implied choice of English law, too. When the Hamburg corn dealer sells corn purchased from an American seller, he customarily incorporates in his sales contract with domestic or foreign buyers the same standard forms under which he himself purchased the corn. Therefore, in the foregoing example, the possibility of choosing English law should not be excluded, even if the final contract does not contain a geographically international element[14].

---

[11] *Cf. Julliot de la Morandière*, in: Act La Haye 6: 1928 (1928) p. 373.

[12] On international corn trade *Schwob*, Les contrats de la London Corn Trade Association (1928); *Großmann/Doerth*, Das Recht des Überseekaufs I (1930) p. 32 note 19; *Ph. Kahn*, La vente commerciale internationale (1961) p. 21 ss.

[13] *Ph. Kahn*, (*supra* note 12) p. 17 ss.; *Goldman*, Frontières de droit et lex mercatoria: Arch. phil. dr. 9 (1964) p. 177, 192.

[14] *Cf. Meijers*, in: Act. La Haye 7: 1951 (1952) p. 21; *M. Wolff*, Private International Law² (1950) p. 420 s.

In this context, mention must also be made of the draft of a European Communities Regulation on Insurance Contracts[15]. That draft enables party autonomy to be applied in insurance contracts without limiting it to international cases. In that draft, the underlying rationale is said to be the following: When an industrial insurance contract is offered by an English company according to English law, it must be possible for the competitors to offer the same legal conditions even if they have their place of business in the same country as the enterprise to be insured[16]. From this example, the general statement may be deduced that law is among the market conditions which affect competition. When the European Common Market aims to offer to the residents of the member states equal access to all markets in the Community, it cannot at the same time worsen the market position of domestic enterprises by refusing to allow them to offer the same legal conditions as those offered by foreigners. Perhaps both examples are covered by the formula "international contracts". Nevertheless, it seems desirable to make it clear in the Report that this term is not to be understood in a narrow geographical sense[17].

Siesby in this context puts stress on one other point: parties should not be allowed the discretionary power to give the contract an international character, *e. g.* by simply inserting a choice-of-forum or by choosing a place of contracting on the other side of the national frontier[18].

3. No Need for a Territorial Connection of the Chosen Law with the Transaction

The Draft does not contain the requirement that the law chosen must have a local connection with the contract. Thus the Draft enables the parties to select a law which inspires particular confidence because the legal system within which it operates is highly experienced in that particular kind of contracts – as, once more, English law is for the corn trade[19].

The Draft does not contain a clause restricting party autonomy in the sense that the choice of law must be "bona fide and legal", to use the phrase familiar to English lawyers[20]. *Siesby* would like to introduce this clause[21]. This restriction seems to be inspired by the fear that the

---

[15] Doc. XIV/59/72.
[16] *Cf. Imbert, infra* p. 31.
[17] *Cf. Lipstein, infra* p. 155.
[18] *Siesby, infra* p. 213.
[19] *Cf. supra* note 12.
[20] Lord *Wright* in *Vita Food Products, Inc.* v. *Unus Shipping Co. Ltd.,* [1939] A. C. 277, 290,
[21] *Siesby, infra* p. 213.

parties could escape by a choice of law from mandatory dispositions of a law closely connected with the transaction. Art. 7, however, seems to provide a good intrument for meeting this danger and for that reason there is perhaps no need to insert these restrictions as to the choice of law.

4. The Splitting of the Contract by the Choice-of-Law Agreement

The Working Group did not propose a provision as to splitting the applicable law by a choice of two or more laws for the different parts of the contract[22]. Practitioners say that this is more a problem for law students. The General Reporter would concur in this lack of interest; the Working Group's omission, then, does not seem to be a matter for reproach.

5. The Subsequent Choice of Law: Art. 3

As to the time of the choice of law, art. 3 provides that the choice may be changed at any time by the agreement of the parties. This change, however must be without prejudice to the rights of third parties. As *Lipstein* says, this reservation in favour of rights of third parties is novel but acceptable[23].

Courts of law have a strong homeward trend: they prefer to apply the well-known law of the forum to applying "nasty" foreign law. Therefore they like to deduce from the conduct of the parties a tacit choice of law. In general, the General Reporter cannot see anything wrong in it. It should be clear, however, that a choice of law made subsequently to the making of the contract cannot have a broader effect than an original choice of law. If some rules protecting weak parties cannot be excluded by an initial choice of law, a subsequent choice cannot have a greater effect. *Lando* puts this idea forward in connection with those specific kinds of contract for which he proposes a total exclusion of the parties' choice of law[24]. *Hoyer* proposes the exclusion of the possibility of a subsequent choice of law in labour contracts rather than excluding, from the parties' choice of law, mandatory provisions of the law of the place where the work is carried out[25]. But will this proposal bring about the desired protection of the employee? A prudent employer, it seems, will always draft a choice-of-law clause.

---

[22] Rapport, *infra* p. 265 s.
[24] *Lando*, RabelsZ 38 (1974) p. 25 s.
[25] *Hoyer*, *infra* p. 116.

[23] *Lipstein*, *infra* p. 158.

II. The Proper Law in the Absence of a Choice of Law by the Parties

1. General Remarks

In the event that the parties have not incorporated a choice-of-law clause in the contract, there are in theory two starting points for the determination of the applicable law. First, one may look at the circumstances surrounding the formation and execution of the particular case, considering *inter alia* the place of negotiation, the language employed, the place for performance, and the *situs* of jurisdiction or arbitration. Sometimes there is a clear preponderance of contacts which tend to point to a certain centre of gravity. Often, however, the contacts are ambiguous, pointing partly to one law and partly to another. Moreover, the boundaries between clear preponderance, slight preponderance and arbitrary location are not easily established. The so-called "subjective" approach offers the possibily of achieving the most satisfactory conflict solution in some cases. But this advantage must to be weighed against the inconvenience of unforeseeability in the majority of cases.

On the other hand, while the so-called "objective" approach does ensure forseeability it does not always guarantee an adequate solution. This objective approach takes from the manifold contacts of a contract one that is typically of decisive importance. Thes approach can either appoint one element for all contracts; it must then choose between the place of conclusion and that of performance. Or it can make a distinction between the different types of contract and indicate the element that characterizes each type of contract.

2. The Approach of the Draft

Art. 4 abolishes the *lex loci contractus* and the *lex loci solutionis* as general points of connection[26].

In the discussion *van Hoogstraten* stressed that this was a progressive solution. The tendency to split up one single contract is thereby eliminated. – Concerning the place of conclusion, *Batiffol* added the remark that it might retain some value as a rule of last resort for contracts in which there is a strict balance between the obligations of either parties, as, *e. g.*, in exchange contracts. It was a "solution of despair".

The Draft attempts to establish a system combining different approaches. The main topic in art. 4 is that of the characteristic obligation

---

[26] The *Austrian Ministry of Justice, infra* p. 81 would prefer to take the place of contracting as a general point of connection of those contracts, for which there is not provided a specific rule of connection.

(para. 2). After a presentation of this concept (a) there will be reported
the general discussion on the system of art. 4 (b). Finally there will
be treated the particular question of the so-called "tacit" choice of
law (c).

a) The Characteristic Obligation: Art. 4 (2). – Art. 4, para. 2, provides
that the connection of a contract is closest with the country in which
the party who is to carry out the characteristic obligation has his
habitual residence or place of business.

Lando supports this approach on the following ground: for all contracts of "sale", in the broader sense, (including lease of movables,
insurance, agency and other contracts for the rendition of services)
the seller's obligations are usually more complex and therefore more
regulated by law than are those of the buyer[27].

In the discussion, *Lando* stated that it was not only the complexity which
should determine the characteristic performance but also the consideration
that an enterprise which has to draw up many contracts should have the
opportunity to have them governed by the same law.

Siehr criticizes the opinion, expressed in the Working Group's Report, that the obligation of the party which has to pay money cannot
be the characteristic obligation[28]. He reasons that in instalment contracts the obligation of the buyer could be regarded as having the
predominant characteristic.

Drobnig stressed the point that the identification of the seller with the party
which carries out the characteristic performance was not covered by the
wording of art. 4, para. 2, but only by a statement in the Report. On the basis
of the text of art. 4, para. 2, one could very well support the idea that the
buyer who has to pay instalments for a period auf 20 or 30 months makes the
characteristic performance. The Convention, however, should not be re-
proached for leaving the question open; for this will enable the courts to
develop particular rules adapted to each type of contract.

As to contracts for the carriage of goods by sea, *Selvig* adds some
critical remarks[29]: art. 4, para. 2, would focus upon the law of the place
in which the carrier has his principal place of business. That law will
be frequently the law of a distant country not linked in any way with
the particular contract. As *Selvig* points out contracts involving time
charterparties would perhaps be the only cases suited to the application of the law of the shipowner. This criticism may be extended to all
kinds of international transport contracts.

It seems to me that the fundamental idea behind art. 4, para. 2,
namely that there should be developed a general criterion of connec-

---

[27] *Lando*, RabelsZ 38 (1973) p. 30.
[28] *Siehr*, p. 576.   [29] *Selvig, infra* p. 197.

tion for each type of contract, merits full approval. The formula of the characteristic obligation, however, is manifestly too narrow to cover all types of contract. Many contracts are not primarily concerned with an exchange of goods and services for money; rather they contain an element of mutual confidence and collaboration, as in contracts of cooperation, sales concession and agency. In these cases it is doubtful whether the obligation of one party can be really identified as being the more complicated one.

Nor can there be held to be a prevailing convenience for one party to calculate its risks by submitting all his contracts to the same law. In contracts of distributorship, *e. g.,* manufacturers as well as distributors often have parallel contracts with partners in different foreign countries and would prefer to have them all submitted to their own law. Then, additional policies must be considered and weighed. In agency contracts, *e. g.,* the law of the agent may be preferred for similar social reasons as to those applying the law of the employee. In several types of contracts it would be possible to develop general criteria of connection by admitting a broader scale of deliberations in order to determine the characteristic performance.

In other contracts it seems that the place of residence of the party which carries out the characteristic obligation is inadequate for determining the applicable law. This is true not only for contracts of transportation, this may also be true for building contracts and some kinds of service contracts. The place of performance could often give an adequate general criterion of connection [29a]. The development of general criteria in those types of contract would not be covered by art. 4, para. 2. Art. 4, para. 1, too, would not allow the development of general rules; this paragraph seems to give prevalence to the individualistic features of the particular contract.

In the discussion, *von Overbeck* raised the question whether art. 4, para. 2, was not drafted in too abstract a way. Obviously it is impossible to establish a complete catalogue containing for each type of contract a specification of the applicable law. It might be useful, however, to enumerate several contracts of particular importance and frequency indicating the applicable law [30]. Such an enumeration can be found in the Austrian draft prepared by *Schwind* [31] and in the Czechoslovakian Act on Private International Law [32]. Such a short

---

[29a] *Cf.* Law Commission p. 31.

[30] This suggestion has already been made by *Siehr* p. 576, with reference to the German Democratic Republic's draft in note 90. *Cf.* Law Commission p. 31.

[31] *Schwind,* Entwurf eines Bundesgesetzes über das internationale Privat- und Prozeßrecht: Z. f. Rvgl. 12 (1971) p. 161–248, § 35.

[32] Art. 10. French translation: Loi sur le droit international privé et de

list of examples could contain, *e. g.*, the contracts of sale of goods, of work on goods, and of commercial agency.

b) The System of Art. 4[32a]. – In the discussion, *Selvig* raised the question of the system followed by art. 4. Para. 2 seems to be the basic rule: whenever there can be identified a characteristic obligation, the law of the habitual residence of the party that carries out the characteristic obligation will generally be applied; the exceptions to this rule are stated in para. 3. The real importance of para. 1 would be in its application to those contracts in which there does not exist a characteristic obligation. In the law of agency, *e. g.*, it seems difficult to say that either supplying or marketing of the goods is more characteristic. Therefore *Selvig* proposed to draft art. 4 in the following way: it should start with the present para. 2, then would follow para. 3; para. 1 should be placed at the end of the article. Concerning the system followed by art. 4, *Lagarde* held that para. 1 gives the general guideline. When the contract contains a characteristic obligation, then it is recommended to the courts to apply para. 2. When there is no characteristic obligation or when this performance does not characterize the whole of the contractual operation (para. 3), the judge will have to select the closest relationship from the elements of the particular case.

Hjerner saw some inconsistency between para. 1 and para. 2 of art. 4. The first paragraph seemed to introduce as a main rule the rule of the closest connection, whereas the second paragraph introduced the rule of the characteristic obligation. It would be useful to clarify the relationship between these two ideas. The question will arise very frequently in so-called "combined contracts". Licence contracts may be combined with sales or with cross licences. The classical example is distributorship. In all those combined contracts, there would arise the question whether the whole transaction should be governed by one and the same law or whether it should be split into several contracts with their respective characteristic obligation and proper law. *Batiffol* was doubtful whether a general answer could be given to the question whether or not the different parts of an agreement made on the same sheet of paper would serve different aims and therefore could be given a separate treatment in the conflicts-of-law field. This question must be reserved for an analysis of the facts of the particular agreement.

Duchek feared that the compromise between strong and flexible rules attempted by art. 4 might break down in practice. In those countries which are accustomed to rigidity, courts would prefer to apply art. 4, para. 2, whereas courts in the other countries would continue to rely on art. 4, paras. 1 and 3. Austria would favour more clarity and precision[33]. *Batiffol* admitted that this concern was justified; he would hope, however, that the jurisdiction of the European Court would achieve some uniformity.

c) The "Tacit" Choice of Law[33a]. – Art. 4 only comes into play when

procédure civile du 4 décembre 1963, in: T.M.C. Asser Instituut, Les Législations de d. i. p. (1971) 261.

[32a] *Cf.* Law Commission p. 32.

[33] *Cf. Republic of Austria, Ministry of Justice, infra* p. 80.

[33a] *Cf.* Law Commission p. 21.

there was neither an express nor a tacit choice of the applicable law by the parties. As to the "tacit" choice of law, both the Draft and the Report are silent upon what this phrase actually means. Other conventions are not so reluctant to define this point. Art. 2, para. 2, of the Hague Convention of 15 June 1955[34] on the Law Applicable to International Sales of Goods has provided a rather restrictive formula. It says: "Such designation must be contained in an express clause, or unambiguously result from the provisions of the contract."

In the discussion, *Schultsz* raised the question why this formula was not adopted for the present Convention.

In several countries, including England and Germany, courts have a more generous attitude towards the assumption of an "implied" or "tacit" choice of law[35]. Those courts, *e. g.*, derive the presumption of choice of law from jurisdiction and arbitration clauses. *Selvig* points out the particularly frequent application of this rule in maritime contracts[36]. A tacit choice of law also will be derived from the language and legal terminology employed, particularly in adhesion contracts[37].

Moreover, *e. g.*, German courts do not attempt to establish a clearcut distinction between the tacit and the hypothetical choice of law[38]. Therefore, if the adjective "tacit" is taken in the broad sense, courts could exclude the application of art. 4, para. 2, in many cases in which a characteristic performance can be established, even if the stringent conditions of art. 4, para. 3, are not fulfilled.

In the discussion, *Volken* was concerned to prevent a possible abuse of art. 4, para. 3, as a means of introducing the hypothetical choice of law. *Lagarde* admitted that the somewhat feeble adjective "tacit" could admit of several different interpretations. The Working Group certainly had the intention to exclude reference to the hypothetical choice of law. The Group, however, thought that one could not impose a solemn formula for the choice of law in order to ensure that only the clear intention of the parties as to the applicable law should always be respected. *Batiffol* illustrated this by the following example: When a Belgian and an English enterprise negotiate a contract which is drafted in English and contains reference to the institution of trust and to other English legal dispositions, then the parties had the real intention to submit the contract to English law, even if the contract contained no express choice of law clause.

---

[34] *Cf. supra* note 9.

[35] For reference to English case law see *Dicey/Morris*, The Conflict of Laws[9] (1973) p. 735 s. notes 89 and 92; for reference to German case law see *Reithmann/Martiny*, Internationales Vertragsrecht[2] (1972) p. 30–34.

[36] *Selvig, infra* p. 199.

[37] *Vischer*, Internationales Vertragsrecht (1962) p. 72–76.

[38] *Kreuzer*, Das IPR des Warenkaufs in der deutschen Rechtsprechung (1964) p. 54 ss.

III. The Protection of the "Weak Party" in International Contracts

Perhaps one of the points in the field of international contract law
that are most rigorously debated today is the scope of mandatory
provisions which aim to protect weak parties in international contracts.
This has been discussed extensively by the French Committee on Private International Law [39]. To an even greater extent, it has been a main
issue in several reports to this Colloquium [40]. The starting point of our
debate is *Lando's* passionate plea in his report [41]. *Hartley*, moving
along similar lines, informs us of the English attitude to consumer
contracts which contain an international element [42]. *Sauveplanne* [43]
criticizes in detail the position of *Lando*, who, on the other hand, is
supported by *Jokela* [44].

In this part of the General Report the general features of the problem
will be highlighted and presented as an introduction (1) leading to a
discussion of the attitude of the Draft on the problem (2).

1. General Remarks

In a great number of contracts there does not exist an equal bargaining power between the parties of the contract. Consumer contracts, employment contracts and some limited production-manufac-
turing contracts are but a few examples of those types of contracts
in which a failure of equal bargaining power is usually manifest. The
weaker party in those cases must generally submit to any and all contractual conditions imposed by the stronger, who negotiates on the
basis of "take it or leave it".

The substantive law of many countries shows an increasing tendency
to protect the weaker party by a set of mandatory rules. Although
"weak-party" contracts are traditionally local contracts, they are
tending more and more to embody international characteristics.

Hartley gives two examples [45]. The first concerns the situation where
a supplier from country A employs a sales representative to solicit
business from consumers in country B (on a door-to-door basis); the
second is drawn from the international mail-order business, where a

---

[39] *Mayer*, p. 376, 378.

[40] *Republic of Austria, Ministry of Justice, infra* p. 80 s.; *Hartley, infra*
p. 105–112; *Jokela, infra* p. 119 s; *Lando, infra* p. 128–136, and RabelsZ 38 (1974)
p. 15–21; *Sauveplanne, infra* p. 188 s.; *Siehr,* p. 573 s.; *Siesby, infra* p. 211 s.

[41] *Lando, infra* p. 126–136, and RabelsZ 38 (1974) p. 15–21.

[42] *Hartley, infra* p. 105–112.   [43] *Sauveplanne, infra* p. 188 s.

[44] *Jokela, infra* p. 119.   [45] *Hartley, infra* p. 111.

supplier from country A advertises through the newspapers of country B and solicits purchase orders from consumers in that country. In each of these cases, it is obvious that the aims of consumer protection will be defeated if the seller avoids the application of mandatory provisions through the use of a choice-of-law clause.

Lando proposes that a general distinction should be made between, on the one hand, contracts where typically equal bargaining power does exist and, on the other, weak-party contracts[46]. Party autonomy, in the broader sense, should be confined to the first category of contracts; for the second category – weak-party contracts – some restrictions should be imposed. He proposes that the law of the habitual residence of the weak party should normally apply.

Batiffol/Lagarde, in their treatise on Private International Law, share *Lando's* basic assumption, namely that the modern state's policy of combating social inequalities must be reflected in the conflict-of-laws field[47]. They, however, demonstrate the difficulty that will arise under the system proposed by *Lando,* by bringing into issue the problems that arise in any attempt to make a distinction between free contracts and those tainted with *dirigisme.* This criticism is shared in the Report of *Sauveplanne*[48]. The following example may illustrate that difficulty in question: The Belgian Law "on unilateral rescission concerning contracts for sole distributorship"[49] contains mandatory provisions which protect the distributor against rescission of the contract by the supplier. According to that statute, those rules cannot be evaded by a choice-of-law clause. I do not know of another country which has enacted a similar statute[50]. If a Belgian lawyer is asked whether a contract for the sole distributorship of a product is a contract tainted with dirigisme, he will affirm this classification. If the same question were to be put to a lawyer of any other country, he would classify the contract as a free one. These distinctions of classification as between the laws of different countries make it difficult to make a bilateral rule in the field of conflicts law as to the exclusion of party autonomy in weak-party contracts. *Batiffol/Lagarde* therefore propose a unilateral approach for these contracts whereby each state would determine whether and to what extent it wishes to apply its own pro-

---

[46] *Lando, infra* p. 131 s., 134 s., and RabelsZ 38 (1974) p. 18 s.

[47] *Batiffol/Lagarde,* D. i. p.[5] II (1971) no. 576, p. 222–224.

[48] *Sauveplanne, infra* p. 188.

[49] Loi relative à la résiliation unilatérale des concessions de vente, Moniteur belge 1961 p. 7518, p. 4996.

[50] The draft of a similar statute, however, was recently proposed to the French National Assembly. *Cf. Langer,* Reform des Alleinvertriebsrechts in Frankreich: AWD 1974, p. 450–453.

tective rules to international contracts[51]. Other states should take account of this claim of application.

The debate continues with *Lando's* dual reply to *Batiffol/Lagarde's* alternative[52]. *Lando* argues, first, that to make the distinction between, on the one hand, simple mandatory rules which can be preempted by a choice-of-law clause in international contracts and, on the other, those which claim absolute application even in international cases is not easier than is his own distinction between free contracts and those tainted with dirigisme. As his second argument, *Lando* maintains that the unilateral approach will split the legal unity of the contractual operation as it is subject to both the law chosen by the parties and to the unilateral mandatory rules. Such a *"dépeçage"* of a contract leads to additional complications which would not exist with *Lando's* approach. – In a similar way, the *Austrian Ministry of Justice* points out that contradictory provisions of several jurisdictions may be applicable and cause difficulties of adjustment[53].

In his Report, *Sauveplanne* replies to *Lando's* second argument[54]. He does not believe that the "splitting" of the contract will bring about serious inconvenience. He argues that those special legislative provisions which intend to achieve consumer protection are not exhaustive regulations imposed upon any specific type of contract, but only regulate particular points of the contract, leaving the other points to the general law of contracts. The effect of splitting a contract is not a feature peculiar to international contracts, but has already been brought about in the field of domestic substantive law. Therefore, there is no reason to exclude splitting in international cases, simply because the general rules of contract belong to a different system of law[55].

Lando's first argument that the distinction between simple mandatory rules and those which claim application to international cases will create a high degree of insecurity in the unilateral approach still awaits a reply. – Of course, you may exhort the legislator to place express limits on the international scope of his mandatory rules.

In the discussion, *Gothot* put forward the view that one of the effects of art. 7 of the Draft Convention could be to invite the legislators to determine the international reach of their mandatory provisions. – *Batiffol*, on the con-

---

[51] *Batiffol/Lagarde (supra* note 47).

[52] *Lando, infra* p. 133 s., note 12, and RabelsZ 38 (1974) p. 19 note 27.

[53] *Republic of Austria, Ministry of Justice, infra* p. 81.

[54] *Sauveplanne, infra* p. 189.

[55] For further discussion of the problems raised by the co-existence of the proper law of the contract and unilateral special rules see *von Hoffmann*, Über den Schutz des Schwächeren bei internationalen Schuldverträgen: RabelsZ 38 (1974) p. 396, 413–417.

trary, was doubtful if the legislators would take pains over the determination whether and to what extent a statute claims necessary application to international cases. Moreover, even if no express rule exists in this respect, parties cannot be prevented from contending that certain mandatory provisions are of necessary application.

At the present stage, however, it seems to the General Reporter that a smooth jurisprudential development of those scope rules is preferable to the harsh and quasi-irrevocable intervention by the legislator.

2. *The Approach of the Draft: Art. 2 (3); Art. 7*

After the foregoing lengthy general remarks the viewpoint of the Draft Convention regarding the protection of the weaker party will briefly be summed up.

(a) The Draft has not excluded any specific type of contract from the parties' choice of law, not even labour contracts. Such a position, by the way, stands in clear disharmony with the Draft Regulation on Labour Relations proposed by the Commission in 1972[56].

(b) However, art. 2, para. 3, provides that, for labour contracts, the choice of law made by the parties shall in no case prejudice the operation of those compulsory rules for the protection of the employee which are in force in the country in which he habitually carries out his work. This is not a reversal of party autonomy, as was proposed by *Lando*, but a special choice-of-law rule for some particular questions; for the rest of the contract, party autonomy is not touched. This is, moreover, a *bilateral* choice-of-law rule which makes applicable the law of the place of work without raising the question whether or not that law claims necessary application to international contracts.

(c) The remainder of the Draft leaves the protection of the weak parties to the operation of art. 7. Following a unilateral approach, it leaves to each disposition which tends to protect weak parties the delimitation of its international scope; the justification of this claim, however, will be examined by the court which has to decide the particular case.

Behind this dualistic approach of the Draft on weak-party contracts there seems to stand the following policy: art. 7 is supposed to have the effect of giving less protection to the weak party than does art. 2, para. 3. If this is correct, then the draftsmen of the Convention will have to explain the reasons which led them to give less protection to consumer contracts than to labour contracts. *Hartley* proposes that it should be considered "whether provision should be made for con-

---

[56] Official Journal of the European Communities, May 18, 1972, no. C 49/26.

sumer contracts along the lines of that for employment contracts" [57]. And in *Lando's* view this could also be considered for insurance contracts [58].

In the discussion *Lando* presented his idea of excluding contracts involving weak parties from party autonomy, instead of leaving their protection to the operation of art. 7. His double argument against art. 7 was (1) that it would lead to unforeseeability of the result and (2) that it would lead to an undesirable piecemeal application of different laws to the contractual relationship. *Hjerner* approved of the idea put forward by *Lando,* as also did *Selvig,* who added the argument that this approach would eliminate in this field the crucial question how to exclude evasive choice-of-law agreements.

Lagarde, defending the solution of the Draft, pointed out two difficulties that stood in the way of formulating *Lando's* suggestion in the text of an international convention: (1) the problem of establishing a uniform distinction between free contracts and weak-party contracts; (2) the problem of delimiting dispositions which pursue public interests from those which aim to protect weak parties.

IV. Rules of Immediate Application: Art. 7

A lively debate arose around the problems of art. 7. The policy underlying this article was critisized particularly by *Hjerner* whilst *Gothot* pleaded for giving the policy an even more authorative tone (1). Lando would have restricted the scope of art. 7 to public law provisions (2); *Drobnig* proposed to extend its scope to non-contractual obligations (3). Other speakers, as *Selvig* and *Siesby,* expressed their doubt that art. 7 could meet the complexity of the problems involved (4). There was broad disapproval on the high degree of discretion given to the courts (5).

1. General Policy

According to *Hjerner* art. 7 was either undesirable or superfluous. In the first place he asked what was the correct meaning of the formula employed in art. 7 that rules of a law other than the proper law "shall be taken into account". If this meant that the foreign law was to be *applied,* then art. 7 laid down a particular choice-of-law rule. – Obviously judges have to apply mandatory rules of the forum state which claim application to a particular case. From that fact, however, one should not draw the conclusion that courts have to apply mandatory rules of a foreign legislator as well. The speaker did not see any reason why a court should pay more attention to the intentions of a foreign legislator than to those of the parties. *Hjerner* illustrated his statement by the following example: A foreign manufacturer appoints a Swedish businessman as his sole distributor. The agreement contains a

---

[57] *Hartley, infra* p. 112.
[58] *Lando, infra* p. 135, and RabelsZ 38 (1974) p. 20.

choice of the law of the manufacturer and a resale-price-maintenance clause. Such a clause is invalid according to Swedish law, but valid according to the law of the manufacturer. The distributor does not obey the resale-price-maintenance clause; consequently the manufacturer stops delivery. The distributor claims damages in the courts of the manufacturer's country. *Hjerner* stated that in such a case foreign public law should not be applied. – *Lagarde,* in the ensuing discussion, made use of the case to defend the opposite conclusion. He modified the facts slightly assuming that the suit would be heard in Sweden. Swedish courts would of course hold invalid the resale-price-maintenance clause. When the courts in the manufacturer's country, following art. 7, took into account the Swedish statute, then an international uniformity of solutions would be achieved.

Hjerner then examined the second possible meaning of the formula that a law "shall be taken into account". It might mean that the foreign law should not be applied, but only paid regard to in another way. Following this interpretation, the provision seems to be superfluous. When, e. g., an act of performance is prohibited by foreign public-law provisions, the question whether or not the judge should pay regard to that obstacle to performance *(Leistungshindernis)* will depend very much upon the circumstances of the particular case. When the injured party claims damages for breach of contract, the courts will have to consider whether or not the other party was aware of the obstacle of performance when entering the contract or whether the obstacle arose unexpectedly after the conclusion of the contract.

A different attitude may be reserved for mandatory rules of those states with which the forum state is closely bound, e. g., between states within the European Community. Art. 7, which does not restrict its scope to mandatory rules of the states of the Community, but is intended to have general application, is too widely drafted.

Gothot expressed his concern that the formula employed in art. 7, by which the rules of a law other than the proper law of the contract "shall be taken into account", might diminish the effect of this article. In order to ensure full effect for art. 7, he proposed to amend the Draft in the sense that the rules of the other law "shall be applied". – *Batiffol* disapproved of this proposal; he considered it dangerous to open the door to foreign law to such a wide extent. This would end in a dismemberment *(dépeçage)* of the situation.

The General Reporter in his final remark could not repress his sympathy with *Gothot's* suggestion. It gave a clear guideline to the reasoning of the courts; the formula actually used, on the other hand, might disguise the rationale of the courts, that the claim of application is not "justifiable by the particular character and purpose of the rules".

2. Restriction of Art. 7 to Public-Law Provisions

Not all mandatory provisions which claim exclusive application in international cases have been enacted solely for the protection of the weaker party; some have been intended for the promotion of both economic and political aims. Restrictions of payment abroad and the restrictions on trading with the enemy are examples of the latter category.

Lando holds art. 7 to be the appropriate means to give respect to the impact of public law on international contracts, whereas he proposes to to remove private-law provisions from its scope [59].

Selvig and *Lagarde* made the point that no clear distinction could be established between rules which aim to protect private parties and rules which are enacted to protect public interest. There are several mandatory provisions which pursue both aims at the same time. *Selvig* held that, in instalment sales, requirements fixing a minimum down payment and a maximum period of credit for payment of the balance are supported by credit-policy considerations as well as by those of consumer protection. Mandatory rules concerning the liability of the carrier as provided in the Convention on the Contract for the International Carriage of Goods by Road (CMR) [60] are designed to protect the sender against stipulations lowering the responsibility of the carrier; on the other hand, the carrier must be prevented from assuming a higher liability in order not to give to this type of carriage a more advantageous position in the competition with carriage by rail.

Lagarde added the example of statutory provisions on certain types of sale (mail-order sales, door-to-door sales). Those provisions which may give the buyer a right to rescind the contract are designed to protect the buyer; at the same time they aim to prevent unfair competition. When art. 7 covered both private- and public-law provisions, it could evade those problems of classification. This point was supported by *Gothot*.

3. Extension of Art. 7 to Non-Contractual Obligations

Mandatory rules do not only concern contractual matters they also have to do with non-contractual claims, as in the restrictions on payments abroad for tort damages. *Drobnig*, therefore, proposes to change the position of art. 7 within the Draft and to place it among the general provisions, perhaps after art. 19 [61].

In the discussion, *Lagarde*, in his quality as a member of the Working Group, held that the spirit of the Draft was not in opposition to this suggestion. The scope of art. 7 had been limited to contractual matters for the simple reason that in the course of the deliberations of the Group there had not appeared case material that might have suggested an extension of art. 7 to torts. Perhaps problems would not in fact arise, because of art. 12. This article

---

[59] *Lando, infra* p. 142, and RabelsZ 38 (1974) p. 35.

[60] U.N.T.S. vol. 399, p. 190, no. 5742 (1961) = *Zweigert/Kropholler* II E 280 (p. 253 ss.).

[61] *Drobnig, infra* p. 82 s. *Cf.* Law Commission p. 42.

provides that, irrespective of the proper law of the tort, account should be taken of such rules issued on the grounds of security and public policy by the law of the place of the accident.

4. Complexity of the Problems Involved

Selvig stressed that art. 7 covers two different situations: That is where the law which claims application is the *lex fori* and that where it is a foreign legal system. According to the traditional approach, the claim of application of the *lex fori* would always be respected, whereas art. 7 seems to have the effect of confining the reference to the *lex fori*. Therefore the speaker raised the question whether it is really possible to cover both situations by art. 7, the application of foreign law and that of the *lex fori*.

Siesby treated the question whether art. 7 was the appropriate means to treat the conflict between party autonomy and mandatory rules in international contracts (he expressly left outside the scope of his remarks the problem of special conflict rules for public-law provisions). A rough distinction could be made between three groups of mandatory rules[62]. (1) For those mandatory rules which apply to all kinds of contract (e. g., concerning its valid formation), the parties should have freedom to choose the applicable law. (2) For mandatory regulations of particular contracts (e. g., labour contracts), the intention of the legislator to make applicable the mandatory rules to international contracts depends upon the extent to which the contract is connected with the central life of the country in question. (3) As to those mandatory provisions which are intended especially to regulate international relations (especially in transport law), a legislator who allows the parties to contract out of them would contradict himself. The speaker doubted whether it would be feasible to find a more elaborate and sufficiently detailed form for art. 7, which would remove the drawbacks of party autonomy. Therefore *Siesby* pleaded for a restriction of party autonomy as an additional method.

5. The High Degree of Discretion of the Courts

Art. 7, in the Reports to this Colloquium, has received broad criticism because of the high degree of discretion which it gives to the courts[63]. *Hartley* argues that the judge in the consumer's country could be expected to apply his own mandatory rules, whereas the judge in the producer's country might be expected to neglect them[64]. *Graue,* on the other hand, fears that the excessive use of mandatory provisions of the *lex fori* would now get a kind of justification[65]. "Forum shopping"

---

[62] *Siesby, infra* p. 212 s.

[63] *Republic of Austria, Ministry of Justice, infra* p. 81; *Drobnig, infra* p. 82 s.; *Graue, infra* p. 100 s., 104; *Hartley, infra* p. 111; Cf. also *Bischoff,* in: *D. Mayer,* p. 378.

[64] *Hartley, infra* p. 111.   [65] *Graue, infra* p. 100.

by the use of jurisdiction clauses, according to *Graue,* would have some importance as to the impact of mandatory rules.

In the discussion *Derain* gave expression to the fear that the foreseeability offered by the admission of party autonomy in art. 2 could be lost through art. 7. It was not possible to foresee to what extent the courts would apply other laws in addition to the proper law of the contract. *Batiffol* added the remark that this need for foreseeability was an argument for the assumption that art. 7 must come into play only in exceptional cases.

The main thrust of *Drobnig's* Report is his proposal for a new text for art. 7[66]. He aims to restrict the quasi-unlimited discretion of the courts to recognize the claim of a closely connected country in applying its mandatory dispositions. According to the wording of the Draft, "these rules shall be taken into account to the extent that the exclusion is justifiable by the particular character and purpose of the rules".

Drobnig also affirms the necessity of including a clause limiting the recognition of a claim for exclusive application of mandatory rules. He proposes that the yardstick which should be used to determine the application of a foreign country's mandatory rules should be that of "international standards". The main purpose of this formula seems to be that it will exclude the natural tendency of a judge to resort to the standards of the *lex fori,* and that it will compel him to find a solution which is acceptable on an international level. Perhaps one may question the utility of introducing a new general clause instead of the old. One can, however, find hints in *Drobnig's* paper on how to give life to the formula of "international standards". Moreover, this formula provides for the judge a guideline which would tend to achieve international uniformity in the application of art. 7. The net effect of that proposal is, therefore, to achieve an increasing degree of foreseeability in the long run.

B. The Scope of the Proper Law of Contract

According to a statement in the Working Group's Report the scope of the contract law covers, in principle, both the formation and the effects of the contract[67].

---

[66] *Drobnig, infra* p. 86.   [67] Rapport, *infra* p. 277, 279.

I. The Formation and Validity of Contracts

1. Formation and Validity

a) Validity. – As to the formation of the contract, art. 8 states: "Conditions governing the validity of the consent of the parties to the contract shall be determined according to the law which is applicable pursuant to the preceding Articles."

The term "validity", however, seems to have a narrower sense than "formation". Under the general term "formation", *Dicey/Morris* [68] treat the problems of offer and acceptance *(i. e.,* whether an agreement has been concluded) and the reality of consent *(i. e.,* the questions of mistake, misrepresentation, duress and undue influence). *Lando* understands "validity" of consent to mean only the reality of consent *(i. e.,* free from the defects of mistake, misrepresentation, duress, and so on) [69]. *Kühne* seems to share this interpretation [70]. This limited application, however, would not allow art. 8 to cover the question of offer and acceptance. Therefore, the net effect of placing offer and acceptance outside the scope of art. 8 is to preclude a uniform conflict rule on this important matter.

b) Silence of the Offeree. – Perhaps the most striking question in the area of offer and acceptance, in international trade, is that of the circumstances under which silence on the part of the offeree amounts to an acceptance of the offer. To this question the Working Group has not yet found a unanimous solution. Three possibilities were discussed by the Working Group [71]. The first was to leave the question outside the scope of the Convention; the other two solutions are to be found in the Annex to the Draft as the first and second variants. *Lando* discusses the problem and its possible solutions in a more general context: that of the meeting of minds [72]. In his conclusion, he expresses doubts as to whether a rule concerning the meeting of minds should be enacted at all. To *Kühne,* on the other hand, it seems advisable to include in the Draft Convention an explicit choice-of-law rule on the effects of silence [73].

Kühne's test is essentially based on the first of the two variants proposed by the Working Group. He approves of the technique employed there, which combines a conflict rule with substantive rules.

---

[68] *Dicey/Morris,* Conflict of Laws[9] (1973) p. 763. The term "validity" is discussed in Law Commission p. 45 s.

[69] *Lando,* RabelsZ 38 (1974) p. 39.

[70] *Kühne, infra* p. 122.   [71] Rapport, *infra* p. 264.

[72] *Lando,* RabelsZ 38 (1974) p. 40–42.

[73] *Kühne, infra* p. 122.

He criticizes, however, the selection of the place of residence of the offeree as the point of connection. He asserts that a connection should be found which takes into account the expectations of the offeror and the offeree alike and proposes as the standard connection the place where the offeree has received the offer. In some cases, however, even this connecting factor may play an inferior role in comparison with other connecting factors. *Kühne* gives the following example: When two persons who are residents of the same country are on a business trip abroad, the place of residence should override the place in which the offer is received.

He therefore proposes to introduce the following exception clause:

If the relation between the parties is characterized by special circumstances and, therefore, is more closely connected with another country than with the place where the offeree has received the offer, the law of that other country shall apply.

c) Formation of the Choice-of-Law Clause. – The problems of formation that exist for the contract in general, are particularly crucial in the choice-of-law agreement. The Draft proposes to submit the validity of the choice-of-law agreement to the chosen law (art. 2, para. 2). In those cases where a choice-of-law clause is accepted by silence, the Draft proposes a disposition which is analoguous to the dispositions on contracts in general.

Lando[74] gives a detailed discussion of the various possible solutions. These are: to leave the question to the *lex fori*; to decide it according to the law chosen or according to the law which would be the proper law in the absence of a choice of law by the parties; or to decide it according to the law of the habitual residence of the silent party; or to leave it to the exercise of court discretion; or to decide it in harmony with the customs established between the parties and the usages of international trade. In his conclusion he dwells on the difficulties of finding a satisfactory solution. It therefore seems to him advisable to delete art. 2, para. 2. *Siesby* also fears that art. 2, para. 2, will create more problems than it solves[75]. He favours the solution of judging validity and formation in accordance with the law which would be applicable in the absence of a choice of law by the parties. If any special rule were to be made on the problem. *Siesby* would prefer the second variant set out in the Annex to the Draft, which is based upon the prior course of dealing between the parties as they conform to the customs and usages of international trade.

Additionally, it may be useful to remind this colloquium of the position taken by *Mezger* in the French Committee on Private International

---

[74] *Lando*, RabelsZ 38 (1974) p. 23–25.

[75] *Siesby, infra* p. 208.

Law [76]. According to *Mezger*, the question of silence as to the choice-of-law clause had to be given a uniform solution in the Convention. He did not find a solution in the reference to the usages of international trade as they do not exist concerning the problem. He prefers the application of the law of the place of business of the silent party.

In the discussion, *von Overbeck* expressed alarm at the idea of introducing particular rules on offer and acceptance into the Convention. The general rule in this field is to apply the proper law of the contract. Even in those examples that *Lando* had given in order to demonstrate that the application of the proper law of the contract was inappropriate, *von Overbeck* held that both parties were aware of the fact that the contract contained an international element. Generally speaking, a party who enters into negotiations with a foreign person must be expected to be more careful than in purely domestic relations. Therefore there would be no need to give a supplementary protection to those parties by applying the law of their habitual residence. Therefore *von Overbeck* preferred not to introduce particular rules on offer and acceptance into the Convention [76a]. In those rather exceptional cases in which the application of the proper law of the contract would stand out as highly inappropriate, recourse could be had to deliberations of *bona fides*, abuse or public policy.

This viewpoint was supported by *van Hoogstraten*. The Convention should not try to make people feel that they can always fall back on their own law when the result of a legal transaction does not please them. In today's world and in the future people will have to realize that foreign law may even apply to their silence.

Hjerner held that validity of the contract should be governed by the proper law of the contract. The problems of formation, however, would be more complex and difficult. Even in the national substantive laws this question has not been treated exhaustively by the legislators; there are merely some particular provisions for particular situations. Therefore the speaker was critical towards the idea that the effect of silence could be solved by substantive-law provisions in the Convention. The substantive-law solution had to be left to the national laws; the proper law to give effect to the silence of a party would be that of its place of business.

The General Reporter expressed agreement with the statements of *von Overbeck* and *van Hoogstraten*. Generally speaking, he who derives profit from international business should also bear its risks. Whenever both parties entered into negotiations, the question of offer and acceptance should be submitted in a uniform way to the proper law of the contract [77]. This will not mean that the substantive-law provisions of the proper law of the contract

---

[76] *D. Mayer*, p. 377.

[76a] Law Commission p. 23. "It may be that it would be preferable to make no express provision on this matter."

[77] *Cf. von Hoffmann*, Vertragsannahme durch Schweigen im internationalen Schuldrecht: RabelsZ 36 (1972) p. 510–525.

will not take account of the fact that a foreigner will not be acquainted with all the peculiar features of that law. Then it may occur that in particular cases the silence of a foreigner – unlike that of a national – cannot be regarded as acceptance.

Selvig raised the problem of the relationship of art. 2, para. 2, and art. 8 to art. 7. When considering the validity of a choice-of-law agreement, art. 7 may come into play, since art. 2 is mentioned in art 7. When considering the validity of a contract, there seemed to be no place for taking into account the mandatory provisions of another law, since art. 8 is not mentioned in art. 7. It would be an unsatisfactory result if the validity of the contract and the validity of the choice-of-law agreement were to be treated in different ways.

2. Capacity

The question of capacity is left outside the scope of the Convention. Art. 20, however, does contain a provision which restricts the possibility for a party to plead his incapacity. Under the terms of this article, one party cannot plead his incapacity against another party who had considered him to have capacity under the law of the place of conclusion, provided, however, that the other party was acting in good faith and prudently. According to *Siehr,* these standards of care imposed upon the other party are not quite clear[78]. It appears that it would be only possible for a conflicts lawyer and thus not for a merchant to determine the capacity of a foreigner. Therefore *Siehr* proposes the deleting of this restriction.

Hoyer, on the other hand, emphazises the notion that protection of the young and the feeble-minded is more in accord with interests of the law than is the safeguarding of those persons who are acting in good faith[79]. He expects that Austria would not ratify a convention which included art. 20.

Lando holds, in a similar way, that in contracts which are not commercial the contractual capacity should be governed by the law of the customer irrespective of the other party's good faith[80]. In commercial contracts, however, the proper law of the contract should govern the question of capacity. – Perhaps it is useful to stress the point that in the majority of member states, capacity is governed by the law of nationality and not by that of domicile or residence. Therefore, in the majority of the member countries, the question is of great importance for resident foreigners. Every merchant who enters into a sales transaction with a resident foreigner needs the protection of art. 20 in order not

---

[78] *Siehr,* p. 577.   [79] *Hoyer, infra* p. 116.
[80] *Lando, infra* p. 154 s., and RabelsZ 38 (1974) p. 55.

to be obliged to take into account the age of majority in the country of each customer's national origin.

In the discussion, *Hoyer* pointed our that Austria is to change from the principle of nationality to the principle of domicile. Therefore there will not exist the need to protect merchants against the resident foreigner. As to the incapacity of non-resident foreigners even when the contract was regarded as invalid, satisfactory practical results would be reached by recourse to unjust enrichment.

Sauveplanne[81] approves of art. 20 as being progressive. He particularly points out that this rule protects not only the merchants dealing within the forum state but – by reason of its bilateral approach – foreign merchants as well.

3. Form

As to the formal validity of contracts, art. 18 provides alternative approaches. The contract is formally valid when it fulfils either the conditions of the proper law of the contract or the conditions of the law of the place where it was made. A hitherto unsettled question was how to determine the place of conclusion of a contract made *inter absentes*. This question is now resolved in accordance with the ingenuous rule suggested by *Zweigert*[82]: when the act is composed of several declarations, the formal validity of each declaration it determined separately by the place where it was made. *Lando*, however, asks why it would not be sufficient for a party to observe the legal formalities of the place where the other party assumes his obligations[83].

II. Performance

1. General Rule: Art. 15 (1)

According the above-mentioned statement of the Working Group the scope of the proper law of the contract should, in principle, cover both the formation and the effects of the contract. Art. 15, para. 1, in accordance with that recommendation, states that the proper law of the contract will govern the following points: the conditions of per-

---

[81] *Sauveplanne, infra* p. 194.

[82] *Zweigert*, Zum Abschlußort schuldrechtlicher Distanzverträge, in: Festschrift Ernst Rabel (1954) I p. 631–654.

[83] *Lando, infra* p. 151 s., and RabelsZ 38 (1974) p. 52 s. *Siehr*, p. 577, is reluctant on this suggestion; it would not be covered by the policies of principle of *lex loci contractus*, but by those of *favor negotii*, the latter being embodied in the draft only in a restricted way.

formance, the various ways in which the contract may be extinguished, and the consequences of non-performance.

Hartley desires that "prescription" may be specified as a matter of the proper law of the contract rather than one of procedure, as it is classified in England[84]. The Working Group's Report expressly mentions that prescription comes under the heading of "ways of extinguishing", the elements of which are subjected to the proper law of the contract[85].

According to that same Report, "set-off" is also regarded as a way of extinguishing an obligation; however, the reporter seems to favour a cumulative application of the laws of both debts[86]. At the present stage of research, a more detailed reglementation of these subjects will be impossible[87].

Lando points out that in common-law systems the rules of specific performance are treated as a question of procedure and submitted to the *lex fori*[88]. Even in the Uniform Law on the International Sale of Goods[89], common-law courts are not obliged to give decrees ordering specific performance except in those cases where they would do so under their own law. According to *Lando,* a similar arrangement could be made in this respect in the present Convention.

Lipstein, on the other hand, holds that there should not be attached excessive significance to the alleged difference between English law and continental law[90]. Rules on specific performance do not concern the substantive duty of a party, but only the procedure of enforcement.

2. Manners of Performance: Art. 15 (2)

Art. 15, para. 2, provides that, in determining the manners of performance, the law of the country in which the performance takes place must be taken into account.

What is the scope and meaning of this term "manners of performance"? The Working Group states in its Report that it "was unwilling

---

[84] *Hartley, infra* p. 112. On the application of foreign statutes of limitation in England cf. *Lipstein, infra* p. 160.

[85] Rapport, *infra* p. 295.

[86] Rapport, *infra* p. 295. In English law – however – set-off is generally governed by the *lex fori*, cf. *Lipstein, infra* p. 160.

[87] Cf. *Rabel,* Conflict of Laws III[2] (1964) p. 485: "More research is necessary to clarify this subject."

[88] *Lando,* RabelsZ 38 (1974) p. 45.

[89] Diplomatic Conference on the Unification of Law Governing the International Sale of Goods, Records and Documents of the Conference I (1966) p. 333 = *Zweigert/Kropholler* I E 137 (p. 41).

[90] *Lipstein, infra* p. 160.

to determine it rigorously"[91]. It must be noted that they were even unwilling to define it roughly. The Report states that the term is to be classified in accordance with the *lex fori*. This will, again, promote unforeseeability of the results.

According to the Group, the rules concerning public holidays, the inspection of goods and the steps which are to be taken in the event of a refusal to comply should be covered by the topic[92].

Public holidays are already covered by art. 7. As for the other two examples, it would perhaps not be desirable to exclude them from the proper law of contracts.

On the other hand, *Lando* and *Siehr* point out that the rules regarding the currency in which a debt must be satisfied should be regarded as manners of performance[93]. Moreover, according to art. 38, para. 4, of the Uniform Law on the International Sale of Goods[94], the methods of examination of goods fall within the law of the place of the inspection. The same could be assumed for the inspection of services. On the whole, it does not seem to be very difficult to define the meaning of that provision. The Working Group will have to reexamine this point.

C. Particular Questions of International Contract Law; Contracts Excluded from the Scope of the Convention

I. Particular Questions of International Contract Law

1. Assignment: Arts. 16, 17

The assignment of a claim involves not only the interests of the assignor and the assignee, but also those of the debtor of the original claim. Substantive law may provide different measures of protection as to the debtor. The most radical measure is to exclude assignability. There are still other measures of protection, such as the delivering of a notification to the debtor as condition for the assignment. It is a traditional postulate of private international law in this field to submit the provisions that aim to protect the debtor to the law which governs the original claim between debtor and assignor.

For voluntary assignment of claims, art. 16, para. 2, follows this traditional approach. According to it, "the conditions under which the

---

[91] Rapport, *infra* p. 297.   [92] Rapport, *infra* p. 297.
[93] *Lando*, RabelsZ 38 (1974) p. 46; *Siehr*, p. 584.
[94] *Cf. supra* note 90.

assignment may be invoked against the debtor" are to be taken from the law which governs the original claim. On the other hand, the question whether or not a statutory assignment has taken place are not to be governed by the law to which the original claim is submitted. Rather it is to be governed – according to art. 17, para. 1 – "by the law to which the body of rules appertains for which that form of assignment was erected".

I will now give an example of this rather complicated question: A person is injured in an accident. The question whether or not the insurer who has compensated the insured will benefit from a statutory assignment of the rights against the liable party should not depend upon the law governing the delictual claim, but on the proper law of the insurance contract.

Sauveplanne deals with this topic and approves of the solution given in art. 17[95]. He goes even further. He favours a uniform rule on the assignment of claims, a rule that would cover both voluntary and statutory assignments. This rule should be modelled on art. 17. The Dutch scholar holds that the distinction between voluntary and statutory assignment is a rather artificial one. In those countries that traditionally do not know statutory assignment it is usual to provide voluntary assignment in insurance conditions. Likewise, social insurance in those countries is obliged to pay indemnification only after receiving an assignment of the insured person's claim. The conditions under which voluntary assignment may be invoked against the debtor should therefore not be subjected to the law of the original claim but to the law governing the obligation between assignor and assignee[96].

This proposal tends towards a radical change in the traditional habits on this point. I must confess that I am impressed by the basic argument, namely that it is often fortuitous whether the legislator has provided for a statutory assignment or whether this assignment is provided in the insurance conditions. However, I am rather hesitant about *Sauveplanne's* proposal in case where the original claim is not created by tort but by an individual contract. In those cases at least, the approach of art. 16, para. 2, seems to be adequate.

2. Transfer of Property: Art. 9

Art. 9 provides that arts. 2–8 should not apply to transfer of property and effects *in rem* arising from the contract. I wonder if this is not a scope rule which belongs to art. 1. – *Lando* points out a problem that

---

[95] *Sauveplanne, infra* p. 192 s.
[96] *Sauveplanne, infra* p. 193.

may arise under this provision: does art. 9 only cover the transfer of property as to third persons or also between the parties[97]? The question may arise in the context of the following problems: when does the risk of loss or damage to goods pass from the seller to the buyer? When will the buyer have the right to enjoy the products and the fruits from the goods sold? May the unpaid seller retake possession of the goods? *Lando* proposes that the present Convention should provide, whether the questions of the transfer of property as between the parties should be covered by art. 9. *Lipstein,* on the other hand, prefers to leave this question to the law of the Member States[98].

3. Evidence: Art. 19

Art. 19, para. 1, provides that presumptions and the burden of proof shall be governed by the law which is applicable to the legal relationship. Art. 19, para. 2, introduces some restrictions on the rule that the law of the forum shall determine the modes of evidence.

Lando has announced that the entire article will have to be renegotiated when Denmark, Ireland and the United Kingdom adhere to the Convention[99]. In the reports to this colloquium the storm has not yet broken out[100].

Perhaps it may be useful in this context to give expression to a feeling that will be widely shared by Continental conflict lawyers. The distinction between substance and procedure is drawn by national traditions in a way that seems not to meet the needs of international cases. In international cases the classification of a problem as procedural has the fatal consequence of submitting it to the *lex fori,* even where it is decisive in the case. This leads to international disharmony and "forum shopping". Therefore it is desirable in the interest of international uniformity to keep the domain that belongs to the *lex fori* as small as possible.

II. Contracts Excluded from the Scope of the Convention: Art. 1 (2)

As to the contracts excluded by art. 1, para. 2, from the scope of this Convention, many questions may arise. These, however, do not seem to stand in the centre of the preoccupation of this colloquium.

There is one important exception. *Selvig* holds that bills of lading are negotiable instruments and therefore excluded from the scope of

---

[97] *Lando,* RabelsZ 38 (1974) p. 43.
[98] *Lipstein, infra* p. 160.   [99] *Lando,* RabelsZ 38 (1974) p. 53.
[100] *Cf.,* however, the remarks of *Lipstein, infra* p. 161 s.

the present Convention by art. 1, para. 2 b[101]. Moreover, he pleads for a general exclusion of maritime transports from this Convention. His main argument, that the present art. 4, para. 2, is not fit for that kind of contracts, was already discussed[102].

In the discussion, *Drobnig* examined in detail the suggestion of *Selvig* to exclude maritime contracts from the scope of the Convention.

(1) From the history of the Draft and especially from its French text it seemed clear that bills of lading are not regarded as negotiable instruments excluded from the scope of the Convention by virtue of art. 1, para. 2 b.

(2) *Drobnig* approved of *Selvig's* opinion that in many cases the criteria of connection set by art. 4, para. 2, would be inadequate for maritime contracts. A contract of carriage by sea from New York to Hamburg concluded by a Swedish shipowner should not properly be governed by Swedish law even if under art. 4, para. 2, the performance of the shipowner is characteristic and his business lies in Sweden. The way out can be found in art. 4, para. 3, which enables regard to be paid to the closer connection with another country. Even where invocation of art. 4, para. 3, seems to be difficult, in practice the relatively limited number of leading maritime courts (e. g., those in Rotterdam, London and Hamburg) will soon be aware that they must find a solution under the paragraph mentioned and it will probably even be possible to find uniform criteria.

(3) As to mandatory provisions in uniform maritime legislation one has to distinguish between two situations: (a) If the international convention is in force in all the countries of the Community, then the application of its mandatory rules is ensured by means of art. 27 of the Draft. (b) If several but not all member states of the Community also adhere to the uniform maritime convention, its mandatory rules may be taken into account by the courts of the non-member states, too, by means of art. 7. – Moreover, *Drobnig* did not see any difficulty in taking into account – by way of art. 7 – the American Harter Act 1893 in a transport by sea from New York to Copenhagen which is governed by Danish law.

(4) *Drobnig* held – in agreement with *Selvig*[103] – that the special conflict-of-law problems arising from the system of global limitation of claims, which are peculiar to maritime claims, are not yet resolved within the system of the Draft in a progressive way. It would be necessary for the Working Group to consider this particular problem. A solution could be found along the lines of that proposed by *Selvig*.

Selvig replied to *Drobnig* he did not doubt that it would be possible to interpret the provisions of the Draft in the way that he suggested. Then, indeed, the existing conflict-of-law solutions could be preserved within the framework of the Convention. The question remains, however, whether it would be advisable to include the matter within the scope of the Convention when everybody is satisfied with the present system of conflict-of-laws solu-

---

[101] *Selvig, infra* p. 196. *Cf.* Law Commission p. 14.
[102] *Supra* p. 8.   [103] *Selvig, infra* p. 202 s.

tions in maritime matters. The inclusion in the Convention would at least entail a risk that the hitherto existing certainty might be disturbed.

As to arbitration and choice-of-forum agreements, which are generally part of the contractual document, one may regret that the uniform rules on the formation and validity of contracts do not relate to them. As it is stressed by *Lipstein,* it would lead to strange results if validity of these clauses and of the contract which contains them should be governed by different laws [104].

As to insurance contracts, the question of their inclusion in the Convention seems to be quite ambiguous.

In the discussion, *Imbert* gave some information on the deliberations of the EC Commission in this field. At the present time the Commission is preoccupied with two questions: (a) ensuring the right of establishment for insurance companies within the Community; (b) removing restrictions on the free use of insurance service within the Community. When opening the right of establishment, there are no difficulties in the conflict-of-laws field: contracts between the domestic subsidiary establishment of a foreign insurance company and domestic customers insuring a risk situated in the same country will be subjected to its law. On the other hand, the question of the law applicable to the insurance contract is a main problem raised in the context of the removal of restrictions on free use of insurance services offered by companies from other EC countries. The solution to this problem seems to be to admit party autonomy. Maybe the choice will be restricted to the laws of member states of the Community. This admission of party autonomy in insurance contracts with foreign companies could introduce new distortions of competition, to the detriment of domestic insurance companies. Therefore the choice of the applicable law will have to be extended also to insurance contracts with domestic companies. When giving such a broad liberty to the parties, evidently the problem of mandatory rule will arise in full force. The question arises whether the member states would have to harmonize their respective mandatory provisions in this field; harmonization, however, would seem to be extremely difficult.

Because of all these unresolved questions it has not yet been decided whether or not insurance contracts should be included into the scope of the Convention.

As to the exclusion of company law, it may be asked how one is to draw the dividing line between contracts of cooperation and company law. As to agreements which restrict competition, art. 7 seems to be a good instrument for meeting their dangers. Is the reluctance of the Working Group grounded in the fear that the provisions of the Sherman Act must be applied or openly excluded as being unjustifiable [105]?

---

[104] *Lipstein, infra* p. 156.

[105] On the need of restricting the application of the Sherman Act by means of art. 7 see the remarks of *Lagarde* in *D. Mayer* p. 378.

Final Remark

Many of the rules on international contracts which have been framed
in this Draft are characterized by a high degree of flexibility. This is
particularly true for art. 4 and art. 7. There exists the danger that the
unifomity which the Convention desires to achieve will be to some
extent lost in the practical application in the courts. *Graue* is rather
sceptical about the Convention when he states: "The Draft Convention
would at best bring about unification of basic conflict rules which are
not really controversial."[106] However *Sauveplanne,* who sees the same
problem, approves of the flexibility followed in this Draft, provided
that uniformity of construction will be ensured by the Court of the
European Communities[107]. If the construction of the Convention were
not to be subjected to the authority of that Court, then the Dutch scholar
sees as the alternative solution that of elaborating strong and precise
rules. It seems to me doubtful that an international legislator, who
wants to rule everything, would be adequate in the field of international contracts law. In my view there is no real alternative to the
present flexible approach, which must be combined with the jurisdiction of the European Court[108]. On some points, however, there could
be achieved improvements in the text, following, *e. g.,* the suggestions
of *Siehr* and *von Overbeck*[109] concerning art. 4, para. 2, and of *Drobnig*[110] concerning art. 7. On other points, *e. g.* the definition of the international character of a transaction (art. 1, para. 1)[111], the requirements
of a tacit choice of law[112], the manners of performance (art. 15, para.
2)[113] it may be sufficient to give further explanations in the Report.

D. Summary

I 1. Art. 1, para. 1, of the Draft delimits the scope of the Convention to
situations of an international character, without indicating the elements which
constitute this "international" character. The Working Group may reconsider
whether or not it would be possible to give some explanations on this point.
The following aspects may be taken into account: (a) a domestic situation
will not acquire an international character by the choice of a foreign court

---

[106] *Graue, infra* p. 103.   [107] *Sauveplanne, infra* p. 187.
[108] For details on this point cf. *Siehr, infra* p. 65.
[109] *Supra* p. 9.   [110] *Supra* p. 18, 20, *infra* p. 82 ss.
[111] *Supra* p. 3–5.   [112] *Supra* p. 10 s.
[113] *Supra* p. 26 s.

or arbitral tribunal *(van Hoogstraten)*; (b) an initially domestic situation may become international through subsequent circumstances, *e. g.* by a change of residence of a party *(Batiffol)*; (c) the international character of a situation should not be constituted only by geographical circumstances, but also by the economic fact that the relevant market involves international competition (*cf. supra* p. 3–5).

2. It has been proposed not to delimit the scope of the whole Convention to international situations, but to extend it to *foreign situations* also (*Lando, Siehr, Hoyer; cf. supra* p. 2). – Moreover, it will have to be reconsidered whether or not the right of the parties to choose the applicable law shall be restricted by the Convention in a uniform way to international situations *(Lando)*. When a contract does not contain a foreign element, there is no doubt concerning the applicable law; then parties should not be allowed to contract out of the mandatory dispositions of their own law (*cf. supra* p. 3). – A particular problem will be raised by the EC "Convention on Jurisdiction and the Enforcement of Judgments in Civil and Commercial Matters" (*cf. supra* p. 3). That Convention will allow the choice of a tribunal of a foreign country within the Community, even when the relationship does not contain an international element *(Schultsz)*. Will the parties then be entitled to choose the law of the forum as the applicable law, too?

II. No objection was raised on *party autonomy*, as it was set out in art. 2, para. 1 (*cf. supra* p. 5 s.). The choice of law should not be restricted to those countries which have a territorial connection with the transaction. A proposal to introduce into art. 2 a clause restricting party autonomy in the sense that the choice of law must be "bona fide and legal" *(Siesby)* did not find further supporters. The question of splitting the applicable law by a choice-of-law agreement does not deserve the attention of the Draft. – The admission of a subsequent choice of law (art. 3) did not evoke reservations; it was made clear that a subsequent choice of law, *e. g.* that of the law of the forum, could not have a broader effect than the initial choice-of-law agreement *(Lando)*.

III. For the determination of the applicable law in the *absence of a choice of law by the parties,* art. 4 follows a double approach. The rule of the closest connection is introduced by para. 1; para. 2 consecrates the rule of the characteristic obligation. In the discussion it became manifest that both notions could be understood in different ways. Moreover, the respective scope of application of these both rules remained in suspense. Finally, the real importance of art. 4 may be restricted by a generous admission of a "tacit" choice of law.

1. The formula of the *closest connection* (*cf. supra* p. 10), if taken in a broader sense, will comprise all those methods of finding a connecting factor which are based on the objective circumstances of the transaction; it is in opposition to the approach which seeks to find a hypothetical subjective intention of the parties. The closest connection may be found either by the search for the proper law having regard to the *circumstances of each particular case* or by developing *general rules of connection* for particular types of contract. With this understanding, para. 1 would be the main rule *(Lagarde)*; para. 2, then, was one of the various possible ways of finding the closest connection.

Taken in a narrower sense, the formula would only mean the search for the proper law on the basis of the circumstances of the particular case *(Lagarde)*. Then, however, it would seem to be appropriate to place para. 1 at the end of art. 4 *(Selvig)*. – On the whole, the broader meaning of "closest connection" seems to be preferable, as it will enable general rules of connection to be developed even in those contracts to which para. 2 will not apply.

2. The question how to determine the *characteristic obligation* remains controversial *(cf. supra* p. 8). Obviously, one of the criteria has to be the complicatedness of the obligations *(Lando)*. The statement of the Report that the obligation to pay money is non-characteristic, was reversed by *Siehr* and *Drobnig*. They held that, e. g., in instalment sales the obligation of the buyer hand the predominating characteristic. – In mass business an additional argument for determining the characteristic obligation would be the convenience for the supplier to submit all his contracts to one and the same law *(Lando)*. Where these two arguments would not be sufficient to give the predominant characteristic to one law, prevalence could be given to the law of the party which is more dependant upon the contractual relationship.

It might be useful to enumerate within the framework of art. 4, para. 2, several particularly important contracts and to specify the applicable law *(von Overbeck)*.

3. In many contracts it will be impossible to establish a characteristic obligation *(cf. supra* p. 10). This is particularly frequent in "combined contracts" *(Hjerner)*. Then it will be necessary to resort to art. 4, para. 1, by considering the elements of the particular transaction. In this context, even the place of conclusion could retain some value as a solution of despair *(Batiffol)*. – In other contracts there can well be established a characteristic obligation. The place of business of the party which carries out the obligation, however, will be a typically improper point of connection *(cf. supra* p. 8 s.). This is particularly true for maritime transports *(Selvig)*. For those contracts there could nevertheless be developed general connections when para. 1 was understood in a broad sense. – In combined contracts there will arise the problem whether separate treatment should be given to each contract by applying art. 4, para. 2, or whether they should be submitted to one law by reference to para. 1 *(Hjerner)*. The question of separability, it seems, cannot be resolved in a general way; it must be decided for each particular contract *(Batiffol)*.

4. A *tacit choice of law* *(cf. supra* p. 10 s.) will be respected. The conditions of a tacit choice of law, however, are not defined in the Draft. In the actual practice of the courts the conditions of a tacit choice of law are understood in different ways. In several countries a tacit choice is inferred from the circumstances, even when the parties have not formed an intention on this point. When the Convention does not exclude the taking of the adjective "tacit" in this broad sense, then art. 4, para. 2, will loose its importance to some extent; international disharmony will subsist.

IV. *Lando's* suggestion of excluding party autonomy for *weak-party contracts* *(cf. supra* p. 13), e. g. consumer contracts and labour contracts, was supported by several speakers *(Jokela, Hjerner, Selvig)*. A less radical suggestion was put forward by *Hartley:* along the lines of art. 2, para. 3, there should be established special bilateral connections for the rules protecting the consumer. – It seems impossible to reach international consensus as to which kinds of contracts should be regarded as weak-party contracts *(Batiffol, Sauveplanne).* Therefore, the Convention cannot establish a uniform distinction between weak-party contracts and free contracts; this would favour the unilateral approach of the Draft *(Lagarde).* – It many be that it is not impossible to agree on a uniform treatment of labour and consumer contracts, following either *Lando's* or *Hartley's* suggestion and to leave remaining mandatory rules protecting weak parties to the operation of art. 7.

V. The policy underlying *art.* 7 to give effect to mandatory rules of a foreign system of law that is not the proper law of the contract, was broadly welcomed *(cf. supra* p. 16). Only *Hjerner* held that art. 7 was either undesirable or useless. *Gothot* proposed even to amend art. 7 in the sense that the foreign law should be applied, not only taken account of.

Lando proposed to remove private-law provisions from the scope of art. 7. The best way to protect weak parties was to apply the law of their residence as the proper law. Such a suggestion not only involves the problem how to define weak-party contracts in an international convention *(supra* IV), but also the question how to establish a distinction between those rules that aim to protect private parties and those that are enacted to protect public purposes *(Lagarde).* There are many provisions which pursue both aims at the same time *(Lagarde, Selvig, cf. supra* p. 18).

Selvig was doubtful whether it was not too simple to treat mandatory dispositions of the *lex fori* on the same basis as those of foreign law.. Courts will give full effect to the *lex fori*, whereas they will carefully examine the claim of application of foreign law *(cf. supra* p. 19). – *Siesby* feared that art. 7 could not meet adequately the conflict between party autonomy and the different groups of mandatory rules which aim to protect private parties *(cf. supra* p. 19). He proposed to introduce into the Draft some restrictions on party autonomy, as an additional method.

The Working Group may wish to consider whether the scope of art. 7 will have to be extended to non-contractual obligations *(Drobnig, cf. supra* p. 18 s.).

The high degree of discretion of the courts to admit the claim of application of foreign law received quasi-unanimous criticism. *Batiffol* held that, in order to ensure the utmost foreseeability, art. 7 would come into operation only in exceptional cases. *Drobnig* proposed a new text for art. 7. It should be so worded that the yardstick used to determine the application of mandatory rules should be that of "international standards", in order to achieve an increasing degree of uniformity and foreseeability *(cf. supra* p. 20).

VI. The proper law should, in principle, cover the formation and the effects of the contract. Art. 8 only submits "validity" to the proper law of the contract. The intricacies of *"offer and acceptance"*, on account of which the Working Group invited a discussion upon alternative propositions (Annex to the Draft), could not be surmounted; they will rather be increased *(cf. supra* p. 21–24).

Von Overbeck and *van Hoogstraten* were partisans of the idea of sub-

mitting offer and acceptance – including the relevance of silence – to the
proper law of the contract; parties who enter into international business
negotiations have to be particularly careful. – *Kühne* approved of the technique employed in the first Variant of the Working Group's proposal, which
combines a conflict rule with substantive rules; he would prefer to take as
the standard connection not the place of residence of the offeree but the place
where the offer was received. *Siesby* showed some preference for a purely
substantive-law provision.

Hjerner rejected the idea of solving the complex problems of the effects
of silence in a substantive-law provision of the Convention. He would prefer
as a connecting factor the residence of the silent party. Finally, *Lando* wanted
to leave the problems of offer and acceptance outside the scope of the Convention.

VII. *Manners of performance* are excepted from the proper law of the
contract (art. 15, para. 2). In order not to risk an evasion of the proper law
of the contract, this notion should be described with some precision (*cf. supra*
p. 26 s.). – The proposal of *Sauveplanne* for a conflict rule on *assignment* that
would cover both voluntary and statutory assignment may be considered
by the Working Group. This rule should be modelled on art. 17: then the
conditions under which voluntary assignment can be invoked against the
debtor would not be subjected to the law of the original claim but to the law
which governs the obligation between assignor and assignee (*cf. supra* p. 27 s.).

VIII. The idea that no person may invoke *incapacity* when he would have
capacity under the law of the place where the act was executed (art. 20) was
welcomed by *Siehr* and *Sauveplanne* (*cf. supra* p. 24 s.). *Sauveplanne* particularly approved of the bilateral shaping of the rule: it did not only give a
privilege to domestic merchants. *Siehr* proposed the deletion of the requirement of art. 20, according to which the other party must have been "in good
faith and not acting imprudently": merchants can be generally supposed not
to be informed about the age of majority in foreign law. – *Hoyer* criticized
the policy behind art. 20: the protection of the young and of the feeble-minded
should have preponderance over the good faith of the other party (*cf. supra*
p. 24). – In a similar way, *Lando* would prefer that in non-commercial contracts capacity should be governed by the law of the customer.

This question will be of greatest importance for resident foreigners; according to the conflict law of of most *EC countries* their capacity will not be
governed by the law of their residence or domicile, but by that of nationality.

IX. The opportunity of excluding *maritime transports* from the scope of
the Convention seems to depend mainly on the understanding of art. 4, para. 2,
in the context of the whole of art. 4 (*cf. supra* p. 8, 30). The place of business
of the carrier is obviously an inadequate point of connection *(Selvig, Drobnig)*.
Drobnig was confident that the courts would find in art. 4, para. 2, a basis for
developing uniform criteria of connection which will be more adequate,
whereas *Selvig* feared that the hitherto well-established practice in this field
could be disturbed by an inclusion in the framework of the Convention. The
special conflict-of-law problems arising from the system of global limitation
of claims will have to be considered by the Working Group (*cf. supra* p. 30).

E. Résumé

I. 1. L'alinéa premier de l'article premier du Projet restreint le domaine de la Convention aux *seules situations qui présentent un caractère international.* Or, les éléments déterminants de cette définition ne sont précisés nulle part. Il serait souhaitable que le Groupe des Experts examine la possibilité de fournir les précisions nécessaires, en tenant compte des aspects suivants: (a) le seul choix d'un tribunal étranger ou d'un arbitre étranger ne suffit pas à qualifier d'internationale une situation qui présente par ailleurs un caractère purement interne *(van Hoogstraten)*; (b) une situation purement interne à l'origine peut acquérir ultérieurement un caractère international par la survenance de certaines circonstances comme le changement de résidence de l'une des parties *(Batiffol)*; (c) la localisation géographique d'une situation déterminée ne suffit pas à lui donner un caractère international: encore faut-il que cette qualification puisse découler de critères d'ordre économique comme la mise en cause de la concurrence internationale (comp. *supra* p. 3–5).

2. MM. *Lando, Siehr* et *Hoyer* proposent d'étendre le champ d'application de la Convention aux *situations internes de droit étranger* (comp. *supra* p. 2). – De plus il faudrait examiner à nouveau l'opportunité d'une restriction aux seules situations internationales du principe de l'autonomie de la volonté *(Lando).* Certes, lorsqu'aucun élément étranger n'est présent dans le contrat, la question de la loi applicable ne se pose pas: dans ce cas, les parties doivent respecter les dispositions impératives de leur propre droit (comp. *supra* p. 3). – Cependant la Convention européenne concernant la compétence et l'exécution des décisions en matière civile et commerciale peut soulever un problème (comp. *supra* p. 3). En effet, elle autorise le choix d'un tribunal d'un Etat contractant, même lorsque la relation juridique ne présente aucun caractère international *(Schultsz).* Dans ce cas, pourrait-on admettre que les parties choisissent la loi du for désigné en tant que loi contractuelle?

II. Le principe de *l'autonomie de la volonté,* tel qu'établi par l'alinéa premier de l'article 2, n'a soulevé aucune objection (comp. *supra* p. 5 s.). Le choix des parties est discrétionnaire: il n'est pas limité aux seuls pays qui ont un lien objectif avec le rapport juridique. Toutefois M. *Siesby* proposa de soumettre la validité du choix effectué par les parties à l'exigence de la bonne foi et de l'absence de fraude *(«bona fide and legal»)*: cet amendement de l'article 2 ne rencontra pas de soutien. D'autre part la question de dépeçage de la loi applicable que peut provoquer l'autonomie de la volonté ne mérite pas les préoccupations du Projet. – Enfin, la possibilité d'un choix postérieur à la conclusion du contrat n'a soulevé aucune objection. M. *Lando* précisa qu'un tel choix, en conduisant par exemple à l'application de la *lex fori,* ne pourrait avoir d'effets plus étendus que le choix primitif.

III. La méthode suivie à l'article 4 pour la désignation de la loi applicable en *l'absence d'un choix* par les parties, repose sur un double principe: l'alinéa premier adopte la règle de la connexion prépondérante; l'alinéa 2 consacre le critère de la prestation caractéristique. Cependant les débats firent apparaître que ces deux concepts peuvent tous deux être compris dans des sens différents. De plus, l'incertitude règne quant au domaine respectif des deux règles. Enfin, la reconnaissance d'un choix «tacite» pourrait réduire l'importance de l'article 4.

1. Prise dans son sens le plus large, la formule de la *connexion prépondérante* (comp. *supra* p. 10) recouvre toute méthode de rattachement fondée sur les éléments objectifs du rapport juridique: cette démarche va à l'encontre de la recherche subjective de la volonté hypothétique des parties. Le critère choisi pour désigner la connexion prépondérante peut être obtenu au terme d'une analyse des *circonstances particulières à chaque situation;* il peut aussi conduire à une *règle générale* de rattachement, commune à certains types de contrats. Dans ce sens, l'alinéa premier constituerait le principe *(Lagarde);* ainsi, l'alinéa 2 ne proposerait qu'une méthode parmi d'autres dans la recherche de la connexion prépondérante. Mais prise dans un sens plus étroit, cette formule n'autoriserait la recherche de la loi contractuelle que sur la base des circonstances particulières de l'espèce *(Lagarde).* Cependant M. *Selvig* fait remarquer que, dans ce cas, l'alinéa premier devrait figurer à la fin de l'article 4. – En définitive, il semble préférable de donner à la formule de la «connexion prépondérante» le sens le plus large possible. Ainsi des règles générales de rattachement pourront être imaginées même pour les contrats laissés hors du domaine de l'alinéa 2.

2. Les débats ne purent dissiper la controverse relative à la détermination de la *prestation caractéristique* (comp. *supra* p. 8). Evidemment un des critères sera la complexité de la prestation *(Lando).* Selon MM. *Siehr* et *Drobnig,* il n'est pas exact d'affirmer, comme le fait le Rapport explicatif du Projet, que l'obligation du payement n'est pas caractéristique dans un contrat. Ainsi, dans le cas d'une vente à tempérament par exemple, l'obligation de l'acheteur serait précisément la plus caractéristique. – D'autre part, dans l'hypothèse des contrats de consommation de masse, la localisation de la prestation caractéristique devrait tenir compte de la commodité que procure au fournisseur la soumission de tous ses contrats à une seule et même loi *(Lando).* Si l'une et l'autre de ces considérations pouvaient ne pas suffire à désigner une loi bien précise qui ait un lien avec la prestation caractéristique, l'application de la loi de la partie qui sur le plan social dépend plus de la prestation de l'autre partie pourrait prévaloir.

M. *von Overbeck* souligna qu'il pourrait être utile d'énumérer, dans le cadre de l'alinéa 2 de l'article 4, les contrats les plus usuels en spécifiant la loi qui leur serait applicable.

3. Dans beaucoup des cas, il est pratiquement impossible de déterminer quelle est la prestation caractéristique (comp. *supra* p. 10). C'est particulièrement vrai pour les contrats à obligations complexes *(«combined contracts»)* *(Hjerner).* Il sera dès lors nécessaire de recourir à l'alinéa premier de l'article 4 et de prendre en considération tous les éléments de la situation particulière. Dans ce contexte, même le lieu de conclusion du contrat pourrait avoir son mot à dire: mais ce serait la solution du désespoir *(Batiffol).* – Par contre d'autres contrats peuvent être caractérisés par une obligation bien spécifique. Pourtant il se peut que le principal établissement du débiteur de cette obli-

gation ne constitue un rattachement nullement approprié (comp. *supra* p. 8 s.) : c'est particulièrement vrai du contrat de transport maritime *(Selvig)*. Néanmoins, une interprétation assez large de l'alinéa premier permettrait l'établissement de critères de rattachement assez généraux pour régir ces contrats. – En ce qui concerne les contrats à obligations multiples, on peut se demander s'il convient de les soumettre à une seule et même loi en vertu de l'alinéa premier ; ou bien faut-il appliquer l'alinéa 2 et prévoir un traitement spécifique pour chaque relation juridique *(Hjerner)*? Il apparaît que cette question ne peut recevoir de réponse globale : la solution doit être adaptée à chaque cas particulier *(Batiffol)*.

4. Un plein effet est reconnu au *choix tacite* de la loi applicable (comp. *supra* p. 10 s.). Mais le Projet ne précise pas les conditions d'un tel choix. Or, l'attitude des tribunaux nous montre que ces conditions peuvent varier d'un pays à l'autre. Ainsi dans certains pays, le choix tacite est déduit des circonstances, même lorsque les parties n'ont manifesté aucune intention en ce sens. Dans la mesure où le texte actuel de Projet n'exclut pas la possibilité d'une interprétation aussi large de l'adjectif «tacite», l'incidence pratique de l'alinéa 2 de l'article 4 est considérablement réduite. Une telle solution ne contribue certes pas à l'harmonie des solutions au niveau international.

IV. Plusieurs orateurs se sont montrés favorables à la suggestion de M. *Lando* d'exclure le choix de la loi applicable en ce qui concerne les contrats ou il y a un déséquilibre entre les positions économiques des parties *(«weak-party contracts»*, comp. *supra* p. 13), tels les contrats de consommation et les contrats de travail *(Jokela, Hjerner, Selvig)*. La proposition de M. *Hartley* est moins radicale : en ce qui concerne l'applicabilité des règles protectrices du consommateur, celui-ci prévoit des règles de rattachement particulières, dans le sens de l'alinéa 3 de l'article 2. – En réalité, il est pratiquement impossible, semble-t-il, de s'accorder au niveau international sur une délimitation exacte des contrats où il existe un déséquilibre entre les positions économiques des parties et des contrats «libres» *(Batiffol, Sauveplanne)*. C'est pourquoi le Projet ne peut opérer aucune distinction sûre entre ceux-ci ; toute solution contraire risquerait d'empêcher une interprétation uniforme de la Convention *(Lagarde)*. – Mais il n'est pas impossible d'aboutir à un traitement commun aux contrats de travail et aux contrats de consommation selon les termes proposés par M. *Lando* ou M. *Hartley*, et de ranger dans le domaine de l'article 7 toutes les autres normes impératives protectrices de la partie la plus faible.

V. Le principe, posé par *l'article 7*, de la prise en considération des règles impératives de droit étranger, c'est-à-dire d'une loi autre que la loi contractuelle, a reçu un acceuil favorable (comp. *supra* p. 16). Seul M. *Hjerner* en conteste l'utilité ou même l'opportunité. D'autre part M. *Gothot* a suggéré d'amender l'article 7 dans le sens de l'«application» des normes impératives étrangères, au lieu de leur simple «prise en considération».

M. *Lando* propose d'exclure les règles de droit privé du domaine de l'article 7 ; le meilleur moyen d'assurer la protection de la partie la plus faible est de prévoir l'application de la loi de sa résidence comme loi contractuelle. Cependant une telle proposition se heurte à la difficulté de circonscrire avec précision les contrats characterisés par le déséquilibre des positions économiques dans le cadre d'une convention internationale (v. *supra* IV). De plus, la difficulté subsiste d'opérer une distinction entre les dispositions qui visent à la protection des intérêts privés et les dispositions de droit public *(Lagarde)*. En effet, un grand nombre de ces dispositions ont ce double objectif *(Lagarde, Selvig,* comp. *supra* p. 18).

M. *Selvig* se demande s'il n'est pas quelque peu simple de prétendre assurer aux normes impératives de droit étranger un traitement identique à celles du for. En effet, si les tribunaux ne font jamais obstacle à l'application pleine et entière de la *lex fori,* il n'en va pas de même de la condition qu'ils réservent au droit étranger (comp. *supra* p. 19). – M. *Siesby,* quant à lui, redoute l'impuissance de l'article 7 à résoudre les conflits éventuels entre l'autonomie de la volonté et les différentes catégories de normes impératives protectrices des intérêts privés (comp. *supra* p. 19). C'est pourquoi il propose de restreindre l'autonomie de la volonté dans une certaine mesure, à titre subsidiaire.

D'autre par le Groupe des Experts devrait examiner la possibilité d'étendre l'article 7 aux obligations non contractuelles *(Drobnig,* comp. *supra* p. 18 s.).

La très grande liberté laissée aux tribunaux quant à l'admission des prétentions à l'application du droit étranger a fait l'objet d'une critique quasiunanime. Dans le but d'assurer le maximum de prévisibilité, M. *Batiffol* suggère de limiter la mise en œuvre de l'article 7 à des hypothèses exceptionnelles. Et M. *Drobnig* propose une version nouvelle de cette disposition. Selon lui, l'applicabilité des règles impératives doit être à la mesure des exigences du commerce international *(«international standards»)*: cette solution permettrait d'obtenir une uniformité plus grande des solutions et un degré croissant de prévisibilité (comp. *supra* p. 20).

VI. En principe, le domaine de la loi contractuelle s'étend aux questions relatives à la formation et aux effets du contrat. D'autre part le texte de l'article 8 se contente de soumettre la «validité» du contrat à la loi contractuelle. Cependant le problème de *l'échange des consentements* peut donner lieu à des difficultés insurmontables; celles-ci avaient d'ailleurs forcé le Groupe des Experts à proposer deux variantes qui puissent servir de base aux discussions ultérieures (v. l'Annexe du Projet, comp. *supra* p. 21–24).

MM. *von Overbeck* et *van Hoogstraten* se sont montrés partisans de l'application de la loi contractuelle à toutes questions relatives à l'offre et à l'acceptation, y compris la portée du silence des parties: En effet, ceux qui négocient à l'échelon international doivent faire preuve de la plus grande prudence. – M. *Kühne,* quant à lui, est plus favorable à la méthode utilisée dans la première variante, à savoir une combinaison de règles matérielles et de règles de conflit. Mais il estime que le lieu de la réception de l'offre constitue un rattachement plus adéquat que le lieu de la résidence de la personne à qui l'offre est adressée. M. *Siesby* préfère une solution de pur droit matériel.

M. *Hjerner* conteste la possibilité de résoudre par une simple disposition de droit matériel, les problèmes complexes relatifs à la portée du silence des parties. Il marque une préférence pour le rattachement à la résidence de la partie qui n'a pas exprimé son consentement. Enfin, M. *Lando* préfère exclure du domaine de la Convention les problèmes de l'offre et de l'acceptation.

VII. L'alinéa 2 de l'article 15 exclut les *modalités d'exécution* du domaine de la loi contractuelle. Cette solution risque d'encourager une réduction de la portée de la loi contractuelle. C'est pourquoi il conviendrait de préciser davantage la notion de «modalités d'exécution» (comp. *supra* p. 26 s.). – D'autre part le Groupe des Experts pourrait examiner la proposition de M. *Sauveplanne* de soumettre à une règle de conflit unique tant la *cession* volontaire d'une créance que celle intervenue par l'effet de la loi; l'article 17 servirait de modèle à cette règle de conflit unique: ainsi les conditions que doit respecter le créancier pour invoquer une cession volontaire ne dépendront pas de la loi applicable à la demande principale, mais de la loi qui régit les rapports entre le cédant et le cessionnaire (comp. *supra* p. 27 s.).

VIII. MM. *Sauveplanne* et *Siehr* ont réservé un acceuil favorable au principe consacré par l'article 20: nul ne peut invoquer sa propre *incapacité* si la loi du lieu de l'acte permet de le considérer comme capable (comp. *supra* p. 24 s.). Tout particulièrement, M. *Sauveplanne* se réjouit de la formulation bilatérale de la règle, en ce qu'elle ne réserve pas sa protection aux seuls commerçants qui agissent dans le pays du for. D'autre part M. *Siehr* propose de supprimer la nécessité, pour l'autre partie, d'avoir agi «de bonne foi et sans imprudence». En effet, n'est-il pas normal qu'un commerçant ignore les conditions auxquelles le droit étranger soumet la capacité de son contractant, notamment quant à l'âge de la majorité? – Par contre, M. *Hoyer* critique la philosophie même de l'article 20: la protection des mineurs et faibles d'esprit devrait prévaloir sur la bonne foi du cocontractant (comp. *supra* p. 24). Dans un même ordre d'idées, M. *Lando* préfère l'application de la loi du consommateur à la question de la capacité dans les contrats non commerciaux.

Cette question revêt une importance toute particulière pour les résidents étrangers. En effet, la plupart des systèmes juridiques des pays de la CEE prévoient l'application de la loi nationale, et non de la loi de la résidence ou du domicile.

IX. Faut-il exclure les *transports maritimes* de la Convention? La réponse à cette question dépend, semble-t-il, essentiellement de la place qu'il convient d'accorder à l'alinéa 2 de l'article 4 dans l'économie générale de cette disposition (comp. *supra* p. 8, 30). Il va de soi que le lieu du principal établissement du transporteur constitue un facteur de rattachement tout à fait inapproprié *(Selvig, Drobnig)*. M. *Drobnig* exprime sa confiance dans l'aptitude des tribunaux à dépasser la lettre de l'aliéna 2 et à établir des facteurs de rattachement uniformes qui soient plus adéquats. M. *Selvig,* quant à lui, pense que l'insertion de ces contrats dans le domaine de la Convention serait de nature à perturber une pratique bien établie jusqu'à ce jour. D'autre part le Groupe des Experts devrait examiner les problèmes particuliers que soulève, au niveau des conflits de lois, un système de limitation globale du montant plafond de la responsabilité de l'armateur (comp. *supra* p. 30).

GENERAL REPORT
ON NON-CONTRACTUAL OBLIGATIONS (ARTS. 10–14), GENERAL PROBLEMS (ARTS. 21–23) AND THE FINAL PROVISIONS (ARTS. 24–36)

By

KURT SIEHR

Hamburg*

My report on those articles of the Draft Convention which have not been discussed by *von Hoffmann* is divided into five major parts: first, the law of torts (A), secondly, the law of quasi-contracts (B), thirdly, the more general problems of renvoi, public policy and uniform interpretation (C), fourthly, the final provisions of the Draft Convention (D) and, finally, a summary of the main topics dealt with in this report, the special reports and the discussion (E).

A. International Law of Torts

The proposed European conflicts law of torts has been criticized mainly in four respects, *viz.* the scope of art. 10 in general (I), the connecting factors (II), art. 10, para. 4, dealing with the problem of several victims (III), and, finally, the scope of the law applicable (IV).

---

* *Abbreviated literature: D. Mayer,* Information (Comité français de d. i. p., Colloque du 24 mars 1973 sur l'Avant-projet ...): Rev. crit. 62 (1973) p. 373 to 380; *Siehr,* Zum Vorentwurf eines EWG-Übereinkommens über das Internationale Schuldrecht: AWD 1973, p. 569–587; *Zweigert/Kropholler,* Sources of International Uniform Law I (1971) and II (1972); The Law Commission and the Scottish Law Commission, Private International Law, E.E.C. Preliminary Draft Convention on the Law Applicable to Contractual and Non-Contractual Obligations, Consultative Document (August 1974).

I. Scope of Art. 10 in General

1. Notion of Tortious Liability: Art. 10 (1)

Art. 10, the main provision of the proposed conflict rules on torts, does not use the word "torts" or any equivalent short term of a European legal system. Instead of this the scope of art. 10, the *"Anknüpfungsgegenstand"* has been fixed by the vague description "non-contractual obligations arising out of an event which has been resulted in damage or injury". Of course, this broad formula may be criticized on several good grounds, as it is done by *von Overbeck* and *Volken*[1]. The main objections to the scope of art. 10, however, do not relate to that formula as such but to specific types of torts which the present version of the Draft Convention either covers or excludes from regulation. It seems appropriate to begin with the excluded types of torts because they are expressly mentioned in the Draft Convention.

2. Torts Excluded from Regulation

There are three different types of torts which are excluded by the Draft Convention: torts in situations of a national character; liability of the state and its officials; and liability for nuclear damage or injury. Only the last exclusion (*cf.* art. 1, para. 2, lit. f) is fully approved with respect to the conventions unifying the substantive law of nuclear liability[2]. The other two exceptions are criticized by various experts.

a) Torts in Situations of a National Character: Art. 1 (1). – According to art. 1, para. 1, the rules of the Draft Convention are to apply to contractual and non-contractual obligations in situations of an *international* character only. This restriction to international situations has already been discussed with respect to contractual obligations and should not be dealt with again at length[3]. It may be sufficient to mention that *Lando*, especially in the field of tortious liability, furnishes good arguments against a general restriction to international situa-

---

[1] *Von Overbeck/Volken* criticize the difficulty to separate clearly between cases of art. 10 and art. 13 (*infra* p. 166) and the lack of special conflict rules for specific types of torts (*infra* p. 171 s.). The critics admit, however, that today it would be premature to draw a detailed codification for all different types of torts (*infra* p. 172). *Cf.* the same authors also in RabelsZ 38 (1974) p. 56, 58 and 65 respectively.

[2] Paris Convention of July 29, 1960, on Third Party Liability in the Field of Nuclear Damage, in: *Zweigert/Kropholler* I E 173 (p. 245), and in: Unidroit 1960 (1961) p. 457 ss.; Vienna Convention of May 21, 1963, on the Liability for Nuclear Damage, in: Unidroit 1964 (1965) p. 253 ss.

[3] *Cf. von Hoffmann, supra* p. 2 ss.

tions[4]. A tort without any foreign connections at the commission and at the causation of damage or injury, e. g. a tort committed in Germany by a German against another German, should be covered by the Draft Convention, so that art. 10 applies if the injured German party of the example happens to sue the tortfeasor in a French court.

The Working Group seems to agree with this result, for *Giuliano* expressly emphasizes in the Report: "Ce n'est en effet que par rapport au *tribunal saisi* d'un litige qu'il est possible de déterminer si la situation résultant d'un contrat ou d'un fait générateur d'obligations extra-contractuelles présente un caractère international ou, au contraire, un caractère purement interne."[5] None the less the General Reporter would omit the ambiguous term "situations of an international character" and simply ask with respect to *contracts* whether it is in these international situations only that the parties can make a valid choice of law. For conflicts rules on *torts* it is also very unusual to provide, for example, as follows: In torts of an international character the law at that place shall govern where the tortious act occurred. There is good reason for the omission of such a restriction to "international situations" inasmuch as there is no definition of the term "international situations". Therefore it is precisely the purpose of the various connecting factors (e. g. place of conduct, place of harm, common nationality, contractual relation, cf. *infra* p. 48 ss. and 51 ss.) not only to determine the applicable law but also to separate the true international fact situations from the merely domestic ones. Hence only that case is "international in character" in which a connecting factor selects as the applicable law that of a jurisdiction *foreign* to the court seized of the case[6].

It is, however, not only unusual to enact the "international situation" as an independent prerequisite. It can also be misleading in practice if such a situation has to be determined without reference to the connecting factors of the individual case. A traffic accident in the forum state could be dealt with as a purely domestic matter not within the scope of the Convention at all although a closer scrutiny of the case and of art. 10 (*infra* p. 53) would have revealed that because of the

---

[4] *Lando, infra* p. 125 s., and RabelsZ 38 (1974) p. 6, 9. *Cf.* also *Hoyer, infra* p. 115; *Siehr*, p. 571 s.

[5] Rapport, *infra* p. 251. Emphasis by the author.

[6] A traffic accident, e. g., between Germans in Germany therefore is purely internal in character for German courts because the Italian descent of a party involved is of no importance for the selection of the applicable law and hence has not been enacted as a connecting factor neither in German conflicts law nor in the Draft Convention.

common foreign nationality of the parties involved the case should have been decided according to the common *lex patriae*[7].

b) Liability of the State and Its Officials: Art. 14. – The other exception to art. 10 is art. 14 dealing with the liability of the state and its officials. *Von Overbeck* and *Volken* criticize this provision with respect to two points. First, they doubt whether non-contractual liability of the state and other legal persons governed by public law should be exempt from the scope of the Convention even if the liability stems from an act performed *iure gestionis* and not *iure imperii*[8]. Admitting, however, that this exemption has to be made for practical reasons (states do not want to submit themselves to foreign jurisdictions and do not like to recognize foreign judgments against them), both authors finally suggest that state organs and agents should be treated in the *same* way as their employers[9]. This means that the non-contractual liability of organs and agents for acts performed *iure gestionis* in the official functions of these persons should also not be covered by the Convention, which in its present version only exempts from the scope of application the "acts of *public* authority performed by the organs or agents in the exercise of their official functions" (art. 14, last part of the provision; emphasis by the General Reporter).

Together with such an improvement of art. 14 one should try at the same time to take account of English law which, as *Hartley* points out, does not have a clear distinction between private law and public law[10].

3. Torts Covered by the Draft Convention

All torts which are not expressly excluded from regulation by arts. 1 and 14 are covered by the Draft Convention. This means that certain torts related to family law and maritime torts are governed by art. 10. It may seem improper to apply the Convention to these two types of non-contractual obligations at all. The question whether other types

---

[7] This may happen, *e. g.*, in England when two Canadians have a traffic accident with a car registered in England.

[8] *Von Overbeck/Volken, infra* p. 178 s., and RabelsZ 38 (1974) p. 56, 74.

[9] *Von Overbeck/Volken, infra* p. 179, and RabelsZ 38 (1974) p. 56, 74 s.; *Siehr*, p. 579, note 116.

[10] *Hartley, infra* p. 113; Law Commission, p. 67. It may, however, be mentioned here that art. 14 does not primarily refer to the distinction between private and public law but rather to categories of public international law (conduct *iure imperii* or *iure gestionis*) also known in common law countries: *Oppenheim/Lauterpacht,* International Law[8] I (1955) p. 271 ss.; critical about this distinction: *Brownlie,* Principles of Public International Law[2] (1973) p. 323 ss.

of torts which ought to be covered by the Convention are properly dealt with by art. 10, will be discussed *infra* at p. 55.

a) Family Torts: Art. 1 (2) (a). – Art. 1, para. 2, lit. a, excludes certain matters of family law from the scope of regulation. Thus this provision does not exempt *all* obligations of family law, so that, *e. g.*, a breach of promise to marry, criminal conversation or alienation of affection are covered by the Convention. Although this may seem to be improper, it must be kept in mind that the European Convention of 1968 on Jurisdiction and Enforcement of Judgments in Civil and Commercial Matters[11] also does not exclude all matters of family law from its application. The above-mentioned family torts, for instance, are not excluded by art. 1, para. 2, no. 1, of the Enforcement Convention[12] and hence it is improper *not* to unify the respective conflicts rules. This, of course, will not guarantee a uniform characterization of these actions[13] but may offer a chance to strive for harmonization and for the elimination of "forum shopping".

b) Maritime Torts. – *Selvig* would like to exclude maritime contracts and maritime torts altogether from the scope of the Draft Convention[14].

In the discussion about the conflicts rules on contractual obligations *Selvig* stressed his conviction with respect to maritime contracts. He was backed by *Schultsz* who wanted to exclude the entire law of transportation from the scope of the Convention. The discussion between *Selvig* and *Drobnig* about problems of maritime contracts has already been reported[15].

Selvig's proposal with regard to maritime torts is mainly based on two arguments: first, the substantive law of maritime law has already been unified internationally to a large extent and such a unification will continue in the years to come, and, secondly, the conflicts rules of the Draft Convention do not properly fill the gaps left by the unification of substantive maritime law[16].

---

[11] Unidroit 1967–1968, vol. 1 (1969) p. 315 ss. = Pasin. belge 1971, p. 19 ss.; French J. O. of Jan. 17, 1973, p. 677 ss.; German BGBl. 1972 II 774, 1973 II 60; Italian G. U. n. 254 of Oct. 8, 1971, p. 6274 ss.; Mémorial of Luxembourg 1972 A, p. 1364 ss., 2131; Dutch Trb. 1969, no. 101, p. 2 ss.

[12] *Cf. Droz*, Compétence judiciaire et effets des jugements dans le Marché Commun – Etude de la Convention de Bruxelles du 27 septembre 1968 (1972) p. 32 ss.; *von Hoffmann*, Das EWG-Übereinkommen über die gerichtliche Zuständigkeit und die Vollstreckung gerichtlicher Entscheidungen in Zivil- und Handelssachen: AWD 1973, p. 57, 58 note 12.

[13] As to the famous French-German differences with respect to the characterization of an action on the breach of promise to marry *cf. Gamillscheg*, in *Staudinger*, Kommentar zum BGB[10/11], EGBGB, part. 3 (1973) App. to Art. 13 EGBGB nos. 28 ss. (p. 461 ss.).

[14] *Selvig, infra* p. 205.   [15] *Cf. von Hoffmann, supra* p. 30 s.
[16] *Selvig, infra* p. 200 ss.

(1) International maritime law has, of course, been unified to a large extent. For the field of maritime torts there may be mentioned the Brussels Convention of 1910 for the Unification of Certain Rules of Law with Respect to Collisions Between Vessels[17] and the Brussels International Convention of 1957 Relating to the Limitation of the Liability of Owners of Sea-Going Ships[18]. These conventions, already in force, prevail over the Draft Convention according to its art. 27 (*infra* p. 67 s.). If a contracting state of the Draft Convention wants to become a party to a *new* multilateral convention unifying other matter of *substantive* maritime law no consultation machinery is required by arts. 26, 28 and 29, although such a requirement would, in the General Reporter's opinion, be useful as well as desirable, and even these new conventions, once they have entered into force, will prevail over the Draft Convention[19]. These proposals will be explained later (*infra* p. 68 s.). Hence it can be concluded that the Draft Convention does not hamper the international unification of substantive maritime law. The important question, stressed by *Selvig*, is therefore whether the Draft Convention properly fills the gaps left by the conventions unifying substantive maritime law[20].

(2) Indeed, the *lex loci* rule of art. 10, para. 1, the exception to this rule provided in art. 10, paras. 2 and 3, the plurality-of-victims clause of art. 10, para. 4, as well as art. 11 about the scope of the law applicable are of no help in finding the law applicable to a collision outside territorial waters between, *e. g.*, a German and an American vessel and to the limitation of the shipowner's liability[21]. In these cases the law of the flag should apply[22] and, according to *Selvig*, the Draft Con-

---

[17] *Cf. Zweigert/Kropholler* II E 205 (p. 3 ss.); or *Singh*, International Conventions of Merchant Shipping[2] (1973) p. 1337 ss. This Convention is in force, among other countries, in all EEC countries except Luxembourg, in all Scandinavian countries except Iceland, in Austria and in Switzerland.

[18] *Cf. Zweigert/Kropholler* II E 209 (p. 17 ss.); or Singh (last note) p. 1348 ss. This Convention is in force, among other countries, in all Scandinavian countries, in France, the Netherlands, Switzerland and in the United Kingdom. The Federal Republic of Germany gave effect to this Convention by including the provisions of this Convention into the German Commercial Code: *cf.* Seerechtsänderungsgesetz of June 21, 1972, BGBl. 1972 II 966; 1973 I 267. *Cf. Abraham*, Das Seerecht[4] (1974) p. 100 ss.

[19] *Siehr*, p. 586; *Selvig, infra* p. 204 s., does not answer the question whether new multilateral conventions unifying substantive law are covered by the final provisions of arts. 24 ss.

[20] *Selvig, infra* p. 200 ss.

[21] Also *Vander Elst*, L'unification des règles de conflit de lois dans la C.E.E.: J. Trib. (Bruxelles) 1973, p. 249, 252 = Foro It. 1973, V, 249, 256, respectively, deplores this gap.

[22] *Siehr*, p. 580 (choice between the laws of the flag of the ships involved); *Selvig, infra* p. 200 s., also favours the law of the flag or the *lex fori* or, in cer-

vention should not cover the limitation of the shipowners' liability[23].
In any case it seems necessary that the Draft Convention should take
account of the special situations in the field of maritime law – and also
pays regard to similar, but somewhat different circumstances in the
law of international land transport[24] and air transport[25]. If these subjects of extensive international unification of substantive law cannot
be properly dealt with as to their decreasing number of genuine conflict-of-laws cases, *Selvig* may be right to exclude the field of international transport altogether from the scope of the Draft Convention.

II. Connecting Factors: Art. 10 (1)–(3)

1. General Rule: Locus delicti: Art. 10 (1)

The only connecting factor precisely mentioned in art. 10 is the
"country in which that event [*i. e.* the event which has resulted in
damage or injury] occurred" (art. 10, para. 1)[26]. This, however, seems
to be the only precise reference which art. 10, para. 1, ventures to
provide. There is no precision either as to the meaning of *locus delicti*
or as to the possibility of a choice between the law at the place of
conduct and that at the place of harm.

a) *Place of Conduct or Place of Harm?* – When the damage occurs
in a country other than that where the conduct causing the damage
took place *(délit commis à distance, Distanzdelikt)*, it may be of vital
interest whether the *locus delicti* is the place of conduct or the place
of harm. The language of art. 10, para. 1, seems to refer to the place
of harm[27], whereas the Report expressly states that the Draft Convention does not prefer either place "afin de ne pas entraver les dévelop-

---

tain cases, the application of the Collision Convention (*supra* note 17). In
case of a collision of ships flying the same flag the law of the common flag
will be applied according to art. 10, paras. 2 and 3, unless the Collision Convention applies: *Selvig, infra* p. 200.

[23] *Selvig, infra* p. 204, and *infra* p. 57 at A IV 1 a. *Cf.* also *Røed, infra* p. 182,
with respect to a Norwegian case.

[24] *Siehr,* p. 580, with respect to land transport cases in which the *locus
delicti* cannot be fixed.

[25] *Selvig, infra* p. 205.

[26] *Fallon, infra* p. 95, suggests that art. 10, para. 1, should be formulated
"Sans préjudice des dispositions de l'article 19 les obligations ..." in order
to make sure that the rules of art. 19 on evidence shall not be forgotten. The
General Reporter does not think that such a clarification is necessary.

[27] *Cf. von Overbeck/Volken, infra* p. 170, and RabelsZ 38 (1974) p. 56, 63;
Siehr, p. 579; *D. Mayer,* p. 379.

pements qui sont en cours dans la jurisprudence de nos pays" [28]. This hesitation is criticized by some authors [29].

In the discussion, too, the rather vague language of art. 10, para. 1, was the focus of some criticism. *Hjerner* asked whether the Draft Convention determines the *locus delicti* at all or whether it is left to the domestic conflicts law of the contracting states to localize it according to their tradition. The consequence would be that in case of the lastly mentioned solution the Court of Justice of the European Communities – if this Court should in fact acquire jurisdiction for a unifying interpretation of the Convention (*infra* p. 65) – could not finally determine the *locus delicti. Lagarde* answered as a member of the EC working group of experts. He confirmed that the Draft Convention "répond peut-être insuffisamment que la loi applicable est celle du lieu où le dommage s'est produit" and he denied that the determination of the *locus delicti* is left to the domestic conflicts law of the contracting states. *Lagarde,* however, had to confess, as already mentioned, that art. 10, para. 1, is not precisely formulated. This deficiency may raise objections as to a lack of foreseeability – foreseeability, especially in cases of products liability, being of the utmost importance even in the law of torts. Such arguments were put forward by *Lando* and *Hjerner;* finally, however they were discarded in favour of the flexible language of art. 10, para. 1. *Van Hoogstraten* joined *Hjerner* in holding that in respect of the still unsettled choice between the place of conduct and the place of harm it seems to be wise not to settle this fundamental question. Some leeway should be given to the judges to adapt their decisions to the merits of the individual case *(van Hoogstraten)* so that, e. g., in the field of products liability the law at the place of conduct would govern *(Hjerner)* irrespective of the fact that other types of torts may be governed by the law at the place of harm.

The somewhat Delphic language of art. 10, para. 1, of the Draft Convention does not only evade an unambiguous decision in favour of the law at the place of conduct *or* that at the place of harm. It also does not expressly rule on another difference between the international law of torts of some European countries, *i. e.* the *choice* between the law at the place of conduct and that at the place of harm in favour of the injured party.

b) Choice in Favour of the Injured Party. – At least in Germany and Switzerland, the vexatious problem of determining the *locus delicti* in cases of a *Distanzdelikt* or *délit commis à distance* has been solved by giving a choice between the law of the jurisdictions concerned in favour of the injured party [30]. In France, however, no choice is given

---

[28] Rapport, *infra* p. 282 s. at no. 3 to art. 10.

[29] *Fallon, infra* p. 96 ss.; *von Overbeck/Volken, infra* p. 170 s., and RabelsZ 38 (1974) p. 56, 63; Law Commission, p. 51.

[30] BGH June 23, 1964, NJW 1964, p. 2012 = IPRspr. 1964–1965 no. 51; *Kegel* in *Soergel/Siebert,* BGB [10] VII (1970) Art. 12 EGBGB no. 48; BG March 30, 1965,

in these cases, and generally the law at the place of harm prevails[31]. The *Comité français de droit international privé* also wants to continue the French tradition[32].

Art. 10, para. 1, of the Draft Convention, without having any clear determination of the *locus delicti,* does not prohibit a choice between the law at the place of conduct and that at the place of harm in favour of the victim. Hence it will be probable according to *von Overbeck* and *Volken* that under the present version of art. 10, para. 1, the national courts will continue their traditional national practice unless a more precise wording is chosen[33]. This would of course encourage "forum shopping". Let me give you an example. Recently a German manufacturer of medical supplies was sued in Norway because a woman died after using contraceptive pills produced by the German firm. The Norwegian courts applied the Norwegian *lex locus delicti* as the law at the place of harm[34]. Perhaps the widower would have succeeded in his action in Germany, where the courts would have applied Norwegian *or* German law according to which was in the victim's favour.

In the discussion, *Batiffol* vigorously opposed the idea of choosing between two different laws in favour of the injured party. He reminded the audience of *Kahn-Freund's* final report given at the 1969 Session of the Institut de Droit International in Edinburgh[35] and of the Hague Convention on the Law Applicable to Products Liability which in a limited number of cases only provides a choice in favour of the victim[36]. According to *Batiffol* the Draft Convention itself has to make the choice and in so doing has to pay regard to the interests

---

BGE 91 II 117, 123. Critical of this practice is *Vischer,* IPR, in: Schweizerisches Privatrecht I (1969) p. 509, 694 ss.

[31] *Batiffol/Lagarde,* D. i. p.[5] II (1971) p. 199 (no. 561).

[32] *D. Mayer,* p. 379. – Also *Fallon, infra* p. 96–98, tacitly does not take into account a choice between the law of several places in favour of the victim.

[33] *Von Overbeck/Volken, infra* p. 170 s., and RabelsZ 38 (1974) p. 56, 63.

[34] Bulletin of Legal Developments 1973, p. 3, and *Roesch,* Norwegische Rechtsprechung zur Produktenhaftpflicht des Pharma-Herstellers: VersR 1974, p. 16–20. – The Court of Appeal of Oslo dismissed the action and the Supreme Court of Norway reviewing this decision upheld the dismissal: Times of November 15, 1974, p. 11.

[35] *Kahn-Freund,* Delictual Obligations in Private International Law: Ann. Inst. Dr. Int. 53 (1969) I, p. 435, 468 s.: "The judge should be given the freedom to find the *locus delicti* in the light" of the circumstances. *Id., ibid.,* p. 398, 404, where the author says that he does not like the German "alternative system".

[36] *Cf.* art. 6 of this Hague Convention, published in: Recueil des Conventions de la Haye (La Haye 1973) p. 193 ss. = Am. J. Comp. L. 21 (1973) p. 150 ss. = Int. Leg. Mat. 11 (1972) p. 1283 ss. = Ned. T. Int. R. 19 (1972) p. 380 ss. = Nord. T. Int. R. 42 (1972) p. 239 ss. = RabelsZ 37 (1973) p. 595 ss. = Rev. crit. 61 (1972) p. 818 ss. = Riv. Dir. Int. Priv. Proc. 8 (1972) p. 901 ss. = Schw. Jb. Int. R. 28 (1972) p. 444 ss.

of the parties, has to take account of the often somewhat weaker position of the victim and, finally, must not forget that even in the law of torts foreseeability is important. *Von Overbeck* renewed his fears that the present version of art. 10, para. 1, will lead to "forum shopping" unless the problem of the *délit commis à distance* is solved by an unambiguous provision. *Van Hoogstraten* suggested that the Draft Convention should show that in each case the court must choose between the law at the place of conduct and that at the place of harm.

c) General Attitude Towards the lex loci. – Apart from the criticism of the absence of a precise definition of the *locus delicti*, it is questioned whether the *lex loci* can serve at all as the general rule in the international law of torts[37]. These doubts make sense if we realize the recent developments in favour of a "proper law of torts" or in favour of specific conflicts rules for specific types of torts. All these doubts and questions, however, did not result in proposals to strike out art. 10, para. 1, altogether. Instead of and despite this the *lex loci* rule has been generally accepted because it may be accompanied by special conflicts rules, as, *e. g.*, by the Hague Conventions on Traffic Accidents[38] and Products Liability[39] and, above all, because art. 10 provides an exception to the *lex loci* rule in paras. 2 and 3.

This general attitude towards the *lex loci* rule also prevailed in the discussion. Nobody questioned this rule as an appropriate principle and *Batiffol*, *Hjerner* and *Lando* expressly described it as a good starting point. It was the exceptions to the general rule of the *lex loci delicti* that aroused some controversies.

2. Exception: Closer Connection: Art. 10 (2) and (3)

a) Two Conditions: Art. 10 (2). – Under two conditions not the *lex loci* but the law of another country applies: On the one hand there must not be any "significant link" between the tort situation and the *locus delicti* and, on the other hand, this situation must have a "closer connection" with the other country. This exception to the *lex loci* rule introduces a sort of a "proper-law-of-torts clause" or the American test of the "most significant relationship" or the "center of gravity" into the Draft Convention[40] and for this reason some members of the

---

[37] *Von Overbeck/Volken, infra* p. 167 ss., and RabelsZ 38 (1974) p. 56, 59 ss.; as to British criticism cp. Law Commission, p. 52.

[38] Hague Convention of May 4, 1971, on the Law Applicable to Traffic Accidents, published in Recueil, *supra* note 36, p. 143 ss. = Am. J. Comp. L. 16 (1968) p. 589 ss. = Int. Leg. Mat. 8 (1969) p. 34 ss. = Ned. T. Int. R. 16 (1969) p. 55 ss. = RabelsZ 33 (1969) p. 343 ss. = Rev. crit. 57 (1968) p. 796 ss. = Riv. Dir. Int. Priv. Proc. 4 (1968) p. 933 ss. = Schw. Jb. Int. R. 25 (1968) p. 342 ss.

[39] *Supra* note 36.

[40] *Fallon, infra* p. 90; *Loussouarn,* Cours général de droit international privé: Rec. des Cours 139 (1973-II) p. 269 ss., 369 s.; *Siehr,* p. 579 s.

Comité français de droit international privé want to apply this exception very restrictively[41]. Most members of the Comité français, including *Lagarde*, however, do not share this view. They want to apply
the Draft Convention faithfully according to art. 23 (*infra* p. 65) and
without French predilections[42].

This controversy within one national group of conflicts specialists
would not justify much attention just now if it did not reflect attitudes
which in other countries meet with strong opposition. At least *von
Overbeck, Volken* and *Sauveplanne* are convinced that there need not
be no significant link between the tort situation and the *locus delicti*
in order to apply the law of another country[43]. They prefer an exception clause like that provided in art. 13 (*infra* p. 63). To disregard the
lex loci it should be sufficient that there be a closer connection with
the law of another country than there is with the *lex loci*. The same
view is likely to be shared in Germany.

As a member of the EC working group of experts *Jenard* addressed the
audience and gave some background information about the difficult birth
of art. 10 of the Draft Convention. He admitted that this provision has been
reached by a compromise. Nevertheless the negative condition of art. 10,
para. 2, should not be omitted. There may be, as he pointed out, situations
which have a closer connection with another country than with the *locus
delicti*, although they have significant links with the place of conduct or
injury at the same time. He gave as an example a ski accident between
Belgians in Switzerland. Normally Belgian law would apply as the law of the
parties' common nationality and habitual residence or domicile. Despite these
common connecting factors within art. 10, para. 3, however, Swiss law might
govern the tortious liability because of special consequences of the accident
and unusual complications of the fact situation. With regard to such cases and
in view of the compromise finally reached, *Jenard* strongly urged that no
change should be made in art. 10.

The difference between art. 10, para. 2, and the exception clause of
art. 13, sent. 2, may, however, be minimal in practice. It is up to the
judge to apply the vague terms of "significant link" and "closer connection" and in fact it may turn out that the lack of any significant link

---

[41] *D. Mayer*, p. 380; cf. also *von Overbeck/Volken*, RabelsZ 38 (1974) p. 56,
67. *Jayme*, Zur Anwendung ausländischer guest statutes im Staate New York:
RabelsZ 38 (1974) p. 583, 588, holds that art. 10, para. 2, of the Draft is unacceptable for Europe because of the bad American experience with such
clauses.

[42] *D. Mayer*, p. 380.

[43] *Von Overbeck/Volken*, *infra* p. 178, and RabelsZ 38 (1974) p. 56, 73;
Sauveplanne, *infra* p. 191; as to the same objection cp. Law Commision p. 53.
Fallon, infra p. 91, correctly points out that the absence of a significant link
as an independent requirement is an additional cause of uncertainty.

with the *locus delicti* is no more than the negative expression of the other prerequisite that there must be a closer connection with another country.

b) Common Connecting Factor, Especially Contractual Relations: Art. 10 (3). – Although art. 10, para. 3, may not be formulated very elegantly[44], it conveys its purpose rather clearly: The closer connection with another country will dispense with the application of the *lex loci* provided that the closer connection is normally based on a connecting factor common to the victim and the tortfeasor or the person responsible for him.

Fallon raises the question whether this common connecting factor has to exist *before* the commission of the tort or whether it would be sufficient that the respective parties have some common relations to a certain country just *at the time* of the tortious act[45]. From the Report and the various comments prepared for this Colloquium it is fairly clear that a common nationality, a common domicile as in the English case *Boys* v. *Chaplin*[46], a common habitual residence or a common flag of the parties at the commission of the tort is a common connecting factor within art. 10, para. 3[47]. If there are more of these common connecting factors, art. 10, para. 3, does not offer a solution. Hence there could be different evaluations in different countries all the more as also art. 10, para. 2, does not give precise directions. Whereas, *e. g.*, the Report applies the Italian *lex loci delicti* to an Italian traffic accident between Italians having their habitual residence in Germany[48], *Sauveplanne* is not quite sure whether Dutch courts would not apply the German law of the parties' common habitual residence[49].

Also pre-existing legal (especially within a family[50]), contractual or any social relations between the victim and the tortfeasor, as, *e. g.*, in the American case *Babcock* v. *Jackson*[51], may furnish a common connecting factor if the tort has been a violation of the tortfeasor's pre-existing duties. This should be expressed more clearly in art. 10,

---

[44] As to this criticism of *Francescakis* cf. *D. Mayer*, p. 380.

[45] *Fallon, infra* p. 90 s.

[46] *Boys* v. *Chaplin*, [1968] 2 Q.B. 1 = [1968] 2 W.L.R. 328 = [1968] 1 All E.R. 283 (C.A.); [1969] 2 All E.R. 1085 = [1969] 3 W.L.R. 322 (H.L.).

[47] Common nationality: *von Overbeck/Volken, infra* p. 173, and RabelsZ 38 (1974) p. 56, 67; *Siehr*, p. 579; *Vander Elst (supra* note 21) p. 252; and col. 256 (critical of this connecting factor). Common habitual residence: *Rapport, infra* p. 286; *von Overbeck/Volken, supra*; *Sauveplanne, infra* p. 191; *Siehr, supra*; *Vander Elst, supra*. Common flag: *Selvig, infra* p. 200; cf. also *Røed, infra* p. 182, with respect to a Norwegian case.

[48] Rapport, *infra* p. 286.　　　　[49] *Sauveplanne, infra* p. 191.

[50] *Fallon, infra* p. 91.

[51] *Babcock* v. *Jackson*, 12 N. Y. 2 d 473, 191 N.E. 2 d 279 (1963). *Cf.* as to a similar fact situation *Fallon, infra* p. 97 s.

para. 3, so that everybody may be fully convinced that especially a
contract between the parties to a tort can be a common connecting
factor [52]. By this it would also be made clear that contractual and
tortious claims of action arising out of the same pre-existing relation
between the parties should be governed by the same law [53]. This would
– as the General Reporter hopes – settle the question of *Anspruchs-
konkurrenz* and the *akzessorische Anknüpfung* in conflicts law [54].

A large part of the discussion was devoted to the questions whether and
to what extent a contract is a common connecting factor within art. 10, para. 3.
At first *Selvig* raised these questions. He agreed with the solution that claims
arising within a contractual relation should be governed by the same law
regardless of whether the action is brought in contract or in tort. The law
to be applied in these cases should be, as *Siesby*, *Schultsz* and *Lagarde* unanimously stated, the law governing the contractual relations. *Selvig* proposed
that it should be expressly mentioned in art. 10, para. 3, that in these cases
all non-contractual obligations arising out of an event which has resulted in
damage or injury, but arising within a contractual relation, should be governed by the *lex contractus*.

Von Hoffmann drew attention to the fact that not in all instances there is
a preponderance of the contractual relation. This may happen with a contract
for delivery if the delivering party sets fire to the receiver's house. This
example demonstrated clearly that a tort to be governed by the *lex contractus*
has to be committed within the tortfeasor's contractual obligations and not
only on the occasion *("bei Gelegenheit")* of the fulfilment of contractual
duties. This was emphasized by *Siesby* and *Schultsz*.

Finally, *Lagarde* mentioned that contractual relations of the tortfeasor and
the victim to the same third party might also be considered as a connecting
factor common to the tortfeasor and to the victim. Under such an evaluation,
the claims arising out of a fight between two employees employed by the
same employer in a foreign country might be governed by the law governing
the employment contracts and not by the *lex loci delicti*.

The fact that pre-existing relations between the parties to a tort
claim in most cases discharge the *lex loci* rule will meet the criticism
of *Fallon* that there might be no foreseeability in the conflicts law of
torts [55]. Foreseeability is important here though to a smaller degree
than in the law of contracts. Where, however, foreseeability is vital,
the relevance of the common connecting factor and a modified art. 12

---

[52] *Lipstein, infra* p. 163; and *von Overbeck/Volken, infra* p. 173, and RabelsZ
38 (1974) p. 56, 67, indicate that there may be some doubts whether a contract
can be a common connecting factor.

[53] Rapport, *infra* p. 286; *Fallon, infra* p. 91; *Siehr,* p. 579.

[54] As to *"akzessorische Anknüpfung"* cf. *Kropholler,* Ein Anknüpfungssystem für das Deliktsstatut: RabelsZ 33 (1969) p. 601, 625 ss.

[55] *Fallon, infra* p. 90.

to be discussed later (*infra* p. 60) take into account the interest of the parties in the application of certain rules of law.

c) Party Autonomy. – In so far as the tortious liability will be governed by the pre-existing *lex contractus,* one could say that the *lex delicti* is *indirectly* chosen by the parties. May it also *directly* be selected after the commission of the tort[56]? Such a choice may perhaps be regarded as a common connecting factor within art. 10, para. 3[57]. The Report states that this question has been left open[58]. As, however, the Draft Convention in general grants full discretion to the parties to regulate their relations (arts. 2 and 3), they should be allowed to alter their non-contractual relations by choice of a specific law different from that applicable under art. 10. If the choice, as in most cases, is made during court proceedings, the procedural law of the *lex fori* has to be consulted, as the Report points out[59].

d) Absence of Common Connecting Factor. – A closer connection to a place different from the *locus delicti* may exist although this connection does not depend on a common connecting factor. This does not mean that the *lex loci delicti* has to prevail according to art. 10, para. 1. Art. 10, para. 3, merely says that *normally* a closer connection must be based on a common connecting factor. Where there is none, art. 10, para. 2, nevertheless may be applied, although this provision gives no further specification.

For some types of cases, one could try to formulate special connecting factors, such as the flag for the collision of ships outside territorial waters[60] or – as *Fallon* proposes[61] – for torts committed at unknown places[62]. For products liability *Hartley* advocates as connecting factor the place where the product is sold to the consumer[63]. *Sundström,* too, is in favour of such a conflicts rule if the place of sale is not unforeseeable by the manufacturer because for some reason he did not intend to sell his products at this place[64]. The General Reporter does not think that such an undertaking to specify the closer connection for a few peculiar types of cases must prove impossible[65].

---

[56] As to party autonomy in the conflicts law of torts *cf. Kropholler* (*supra* note 54) p. 624 ss.

[57] *Von Overbeck/Volken, infra* p. 173, and RabelsZ 38 (1974) p. 56, 67; *Siehr,* p. 580.

[58] Rapport, *infra* p. 288.   [59] Rapport, *infra* p. 267.

[60] *Supra* p. 47 at note 22.   [61] *Fallon, infra* p. 96 s.

[62] This type of cases should not be mixed with cases in which it is not proved who has caused the damage or injury. If there are more known places, a choice may be given in favour of the victim (*supra* p. 49 ss.).

[63] *Hartley, infra* p. 112. *Fallon, infra* p. 97, wants to apply the law at the producer's residence if the *locus delicti* cannot be fixed.

[64] *Sundström, infra* p. 218.

[65] As to the same conclusion *Fallon, infra* p. 92.

3. Renvoi

If the *lex delicti* is the law of a foreign country, the court has to apply
the foreign substantive law only. According to art. 21 a renvoi by
foreign conflicts rules has to be disregarded completely (*infra* p. 64).

III. Several Victims: Art. 10 (4)

As in art. 4, lit. a, sent. 2, of the Hague Convention on Traffic Accidents [66], the applicable law has to be determined separately for every
victim of the same tort (art. 10, para. 4). Although *Selvig* does not expressly mention art. 10, para. 4, his discussion of maritime torts furnishes ample argument against this provision [67]. In case of a collision
of ships, of an air crash or also of a road traffic accident, it may be
extremely unpractical or even impossible to treat the relationship of
every victim against the tortfeasor separately. Under these circumstances it would be better to omit art. 10, para. 4, and leave the problem of plurality of victims unregulated, as the Draft Convention has
abstained from any provision on the plurality of tortfeasors.

IV. Scope of the Applicable Law

1. General Rule: Art. 11

Art. 11 of the Draft Convention is almost identical with the respective
provisions of the Hague Conventions on Traffic Accidents (art. 8) and
on Products Liability (art. 8) and it enumerates the questions to be answered by the law applicable under art. 10 [68].

In the discussion, *Røed* was worried about art. 11. If liability is no longer
in dispute between the parties, but questions as to, *e. g.,* contributory negligence or the extent of compensation are still open, art. 11 would compel the
courts to determine first the law governing under art. 10 in order to answer
the unsettled questions with respect to minor problems. These problems
should be solved separately, for instance according to the standards laid
down in art. 10. In his answer to *Røed's* question *Lando* affirmed the solution
of the Draft Convention: If there is no settlement with respect to the governing law (*supra* p. 55), one has in fact to determine the *lex delicti* first in
order to find the law applicable to the questions enumerated in art. 11.

---

[66] *Supra* note 38.   [67] *Selvig, infra* p. 200 ss.
[68] As to the Hague Conventions *cf. supra* notes 38 and 36.

Not all reporters are convinced that every problem mentioned in art. 11 should be determined by the same law[69]. This will now be examined separately for every single topic which has been criticized individually.

a) Limitation of Liability: Art. 11 no. 2. – It has already been mentioned that according to *Selvig* the limitation of shipowners' liability should not automatically be governed by the *lex delicti* under art. 10 (*supra* p. 47 s.). The *lex fori* should be applied as in the Limitation Convention of 1957[70] or the law of the flag of the responsible ship[71]. Exemption clauses, however, agreed upon by the parties to a contract should be governed – without prejudice, of course, to arts. 7 and 22 – by the *lex contractus*[72] which according to art. 10, para. 3, normally will be also the law governing the liability in tort (*supra* p. 53 ss.).

b) Form and Extent of Compensation: Art. 11 no. 4. – Since the form of compensation may be closely tied up with local enforcement procedures, *Lipstein* has some doubts as to whether it should be determined in accordance with foreign law[73]. Which law, however, should govern? The application of the *lex fori* would take account of this connection between the form of compensation and enforcement procedures only in those cases where the court decision will be enforced in the forum state. But in view of the EEC Convention on Jurisdiction and Enforcement of Judgments[74] there will be many cases in which enforcement will be sought abroad, perhaps at a place which is still unknown to the judgment creditor. Which law should be applied in these instances? With respect to such situations it seems easier to adjust local enforcement procedures to certain forms of compensation governed by foreign law than to adjust the form of compensation to local enforcement procedures.

Whereas *Lipstein* draws attention to the fact that it may be difficult to determine the extent of damages according to *foreign* law[75], *Røed* and *Sundström* would like to pay regard to the law of the victim's residence or domicile[76]. As to both authors it is only this law which can ensure that the victim will be adequately compensated by taking

---

[69] *Lipstein, infra* p. 163 s.; *Røed, infra* p. 184 s.; *Selvig, infra* p. 200 ss.; *Sundström, infra* p. 216 s. Cp. also Law Commission, p. 59 ss.

[70] *Supra* note 18. [71] *Selvig, infra* p. 204.

[72] *Cf. Graue, infra* p. 99 ss.; *Hartley, infra* p. 113, with reference to *Sayers* v. *International Drilling Co NV*, [1971] 3 All E.R. 163 (C.A.). – The latter decision has not been followed in Scotland: *Brodin* v. *A/R Seljan and Another*, S.L.T. 1973, 198 (Outer House), with note by *Thomson* in: Int. Comp. L. Q. 23 (1974) p. 458–461.

[73] *Lipstein, infra* p. 163. [74] *Supra* note 11.

[75] *Lipstein, infra* p. 163.

[76] *Røed, infra* p. 184 s; *Sundström, infra* p. 216 s.

account of his living costs, of the price level at his place of residence, and of fiscal regimes, bank rates or currency regulations which may influence payments in compensation for the injury suffered. I am not quite sure whether this is a stringent argument against art. 11 no. 4. This conflicts provision merely determines the scope of the law applicable and the latter, of course, in its rules of substantive law will in most jurisdictions take account of the victim's living costs at his place of residence and the other facts mentioned above [77].

c) Transmissibility by Succession: Art. 11 no. 5. – The law of succession is excluded from the Draft Convention (art. 1, para. 2, lit. a) and the assignment is dealt with separately by art. 16. From this and from the Report it is pretty clear that art. 11, no. 5, does not touch the national rules as to the determination of the heir of a deceased person [78]. Art. 11, no. 5, simply aims to determine the law which has to answer the question whether the deceased's cause of action survives and is transmissible to his heirs or whether it is extinguished by the injured person's death as, *e. g.*, in common law. This meaning of art. 11, no. 5, has to be formulated in clearer language. Then, perhaps, even *Sundström* may be satisfied with this provision [79].

d) Compensation of "Indirect Victims": Art. 11 no. 6. – Art. 11, no. 6, particularly aims to refer to those persons who are not "direct victims" but have suffered damage or injury indirectly by *"ricochet"* [80]. This aim, too, could perhaps be better expressed and formulated.

e) Vicarious Liability: Art. 11 no. 7. – According to *Lipstein* the problem of vicarious liability may raise a preliminary question as to the private-law relations between master and servant [81]. This may be true, but does not ensue that the relation with respect to the liability of the master has to be determined by the law governing this relation. Whether a manufacturer is liable for acts of other persons, should be decided according to the *lex loci delicti*, whichever law this may be under art. 10.

f) Statute of Limitations: Art. 11 no. 8. – It is also *Lipstein* who points out that the limitation of actions (as distinct from matters destroying

---

[77] *Cf.* a case which goes far beyond that: BGH Sep. 23, 1969, VersR 1969, p. 1040, compensating costs and travel expenses of Americans, living in Germany, for medical treatment in the United States although the tort, for which the responsibility was not in dispute, was governed by German law and according to German substantive law normally the costs for medical treatment in Germany have to be paid by the tortfeasor.

[78] Rapport, *infra* p. 290.   [79] *Sundström, infra* p. 217.

[80] Rapport, *infra* p. 291.

[81] *Lipstein, infra* p. 163 s., referring to *Lipstein,* Phillips v. Eyre, a Re-interpretation, in: Jus privatum gentium, Festschrift für Max Rheinstein I (1969) p. 411, 414, 420 s.

a substantive right) is governed by the *lex fori* according to English conflicts law. Therefore the Draft Convention will meet English objections in so far at least as the *lex loci delicti* should apply even if it provides a longer period of time in which an action may be maintained[82].

Von Overbeck and Volken draw the attention to another problem connected with art. 11 no. 8 and to a distinction to be made there[83]. Under this provision the *lex delicti* correctly also applies to the extinction or limitation of causes of action and to the question how the running of the statute of limitations can be interrupted. If, however, the interruption has to be made by certain acts of procedure, it is the *lex fori* which determines whether, e. g., an action has been validly instituted or not.

g) *Capacity to Do Wrongful Acts.* – The capacity to do wrongful acts is not mentioned in art. 11. This may be explained by art. 1, para. 2, lit. a, which expressly excludes the capacity of natural persons from the Draft Convention. As, however, in most European countries the capacity to do wrongful acts is determined by the law applicable to the tort itself, *von Overbeck* and *Volken* urge that this capacity should be added to the questions mentioned in art. 11[84]. *Hoyer* seems to agree with this proposal[85].

h) *Direct Actions.* – The Working Group intentionally did not incorporate into the catalogue of art. 11 the question whether the victim can directly sue the insurer of the tortfeasor[86]. This does not mean that this question, too, is not answered by the *lex delicti*, since art. 11 expressly states that the enumerated topics "in particular" are governed by the law applicable under art. 10. At the reconsideration of the Draft Convention it should be discussed once more whether the problem of direct actions, because of their importance, should be dealt with in the Convention as has been done in art. 9 of the Hague Convention on Traffic Accidents[87].

2. Special Provisions

The scope of the law applicable to tortious liability is, as just mentioned, not exhaustively delimited by art. 11. There are some

---

[82] *Lipstein, infra* p. 164.

[83] *Von Overbeck/Volken, infra* p. 176 s., and RabelsZ 38 (1974) p. 56, 71 s.

[84] *Von Overbeck/Volken, infra* p. 177, and RabelsZ 38 (1974) p. 56, 72.

[85] *Hoyer, infra* p. 115.   [86] Rapport, *infra* p. 292.

[87] *Cf. supra* note 38. The exclusion of insurance contracts (art. 1, para. 2, lit. d) would be no obstacle for an inclusion of the direct action problem into the Draft Convention.

other provisions which extend the *lex delicti* to additional matters or
which restrict its scope of application.

   a) Rules of Security and Public Interest: Art. 12. – There is no doubt
that account has to be taken of the rules in force at the *locus delicti*
and issued on grounds of security or in the public interest. This is
provided by art. 12. The Draft Convention had to insert such a provision
especially for those cases which, according to art. 10, paras. 2 and 3,
are not governed by the *lex loci delicti*. English traffic regulations, of
course, have to be consulted as local data even if a traffic accident
between Germans in England and the resulting claims for damages
are governed by German Law (art. 10, para. 2 and 3) [88].

   However self-evident the rule of art. 12 may be in these cases, there
may arise problems in the normal situation of art. 10, para. 1 as *Fallon*
correctly points out [89]. Let me once more take as an example the recent
Norwegian case against a German producer of contraceptives [90]. Can
the defendant in such a case plead German rules of safety if they are
less rigid than the Norwegian ones? According to the Hague Convention on Products Liability he cannot do so if, as in the Norwegian case,
the product was introduced into the Norwegian market [91]: the German
producer has to comply with the safety regulations of those countries
to which he sells his products. But what about the case where the Norwegian customer had bought the product in Germany and the product
had been introduced in the German market only? In these situations
the producer should be allowed to plead the German safety regulations
even if the cause of action is determined by the Norwegian law as the
law at the place of harm. The result would be that despite the same
language of the French version in art. 12 and art. 10, para. 1, (country
or place "où le fait dommageable s'est produit") the *locus delicti* could
reasonably be qualified differently for both provisions. Therefore art.
12 should be drafted more clearly, indicating that for reasons of safety
rules the tortfeasor should pay regard to the law of that country where
he has acted or where his acts, foreseeably to him, could cause harm.

   Fallon suggests that art. 12 should discard the application of the
lex loci altogether and should instead take into consideration the
safety rules which the victim could reasonably rely on at the time of
injury [92]. Similar problems may arise as to standards of competition in
the field of unfair competition.

---

[88] *Cf.* also art. 7 of the Hague Convention on Traffic Accidents (*supra*
note 38). In agreement *Lipstein, infra* p. 164, and *Sundström, infra* p. 217.
   [89] *Fallon, infra* p. 93 ss.   [90] *Supra* note 34.
   [91] Art. 9 Hague Convention on Products Liability (*supra* note 36).
   [92] *Fallon, infra* p. 94.

b) Arts. 15, 16, 17 and 19. – The provisions about the performance of an obligation (art. 15)[93], the assignment (arts. 16 and 17) and about presumptions of law, as well as the burden of proof (art. 19)[94], have already been dealt with by *von Hoffmann* in his general report on the international law of contractual obligations[95]. These articles, however, also apply to non-contractual obligations arising out of tortious acts. In all of these provisions the *lex delicti* is important (arts. 15, para. 1, art. 16, para. 2, art. 17, para. 2 and art. 19, para. 1). Of special interest to tort obligations is art. 19, para. 1, concerning the presumptions of law and the burden of proof to be determined by the *lex delicti* and especially art. 17, para. 1. The latter rule about the assignment by operation of law, correctly does not apply the law of the assigned claim, *i. e.*, for example, the claim against the tortfeasor but applies the law governing the relation which provides, as for instance an insurance contract, the assignment by operation of law. The protection of the debtor, however, who pays his original creditor, should be determined by the *lex delicti*. This could perhaps be expressly stated for all cases in art. 17.

c) *Extension of Art. 7.* – Art. 7 has already been discussed extensively by *von Hoffmann*[96]. It is sufficient to repeat here that *Drobnig* reasonably proposes the extension of the scope of art. 7 to non-contractual relations also, especially to tort claims[97].

V. Conclusion as to the International Law of Torts

It is rather ambitious to codify the international law of torts, this being the part of conflicts law which, above all, has caused the so-called "crisis of conflicts law" and which still is in process of development. From that I would not draw the conclusion of *Fallon* that the codification might be premature[98]. The Draft Convention is rather flexible and could be made even more flexible to ensure fair court decisions and to encourage a further evolution of conflicts law. This flexibility may impair the uniformity of interpretation of the Convention but, sooner or later, a start has to be ventured on in order to achieve greater harmony in times to come.

---

[93] According to *Fallon, infra* p. 95, art. 15 expressly should state that it has to be applied without prejudice to arts. 10 and 19.

[94] *Cf. supra* note 26. [95] *Von Hoffmann, supra* p. 25 ss.

[96] *Von Hoffmann, supra* p. 16 ss.

[97] *Drobnig, infra* p. 82 s. [98] *Fallon, infra* p. 92 s.

B. International Law of Quasi-Contracts: Art. 13

Unlike the international law of torts the international law of quasi-contracts does not play an important role in court practice. This may be the reason why art. 13 did not attract much attention[99]. Some comments, however, have been made on this provision.

I. Scope of Art. 13 in General

Art. 13 does not specifically enumerate the non-contractual obligations arising from an event which does not result in damage or injury. But there is no doubt that the *negotiorum gestio,* unjust enrichment and the payment of money not owed are covered by this provision[100]. This is quite a large scope comprising some very heterogeneous causes of actions. In view of this it is of minor importance that even here the liability of the state and its officials is excluded (art. 14; *supra* p. 45) and that perhaps other matters should also be exempt as with the law of torts (*supra* p. 46 ss.)[101]. The main question is whether art. 13 can manage to deal with all these different actions properly – whether the connecting factors are well chosen.

II. Connecting Factors

1. General Rule: Locus actus: Art. 13 s. 1

In cases of a voluntary agency, *i. e.* a *negotiorum gestio,* or of an interference with property of others, by consumption for example, the *lex loci actus* may be the proper law for determining the reciprocal causes of action based on a quasi-contract[102]. But is this also true with

---

[99] *Lipstein, infra* p. 164; *von Overbeck/Volken, infra* p. 177 s., and RabelsZ 38 (1974) p. 56, 72 s.; *Siehr,* p. 581 s. (based on comparative law and an analysis of different fact situations); *Vander Elst (supra* note 21) p. 252 s. and col. 257.

[100] *Rapport, infra* p. 293. Problems arising from assistance and salvage at sea are within the scope of the Brussels Convention of 1910 for the Unification of Certain Rules of Law With Respect to Assistance and Salvage at Sea, in: *Zweigert/Kropholler* II E 206 (p. 7 ss.). Doubts as to the coverage of trusts are raised by the Law Commission, p. 64 s.

[101] But also here is true what has been said *supra* at p. 43 ss. about situations of a national character.

[102] *Siehr,* p. 581 (sub III 2) and 582 (sub 3 b); *Zweigert/Müller-Gindullis,* Quasi-Contracts, in: Int. Encyc. Comp. L. III (1974), Ch. 30, s. 40 and s. 36.

respect to other situations such as, for instance, the buyer's action for money had and received against the seller on the ground that the sale violated certain rules of foreign trade and therefore was null and void? It would be very unreasonable to apply the law of the country where the money happened to be paid. For these situations, however, art. 13, sentence 2, provides an exception to the general rule of the *lex loci actus*. But in any case a renvoi will not be accepted (art. 21; *infra* p. 64).

2. Exception: Closer Connection: Art. 13 s. 2

a) Common Connecting Factor. – The common connecting factor mentioned in the second sentence of art. 13 may be, among other things, any legal or contractual relationship between the parties. Hence there will be a closer connection with the law governing this relationship for all quasi-contractual claims arising out of this relationship. This is true even if the relationship, as in the afore-mentioned contract, did not become a valid one. In these cases the failed relationship has to be liquidated according to the law which would have governed the relationship[103].

b) Absence of Common Connecting Factor. – Although in many cases the *locus actus* or a common connecting factor will determine the applicable law in a reasonable way, there may be situations which cannot properly be solved either by the first or by the second sentence of art. 13. This may happen with cases of payment of other people's debts or with the *actio de in rem verso*. In order to meet these problems the second sentence of art. 13 should be altered. It should be provided that the closer connection, as in art. 10, para. 3, only *normally* should be based on a common connecting factor so that even *without* it a closer connection to another jurisdiction may prevail over the *locus actus* of art. 13 sent. 1.

III. Scope of the Applicable Law

Of course, the arts. 15, 16, 17 and 19 also apply to quasi-contractual claims. Whether a modified art. 7 will have a great influence in the field of quasi-contracts cannot be said in advance. As it is pointed out by the Report, art. 11 may be consulted in analogous situations[104].

---

[103] *Lagarde,* according to *D. Mayer,* p. 380; *Siehr,* p. 581; *Zweigert/Müller-Gindullis* (last note) s. 20; *E. Mezger,* according to *D. Mayer,* p. 380, wants to apply art. 15.

[104] Rapport, *infra* p. 296. Perhaps also art. 12 should be applied, cp. Law Commission, p. 66.

C. General Problems: Arts. 21–23

There are three general problems which remain before the General Report finishes with the Final Provisions of the Draft Convention: renvoi, public policy and uniform interpretation.

I. Renvoi: Art. 21

In Germany, for example, you may find contract and tort cases applying the renvoi[105]. Art. 21 of the Draft Convention excludes the renvoi *altogether* and this is accepted unanimously as the right decision[106].

II. Public Policy: Art. 22

Art. 22 of the Draft Convention about public policy is taken from the formulas used by the Hague Conference of Private International Law since 1965[107]. There is nothing to be said on art. 22 except perhaps two short remarks. First, public policy should not be mixed with the idea of *"fraude à la loi"*, as has been done in the Report[108], and, secondly, art. 22 should be kept separate from art. 7, as *Drobnig* correctly points out[109].

---

[105] BGH Feb. 14, 1958, AWD 1958, p. 57 = IPRspr. 1958–59 no. 39; BGH June 6, 1960, NJW 1960, p. 1720 = IPRspr. 1960–61 no. 23; *Graue,* Rückverweisung und Weiterverweisung im internationalen Vertragsrecht: AWD 1968, p. 121–131; *Kegel* in *Soergel/Siebert* (*supra* note 30) pre-notes to Art. 7, no. 278 (p. 131 s.).

[106] *Lipstein, infra* p. 163; *von Overbeck/Volken, infra* p. 180, and RabelsZ 38 (1974) p. 56, 75 s.; *Siehr,* p. 584. The Law Commission, p. 84, proposes to define what is meant by the word "country" used in art. 21. As in the latest Hague Conventions (*supra* note 36, art. 12; note 38, art. 13) a clause for non-unified legal systems may be inserted into the Draft Convention.

[107] *Cf., e. g.,* art. 10 of the Hague Convention on Traffic Accidents (*supra* note 38) and art. 10 of the Hague Convention on Products Liability (*supra* note 36).

[108] Rapport, *infra* p. 311.

[109] *Drobnig, infra* p. 86. – In the *Brodin* case (*supra* note 72) the accident took place in Scotland and the contract of employment was governed by Norwegian law. The court did not apply the contracted exemption clause valid under Norwegian law but applied Scottish law because the exemption clause was void by virtue of s. 1 (3) of the British Law Reform (Personal Injuries) Act 1948 (11 & 12 Geo. VI, c. 41). This Act was intended to alter the law of Scotland and to rid it of the defence of common employment. The

III. Uniform Interpretation

1. Interpretation Rule of Art. 23

It is obvious that the Convention has to be interpreted in a manner taking account of its international character. This exhortation to forget national niceties and qualifications has been laid down in art. 23. This provision, however, does not indicate how the uniform interpretation will be enforced. It merely urges the courts to strive for uniformity.

2. Jurisdiction of the European Court of Justice

One way to meet the problem of uniform interpretation would be to give jurisdiction to the Court of Justice of the European Communities in order that this body may review the application of the Convention by national courts. With respect to the European Convention on Jurisdiction and Enforcement of Judgments the original member states of the EEC have declared themselves willing to pursue such a way[110]. The same should be done concerning the Draft Convention[111]. The jurisdiction of the European Court of Justice, of course, would not guarantee uniform interpretation. On the other hand, it would not hamper a further improvement of the international law of obligations. The European Court of Justice could make of art. 23 more than a mere request to be internationally-minded, it could make of it an obligation subject to review on a supranational level.

In the discussion, *Jenard* strongly supported the proposition that the European Court of Justice should be empowered to review national decisions on the Convention and that the Draft Convention should be amended accordingly.

---

court decision may be interpreted that way: The court applied the Scottish public policy against Norwegian law. If the claim were brought in a third country, the courts of that country might be obliged by a new art. 7 of the Draft Convention to pay regard to s. 1 of the Law Reform (Personal Injuries) Act 1948.

[110] *Cf.* the Common Declaration annexed to the Convention of September 27, 1968 (*supra* note 11) and the Protocol of June 3, 1971, Concerning the Interpretation of this Convention by the Court of Justice of the European Communities, published by *Droz* (*supra* note 12) p. 506 ss.

[111] *Sauveplanne, infra* p. 187; *Siehr*, p. 585.

D. Final Provisions: Arts. 24–36

With reference to the Final Provisions of the Draft Convention, I should like to stress three main problems, *viz.* the scope of application according to art. 24 (I), the relation of the Draft Convention to already-existing and to future rules of law (II), and the coming into force of the Convention (III).

I. Scope of Application According to Art. 24

According to art. 24 the Convention is to apply independently of any requirement of reciprocity and even if the applicable law is not that of a contracting state. This provision is not an invention of the Working Group. In recent years the Hague Conventions have the same provisions and thereby ensure that within the scope of application as to the subject matter there will be only *one* set of conflicts rules in the contracting states and not two of them, namely a contractual one for conflicts between members of the contracting parties and another, non-contractual but local one for all other conflicts[112]. This is a reasonable approach and should be followed despite some American complaints against it[113].

II. Draft Convention and Other Rules of Law

With respect to the relation of the Draft Convention to other rules of law, the Final Provisions distinguish three different bodies of law, *viz.* first, law of the EEC (1), secondly domestic rules of law (2) and, finally, international treaties outside the EEC (3).

---

[112] *Cf., e. g.,* art. 11 of the Hague Convention on Traffic Accidents (*supra* note 38) and art. 11 of the Hague Convention on Products Liability (*supra* note 36). *Cf.* also art. 7 of the Hague Convention of June 15, 1955, on the Sale of Movables (Recueil, *supra* note 36, p. 12).

[113] *Cf. Nadelmann,* The Twelfth Session of the Hague Conference on Private International Law: Am. J. Comp. L. 21 (1973) p. 136–139; *id.,* The EEC Draft of a Convention on the Law Applicable to Contractual and Non-Contractual Obligations: Am. J. Comp. L. 21 (1973) p. 584, 586; *id.,* Conflicts Between Regional and International Work on Unification of Rules of Choice of Law: Harv. Int. L. J. 15 (1974) p. 213, 214, 228–231. *Cf.* also *Siehr,* p. 570 (sub B II).

1. Law of the EEC: Art. 25

It is obvious that special conflicts rules promulgated by institutions of the EEC or being part of conventions concluded within the framework of the Rome Treaties will derogate conflicting provisions of the Draft Convention (art. 25, paras. 1 and 2). Therefore the proposed Regulation of the Council on the Law Applicable to Labour Contracts Within the Community will, when it enters into force, take priority over the respective provisions of the Draft Convention [114].

2. Domestic Rules of Law

a) Domestic Conflicts Rules in Force. – It goes without saying that the Draft Convention will replace all domestic conflicts rules for contractual and non-contractual obligations in force within the EEC member states [115].

b) Future Domestic Legislation: Art. 26. – As to future domestic legislation affecting the unified conflicts rules of the Draft Convention, art. 26 creates an obligation for every member state to communicate its legislative intentions to the other signatory states. This provision may be called a "system of controlled freedom" [116].

3. International Treaties Outside the EEC

The relation of the Draft Convention to international treaties outside the EEC is to some extent obscure.

a) International Treaties Already in Force: Art. 27. – With respect to international treaties already in force, art. 27 provides that the Draft Convention shall be applied without prejudice to these treaties. This means that the Hague Convention of 1955 on the *Law Applicable to the International Sale of Goods* [117], the Hague Conventions of 1964 Relating to a *Uniform Law* on the International Sale of Goods [118], as

---

[114] *Cf.* J.O.C.E. no. C 49/26 of May 18, 1972 = RabelsZ 37 (1973) p. 585–588 = Rev. trim. dr. europ. 9 (1973) p. 152–155.

[115] As to the relevant written German conflicts rules *cf. Siehr*, p. 585 (sub D I 1). Mandatory national rules within art. 7 are not touched by the Convention, neither the present ones nor the future ones: *Drobnig, infra* p. 85 s.

[116] Rapport, *infra* p. 313 (commentary to art. 26), speaks of a "système de liberté surveillée".

[117] *Supra* note 112.

[118] *Zweigert/Kropholler* I E 137 and 138 (p. 41 ss.); Unidroit 1964 (1965) p. 71 ss.; Pasin. belge 1970, p. 1156 ss.; German BGBl. 1973 II 892 ss., 1973 I 856 ss.; Italian G.U. suppl. to no. 258 of Oct. 13, 1971; Riv. Dir. Int. Priv. Proc. 8 (1972) p. 629 ss.; Dutch Stbl. 1971 no. 779. *Cf.* also the British Uniform Laws on International Sales Act 1967 (1967 c. 45).

well as the Brussels Conventions on Maritime Law mentioned above
(*supra* p. 47), will stay in force between the contracting states.

b) Future Multilateral Treaties on Conflicts Law: Art. 28. – A procedure similar to that of art. 26 has to be pursued if a member state of
the European Communities wants to become a party to such a multilateral treaty on private international law concerning one of the matters governed by the Draft Convention (art. 28). If, for instance, an
EEC member state wants to introduce the Hague Convention on Products Liability[119] after the present Draft Convention has entered into
force, this intention has to be communicated to the other EEC member
states in order that they may try to come to a common arrangement
and to maintain uniformity.

*c) Remaining Future Conventions, Especially on Uniform Substan-
tive Law: Art. 29?* – There seems to be no doubt that the conclusion
of *bilateral* conventions on conflicts law does not require a communication of this fact to the other EEC member states[120]. The same is true
of *multilateral* treaties the conflicts rules of which are not a principal
aim of these treaties[121]. The Draft Convention is not clear, however,
as to the impact of treaties unifying *substantive* law. Are such treaties
also comprised by art. 29 or are they not[122]? Take, for example, a Council of Europe Convention on Products Liability[123], if such a convention
eliminates the question as to the applicable law, or the Hague Conventions of 1964 of a Uniform Law on the International Sale of Goods[124].
Although such a treaty does not embody conflicts rules of the usual
type, it may in fact lead to a non-application of the Draft Convention:
the judge simply applies the Uniform Law and does not have to determine the Law applicable according to the Draft Convention. To this
extent a multilateral convention on uniform law may impair the uniformity of European practice in international cases just as seriously
as a treaty on conflicts law does. In view of this situation, two things
should be made clear. First, the unification of substantive law for at
least international transactions must remain the ultimate aim of international legislation. Therefore all conventions on uniform *substantive
law* should prevail over treaties on *conflicts law* with regard to the

---

[119] *Supra* note 36.   [120] Rapport, *infra* p. 313 s.

[121] Rapport, *infra* p. 313 s.

[122] The Report (*infra* p. 314) denies this question without going deeper into
the problem.

[123] Cp. the Draft European Convention of March 20, 1975, on products liability in regard to personal injury and death and Draft Explanatory Report
[DIR/JUR (75) 1]. The Draft obliges the Contracting States to make their
national law conform with the provisions of the Convention (Art. 1) and,
therefore, does *not* eliminate the question as to the applicable law.

[124] *Supra* note 118.

same subject matter[125]. The same should be true for domestic legislation of those states which do not ratify these unifying conventions but promulgate a domestic statute with provisions identical to those provided in the convention. This prevalence of internationally unified law should be guaranteed even for future conventions on uniform substantive law.

The second point to be made refers to the question how, despite this prevalence, uniformity of European practice in the international law of obligations can be maintained. This could be tried by extending art. 28 of the Draft Convention to *all* multilateral conventions, *i. e.* also to those on uniform law if they affect the Draft Convention by its non-application.

This second point may be of minor importance. However, the General Reporter completely agrees with *Selvig* that the Draft Convention should not impair the unification of substantive law[126]. Conflicts law is merely an emergency device. The genuine international private law is – as *Ernst Rabel,* the founder of the Max-Planck-Institute in Hamburg once said[127] – the internationally unified private law. Today we still have to be modest and to find a common emergency device, but we should not hamper the movement towards a more ambitious unification of substantive law. This door should be left open by the final provisions of the present Draft Convention.

III. Coming into Force of the Convention: Art. 33

According to sentence 1 of art. 33 the Convention is to enter into force after the *fifth* instrument of ratification has been deposited with the Secretary General of the Council of the European Communities. This provision should not be altered because of the entrance of Denmark, Ireland and the United Kingdom into the Common Market. With respect to this new situation, it is true, one could argue that art. 33 should be redrafted and the coming into force of the Convention should be postponed until for example, the *eighth state,* has ratified it. One should not forget, however, that the Convention applies without any requirement of reciprocity and that it replaces the national conflicts rules on contractual and non-contractual obligations (*supra* p. 66 s.). Also several Hague Conventions of the last twenty years do not require any reciprocity and therefore provide that they shall enter

---

[125] *Siehr,* p. 586, with further references.

[126] *Selvig, infra* p. 204 s.

[127] *Rabel,* Privatrecht auf internationaler Ebene, in: Festgabe Erich Kaufmann (1950) p. 309, 311 = Gesammelte Aufsätze III (1967) p. 369, 371.

into force very quickly, *i. e.* some time after the deposit of the *third* instrument of ratification [128].

Jenard touched these problems already in his introductory remarks to the discussion of the whole Draft Convention. He pleaded for a speedy coming into force of the Convention and therefore did not favour a redrafting of art. 33. The sooner the Convention enters into force, the earlier the European Court of Justice, vested with the necessary jurisdictional powers (*supra* p. 65), can interpret the Convention and thereby contribute to its uniform application by the courts of the present and future contracting states.

E. Summary

I. The *international law of torts* as provided by the Draft Convention may be criticized in four respects, *viz.* the scope of art. 10, the connecting factors used by art. 10, the provision as to several victims (art. 10, para. 4) and the scope of the applicable law (art. 11).

1. The *scope of art. 10* is not conclusively delimited by this main conflicts rule on torts itself. Regard must be paid to arts. 1 and 14 not only as to what they expressly provide but also as to matters they do not mention in particular.

a) *Situations of an international character* only are to be regulated by the Convention (art. 1, para. 1). This restriction is criticized with respect to contractual obligations [129]. But in the present context, too, it turns out that the restriction should be omitted, at least for torts, particularly as the Report of the Working Group itself admits that it is only possible to determine by reference to the court seized of a dispute whether a certain situation is international in character or is a purely internal one (*cf. supra* p. 43 ss).

b) The *liability of the state and state officials,* according to art. 14, is, at least to a large extent, not covered by the Draft Convention. *Von Overbeck* and *Volken,* however, convincingly argue that the state liability for acts performed *iure gestionis* should also be included in the scope of the Convention or that the responsibility of state officials for such acts should be excluded too. To treat a state and its officials differently, does not make sense (*cf. supra* p. 45).

c) Certain *family torts,* as, *e. g.,* criminal conversation, are not exempt from application of the Convention. This should not be altered by redrafting

---

[128] *Cf., e. g.,* the Hague Convention of 1956 on the Law Applicable to Maintenance Obligations in Respect to Children, and the Hague Convention on the Law Applicable to Maintenance Obligations, prepared at the 12th session of the Hague Conference in 1972, *cf.* Recueil (*supra* note 36) p. 32 and p. 218.

[129] *Von Hoffmann, supra* p. 2 ss.

ar. 1, para. 2, lit. a, because the European Convention of 1968 on Jurisdiction and Enforcement of Judgments in Civil and Commercial Matters also covers these tort claims (*cf. supra* p. 46).

d) *Maritime torts,* too, are subject to the conflicts rules of the Draft Convention owing to the fact that the entire law of transport, although extensively unified by international conventions already in force, is not excluded by art. 1, para. 2. This is criticized, especially by *Selvig.* The Convention will be without prejudice to the application of international conventions already in force and it will not hamper further unification (*cf. supra* p. 47, 67 ss.). It has, however, to be admitted that the present Draft does not satisfactorily cope with special problems of maritime law, such as the law applicable to collisions on the high seas or to the limitation of the shipowner's liability. To meet this criticism the Working Group should also take into account these somewhat unique situations of international transport unless it prefers to exclude this field of law altogether from the scope of this Convention (*cf. supra* p. 46 ss.).

2. As *connecting* factors the Draft Convention generally favours the *locus delicti commissi.* But if there is a closer connection with another country, then the law of the other country should apply.

a) The *lex loci rule is,* in the discussion, too, generally accepted as the appropriate starting point for the determination of the law governing tortious liability (*supra* p. 51). Yet there is no agreement as to the definition of the *locus delicti* (*supra* p. 48 s.). Art. 10, para. 1, seems to prefer the law at the place of harm. On the one hand this presumption was endorsed by *Lagarde* (*supra* p. 49). On the other hand the Report expressly states that the Draft Convention intentionally avoids a preference in favour of the place of conduct or the place of harm because art. 10, para. 1, does not want to impede ongoing developments in European case law.

This indifference or, at least, ambiguity of art, 10, para. 1, has been attacked because it might cause uncertainty and "forum shopping" in general and with respect to a *Distanzdelikt* or *délit commis à distance* in particular (*supra* p. 49 ss.). An the latter cases German and Swiss courts would continue their standing court practice according to which neither the law at the place of conduct nor that at the place of harm exclusively governs but that one of these laws which is more favourable for the victim. *Batiffol* vigorously opposed the idea of such a choice whereas others, especially *Hjerner* and *van Hoogstraten,* pleaded for the language of art. 10, para. 1, which will give some leeway to the courts to find reasonable answers to a still unsettled problem (*supra* p. 49 s.).

b) A *closer connection* with another country shall discard the *lex loci* only if there is "no significant link" between the tortious act and the *locus delicti* (art. 10, para. 2). Although there is not much enthusiasm about this novel sort of "missing link" as an independent prerequisite, *Jenard* strongly urged that art. 10 should not be changed in this respect, as there may be cases in which this prerequisite will be helpful, and, above all, an omission of the "significant link" would destroy a compromise finally reached (*supra* p. 51 s).

As the closer connection must normally be based on a connecting factor *common* to the victim and the tortfeasor (art. 10, para. 3), the discussions concentrated on this common connecting factor and especially on the question whether and to what extent preexistent contractual relations may establish a closer connection to a jurisdiction different from the *lex loci* (*supra* p. 53 ss.). There was unanimous agreement that claims arising within a contractual relation (not, however, on occasion of it) are governed by the law governing the contract *(lex contractus)* regardless of whether the action is brought in contract or in tort *(von Hoffmann, Lagarde, Schultsz, Selvig, Siesby)*. Nevertheless this kind of *akzessorische Anknüpfung* might be expressly mentioned as perhaps the solution of typical conflicts between *several* connecting factors common to the parties, e. g. the common domicile of fellow-countrymen in a country of which they are not citizens.

A subsequent contractual choice of law with respect to an already existing tort claim should also be admitted (*supra* p. 55).

If there is *no* common connecting factor, the *lex loci* may nevertheless have to give way to the law of a jurisdiction more closely connected with the tort. Art. 10, para. 3, *normally* only requires a connecting factor common to the parties.

Especially for such situations without a *common* connecting factor it might be helpful for daily practice to formulate *special* connecting factors for certain types of torts, such as, e. g., the flag for collisions on the high seas or the place of sale for products liability (*supra* p. 55).

c) As a *renvoi* is not recognized (art. 21), the conflicts rules of an applicable foreign *lex delicti* are of no importance (*supra* p. 56).

3. If there are *several victims* of the same tort, the applicable law should not be determined for every victim separately as art. 10, para. 4, provides. This question need not be answered by the Draft Convention as it is not done with regard to the problem of plurality of tortfeasors. Courts should not be impeded from applying the same law to all responsible persons and to all victims of a disaster such as, let us say, an air crash or a collision of ships (*supra* p. 56).

4. The *scope of the applicable lex delicti* is described and deliminated by art. 11 and some special provisions.

a) Nearly all parts of *art. 11* are criticized by various experts. *Selvig* does not like the limitation of liability (art. 11, no. 2) to be governed automatically by the *lex delicti* (*supra* p. 57). With respect to the form and extent of compensation (art. 11, no. 4) *Lipstein* prefers to apply the *lex fori* whereas *Røed* and *Sundström* want to pay regard to the victim's residence and domicile. Despite these objections to art. 11, no. 4, there are some doubts, however, whether this provision has to be redrafted (*supra* p. 57 s.). The case is different with art. 11, no. 5, on the transmissibility of tort claims by succession and art. 11, no. 6, on the persons entitled to compensation. These rules could be formulated in clearer language (*supra* p. 58).

Vicarious liability (art. 11, no. 7) and the statute of limitations (art. 11 no. 8) are also subject to the *lex delicti,* although with respect to the latter problem some qualification must be made (*supra* p. 58 s.).

The capacity to do wrongful acts is not mentioned in art. 11. Art. 1, para. 2, lit. a, however, which excludes questions of capacity from the scope of application altogether, need not be a bar to regulating this capacity. This question should be treated by the Convention (*supra* p. 59) as direct actions should not be omitted from regulation (*supra* p. 59).

b) Some *special provisions* take into account the law of jurisdictions, which is sometimes different from that of the *lex delicti*.

According to art. 12 certain local data (*e. g.* traffic regulations) have to be recognized irrespective of the law applicable under art. 10. However self-evident this may be, *Fallon* has demonstrated that a more flexible language in art. 12 should be chosen. Courts should take into consideration all safety rules which the victim could reasonably rely on at the time of injury (*supra* p. 60).

It goes without saying that arts. 15, 16, 17 and 19 also apply to torts. Art. 17 on assignments could perhaps be amended in order to make sure that the debtor be protected if he *bona fide* pays his original creditor (*supra* p. 61). Art. 7, too, should be redrafted and extended to tort claims (*supra* p. 61).

II. The *international law of quasi-contracts* is regulated in art. 13.

1. As to the *scope of art. 13*, this provision does not enumerate specific types of non-contractual obligations not arising out of a tort. Only the liability of the state and its officials (art. 14; *supra* p. 45) is expressly excluded from the broad field of application of art. 13 (*supra* p. 62).

2. The *connecting factor* for quasi-contractual liability generally is the *locus actus*, and exceptionally a closer connection with another jurisdiction prevails.

a) Whether the *locus actus* is an appropriate connecting factor for all types of quasi-contracts seems to be rather doubtful (*supra* p. 62 s.). Therefore a general evasion clause is one of utmost importance.

b) This evasion clause refers to a *closer connection* of the situation with a country different from the *locus actus*. Art. 13, sent. 2, requires that this closer connection has to be created by a *common connecting factor*, for example by a contractual relationship even if it did not become a valid one. Then the hypothetical *lex contractus* should govern (*supra* p. 63).

If there is *no* common connecting factor, the *lex loci actus* would apply according to the general principle of art. 13. To achieve better results, art. 13, sent. 2, should be redrafted. A closer connection *normally* should depend only on a common connecting factor (*supra* p. 63).

3. The *scope* of the law applicable to quasi-contracts is described by arts. 15, 16, 17 and 19, by a modified art. 7 and by art. 11 in analogous situations of the law of quasi-contracts (*supra* p. 63).

III. Three *general problems* of conflicts law are dealt with in arts. 21–23.

1. The exclusion of any *renvoi* (art. 21) has been accepted unanimously (*supra* p. 64).

2. *Public policy* (art. 22) should be distinguished from a more comprehensive art. 7 (*supra* p. 64).

3. With respect to the *uniform interpretation* of the Convention (art. 23),

Jenard strongly supported an amendment giving jurisdiction to the European Court of Justice to review national decisions on the Convention (*supra* p. 65).

IV. The *final provisions* of the Draft Convention (arts. 24–36) relate to three major problems.

1. First, *no requirement of reciprocity* is necessary for the application of the Convention. Hence it applies even if the law governing is that of a non-contracting party (art. 24; *supra* p. 66).

2. Secondly, the relation of the Draft Convention to *other rules of law* is extensively regulated by the final provisions.

a) It goes without saying that *EEC conflict rules* on *special* problems will prevail over the present Convention on the law of obligations in *general* (art. 25; *supra* p. 67).

b) *Domestic conflicts law* already in force will be replaced by the respective conventional rules (*supra* p. 67). As to *future* domestic legislation in this field, the contracting parties have to communicate their legislative intentions to the other signatory states (art. 26; *supra* p. 67).

c) International *treaties concluded outside the EEC* are not touched by the Convention if they are already in force (art. 27; *supra* p. 67 s.). If an EEC member state wants to ratify a *multilateral* treaty on conflicts law, it also has to communicate this intention to the other EEC member states (art. 28; *supra* p. 68). This communication is not necessary with respect to future *bilateral* treaties. A problem still unsettled, however, is whether future conventions on *substantive* law (*e. g.* a Council of Europe Convention on Products Liability) requires any communication procedure. An affirmative answer should be given although there should be no doubt that the present Convention must not hamper the more ambitious aim to unify substantive law (*supra* p. 68 s.).

3. Finally, the Convention is to *enter into force* at a certain date after the deposit of the fifth instrument of ratification (art. 33). This provision should not be redrafted on account of the entrance of the three new members into the Common Market. *Jenard* pleaded for a speedy coming into force of the Convention (*supra* p. 69 s.).

F. Résumé

I. La solution que le Projet apporte aux problèmes de conflits de lois en matière d'*obligations aquiliennes* est susceptible de plusieurs critiques. Celles-ci concernent (1) le champ d'application de l'article 10, (2) le rattachement qui y est prévu, (3) la solution de l'alinéa 4 de l'article 10 relatif à l'hypothèse de la pluralité des victimes, et (4) le domaine de la loi délictuelle (art. 11).

1. Le *domaine d'application de l'article 10* n'est pas déterminé de façon exclusive par cette règle principale de conflit en matière de droit délictuel. De plus, il convient de se référer aux articles 1 et 14. En effet, ces dispositions

insèrent ou excluent expressément une série de délits du champ d'application de la Convention; mais les limites du domaine peuvent également être déduites de l'omission de certaines matières.

a) Le domaine de la Convention est limité aux seules *situations qui présentent un caractère international* (alinéa premier de l'art. premier). Dans son rapport, M. *von Hoffmann* fait état des objections auxquelles cette limitation a donné lieu lors des débats sur l'article premier (v. *supra* p. 2 ss.). Ces objections restent valables en ce qui concerne les obligations délictuelles: cette limitation devrait être supprimée du moins quant à la responsabilité delictuelle; d'ailleurs le Groupe des Experts lui-même a reconnu l'impossibilté d'opérer une distinction *a priori* entre les situations qui ont un caractère international et les situations purement internes: seul le juge saisi d'un litige est à même d'effectuer cette appréciation (v. *supra* p. 43 ss.).

b) Le Projet exclut, dans une certaine mesure, la *responsabilité de l'Etat et de ses agents ou organes* (art. 14). Cependant MM. *von Overbeck* et *Volken* avancent des arguments fort pertinents en faveur de l'inclusion de la responsabilité de l'Etat dans le champ d'application de la Convention en ce qui concerne les actes accomplis *jure gestionis*; si cette responsabilité était exclue, il devrait alors en aller de même de la responsabilité des organes ou agents de l'Etat à propos de ces mêmes actes. Toute solution contraire serait dépourvue de sens (comp. *supra* p. 45).

c) La Convention s'étend à certains *délits de droit familial,* comme l'adultère. Or, ceux-ci sont également couverts par la *Convention européenne concernant la compétence judiciaire et l'exécution des décisions en matière civile et commerciale.* C'est pourquoi un amendement éventuel de l'alinéa 2, litt. a), de l'article premier du Projet ne devrait apporter aucune modification sur ce point (*supra* p. 46).

d) En ce qui concerne les *délits de droit maritime,* ceux-ci sont également couverts par les règles du Projet. En effet, l'alinéa 2 de l'article premier n'exclut nullement le droit des transports, quoique celui-ci soit déjà largement unifié par des conventions entrées en vigueur. M. *Selvig* s'est fermement opposé à l'insertion de cette matière. S'il est vrai que la Convention ne porte aucune atteinte à l'application d'autres instruments internationaux déjà entrés en vigueur et ne constitue aucun obstacle à une unification plus poussée (comp. *supra* p. 47, 67 ss.), il faut néanmoins reconnaître que le Projet actuel ne répond pas de manière satisfaisante à tous les problèmes spécifiques que pose le droit maritime: ainsi en est-il des accidents survenus en haute mer, hors des eaux territoriales, ou encore de la limitation de la responsabilité du propriétaire du navire. C'est pourquoi le Groupe des Experts devrait tenir compte de ces situations quelques peu uniques en leur genre, à moins qu'il ne préfère exclure purement et simplement toute cette matière du champ d'application de la Convention (comp. *supra* p. 46 ss.).

2. Le *principe de rattachement* qu'utilise le Projet est l'application de la *lex loci delicti commissi.* Toutefois, s'il existe une connexion prépondérante avec un autre pays, il fait application de la loi de ce pays.

a) Les rapports tout autant que les débats ont approuvé l'application de la *lex loci* comme principe de base, servant de point de départ à la recherche de la loi délictuelle (*supra* p. 51). Cependant le problème de la détermination du *locus delicti* fait toujours l'objet de vives controverses (*supra* p. 48 s.). M. *Lagarde* déduit de l'alinéa premier de l'article 10 que la localisation peut être faite au lieu du préjudice. Mais d'autre part, le Rapport explicatif souligne en toutes lettres le souci du Projet de laisser cette question sans réponse, de manière à ne pas entraver l'évolution de la jurisprudence dans les divers Etats membres.

Cette neutralité de l'alinéa premier de l'article 10 a fait l'objet de vives critiques en raison de son ambiguïté et de l'incertitude qu'elle peut engendrer: non seulement elle encourage le *forum shopping,* mais en outre elle n'apporte aucune solution aux problèmes particuliers que posent les délits commis à distance *(Distanzdelikte)* (*supra* p. 49 ss.). Ainsi en Allemagne et en Suisse, les tribunaux appliquent à de tels cas la loi la plus favorable à la victime et rejettent le rattachement exclusif au lieu du fait générateur ou au lieu du préjudice; et rien ne laisse supposer qu'ils abandonnent cette pratique devenue constante. Au cours de débats, M. *Batiffol* s'est violemment opposé au principe de l'option, tandis que d'autres, tout particulièrement MM. *Hjerner* et *van Hoogstraten,* approuvèrent le silence de l'alinéa premier de l'article 10, préférant laisser au juge le pouvoir d'apprécier lui-même, en toute objectivité, la solution à donner à un problème non encore assez mûr pour recevoir une réponse globale (*supra* p. 49 s.).

b) Lorsque la situation délictuelle présente une *connexion prépondérante* avec un autre pays, la *lex loci delicti* est écartée au profit de la loi de ce pays, mais à condition qu'il n'existe aucun «lien significatif» entre le fait générateur du dommage et le pays où ce fait s'est produit (art. 10, alinéa 2). Présentée comme une condition préalable, cette dernière exigence n'a guère suscité d'enthousiasme. Néanmoins M. *Jenard* insista vivement sur la nécessité de ne modifier en rien l'article 10 sur cette question. En effet, cette condition préalable pourra s'avérer extrêmement utile dans certains cas; mais surtout, sa suppression risquerait de mettre à néant un compromis fort précieux en raison des efforts accomplis pour y arriver (*supra* p. 51 s.).

L'alinéa 3 de l'article 10 précise que la connexion prépondérante se fondera normalement sur un élément de rattachement *commun* à la victime et à l'auteur du dommage. Ce critère du rattachement commun suscita de vives discussions, tout particulièrement quant à la question de savoir dans quelle mesure des relations contractuelles pré-existantes peuvent constituer un lien assez étroit pour attribuer la compétence législative à une loi autre que la *lex loci* (*supra* p. 53 ss.). En ce qui concerne les litiges survenant dans le cadre de rapports contractuels – à l'exclusion toutefois de ceux soulevés uniquement à l'occasion d'un contrat –, le principe unanimement admis est l'application de la loi contractuelle même si l'action portée devant le juge reçoit une qualification aquilienne *(von Hoffmann, Lagarde, Schultsz, Selvig, Siesby).* Quoiqu'il en soit, un «rattachement dépendant» *(akzessorische Anknüpfung)* devrait être mentionné de façon expresse comme devrait l'être peut-être egalement une solution satisfaisante aux conflits que suscite l'hypothèse où *plusieurs* facteurs de rattachement sont communs aux parties, par exemple lorsque deux personnes de même nationalité possèdent un domicile commun à l'étranger.

De plus, il faudrait reconnaître un plein effet au choix de la loi applicable au contrat effectué postérieurement à l'intentement de l'action délictuelle *(supra* p. 55). D'autre part, même en l'*absence* d'un élément de rattachement commun, la *lex loci* peut encore devoir céder le pas à la loi d'un pays qui possède un lien plus étroit avec le délit. En effet, l'alinéa 3 de l'article 10 stipule uniquement que la connexion sera *normalement* un rattachement commun aux parties.

Précisément, dans ces cas où fait défaut un rattachement *commun* aux parties, il faudrait peut-être aider le praticien du droit en prévoyant des facteurs de rattachement *spéciaux* qui soient adaptés à certains types de délits. Par exemple, la loi du pavillon conviendrait fort bien aux accidents survenus en haute mer, et la loi du lieu de la vente d'un produit à la responsabilité des fabricants *(supra* p. 55).

c) L'article 21 rejette la théorie du *renvoi.* Par conséquent, les règles de conflit de la loi délictuelle ne retiennent pas l'attention *(supra* p. 56).

3. N'abordant pas l'hypothèse de la pluralité de défendeurs, le Projet ne devrait pas non plus traiter du cas où *plusieurs personnes sont victimes* d'un même fait générateur de dommage. En effet, il est préférable de ne pas prévoir l'application d'une loi différente à l'égard de chacune des victimes. Or, c'est ce que fait l'alinéa 4 de l'article 10. Au contraire, il faudrait laisser la possibilité aux tribunaux de soumettre toutes les personnes dont la responsabilité est invoquée à la même loi, de même que toutes les personnes victimes d'une même catastrophe comme un accident d'avion ou une collision de navires *(supra* p. 56).

4. Le *domaine* de la loi délictuelle fait l'objet de l'article 11 ainsi que de quelques dispositions éparses.

a) Pratiquement tous les points de l'*article 11* ont fait l'objet de l'une ou l'autre critique. Ainsi, en ce qui concerne les limitations de responsabilité (litt. 2), M. *Selvig* désapprouve l'application mécanique de la *lex loci delicti* *(supra* p. 57). M. *Lipstein* préfère l'application de la *lex fori* aux modalités et à l'étendue de la responsabilité (litt. 4), tandis que MM. *Røed* et *Sundström* sont partisans de l'application de la loi de la résidence ou du domicile de la victime. Malgré ces objections, l'on peut néanmoins s'interroger sur l'opportunité d'amender le litt. 4 de l'article 11 *(supra p. 57 s.).* Mais il en va tout autrement du litt. 5 sur la transmissibilité du droit à réparation aux héritiers, et du litt. 6 relatif aux personnes ayant droit à la réparation: leur formulation gagnerait à être plus claire *(supra* p. 58).

Le domaine de la loi délictuelle s'étend également à la responsabilité du fait d'autrui (litt. 7) ainsi qu'aux prescriptions et déchéances (litt. 8). Le texte actuel du litt. 8 devrait recevoir une formulation plus nuancée en raison de certaines distinctions auxquelles peuvent donner lieu les questions relatives à l'interruption et à la suspension des délais *(supra* p. 58 s.).

L'article 11 ne traite pas de la capacité délictuelle, alors que l'alinéa 2, litt. a), de l'article premier exclut expressément les questions relatives à l'état et à la capacité. Pourtant, il n'est pas nécessaire que le Groupe des

Experts exclût la capacité délictuelle de la Convention. Une rectification en ce sens devrait être faite dans le texte définitif (*supra* p. 59). La Convention devrait également régler le problème de l'action directe (*supra* p. 59).

b) Quelques dispositions du Projet imposent certaines *limites au domaine* de la *lex loci delicti.*

D'après l'article 12, le juge doit considérer comme un donné de fait certaines réglementations en vigueur au lieu où le fait dommageable s'est produit – par exemple les lois sur la circulation routière –, quelle que soit la loi délictuelle désignée en vertu de l'article 10. Quoique ce rattachement aille de soi, M. *Fallon* préconise une formule plus souple: les tribunaux devraient prendre en considération toutes les règles de sécurité sur la protection desquelles la victime pouvait légitimement compter au moment de la lésion (*supra* p. 60).

Il va sans dire que les articles 15, 16, 17 et 19 s'appliquent également aux délits. Peut-être faudrait-il modifier l'article 17 relatif à la cession de créance et protéger le débiteur qui s'est exécuté de bonne foi auprès de son créancier originaire (*supra* p. 61). De même, l'article 7 devrait recevoir une nouvelle formulation, pour s'appliquer également aux obligations délictuelles (*supra* p. 61).

II. L'article 13 traite des conflits de lois en matière de *quasi-contrats.*

1. En ce qui concerne le *domaine* de l'article 13, il n'y figure aucune liste énumérant les principaux types d'obligations non contractuelles qui trouvent leur source en dehors d'un délit. Seul l'article 14 exclut expressément la responsabilité de l'Etat et de ses organes ou agents (*supra* p. 45) du champ d'application très étendu de l'article 13 (*supra* p. 62).

2. Le *principe de rattachement* de la responsabilité quasi-contractuelle est l'application de la loi en vigueur au lieu où le fait s'est produit (*locus actus*); exceptionellement, référence est faite à une connexion prépondérante avec un autre pays.

a) Il est peu probable que le *locus actus* constitue un facteur de rattachement vraiment adapté à toutes les catégories de quasi-contrats (*supra* p. 62 s.). Ceci mesure toute l'importance d'un rattachement subsidiaire.

b) Celui-ci a trait à une *connexion prépondérante* de la situation avec un pays autre que celui où le fait s'est produit. Mais l'alinéa 2 de l'article 13 exige en outre que cette connexion soit constituée d'un *élément de rattachement commun,* par exemple une relation contractuelle même restée sans effet. Dans ce cas prévaudra la *lex contractus* présumée (*supra* p. 63).

En l'*absence* d'un rattachement commun, la *lex loci* est applicable en vertu du principe général de l'article 13. Mais peut-être conviendrait-il d'amender l'alinéa 2 en exigeant uniquement que la connexion prépondérante soit *normalement* un rattachement commun aux parties (*supra* p. 63): en effet, la formulation actuelle de l'alinéa 2 risque d'amoindrir son incidence pratique.

3. Le *domaine* de la loi applicable aux quasi-contrats est fixé par les articles 15, 16, 17 et 19, par l'article 7 modifié et par l'article 11 en tant qu'applicable à des situations analogues aux quasi-contrats (*supra* p. 63).

III. Les articles 21 à 23 traitent de trois questions qui ont une *portée générale*.

1. L'exclusion de tout *renvoi* (art. 21) a été accueillie à l'unanimité (*supra* p. 64).

2. L'article 22 distingue nettement la notion d'*ordre public* des normes visées à l'article 7 étendu aux délits (*supra* p. 64).

3. Ayant en vue la nécessité d'une *interprétation uniforme* de la Convention (art. 23), M. *Jenard* se montra un partisan résolu d'une modification au texte qui attribuerait compétence à la Cour de Justice Européenne pour connaître de litiges d'interprétation soulevés par toute décision d'un tribunal national (*supra* p. 65).

IV. Les *dispositions finales* du Projet portent essentiellement sur trois types de questions.

1. Tout d'abord, l'application de la Convention est indépendante de toute *condition de réciprocité*. Cela signifie que la Convention s'applique même si la loi applicable n'est pas celle d'un Etat contractant (art. 24; *supra* p. 66).

2. En deuxième lieu, les dispositions finales s'étendent longuement sur l'éventualité de *conflits avec d'autres sources de droit*.

a) Il va sans dire que la présente Convention, portant sur les obligations *en général*, ne doit préjuger en rien de l'application des *règles de conflit* établies *à un niveau européen* sur des matières *spéciales* (art. 25; *supra* p. 67).

b) La Convention se substitue aux *règles nationales* de conflit correspondantes qui sont déjà entrées *en vigueur* dans les divers Etats membres (*supra* p. 67). Quant aux modifications nationales *postérieures* à l'entrée en vigueur de la Convention, les Etats membres devront communiquer leur intention d'y procéder aux autres Etats signataires (art. 26; *supra* p. 67).

c) La Convention ne porte pas atteinte aux *instruments internationaux élaborés en dehors de la CEE*, à condition qu'ils soient entrées en vigueur antérieurement (art. 27; *supra* p. 67 s.). Si un Etat membre de la CEE désire devenir partie à une Convention *multilatérale* de conflits de lois, elle doit également communiquer son intention de la faire aux autres Etats membres (art. 28; *supra* p. 68). Cette communication ne s'impose pas pour les instruments *bilatéraux* entrés en vigueur postérieurement. Mais un problème est resté sans solution: les Conventions futures de *droit matériel* – par exemple une Convention du Conseil de l'Europe sur la responsabilité du fait des produits – nécessitent-elles une procédure quelconque de communication aux Etats signataires? Quoique la présente Convention ne doive certainement pas constituer un obstacle à l'objectif plus ambitieux de l'unification du droit matériel, une telle procédure paraît devoir s'imposer (*supra* p. 68 s.).

3. Enfin, la Convention *entrera en vigueur* un certain temps après le dépôt du cinquième instrument de ratification (art. 33). Cette disposition ne doit faire l'objet d'aucune modification, en raison de l'entrée des trois nouveaux membres au sein du Marché Commun. M. *Jenard* plaida une entrée en vigueur aussi prompte que possible de la Convention (*supra* p. 69 s.).

SOME COMMENTS ON CONTRACTUAL OBLIGATIONS

By

the Austrian Ministry of Justice

Vienna

In cases of bilateral contracts the Draft Convention prefers as connecting factors the habitual residence or the principal establishment of the party who is to carry out the characteristic obligation rather than those factors pertaining to the other party (art. 4, sub-para. 2). Thus, according to the Report, a contract can be linked to its economic background. Theoretically, however, it may be doubtful whether this background always can be located properly by the concept of characteristic performance. There may be for instance contracts for sale which have also strong relations to the economic and social life of the country where the buyer lives.

With respect to some provisions of the Draft Convention it may be anticipated that they will be difficult to handle in practice and that they may impair legal certainty by giving wide discretion to the judges. The articles 4 (sub-para. 2), 5 and 6, for example, provide objective points of contact (habitual residence of the party who has to perform the characteristic obligation, country where the work habitually has to be carried out, place where the immovable property is situated) and these objective connecting factors shall not be decisive if in all the circumstances it is clear that the contract is more closely connected with another country not yet selected by the above mentioned objective connecting factors. These provisions may have the result that in all cases, despite the objective points of contact, the judges have to make up their minds as to the country with which the case has the closest connections. This has to be emphasized because even the Report is very critical about these difficult and eventually often uncertain determinations of the closest connection (Report, *infra* p. 271).

Courts will also have problems with the application of art. 7. According to this provision compulsory rules different from those which govern the contract, the assignment or the formal validity of an act, shall be taken into account under three conditions: The case must have connections with the country providing these compulsory rules, the compulsory rules must govern the case in such a way that they exclude the application of every other law and this exclusion must at least be partially justifiable by the particular character and purpose of these rules. On the one hand, this provision again gives wide discretion to the courts. On the other hand, it will be necessary to analyse and compare the law of all those countries which have any contact with the case. Eventually some provisions of several jurisdictions may be applicable and cause difficulties of adjustment if they are contradictory.

It is the opinion of the Ministry of Justice that several of all these difficulties might be avoided by three different rules: Firstly, there should be a very broad provision on party autonomy which also takes account of an implied choice of law to be gathered from the particular circumstances. Secondly, it would be better to provide strict rules without any exception for certain contracts if the parties did not determine the law applicable. Banking contracts, *e. g.,* transport contracts, as well as contracts to store or to forward goods might be governed by the law at the principal establishment of the bank, the transport, storing or forwarding business respectively. Hire purchase agreements and other consumer contracts should be connected with the law at the habitual residence of the purchaser or the consumer. Labour contracts without any choice of law might be governed by the law of the country where the employee habitually carries out his work. Finally, all other contracts, for which no specific rule is provided in cases of no express or implied choice of law by the parties, should be performed according to the law at the place of contracting.

These comments do not mean that the Ministry of Justice in general disapproves the Draft Convention. If the Draft Convention will obtain public consent and a corresponding Convention will be ratified by the member countries of the EEC, the Ministry of Justice would probably support the Convention as soon as the accession of Austria becomes relevant. This statement, of course, cannot prejudice future decisions.

COMMENTS ON ART. 7 OF THE DRAFT CONVENTION

By

ULRICH DROBNIG

Hamburg

1. General Comment

Art. 7 attempts to resolve the difficult and controversial problem of fixing the legal incidents flowing from the exclusive mandatory provisions of a country other than that of the *lex contractus.*

It is fortunate that the committee has proposed a special rule to deal with this problem in light of the increasing number of exclusive mandatory provisions which have been enacted in all countries for the promotion of specific economic, social or political aims.

Although the general contents of the proposed rule can be approved, it would seem that art. 7, in its present form, could be improved in several respects.

2. Scope of Application

The scope of art. 7 is limited to: contractual obligations, including their formal validity, and the voluntary and statutory assignments of all claims regardless of their legal character. It is, perhaps, the limited scope of the article which explains why the provision has been placed amidst the rules on contractual obligations.

It is certainly true that the provision will most often be applied in the context of contractual obligations. This explicit limitation appears to be too narrow, however, for two reasons. First, contractual obligations are often combined with non-contractual obligations. This is especially true in the area of tort claims (art. 10 para. 3 of the draft envisages such a combination). Is art. 7 inapplicable in such a case?

Second, even in the situation which involves purely non-contractual obligations (such as a tort claim or a claim based upon unjust enrichment) it may be necessary to take into account the exclusive, mandatory provisions of a law outside the *lex obligationis*, *e. g.*, the foreign exchange rules of another country.

For these reasons, it is submitted that the scope of application of art. 7 should be extended to encompass all of the conflicts rules within the proposed draft. It also follows that the provision should be placed among the general rules of the draft, perhaps after the present art. 19.

3. Raison d'être

The comments to art. 7 assume the necessity of the provision despite the fact that it is without statutory precedent. Perhaps, the assumption is made too readily, when the only justification offered is that "the need for it is incontestable". If a more explicit justification were offered, this would be helpful to achieve the desired uniform application of this novel provision, especially in determining its outer limits.

Two justifications for taking into account a third country's exclusive, mandatory provisions deserve particular attention. First, states should mutually pay regard for each other's interests; and second, citizens should not be exposed to contradictory rules. These two principles are of primary importance in the relationships among states which share common political convictions, and even to a greater extent where they pursue common goals. A third principle, that of achieving substantive justice, comes into play with regard to mandatory rules which aim at the protection of the weaker, or the less experienced, contracting party.

4. Contents of the Conflicts Rule

On close examination, the proposed art. 7 contains three requirements which must be met before taking into account the exclusive, mandatory rules which are outside the *lex contractus*. These requirements are: (1) the contract must "also" have a connection with the other country; (2) the rules of the other country must govern the matter compulsorily and to the exclusion of any other law; and (3) the particular character and purpose of the rules must justify their exclusive application.

a) In General. – It would facilitate the application of the difficult new conflicts rule if these three requirements, as such, were expressed more clearly. As to substance, the first two requirements call for brief comment only, while the third requirement deserves closer analysis and more extended discussion.

b) "Connection". – The draft requires no more than "a" connection

6 *

between the contract and the other country. "A" connection implies "any" connection, and "any" connection seems to be too loose and too broad to justify the other country's law being taken into account. It is submitted that only a *close* connection of the legal relationship with the other country would justify the intervention of the latter's mandatory rules. Also two practical considerations militate in favour of this restriction: first, only a very limited number of countries (often only one or two) will have a close connection with the contract, so that only the mandatory rules of these few countries need to be taken into account; second, a possible conflict between the mandatory rules of various countries is less likely in these circumstances.

c) *Claim of exclusive application.* – The draft correctly demands that the mandatory rules of the other country must exclude the application of any other law. A very minor suggestion is offered and it relates to the form of this requirement: from the viewpoint of the *lex fori,* the other country's mandatory rules can merely *claim* exclusive international application rather than effect this exclusion, as the wording of the draft suggests.

d) *The justification for the exclusive application* is derived in the draft from "the particular character and purpose of the rules" (art. 7, *in fine*). This aspect of the rule deserves the closest scrutiny.

In effect, the rule promises to honour any legislator's purpose, however whimsical or wicked it may be. In light of the experiences of the last forty years, no one would be bold enough to deny the very real possibility of repulsive legislation. It should not be necessary to invoke the public policy clause of art. 22 in order to prevent the application of such legislation. This is especially true in light of the fact that art. 22 demands that the incompatibility of the foreign law with the forum's public policy must be "manifest".

On the contrary, it appears to be necessary that art. 7, itself, should contain a limiting clause. The yardstick that should be used to determine the application of a third country's mandatory rules, should be that of "international standards". Neither the foreign country's intentions nor the rules of the *lex fori* are relevant in this particular instance. It is submitted that the course of international academic discussion has evolved standards for the extraterritorial application of many types of mandatory rules. For example, the standards which have evolved in the areas of foreign exchange and anti-trust law are sufficiently precise to be applied in concrete cases. Wherever precise standards of this kind are still lacking, it is within the mission of the court to evolve them for the concrete situation. Some of the issues which may be considered relevant in this connection are: (1) whether the purpose(s) of the other country's mandatory rule appears to be reasonable (as, for example, the rules for the protection of the consumer, or, more generally, of the weaker party); (2) whether similar rules have been enacted in other countries, thereby expressing an international trend; and, (3) whether the application of the mandatory rule in question will promote uniformity of decision *("Entscheidungsharmonie")* within the EEC-countries.

5. Mandatory Rules of the lex fori

Apparently, art. 7 also covers the situation where the forum's own mandatory rules claim exclusive application to an obligation which is governed by foreign law. Certainly, in such a case art. 7 can only be applied in a subsidiary function. The authorities of the forum are bound to apply the exclusive, mandatory rules of their own law according to the geographical criteria established in these rules, even if these criteria are wider than is permitted by art. 7. However, each national legislator should use art. 7 as a yardstick in determining the geographical scope of his enactments.

Frequently the legislator does not regulate the international scope of his mandatory rules, leaving the solution of this thorny problem to an appreciation of the circumstances of each individual case. In this situation art. 7 regains its relevance. This provision is binding upon the authorities of the forum in their determing the international scope of application of their own mandatory rules.

It may be desirable, and in view of the considerations set out *infra* no. 6 even necessary, to spell out clearly the priority that must be accorded to the forum's rules which fix the geographical scope of application of its own mandatory rules. In order to promote the desired uniformity and to extend art. 7 as much as possible, only the express "scope rules" of the forum should be excepted from the operation of art. 7.

6. Freedom to Reserve and to Enact National "Scope Rules"

This brings us to a brief formal point. "Scope rules" of a member state (as defined *supra* no. 5) may be considered to be conflicts rules. Existing national conflicts rules will be derogated by the proposed convention, while future national conflicts rules will be subject to the time-consuming consultation procedure under art. 26. It would seem that both of these effects of the proposed convention are undesirable and probably unintended as far as "scope rules" are concerned. For national legislatures which enact mandatory rules in order to achieve certain economic and/or social purposes should not be bound by the ordinary bilateral conflicts rules laid down in the draft convention and established for very different purposes.

How can the desired exclusion of the "scope rules" from the purview of the convention optimally be achieved? The simplest way is probably a statement to the effect that the unilateral rules which mandatorily circumscribe the geographical scope of application of rules of law are not rules of private international law in the sense of art. 1 para. 1 of the convention.

7. Public Policy

Art. 7 does not expressly settle the question whether it excludes or reserves the public-policy clause of art. 22. In order to dissipate any doubts and to facilitate application of art. 7, the public-policy clause of art. 22 should expressly be declared to be applicable.

8. Suggested New Text

In lieu of a conclusion the following revised text is offered:
Art. 7 should be replaced by an art. 19 a, worded as follows:

"In applying any law indicated by the preceding provisions, mandatory rules of another legal system must be taken into account if
(a) the case is closely connected with that other legal system;
(b) the relevant rules of the other legal system claim to be applied to the exclusion of any other law; and
(c) this claim for exclusive application is justified according to international standards.
Express rules of the *lex fori* and art. 22 are reserved.
Unilateral mandatory rules circumscribing the geographical scope of application of national rules of law are not rules of private international law in the sense of art. 1 para. 1."

LES DISPOSITIONS DE L'AVANT-PROJET C.E.E. RELATIVES À LA LOI APPLICABLE AUX OBLIGATIONS AQUILIENNES

Par

MARC FALLON

Louvain

Avant-propos

Le présent Rapport s'efforce de situer les dispositions de l'avant-projet relatives aux obligations aquiliennes dans leur contexte historique. Prenant en considération les divers mouvements, parfois contradictoires, qui se manifestent dans ce domaine du droit international privé, il examine la réponse que l'avant-projet apporte aux questions que ceux-ci ne cessent de poser.

Le Rapport est divisé en trois sections. La première est consacrée au principe de détermination de la loi applicable et contient un commentaire des articles 10 – plus précisément des alinéas 2 et 3 – et 12. La deuxième section traite succinctement du domaine de la loi applicable (arts. 11, 15 et 19). La troisième section est plus large qu'une conclusion. Sans reprendre les diverses appréciations critiques qui accompagnent les commentaires des articles 10 et 12 dans les deux premières sections, elle contient des observations d'ordre plus général. Alors que la première section porte principalement sur un examen du facteur de rattachement subsidiaire utilisé par l'article 10, le no. 12 évoque les problèmes que pose la détermination du facteur de rattachement lorsque la loi applicable est la *lex loci delicti* elle-même. Le no. 13 contient un essai de réponse aux problèmes que pose la détermination des facteurs choisis, qu'il s'agisse du *locus delicti* ou de la «connexion prépondérante». Enfin, le no. 14 reprend, en guise de conclusion, les diverses interrogations que suscite l'avant-projet relativement aux obligations aquiliennes.

Le Rapport se limite à un aperçu des diverses questions que pose l'avant-projet dans la matière étudiée. Sans doute certaines critiques paraîtront-elles trop extrêmes, et certaines solutions proposées quelque peu vagues. Ces défauts sont à la fois involontaires et voulus: involontaires en raison du peu de temps dont l'auteur a pu disposer pour l'élaboration du Rapport; voulus, car l'objectif premier de celui-ci est de suscitre des réactions, des réflexions, des discussions, une ouverture éventuelle de débats, mais certainement pas de dire le dernier mot.

Section 1 : Détermination de la loi applicable

§ 1er: Commentaire de l'article 10 (al. 2 et 3)

1. *Règle générale de conflit.* – Le groupe des Experts chargés d'élaborer l'avant-projet de Convention a opté pour le principe d'une règle générale de conflit qui puisse s'appliquer à toutes les matières de responsabilité aquilienne. Il n'y a donc pas lieu de distinguer les cas de la responsabilité des conducteurs d'automobiles, ni celle des producteurs, ni celle des auteurs d'actes de concurrence déloyale[1].

L'avant-projet se conforme ainsi au droit en vigueur dans les six pays originairement membres de la C.E.E. La règle générale de l'application de la *lex loci delicti* y est reconnue fermement[2].

Certes, des réactions se sont fait jour, surtout depuis une vingtaine d'années[3]. De plus, le «phénomène social et économique» a profondé-

---

[1] La réparation des dommages résultant de l'utilisation pacifique de l'énergie nucléaire est exclue par l'article premier, afin d'éviter tout conflit avec la Convention de Paris du 29 juillet 1960.

[2] Il est à noter qu'au Royaume-Uni, référence est faite non seulement à la loi du lieu du délit, mais également à la loi anglaise: l'acte générateur du dommage doit d'abord être considéré comme illicite s'il avait été commis en Angleterre. V. *Graveson*, Rec. des Cours 99 (1960-I) p. 100–111; sur la portée de *Chaplin* v. *Boys*, v. *Graveson*, Rev. crit. 59 (1970) p. 81–87.

Quant au principe de l'application de la *lex loci delicti* v. en France *Arminjon*, Précis de d. i. p.[2] II (1934) p. 340–343; *Batiffol/Lagarde*, D. i. p.[5] II (1971) nos. 554–559; Cass. civ. 25 mai 1948 *(Lautour c. Guiraut)*, Rev. crit. 38 (1949) p. 89 (note *Batiffol*). – En Belgique *De Vos*, Le problème des conflits de lois I (1946) no. 37, II (1946) nos. 715–719; *Graulich*, Principes de d. i. p. (1961) p. 35–39; *Rigaux*, D. i. p. (1968) nos. 423–428; Cass. (1ère ch.) 26 novembre 1908 *(Soc. Gérard et Cie. c. V. Monseur et consorts)*, Rev. crit. 5 (1909) p. 951; Cass. (aud. plén.) 17 mai 1957 *(Bologne c. Sainte)*, Clunet 85 (1958) p. 1158.

[3] V. *Beitzke*, Rec. des Cours 115 (1965-II) p. 70, 73–79, 95–119. Dès le début du siècle, certains auteurs se sont opposés à l'application de la *lex loci delicti*: *Fiore*, Clunet 27 (1900) p. 720; *Poullet*, Manuel de d. i. p.[3] (1947) no. 318; *Weiss*, Traité théorique et pratique de d. i. p.[2] IV (1912) p. 415; *Mazeaud/Mazeaud*, Traité théorique et pratique de la responsabilité civile délituelle et contractuelle[4] III (1950) p. 337. Dans le sens de la théorie du «centre de gravité» ou «sphère juridique», v. *Binder*, RabelsZ 20 (1955) p. 401 ss.; *Morris*, Harv. L. Rev. 64 (1950/51) p. 881–885; *Castel*, Rev. crit. 53 (1964) p. 298; v. la synthèse

ment évolué depuis le siècle dernier, sans que les règles substantielles de responsabilité n'aient toujours suivi les changements intervenus.

Ce double facteur a suscité un nouvel examen de la solution traditionelle de l'application générale de la *lex loci delicti commissi.*

2. *Un antécédent: la Loi Uniforme Benelux.* – La Loi Uniforme Benelux constituait un premier effort d'adaptation. Si le principe de la *lex loci delicti* y était encore affirmé, c'était sous la réserve d'un rattachement plus fort de la situation délictuelle – plus précisément des conséquences de l'acte illicite – à la «sphère juridique» d'un autre pays (art. 14).

Aujourd'hui, cette solution paraît critiquable et sa formulation imparfaite.

D'une part, le rattachement des conséquences d'un acte illicite à une loi différente de celle applicable aux conditions de la responsabilité, revient à disséquer une situation juridique qui doit être considérée comme une. Il rend en outre plus difficile la tâche du juge à qui incombe de distinguer les «éléments constitutifs» des «conséquences dommageables» et d'appliquer deux lois différentes. Ce «dépeçage» a été violemment combattu[4].

D'autre part, le concept de «sphère juridique» était de nature à soulever quelques difficultés. S'il est justifié de faire confiance au juge dans la détermination de cette sphère, une telle solution place cependant les parties dans une incertitude trop grande quant à la prévisibilité de la loi applicable[5].

3. *Le principe adopté par l'avant-projet.* – Tout en se situant dans la même ligne que l'article 14 de la Loi Uniforme Benelux qu'il est appelé à remplacer, l'article 10 s'en éloigne par les précisions qu'il apporte.

Tout d'abord, il n'est plus question de dépeçage de la *lex causae:* la situation issue d'un fait dommageable est une – du moins entre les mêmes parties – et, s'il faut appliquer une loi autre que la *lex loci*

---

faite, au sujet des doctrines américaines, par *Cavers*, Rec. des Cours 131 (1970-III) p. 143–151.

[4] *Beitzke* (*supra* note 3) p. 123 s.; Ann. Inst. Dr. int. 53 (1969) I, p. 335–341, II p. 194, 202, 210–216. V. également *Lerebours-Pigeonnière/Loussouarn*, D. i. p.[9] (1970) no. 355; *De Vos* (*supra* note 2) II (1946) nos. 719–722.
Cependant *Kahn-Freund*, Rec. des Cours 124 (1968-II) p. 88–102, admet un dépeçage dans les situations se trouvant dans une «twilight zone», c'est-à-dire dans les cas de «special relationship» ou de «insulated environment». En faveur du dépeçage, v. également *Wengler*, Ann. Inst. Dr. int. 53 (1969) I, p. 505–546.
[5] *Beitzke* (*supra* note 3) p. 70; *Bourel,* dans: *Dalloz,* Rep. dr. int. II (1969) Responsabilité civile no. 16; *Cavers* (*supra* note 3) p. 145 et 163; *Kahn-Freund* (*supra* note 4) p. 49–52; *Lerebours-Pigeonnière/Loussouarn* (*supra* note 4) p. 447–452; *Wengler* (*supra* note 4) p. 505–546.

delicti, celle-ci régit «l'ensemble des éléments constitutifs de la responsabilité» et non pas seulement les conséquences dommageables[6].

Ensuite, l'avant-projet précise le facteur de rattachement subsidiaire utilisé: à l'image, empruntée aux mathématiques modernes, de «sphère juridique» se substitue la «connexion prépondérante». Cette notion correspond aux termes anglais *«the most significant relationship»,* utilisés par le *Restatement Second* américain. Il faut toutefois préciser que le *Restatement Second* américain utilise le critère de la *«most significant relationship»* comme principe de base et non comme exception.

La «connexion prépondérante» est une forme concrète de la «sphère juridique», appelée aussi le «centre de gravité» ou le «groupement des points de contact».

4. Détermination de la connexion prépondérante. – La théorie de la *«most significant relationship»* a fait l'objet de certaines critiques, tant aux Etats-Unis qu'en Europe[7].

Le principal reproche touche à l'incertitude et à l'imprévisibilité, comme c'était le cas à propos du critère de la «sphère juridique» utilisé par la Loi Uniforme Benelux: une entière discrétion étant laissée au juge, les parties ne peuvent prévoir quelle loi sera ou serait appliquée par celui-ci.

C'est pourquoi l'alinéa 3 de l'article 10 de l'avant-projet précise utilement en quoi peut consister cette connexion prépondérante: il s'agira «normalement (d'un) élément de rattachement commun à la victime et à l'auteur du dommage . . .»

On eût préféré encore d'avantage de précisions. En effet, la question est controversée de savoir s'il suffit que les parties aient une résidence commune[8], ou si une véritable «relation préexistante» est néces-

---

[6] *Vander Elst,* L'unification des règles de conflit de lois dans la C.E.E.: J. Trib. 88 (1973) p. 252.

[7] V. notamment *Kahn-Freund (supra* note 4) p. 226; *Batiffol/Lagarde (supra* note 2) nos. 554–559; *Cavers (supra* note 3) p. 144 s., 163.

[8] Aux Pays-Bas, un certain nombre de décisions jurisprudentielles se sont prononcées en faveur de l'application de la loi de l'Etat de la nationalité ou de la résidence commune des parties: V. Rb. Maastricht 8 décembre 1927 *(Callemeyn c. Murkens),* Ned. Jur. 1929, p. 130; Hof s'Gravenhage (1ère ch.) 16 juin 1955 *(de Beer c. de Hondt),* Ned. Jur. 1955, no. 615 (cas de transport bénévole); Rb. Breda 2 octobre 1962 *(Backx c. Fransen),* Ned. Jur. 1963, no. 109; Hof Amsterdam (4ème ch.), 21 janvier 1972 *(Vogels en Van Loon c. Land Nordrhein-Westfalen),* Ned. Jur. 1972, no. 280; Rb. Amsterdam 8 février 1972 *(J. van den Oever c. Delta Lloyd Autoverzekering N. V.),* Ned. Jur. 1972, no. 475 (application de l'art. 14, al. 2, de Loi Uniforme Benelux).
En France, la jurisprudence semble hostile à la prise en considération d'un rattachement commun aux parties: V. *Bourel (supra* note 5) no. 16; *id.,* note de jurisprudence, Rev. crit. 60 (1971) p. 514–517; dans l'arrêt de principe, Cass.

saire[9]. Par relation préexistante il faut entendre un rapport qui ne rende pas fortuite la rencontre des parties, tel un lien de famille ou un contrat. Par exemple il ne suffirait pas que deux individus résident chacun en Belgique pour que la loi belge soit appliquée à une collision survenue en France; il en irait autrement s'il y avait eu entre les parties un lien contractuel, par exemple un contrat de transport.

La formulation actuelle de l'alinéa 3 de l'article 10 laisse croire que la résidence commune des parties suffirait pour que soit appliquée la loi du pays où elle est localisée[10].

Encore faut-il qu'il «n'existe aucun lien significatif entre la situation résultant du fait dommageable et le pays où s'est produit ce fait» (al. 2)[11]. Cette restriction répond à la logique de la solution adoptée par l'article 10, à savoir l'application générale de la *lex loci delicti* tempérée par certaines exceptions; cependant, elle introduit un élément supplémentaire d'incertitude.

5. *Examen de l'opportunité de l'article 10.* – Il apparaît que la matière des conflits de lois est en pleine évolution en ce qui concerne la responsabilité aquilienne.

D'une part cette évolution est marquée par le souci de rechercher une nouvelle règle de conflit plus nuancée, plus souple que la règle traditionnelle, mais qui ne perde pas pour autant la certitude que

---

civ. 25 mai 1948 (*supra* note 2), la loi espagnole fut appliquée comme *lex loci delicti* malgré la nationalité française commune des parties; également Cass. civ. (1ère sect.) 30 mai 1967 *(Kieger c. Amigues)*, Rev. crit. 56 (1967) p. 728 (note *Bourel*).

En Belgique: Cass. 26 novembre 1908 (*supra* note 2) note, admet que lorsque les parties ont même nationalité, la loi du rattachement commun doit prévaloir sur l'application de la *lex loci delicti*. Cependant, Cass. 17 mai 1957 (*supra* note 2) note, applique la loi néerlandaise comme *lex loci delicti* malgré la nationalité belge commune des parties. V. cependant l'arrêt rendu par Bruxelles (4ème ch.) 14 mai 1973 (*Al Ahli c. Kop, Laruelle et Thirion*), J. Trib. 88 (1973) p. 731.

[9] Parmi les auteurs qui souhaitent une relation préexistante, citons *Beitzke* (*supra* note 3) p. 103 s.; il souligne que dans *Babcock* v. *Jackson*, décision considérée comme élément fondamental du développement de la théorie du «centre de gravité», il s'agissait d'un cas de transport bénévole, c'est-à-dire qu'il existait entre les parties un «groupement social spécial» (p. 104); v. également *Batiffol*, Ann. Inst. Dr. int. 53 (1969) II, p. 228; *Fragistas*, Ann. Inst. Dr. int. 53 (1969) II, p. 229; *Kahn-Freund* (*supra* note 4) p. 77 et 78. La Résolution adoptée par l'Institut de Droit international lors de la session d'Edimbourg en 1969 semble soumettre l'application d'une loi autre que celle du pays où le délit a pu être localisé, à l'existence d'une relation préexistante entre les parties (article 3 de la Résolution): V. Ann. Inst. Dr. int. 53 (1969) II, p. 370–374.

[10] V. le Rapport concernant l'avant-projet, *infra* p. 286.

[11] Cette double condition était déjà préconisée par *van Brakel*, Grondslagen en beginselen van Nederlandsch IPR (1946) § 149.

celle-ci apportait abstraction faite du problème de la détermination du *locus*. Or le choix d'une telle règle ne semble pas pouvoir déjà être fait: d'aucuns estiment qu'il faut se contenter de la règle traditionnelle, d'autres sont partisans de la théorie de la «connexion prépondérante» ou même de la «*proper law*»; certains se contentent, dans le choix d'un facteur subsidiaire de rattachement, d'un rattachement commun aux parties alors que d'autres exigent une «relation préexistante».

D'autre part une tendance apparaît dans le sens de la création de règles spéciales de conflit, c'est-à-dire propres et adaptées à des matières bien précises de responsabilité [12]. Alors que la Convention de La Haye sur la loi applicable en matière d'accidents de la circulation routière s'est en quelque sorte contentée d'entériner la tendance amorcée par la loi Uniforme Benelux en l'adaptant, la Convention sur la loi applicable à la responsabilité du fait des produits va plus loin en créant une solution propre à la matière, faite d'une combinaison – relativement complexe il est vrai – de rattachements multiples. La création de règles spéciales du conflit n'est certes pas à dédaigner car elle permet de cerner de plus près les problèmes à traiter et d'y apporter des solutions plus adéquates.

Dès lors, on peut se demander s'il est opportun d'établir une règle de conflit générale pour les obligations aquiliennes et de figer dès à présent le droit des conflits en cette matière, même si les articles 25 à 29 de l'avant-projet prévoient des assouplissements, notamment en autorisant les Etats Parties à la Convention d'adhérer à une Convention multilatérale ayant pour objet principal l'une des matières régies par l'avant-projet.

6. *L'exemple de l'Institut de Droit international.* – Il est intéressant de relever les considérations suivantes extraites du Préambule de la Résolution que l'Institut de Droit international a prise lors de la session d'Edimbourg en 1969 relativement aux «obligations délictuelles en droit international privé».

«L'Institut de Droit international,

  . . .

Estimant . . . que l'étendue et les modalités de la substitution à la loi du lieu du délit d'un autre système juridique doivent faire l'objet d'une étude particulière pour chaque type de délit (accidents de la circulation, accidents du travail, diffamation et violation de la sphère privée par les moyens de communication, concurrence déloyale et autres délits économiques, délits commis en haute mer, dans l'air, dans l'espace, etc.), et excède le cadre d'une Résolution générale sur la responsabilité délictuelle;

---

[12] *Beitzke* (*supra* note 3) p. 70; *Vallindas*, Rec. des Cours 101 (1960–III) p. 361.

...

Considérant qu'en raison du développement rapide et souvent contradictoire du droit dans de nombreux pays, le temps n'est pas venu de formuler un projet de législation précise mais que des directives générales de nature à orienter la jurisprudence et la doctrine sont requises» [12a].

§ 2: Commentaire de l'article 12

7. *Principe de la «prise en considération» des «règles de sécurité et de police».* – Les dispositions de l'article 12 de l'avant-projet reprennent celles de l'article 7 de la Convention de La Haye sur la loi applicable en matière d'accidents de la circulation routière. Seule la formulation en a été élargie. Quant au fond, ils prévoient tous deux la prise en considération des lois de police en vigueur au *locus delicti* dans le cas où la *lex causae* n'est pas la loi de l'Etat où le fait dommageable s'est produit.

Dans son principe, la prise en considération des lois de police du *locus delicti* correspond, dans la Loi Uniforme Benelux, à l'application de la loi du lieu du fait dommageable aux conditions de la responsabilité lorsque la «sphère juridique» appartient à un Etat autre que celui de *locus delicti*. Toutefois il existe une différence essentielle: lorsque le juge «prend en considération» des lois de police, il ne les applique pas: il ne fait que les utiliser comme un instrument dans l'appréciation de la responsabilité du défendeur. L'article 12 de l'avant-projet ne conduit donc pas à un «dépeçage» de la *lex causae*.

8. *Technique du rattachement.* – Le facteur utilisé à l'article 12 est le lieu où «le fait dommageable s'est produit».

Dans la mesure où la *lex loci delicti,* retenue comme principe de base, peut être aisément déterminée, cette solution ne pose aucun problème. Cependant, si une telle localisation se révèle difficile, voire impossible, le rattachement choisi est-il encore adéquat? Il va de soi qu'en cas d'accident de voiture, les lois de police dont il faut tenir compte sont celles en vigueur au lieu de l'accident. En est-il de même lorsque le caractère délictuel passe au second plan, comme c'est le cas dans les matières de responsabilité sans faute et notamment en responsabilité du fait des produits? L'aspect délictuel y est souvent absent, que le «fait illicite» soit indécelable ou même inexistant (v. *infra*, no. 12).

Il serait plus adéquat de choisir un rattachement se rapprochant d'avantage de la raison d'être des lois de «sécurité et de police», et susceptible d'être utilisé indépendamment de l'applicabilité de la *lex loci delicti.*

[12a] Ann. Inst. Dr. int. 53 (1969-II) p. 370 et 372.

Cette raison d'être fondamentale réside, à travers le maintien du
bon ordre social ou économique sur un territoire donné, dans la protection de la personne lésée, de l'individu qui, par le fait dommageable,
subit la lésion d'un droit et se trouve projeté dans un état de déséquilibre[13]. Par conséquent doivent être prises en considération les
«règles de sécurité et de police» sur la protection desquelles la personne lésée pouvait légitimement compter au moment de la lésion.
En matière d'accidents de la circulation routière, ce seront les lois de
police en vigueur au lieu de l'accident: elles constituent le Code de la
route et visent à la protection des individus en garantissant le bon
ordre de la circulation; en matière de responsabilité du fait des produits, il s'agira des diverses normes réglementaires en vigueur au lieu
d'acquisition du produit et établissant un standard minimum de qualité
en vue de la protection des utilisateurs[14]; dans le cas de la concurrence
déloyale, il s'agira des lois de police du commerce en vigueur dans le
marché où le préjudice a été ressenti, ces lois visant à l'organisation
du marché dans le but de garantir le droit de chacun à exercer le commerce. Dans chacune de ces hypothèses, le critère proposé correspond
bien à la volonté d'application de ces normes de sécurité et de police.

9. *Une confusion à éviter: les «lois de police» et les règles civiles
de la responsabilité.* – Les véritables lois de police visées à l'alinéa
1er de l'article 3 du Code civil sont ces diverses dispositions décrites
supra nos. 7 et 8. Pourvues d'une volonté d'application bien précise,
elles sont prises en considération dans les limites que ces normes
déterminent elles-mêmes.

Elles sont à distinguer des règles de droit civil à caractère essentiellement privé qui règlent quant au fond les conditions et les conséquences de la responsabilité. Ce droit a principalement en vue le
règlement des conflits d'intérêts entre les parties en cause, protégeant
tantôt l'une, tantôt l'autre. Mais il n'a aucune vocation particulière
à garantir, plus spécialement qu'une autre règle de droit, le respect

---

[13] Les termes «bon ordre social» sont pris ici dans le sens familier, à savoir
le bon fonctionnement des rouages de la vie quotidienne, et non pas le respect
de l'ordre public.

Sur la question de la détermination des «lois de police», v. notamment: *De Vos*
(*supra* note 2) II (1946) nos. 686–701; *Niboyet,* Traité de d. i. p. IV (1947) nos.
1110 et 1111; *Graulich* (*supra* note 2) no. 40; *Vander Elst,* Rép. prat. dr. belge,
Compl. 2 (1966) V: Conflits de lois, no. 91; *Francescakis* dans: *Dalloz,* Rép. dr.
int. I (1968) V: Conflits de lois, nos. 89–149, particulièrement no. 137; *Lere-
bours-Pigeonnière/Loussouarn* (*supra* note 4), p. 401–405; *Batiffol/Lagarde*
(*supra* note 2) I (1970) no. 251; II no. 557; *Gothot,* Rev. crit. 60 (1971) p. 212–243,
particulièrement p. 214 et 239–242.

[14] V. cependant la Convention de La Haye sur la loi applicable à la responsabilité du fait des produits, art. 9; *Fallon,* J. Trib. 89 (1974) p. 78.

de la «règle morale» ou le maintien de l'intérêt général dans une société donnée.

Ainsi, les règles civiles de la responsabilité ne font pas partie des lois de police et de sûreté visées à l'alinéa 1er de l'article 3 du Code civil[15]. Les conséquences de cette proposition peuvent être importantes (v. *infra* no. 12).

Section 2: Domaine de la loi applicable

10. Rapprochement des articles 11, 15 et 19. – Le domaine d'application de la *lex causae* est déterminé par l'article 11 de l'avant-projet. Celui-ci reprend essentiellement les dispositions correspondantes de la Convention de La Haye sur la loi applicable en matière d'accidents de la circulation routière et de celle relative à la responsabilité du fait des produits.

Il convient de mentionner également les articles 15 et 19. La première de ces dispositions porte sur le domaine d'application de la loi applicable aux obligations en général, mais concerne principalement les obligations contractuelles et quasi-délictuelles vu l'existence de l'article 10. Par contre l'article 19, qui porte sur les questions relatives à la preuve – et dont l'article 10 ne fait pas mention – concerne aussi bien les obligations contractuelles que les obligations extracontractuelles.

Par conséquent il serait peut-être souhaitable pour la clarté du texte, d'ajouter au début de l'article 10: «Sans préjudice des dispositions de l'article 19», et au début de l'article 15: «Sans préjudice des dispositions des articles 10 et 19 . . .»

Section 3: Observations finales

11. Mérites de la solution proposée par l'avant-projet. – Du point de vue du droit belge, la solution proposée par l'article 10 de l'avant-projet est acceptable. Elle constitue un progrès par rapport à l'article

---

[15] En ce sens v. *Lerebours-Pigeonnière/Loussouarn* (*supra* note 4) p. 403, 447–452; *Dayant,* Clunet 99 (1972) p. 73–75; *Beitzke* (*supra* note 3) p. 79–82; et, semble-t-il *Bourel* (*supra* note 5) no. 11.

En faveur de la qualification comme lois de police, v. notamment: *De Vos* (*supra* note 2) II, nos. 686 et 701; *Niboyet* (*supra* note 13) nos.1110–1126bis; *Vander Elst* (*supra* note 13) no. 91; *Graulich* (*supra* note 2) no. 40; *Batiffol/ Lagarde* (*supra* note 2) nos. 554–559, n'attribuent à l'alinéa 1er de l'article 3 du Code civil, en raison de l'obscurité du texte, qu'une valeur confirmative quant à l'application de la *lex loci delicti*.

14 de la Loi Uniforme Benelux. De plus, elle semble correspondre, dans son principe, aux souhaits de la doctrine récente qui, refusant l'excessive souplesse du *Restatement Second* américain, reste fidèle à l'application de la *lex loci delicti* tempérée par des exceptions bien précises.

D'autre part les articles 25 à 29 de l'avant-projet rendent notamment possible l'élaboration de règles de conflit spéciales portant sur des matières précises de responsabilité.

12. Le silence de l'avant-projet sur le problème de la détermination du facteur de rattachement lorsque celui-ci est le locus delicti. – L'avant-projet laisse de côté le problème, combien épineux, de la détermination du *locus delicti,* aussi bien lorsque ce lieu est éparpillé en plusieurs endroits que lorsqu'il est impossible de le localiser en un lieu précis. Or cette question présente un caractère primordial: dans la mesure où le *locus delicti* – terme dont la traduction française est d'ailleurs malaisée – ne peut être déterminé avec certitude, la règle de l'application de la *lex loci delicti* n'apporte pas toute la sécurité juridique (prévisibilité) désirée, et est impraticable [16].

Un exemple récent illustre le caractère souvent abstrait du *locus delicti,* lorsqu'il est irréductible à une forme réelle. Le 3 mars 1974 un avion «DC-10» des «*Turkish Airlines*» s'est écrasé dans la Forêt d'Ermenonville, en France, après avoir littéralement explosé en plein vol. Il semblerait que la catastrophe trouve son origine dans une déficience du système de fermeture de la porte de la soute à bagages. La veuve d'une des victimes, de nationalité britannique mais résidant en France pour affaires, a porté plainte contre la société «*Mc Donnel-Douglas*» constructice de l'appareil et réclame 125 millions de dollars d'indemnités pour l'ensemble des 345 familles lésées. Or, le système de fermeture de la porte arrière des «DC-10» semble bien affecté d'un vice de conception puisque plusieurs fois on essaya d'y remédier, mais de façon insatisfaisante paraît-il. La plainte a été déposée devant une Cour de Los Angeles, région où le fabricant a plusieurs de ses usines [17]. Dans une telle situation, le lieu du délit doit être considéré ou bien comme inexistant (l'explosion a eu lieu en plein air et peut-être au-dessus de l'espace aérien français) ou bien comme réparti entre la France et les Etats-Unis. Le critère de l'application de la *lex loci delicti* n'est donc ici d'aucune utilité, et force est d'en chercher un autre! Il en est de même en cas de «sinistre processus» [18], lorsque le fait générateur

---

[16] V. Rapport *infra* p. 287 s.; V. également *Beitzke* (*supra* note 3) p. 82, citant *Rabel,* The Conflict of Laws II (1960) p. 251–254.

[17] Informations recueillies dans un quotidien belge, La Libre Belgique, du 20 mars 1974. V. également The Observer, 24 mars 1974.

[18] Terme utilisé dans le domaine de l'assurance «responsabilité civile produits» et destiné à remplacer la notion, inadéquate, d'accident considéré comme un événement soudain.

du dommage (par exemple la fabrication défectueuse d'un médicament) est distinct du fait dommageable (par exemple l'absorption du médicament) et des conséquences dommageables (par exemple l'apparition des premiers symptômes de maladie): l'on ne peut dire qu'il y ait un accident, c'est-à-dire un événement soudain. Bien plutôt, il y a une multiplicité de circonstances conduisant au dommage ressenti par la personne lésée. Il paraît dès lors arbitraire de choisir, parmi ces événements, celui qui sera déterminant pour le choix de loi. En réalité, tous sont nécessaires à la réalisation du dommage tel qu'il est survenu.

Dans la mesure où la catégorie des lois de police et de sûreté ne recouvre pas les règles civiles de la responsabilité qu'il faut distinguer des lois pénales et des normes réglementaires dites de sécurité et de police (*cf. supra* nos. 8 et 9), le juriste n'est pas lié par l'impératif de la localisation de la situation aquilienne au *locus delicti*.

Par conséquent lorsque le *locus delicti* n'est pas localisable en un lieu précis et unique, il doit être possible d'utiliser un facteur de rattachement approprié, par exemple la localisation de la prestation caractéristique, à savoir l'obligation même de réparer. En matière de concurrence déloyale cette localisation pourrait se faire au lieu où se trouve le marché qui subit une telle concurrence; en cas de responsabilité du fait des produits, au lieu de la résidence du débiteur.

13. Perspective de solution. – On constate que le maintien de la *lex loci delicti* comme règle générale n'est plus possible que si le principe est accompagné d'une multitude fort complexe d'exceptions dont il convient de délimiter avec soin les champs respectifs d'application pour réduire au maximum les difficultés de qualification. La Convention de La Haye sur la loi applicable à la responsabilité du fait des produits en est un exemple récent.

Deux types d'exceptions doivent pouvoir être prévus, de telle sorte que la hiérarchie des rattachements pourrait se présenter comme suit:

(1) Lorsque la situation aquilienne a un lien, direct ou indirect, avec un rapport légal préexistant, elle est régie par la loi applicable à ce rapport. Par «lien indirect avec un rapport légal préexistant», il faut entendre une situation aquilienne dont un rapport légal préexistant est l'occasion, même s'il n'en est pas l'origine. Ainsi, lorsque des amis partent en voyage à l'étranger, il ne se forme généralement entre eux aucun contrat de transport, malgré l'existence d'accords concernant le partage des frais d'essence, de nourriture, etc. Le passager de la voiture accidentée n'a contre le conducteur qu'un recours aquilien. Cependant, en raison du caractère privilégié de leurs rapports, il est indiqué que la partie lésée puisse demander au juge, bien souvent plusieurs années après la survenance de l'accident à l'étranger, de lui accorder une réparation sur la base de la loi qui régit les relations

légales qu'il a eues avec l'autre partie et qui ont préparé ou contribué à la préparation de l'événement dommageable.

L'exigence d'un rapport «légal préexistant», tel un lien de famille ou un contrat, paraît préférable à la notion «d'environnement social» parfois utilisée: celle-ci est en effet beaucoup moins précise; et la possibilité d'un lien *indirect* avec la relation légale préexistante en atténue le caractère restrictif.

(2) Dans les autres cas, la *lex loci delicti* conserve sa vocation à s'appliquer.

(3) Toutefois, lorsque le lieu précis et unique où le fait dommageable s'est produit est raisonnablement indéterminable, il faut pouvoir rejeter le critère du rattachement au lieu du délit, comme développé *supra* no. 12.

14. Le pari de l'unification du droit des conflits en matière d'obligations aquiliennes. – Alors que la Conférence de La Haye en 1966 et l'Institut de Droit international en 1969 – organismes regroupant un nombre plus large d'Etats que la C.E.E., il est vrai – ont déjà refusé d'établir une règle générale de conflit qui régirait l'ensemble des obligations aquiliennes, la première en procédant à un découpage de la matière, le second en se limitant à des recommandations de nature à orienter la doctrine et la jurisprudence des divers pays, les Etats Membres de la C.E.E. sont-ils disposés à fixer le droit des conflits dans la matière des obligations aquiliennes par une règle générale? Certes, l'œuvre d'unification est souhaitable et vivement souhaitée; mais doit-elle se faire à n'importe quel prix et le plus rapidement possible? Puisque le problème de la détermination du *locus delicti* n'est pas résolu par l'avant-projet malgré la grande importance qu'il revêt, ne pourrait-on pas également laisser – temporairement – ouverte à l'évolution jurisprudentielle l'ensemble de la matière des obligations aquiliennes?

Si le présent Rapport, en posant ces questions, parvenait à susciter de nouveaux débats, son objectif serait atteint même si, malgré ceux-ci, les Etats Parties à la Convention se décidaient à courir le risque d'une unification peut-être prématurée de la matière.

EXCEPTION CLAUSES UNDER THE DRAFT CONVENTION ON THE LAW APPLICABLE TO CONTRACTUAL AND NON-CONTRACTUAL OBLIGATIONS

By

EUGEN DIETRICH GRAUE

Kiel

In view of the considerable importance of contractual clauses limiting or excluding liability of contracting parties, an attempt may be justified to test the practicability of the Draft Convention under this particular aspect.

I. Exception Clauses Connected with a Contractual Choice of Law

If the contracting parties have made an express or implied choice of law, such choice will be covered by art. 2 (1) of the Draft. If such choice is connected with an exception clause agreed upon, the interpretation and validity of such a clause will be governed, in the first place, by the law the parties have chosen. If such clause limits or excludes a party's liability to an extent incompatible with mandatory rules of the law chosen, it will be void, voidable, or subject to judicial modification, in conformity with the sanctions provided for under that law. Thus, if German law is chosen, the exception clause will validly limit or exclude damages for delictual negligence [§§ 276 (2), 823 BGB]; if, however, French law is chosen, such a clause will be held repugnant to the principle that the provisions of the Code civil on torts are instruments of public policy *(ordre public)* and cannot be modified by contract. It follows that, if parties choose a legal system, they must adopt it in its entirety, which includes the borderline between mandatory and other provisions. This will also be true where the parties split their relationship between two or more legal systems, e. g., if a contract of affreightment is governed by one legal system, and the bill of lading by another.

7 *

Yet it may happen that liberal rules of the legal system chosen are repugnant to the public policy of another legal system, with which such a case may be connected. If liability for delictual negligence is covered by an exception clause in an agreement governed by German law, a French judge assuming jurisdiction will deny recognition to this clause, on the ground that, however valid under German law, it runs counter to French public policy. The vague language of art. 7 of the Draft, which refers to such cases, will hardly encourage French courts to depart from their traditional reasoning. A more subtle conflict will arise where contractual negligence is concerned. According to the so-called "court law" *(droit jurisprudentiel)* developed in France, and to the provisions of the Austrian, Swiss and Italian civil codes, liability for gross negligence *(faute lourde, grobe Fahrlässigkeit, colpa grave)* cannot be validly excluded or limited. Under Federal German law, liability may be excluded, as a matter of principle, for any case of negligent violation of contractual duties; this general rule has been restricted by the courts, to the extent that contracting out of liability for gross negligence may be immoral and void where such clauses are employed by all, or almost all of the members of the economic branch concerned, or where denial of liability for gross negligence is unconscionable under the circumstances of the case. Thus, to the extent that German law permits contracting out where other legal systems do not permit it, the application of German law, even though it may have been chosen by the parties, may be refused by foreign courts assuming jurisdiction over the matter.

A specific conflict may appear in the field of commercial agency. It is well known that in several countries commercial agents are given sweeping protection by mandatory rules, such as the rule entitling the agent to an indemnity where the contract of agency is terminated through no fault of his. Now the German Commercial Code says that, where the agent does not have a commercial establishment within the territory of the Federal Republic, the mandatory rules are subject to contractual modification just as well as the others [§ 92 c (1) HGB]. Trying to make the most of this provision, the Association of German Machinery Manufacturers, in which about 4000 firms of all sizes are grouped together, worked out a standard contract for agents domiciled abroad, which provided that (a) the agreement with a foreign agent is governed by German law, and (b) that the mandatory rules of the German Commercial Code will not apply. This means that the agent cannot claim an indemnity under either law concerned; he cannot under the law of his domicile because German law has been chosen, and he cannot under German law because the mandatory provisions of German law may be, and have been, excluded. The question remains, of course, whether a foreign court having jurisdiction will deny recognition to such a clause – in other words, whether a foreign court will regard its domestic rules as an instrument of public policy. It should be noted that the German Supreme Court *(Bundesgerichtshof)* held an agreement valid under which a German agent submitted to the domestic law of his foreign principal, thus renouncing protection under German law; the Court stated that a commercial agent, who after all is supposed to be an independent businessman, must know what he is doing if he signs such an agreement. It is very doubtful, however, whether this reasoning will be adopted by courts in other countries, especially in those cases where the agent depends, as a practical matter, upon one particular principal; it is known that under French law subtle distinctions are made between commercial agents in the traditional sense and those referred to as VRP *(voyageurs, représentants, placiers)*. In any event, it is impossible to predict to what extent art. 7 of the Draft will influence the decision by a court to grant or deny recognition of exception clauses valid under a foreign law chosen by the parties, and repugnant to mandatory rules of domestic law.

It is obvious that in many cases the above question is connected with another, namely, the jurisdiction of the court granting or denying recognition. International contracts will often attempt to concentrate jurisdiction in the courts of one country, generally the one whose legal system is preferred; they may also submit to commercial arbitration by representatives of a trustworthy institution, such as the arbitrators of the corn, coffee or cotton trade associations in such cities as London, Liverpool, Hamburg or Bremen. In such cases, the legitimate inference will be that such jurisdiction is meant to be exclusive of any other, and that the parties are submitting, by the same token, to the law of the court or of the arbitrator's seat. There are countries, such as Federal Germany, which will allow the international jurisdiction of their courts to be excluded by agreement; even in France, the specific jurisdiction vested in French courts whenever a French national is a party (arts. 14, 15 Code civil), may be renounced by express agreement. In Italy, however, international jurisdiction of the courts will generally not be excluded by agreement in favour of a foreign jurisdiction or of arbitrators sitting abroad (art. 2 Codice de procedura civile).

More recently, a tendency has become apparent to apply constitutional standards both to exception clauses and to conflict rules. In Federal Germany, it has been argued that the constitutional provision imposing the rule of law and social justice *(Rechtsstaatlichkeit und Sozialstaatlichkeit,* art. 20 Basic Law) should be employed as an instrument against unconscionable exception clauses. On the other hand, the Federal Constitutional Court *(Bundesverfassungsgericht)* held in

1971 that conflict rules are not exempt from constitutional scrutiny. Both lines of thought might eventually converge in a new rule, to the effect that even a contractual choice of law, if arbitrarily imposed by one party upon another, may be denied recognition on the ground that it is unconscionable, hence not binding in the circumstances of the case.

II. Exception Clauses not Connected with a Contractual Choice of Law

In the absence of an express or implied choice of law, a court taking jurisdiction of the case will have to follow the conflict rules of its domestic law. A French or Italian court will look for the place where the contract was entered into, an English court will try to find the proper law of the contract, a Swiss court will start out from the center of gravity *(Schwerpunkt)*, and a German court will follow what is called the hypothetical choice of law by the parties. As a practical matter, the English, Swiss and German lines of approach are largely identical. More recently, a tendency has become apparent to simply refer to the country of the party undertaking to perform the character-istic obligation within the contractual relationship. In the field of inter-national sales contracts, both the Convention on the Law applicable to International Sales of Movables, of 1955, and the Comecon Rules are supporting this principle, and so is art. 4 (2) of the Draft Conven-tion. The question remains, however, whether French and Italian courts will adopt this rule in their daily practice, the more so because art. 4 (3) will offer them a loophole enabling them to hold in any given case that the contract is more closely connected with the law of the *"lieu de conclusion"*.

In any event, the problems sketched before will emerge here as well, and even more generally. In the absence of a choice of law, a court may give vent to its dislike of certain exception clauses by simply applying a legal system – preferably its own – which tends to declare such clauses void as soon as they go beyond certain narrow limits of fairness.

Thus, the main difference between exception clauses connected and those not connected with an express or tacit choice of law will be that in the first case the courts will have to refer to public policy if they want to strike down certain clauses, whereas in the second case all they must do is apply a law seemingly connected with the matter and enabling them to impose rigid standards. Under the Draft Convention, the first type of judicial reaction will be covered by art. 22, and the second by art. 4.

III. Validity of Exception Clauses and/or Choice of Law

Neither the exception clause nor the choice of law, if any, will bind the other party in the absence of a valid contract. This may be due to failure by the parties to reach agreement *(dissensus)*, or to statutory invalidity of a party's declaration. Such delicate situations are governed by art. 8 of the Draft Convention, a rule based on the assumption that it would be unreasonable to test the validity of a contract by a legal system other than the one chosen or found in the case of a valid contract.

The question remains, however, whether this rule also applies to those cases where the mere validity of exception clauses is at stake. Thus, the Italian civil code says that exception clauses and other specific clauses modifying statutory rules will be invalid unless they have been accepted in writing by the other party (art. 1341 Codice civile). Thus, whichever law may have been chosen by the parties, an Italian court will most certainly hold the exception clause invalid on the ground of this rule, if the party invoking such invalidity is an Italian national and received the offer in Italy. Another problem will arise in connection with the commercial practice of first making an agreement by words of mouth and then sending the other party a letter confirming the agreement subject to certain conditions including exception clauses. In Federal Germany, the rule is that such a letter, if accepted by the other party without objection, will be binding even though it may contain various conditions not discussed at the time of the oral agreement. If, however, one party makes an offer subject to his conditions, and the other replies subject to his own, the rule prevailing in Federal Germany is that no agreement has been reached on the conditions, the effect being that the contract will be governed by the statutory provisions. In theory, all this may be covered by art. 8, but it is highly doubtful whether in a given case a court will resist the temptation of applying its domestic law.

IV. Conclusions

However desirable the harmonisation or even unification of conflict rules may be, this sketchy attempt made to analyse the effects of the Draft Convention in a restricted but important field will have demonstrated that it would only amount to shifting the real problems from one level to another. The Draft Convention would at best bring about unification of basic conflict rules which are not really controversial.

As soon, however, as it attempts to go right into the melée between the choice of law principle and deeply entrenched views of what is right or wrong, it must resort, as it does in art. 7, to vague language permitting all kinds of interpretation.

It follows that harmonisation of conflict rules cannot serve its purpose unless either the national concepts of law and social justice are largely identical from one country to another, or such harmonisation extends to substantive law as well. The first requirement seems to be met in the relations between the Nordic, the Latin American and the Socialist countries where conflict rules have been harmonised through multilateral or bilateral agreements. An attempt along the second line has been made through such legislation as the Uniform Commercial Code within the United States, or the Uniform Laws on International Sales of Movables and on the Conclusion of Sales Contracts. It should be noted that the two Uniform Laws, which have already been ratified by numerous countries, are now in force in Federal Germany: having been ratified by the legislative bodies, they were published on July 17th, 1973[1], and have become effective on April 16th, 1974. This uniform legislation seemed inacceptable to representatives of German export industries for a long time, on account of its sweeping rules on liability for failure to perform contractual duties. But at this very moment, German lawyers are being informed that the application of the Uniform Laws can be avoided by express choice of a national law, such as the German, plus express exclusion of the Uniform Law[2]. Thus, even harmonisation of substantive law, limited as it is to international sales, will not suffice to discard national traditions and abuses. Harmonisation of conflict rules cannot be expected to do better.

---

[1] BGBl. 1973 I 856, 868.

[2] *H.-G. Landfermann*, Neues Recht für den internationalen Kauf: NJW 1974, p. 385 ss.

SOME ASPECTS OF THE DRAFT CONVENTION FROM THE POINT OF VIEW OF BRITISH LAW

By

T. C. HARTLEY
London

The main topic I wish to consider in this paper is the extent to which the principles of the Draft Convention are compatible with the policies of United Kingdom legislation designed to protect the consumer. Brief consideration will also be given to some other problems.

I. Consumer Protection

A. Contracts

The rationale of the doctrine of private international law that the parties to a contract are free to chose the law governing that contract is that this will produce the result most in accord with the common interests and expectations of the parties. The same considerations underlie the widespread acceptance of the principle of freedom of contract in internal law. However, the belief that the agreement arrived at by the parties represents the fairest compromise between their conflicting interests is based on the implicit assumption that the parties have approximately equal bargaining power. Where this is not the case the principle of freedom of contract permits the economically strong to exploit the economically weak. This is especially true in the case of contracts of adhesion – *i. e.* where the economically stronger party presents the other with a standard form contract on a "take it or leave it" basis.

One area in which the untrammelled application of the doctrine of freedom of contract can cause problems is that of consumer transactions. In recent years in Britain there has been a considerable growth in the size and influence of the consumer movement (*i. e.* those who are campaigning for a better deal for the consumer) and since the aims of this movement enjoy wide-spread support among the electorate, politicians have not been slow to realise the electoral value of "standing up for the consumer". This has resulted in the enactment of a number of statutes designed to help the consumer by redressing the balance in the consumer-supplier relationship. It is likely that this trend will continue in the future and there is now a special Ministry to promote the interests of the consumer, the Ministry of Prices and Consumer Protection.

The exact meaning of a "consumer transaction" may vary according to the context but the typical consumer transaction is one in which goods are supplied by someone acting in the course of business to a person who requires them for his own personal consumption and not for commercial purposes. The concept can also apply to the provision of services, including financial services (such as insurance and loans of money) and transport.

One feature of the legislation designed to protect the consumer is the granting to the consumer of certain rights that cannot be taken away by the terms of the contract. This clearly involves a limitation of the principle of freedom of contract but it is justifiable in view of the inequality of bargaining power between consumer and supplier. It is obvious that the purpose of a statute of this kind would be defeated if the parties could avoid its application by means of a choice of law clause: in other words, the same considerations which require the restriction of the principle of freedom of contract in internal law also require its limitation in private international law.

The private international law aspects of consumer protection law have not been studied in any great depth in England but they are clearly of interest both from the point of view of international business and from that of social policy. Before discussing the provisions of the Draft Convention that are relevant to this problem it is desirable to outline some of the relevant British statutes.

The problem can best be considered by taking the supply of goods as an example. Two pieces of legislation are of particular importance in the United Kingdom in this area: The Hire Purchase Acts and the Supply of Goods (Implied Terms) Act. The former apply only to credit transactions but the latter applies to all sales.

The Hire Purchase Acts[1] apply to hire purchase transactions and conditional sales provided, in each case, that the price is less than

---

[1] In England the relevant legislation is the Hire Purchase Acts of 1964 and 1965. The 1964 Act applies in Scotland but not the 1965 one. However, similar provisions are found in the Hire Purchase (Scotland) Act 1965. The relevant legislation in Northern Ireland is the Hire Purchase Act 1966 (a statute of the Northern Ireland Parliament).

£ 2000 and the buyer/hirer is not a company. (Hire purchase is the most important vehicle for consumer credit sales in the United Kingdom. It is a contract under which the buyer/hirer hires the goods on payment of regular sums of money ["rent"] on the condition that he will have the option, after paying a certain number of instalments, to purchase the goods for a small additional sum. Its economic function [but not its legal form] is that of a credit sale in which the price is paid in instalments and the ownership of the goods remains with the seller until the price has been fully paid. A conditional sale is simply a credit sale in which the buyer becomes owner only when he has fully paid the price. In both cases the buyer is given possession of the goods as soon as the contract is signed.)

The Hire Purchase Acts contain a large number of provisions designed to protect the consumer, including requirements relating to the form of the contract and provisions giving the consumer the right to cancel the contract in certain circumstances. Draft legislation, the Consumer Credit Bill[2], is now before Parliament to replace the Hire Purchase Acts with more comprehensive legislation which will apply to almost all consumer credit transactions, including hire purchase, conditional sales, credit sales, loans and ancillary transactions such as suretyships. There are a wide range of obligatory terms designed to protect the consumer from unscrupulous suppliers. The obligatory nature of the provisions of the Bill is made clear by clause 169 (1) which provides[3]:

> „A term contained in a regulated agreement or a linked transaction, or in any other agreement relating to an actual or prospective regulated agreement or linked transaction, is void if, and to the extent that, it is inconsistent with a provision for the protection of the debtor or hirer or his relative or any surety contained in this Act or in any regulation made under this Act."

Unfortunately there is no provision in either the Hire Purchase Acts or the Consumer Credit Bill for conflict of laws. It would, however, defeat the whole purpose of these Acts if the supplier in any transaction covered by them could avoid the application of an obligatory term by a simple choice of law clause stipulating that the law of a foreign country is to apply. If the parties cannot exclude the obligatory term directly, they cannot be permitted to do so indirectly.

What means might a British court use to safeguard the policy of these Acts in the case of international transactions? The concept of

---

[2] This legislation will apply throughout the United Kingdom.

[3] This is the version of the Bill that was introduced into the House of Lords (28 March 1974). It may be amended in the course of its passage through Parliament.

public policy is more restricted in Britain than that of *ordre public* in many Continental countries and this is unlikely to prove a very satisfactory means of preventing evasion of the law. Another Continental doctrine, *fraude à la loi*, is virtually unknown in Britain and is anyway too subjective to meet the case. What is most likely is that the courts will resort to statutory interpretation to discover the real or assumed intention of Parliament as to the international scope of the Act; once this has been ascertained the Act will be applied to all transactions within its scope, irrespective of normal conflict of laws principles.

This approach was adopted in the Scottish case of *English* v. *Donnelly*[4]. This case concerned a hire purchase contract entered into between an English company (the Twentieth Century Banking Corporation Limited) and a consumer who was domiciled and resident in Scotland. The negotiations took place in Scotland and the consumer signed the form in Scotland. Legally speaking, this form was an offer and the contract only came into existence when this offer was accepted by the Company. This was done when the latter signed the form in England. The subject of the contract, a motor car, was delivered in Scotland but under the contract the payments had to be sent to the company in England.

The contract contained a choice of law clause stating that English law applied. The court, however, held that this did not prevent the application of Scottish legislation designed to protect the consumer. (The legislation was the Hire Purchase and Small Debt [Scotland] Act 1932 which applied only in Scotland. It has now been replaced by the legislation mentioned above.) Although the Act had no provisions concerning conflict of laws, the court held that it was intended to apply to all contracts entered into in Scotland and they regarded the contract as being entered into in Scotland since it was signed there by the consumer (even though the company signed it in another country). Lord *Clyde*, the Lord President of the Court of Session, gave the following reasons for his decision:

> "It is quite true that in general under private international law it can be said that the validity of a contract is governed by the proper law of the contract, namely, by the law which the parties intend or may fairly be presumed to have intended to invoke (see Dicey, Rules 153 and 148). But that general rule is displaced where an Act of Parliament has expressly provided otherwise, and has applied certain conditions as necessary for

---

[4] *English* v. *Donnelly*, [1958] S.C. 494; [1959] S.L.T. 2 (the quotations are from pp. 6 and 7 of the S.L.T). The same approach was adopted by the House of Lords in the English case of *Boissevain* v. *Weil*, [1950] A.C. 327 (a case concerning exchange control regulations).

the validity of the contract. The situation might have been different if the statutory provisions had not been mandatory (see *Vita Food Products Inc.* v. *Unus Shipping Co. Ltd.*, [1939] A.C. 277).

In the present case, however, the statutory provision contained in the Scottish Act of 1932 (as amended in 1954) is mandatory. The object of section 2 of the Scottish Act is to lay down certain conditions precedent for valid hire purchase contracts, designed to ensure that persons who hire goods under them are properly certiorated of the conditions contained in the agreements into which they are entering. The Act is a piece of social legislation designed for the protection of certain persons, i. e. members of the public who hire articles through companies such as the Twentieth Century Banking Corporation Limited. It is not intended to benefit nor to protect these companies. The way the protection operates is the avoidance of the contract of hire if certain statutory safeguards in the hirer's interest are not satisfied. Hence it follows that the test for the applicability of the Act, which under section 11 extends only to Scotland, is whether or not the contract was entered into in Scotland (see section 1), irrespective of where that contract is ultimately completed or is to be executed. The first defender in the present case undoubtedly entered into this contract in Scotland, and it necessarily follows that the Scottish Act therefore applies. If so the general rules of private international law applicable to contracts are superseded by this express statutory provision. Such a situation is envisaged by Dicey in Rule 149."

It should be mentioned that, in spite of what Lord *Clyde* said, the Act in question here did not make any "express" provision for conflict of laws. Section 11 of the Act states that the Act applies in Scotland and not in England. Section 1 merely says that the Act applies notwithstanding anything contained in the contract[5].

A passage from the judgment of another judge, Lord *Sorn*, illuminates the policy considerations which influenced the court. He said that the manifest purpose of the Act was:

"to give to persons entering into hire purchase contracts in Scotland a measure of protection against those persons with whom they are dealing. This just means that, if financiers from the other side of the border wish to do valid business with hirers in Scotland, they must do so with due regard to the Scottish Act and that they cannot get round the Act by putting in a clause to the effect that some other law is to apply to the contract."

The other piece of legislation to be considered is the Supply of Goods (Implied Terms) Act 1973. The most important effect of this is to make it impossible for the parties in a consumer sale or hire purchase transaction to exclude certain terms from the contract. These terms, which

---

[5] The reference to "Dicey" in Lord *Clyde's* judgment is to *Dicey's Conflict of Laws.*

previously applied only in the absence of a provision to the contrary in the contract, relate to matters such as the quality of the goods, their correspondence with the seller's description, and the seller's title to them.

The Act contains specific provisions relating to conflict of laws and it is interesting to note that there is an important difference between the case of a sale and a hire purchase contract. Section 13 of the Act covers hire purchase contracts and provides:

"Where the proper law of a hire purchase agreement would, apart from a term that it should be the law of some other country or a term to the like effect, be the law of any part of the United Kingdom, or where any such agreement contains a term which purports to substitute, or has the effect of substituting, provisions of the law of some other country for all or any of the provisions of sections 8 to 12 above, those sections shall, notwithstanding that term, apply to the agreement."

There is a similar provision, section 4, dealing with sales but in this case there is a proviso which excludes its operation in the case of an international sale.

Section 7 gives the following definition of an international sale:

"'contract for the international sale of goods' means a contract of sale of goods made by parties whose places of business (or, if they have none, habitual residences) are in the territories of different States (the Channel Islands and the Isle of Man being treated for this purpose as different States from the United Kingdom) and in the case of which one of the following conditions is satisfied, that is to say –

(a) the contract involves the sale of goods which are at the time of the conclusion of the contract in the course of carriage or will be carried from the territory of one State to the territory of another; or

(b) the acts constituting the offer and acceptance have been effected in the territories of different States; or

(c) delivery of the goods is to be made in the territory of a State other than that within whose territory the acts constituting the offer and the acceptance have been effected."

This definition is based on art. 1 (1) of the Uniform Law on the International Sale of Goods.

It will be seen from this discussion of these British statutes that there is no uniform approach to the problem of conflict of laws. The Hire Purchase Acts (and the Consumer Credit Bill when it is enacted) probably apply whenever the transaction is concluded in the United Kingdom (including a postal contract where the consumer is in the United Kingdom). The provisions of the Supply of Goods (Implied Terms) Act 1973 will apply if the proper law of the contract is that of a part of the

United Kingdom but in determining the proper law no account is to be taken of the intention of the parties except in the case of an international sale of goods.

How does the Draft Convention affect consumer transactions? The first point, of course, is that the Draft Convention applies only to "situations of an international character" (art. 1) and this will no doubt exclude the great bulk of consumer transactions. The Draft Convention deliberately refrains from defining this phrase and it is therefore impossible to say exactly what transactions would come within its scope. However, it is possible to think of several kinds of consumer transactions that would come within the scope of the Draft Convention.

One example would be where a supplier in Country A employs a representative in Country B to solicit business (possibly by door to door canvassing). If the representative lacks the power to enter into transactions on behalf of the supplier (*i. e.* is not an agent in the legal sense) the procedure followed will probably be similar to that in the case of *English* v. *Donnelly* (discussed above): the consumer will be asked to sign a form which is in law an offer (on the supplier's terms) and this will be transmitted to the supplier who will sign it in Country A.

A second example is that of an international mail order business. Here the consumer sends in his "order" (in law probably an offer) through the post in response to advertisements. It is quite possible that a supplier in one country might wish to extend his operations to another country and would decide to advertise in that country. The resulting contracts would plainly be of an international nature.

Both these situations would come within the scope of the Draft Convention. They are also cases in which the consumer protection law of the consumer's country ought to apply. This would probably be the case under the present United Kingdom law except that, if the transaction is one of sale and not hire purchase, the parties would be free to exclude the provisions of the Supply of Goods (Implied Terms) Act.

A solution to the problem could of course be obtained by means of art. 7 of the Draft Convention. The weakness of this article is that it is extremely general and while it would probably be used by a court of the consumer's country to justify the application of the law of that country, it is by no means certain that a court in the supplier's country would consider itself bound to do this.

The problem of consumer protection has been considered in this paper from the point of view of the United Kingdom. It is, however, a matter which affects all countries and could have a bearing on free competition within the Community. If a supplier wants to enter a certain market he should abide by the same rules for consumer protection as local suppliers; otherwise he would have an unfair advantage.

In view of these problems it might be worth considering whether provision should be made for consumer contracts along the lines of that for employment contracts (art. 2, para. 3, and art. 5).

B. Torts

Another aspect of consumer protection involves products liability (*i. e.* liability of a manufacturer for injury or damage caused by defective products: in English law there is an action in tort in this situation). A conflict of laws problem can arise where the product is manufactured in one country and sold to a consumer in another. For example:

A pharmaceutical company in Country A manufactures a drug which is sold to a patient in Country B. As a result of faulty manufacture the drug is impure and the patient suffers injury.

This raises the problem of defining the *locus delicti* in the case where the elements of the tort are spread over two or more countries. The comment to art. 10 states that the Draft Convention is not intended to give a definite answer to this problem.

The desirable result from the point of view of consumer protection is that the law of the place where the product is sold to the consumer should apply: if a manufacturer wishes to sell in a particular market he should comply with the consumer protection laws of that market. It should be noted that the place where the product is sold is not necessarily the same as the place where the injury occurs: the consumer might take the product to another country and use it there.

II. Brief Comments

1. Prescription (Statute of Limitations)

In England prescription is often regarded as a matter for the *lex fori*. Article 11, no. 8, specifically deals with this point as regards non-contractual obligations but it is not covered with regard to contractual obligations (unless it is thought to come within art. 15). It might be desirable to specify that this is a matter for the law governing the contract.

2. Contracts of Public Authorities

The torts of public authorities are excluded by art. 14 from the scope of arts. 10 to 13. Are the contracts of public authorities intended to come within the scope of the Draft Convention? (It should be noted that in English law the distinction between public law and private law contracts is not very well developed.)

3. Article 17

The meaning of this article is not very clear in the English version. It might be desirable to re-draft it or at least provide a fuller comment explaining the meaning of the decisions on which it is based.

4. Article 19

The English translation of the second sentence of the first paragraph does not adequately convey its meaning. It reads:

"However, the consequences arising from the conduct of a party to proceedings shall be determined by the law of the forum."

This does not make clear that it is the conduct of the party *in the course* of the proceedings that is in issue, not his conduct when the obligation was created.

5. Exemption Clauses

The Draft Convention does not consider the problem of contracts which exempt one of the parties from liability in tort towards the other. Is the legality of such a contract to be determined by the law governing the contract or that governing the tort[6]?

6. Money

The Draft Convention does not cover the question of the time element in the conversion of currency. This can arise if a debt owed in the currency of one country is sued upon in another country; or if damages in contract or tort are payable in a foreign currency. Under English law a court can give judgment only in United Kingdom currency and the rate of exchange used is not that prevailing when judgment is given but that prevailing when the cause of action arose (e. g. when the debt was due, the contract broken or the tort committed). These rules are applied in England as part of the *lex fori*.

---

[6] See *Sayers* v. *International Drilling Co N. V.*, [1971] 3 All E.R. 163 (C.A.).

SOME REMARKS ON ARTS. 1, 2
AND 20 OF THE EC DRAFT CONVENTION

By

HANS HOYER

Vienna

I.

The conventions between the European Communities and Austria did not lead to full Austrian membership. Austria was forced to refuse full membership in accordance with its Declaration of Permanent Neutrality in fullfilling the Convention of Vienna of Mai 1955, but wanted to become associated to the European Communities in economic relations as close as possible.

The convention between Austria and the European Communities does not include unification of private law or of conflicts law. Nevertheless art. 32 of Austria-EC convention includes – similar to art. 220 of the EEC Treaty of Rome – the possibility of evolution in the relations between the partners. As trade and personal mobility in relation between the members of EEC and Austria grow rapidly as rapidly grows the need of a safe platform in the choice-of-law problem for international trade and employment contracts. There are two ways to approach this: unification of private law or unification of conflicts law. Both ways are to meet predictability of decisions in case of lawsuit.

Austria's obligations to keep strictly neutral is no principal obstacle against its participation in international conventions relating to the law of conflicts of law, not even in conventions proposed by the EEC for the use of its own members and associates. The law of conflicts of law cannot be involved by war in such an extent that political decisions of any neutral state could be prejudiced.

It is right time now to deal with the subject of this colloquium, at least for Austrian participants: Austrian government prepares new statutory orders of conflicts law. Tentative drafts have been made by

Fritz Schwind[1] and are still under discussion of an ad-hoc commission at *Bundesministerium für Justiz.* Their accomodations still are possible.

II.

The following remarks happen to indicate my personal interest in special articles of Draft Convention and certain items dealt with in this convention.

III.

1. Art. 1 (Scope of the Convention)

a) The Convention is intended as a multilateral convention to apply independently of any requirement of bilateralisation, even by reciprocity. Application of Convention and of its uniform law of conflicts (arts. 2–23) does not depend on the need of the substantive law to apply under the rules of Convention being the law of a contracting state. That modification of art. 1 by art. 24 must not be put out of sight.

Art. 1 excludes matters of status and capacity, of bills and notes, of arbitration and jurisdiction clauses, of insurance contracts, of companies, of cartels from the scope of the Convention. I agree to the exclusion of most of the mentioned matters but capacity. Art. 20 includes special rules on contractual capacity but leads to a result being the wrong one in my views. Art. 20 shows the urgent need of rules on capacity not only for closing agreements but also for committing torts. If such rules are lacking the Convention cannot guarantee the predictability of sentences, the most inportant reason to deal with contractual instruments in the field of conflicts law. Without entire rules on capacity the Convention seems to be defective in fullfilling all purposes wanted by its contractants.

b) The Convention restricts its scope to obligations arising of situations of international character. To discuss problems of obligations of international character means to do double characterisation of case, on behalf of jurisdiction as well as on behalf of choice of law. Undoubtedly the situation is an international one if only one element of the case does indicate application of another law than the *lex fori.* Does it make any difference whether the international element of the case is one relating to jurisdiction or with regard to the choice of law? That is the reason why I agree with *Ole Lando*[2] in characterising cases like *"The Halley"*[3] as international ones.

---

[1] *Schwind,* Z. f. Rvgl. 12 (1971) p. 161.
[2] *Lando,* RabelsZ 38 (1974) p. 9.
[3] *The Halley* (1868), L.R. 2 P.C. 193.

2. *Art. 2* of Convention orders contracts being governed by the law chosen by the parties.

The question is whether party autonomy prevails all other kinds of choice of law. Art. 2 seems to affirm the principle which is obstracted by arts. 7, 9 and 15, so that predictability of sentences hardly can be guaranteed. Identity of sentences independent to the *lex fori* as the aim fixed by conflicts law is called in question again by the proposed procedure of choice of law.

Choice of law is restricted on behalf of contracts of employment by art. 2 (3) of Convention. The idea seems to be to prevent persons in weak position because of social inequality from escaping mandatory provisions protecting workers. But is this idea the proper one?

Provisions protecting persons in weak positions are to be made not by conflicts law but within the substantive law to apply under the rules of Convention. The way to protect workers is a quite variable one, there is none acknowledged as the only or the proper one. Some purposes of protection are to be reached by social insurance as well as by mandatory law rules governing employment contracts and relations. Within the members and associates of EEC comparison of social standards shows them to be equal in protection of employees to a high degree. There is no need to exclude choice of law by the parties of employment contracts, as far as the minimum protection of the weak is granted by the law applicable. If there needs to be restriction of freedom of parties, suitable is restriction to the law of members of Convention, indifferent where the employee habitually carries out his work.

To grant freedom of choice of law to the parties at any moment, especially after conclusion of employment contract (see art. 3), is not necessary but may cause some danger for the employee in a weak position. Therefore it is wanted to exclude choice of law within art. 3 from applying to employment contracts.

3. *Art. 20.* – Capacity as an institution of law has to prevent persons of less than average mental vigour in critics of their own acting from damage disadvantage caused to themselves by themselves. Lack of capacity limits responsibility in any way, lack of capacity prevents from beeing bound by contracts in consequence to incompetence, inexperience, ignorance, inequal bargaining power. Protecting the young and the feeble-minded is much more necessary and within the interests of law than to safeguard persons acting in good faith and without imprudence against the consequences of their partners lacking in contracts capacity. Therefore good faith is not committed to lead to contracts to be hold if one partner lacks capacity in Austrian law. In consequence with this art. 866 ABGB orders responsibility of a person

who makes his partner trust into his full capacity without imprudence if only a certain extent of capacity is granted to him by law: The marginal age of responsibility for torts is 14, the one for contracting 19.

I cannot expect Austria ratifying a convention including an order like art. 20, although the same convention tries to protect the young and feeble-minded in any way, because art. 20 would destroy the system of capacity and responsibility in legal protection of dependent persons.

SOME GENERAL REMARKS ON THE POLICY OF THE DRAFT CONVENTION AND THE LAW APPLICABLE TO CONTRACTUAL OBLIGATIONS

By

H. JOKELA

Helsinki

Preliminary Draft Convention on the Law Applicable to Contractual and Non-contractual Obligations produced by the Working Group of Experts of the European Communities is a document of great importance to all those who are interested in the unification of the rules of conflict. Coming from a country outside the Communities I confine myself to some general remarks.

I. Question of Policy

There seems to be a common interest of the countries both within the EC and outside the Communities in establishing unified rules of conflict of laws in contracts and torts. This is illustrated by two facts. First, the EC Working Group has presented a Preliminary Draft Convention. Second, the activities within the EC have awaked those member states of the Hague Conference on Private International Law which are not members of the Communities.

Assuming that it is the purpose of all those countries involved to achieve a wide unification of the rules of conflict there still remains a question of policy to be answered at the outset: What would be the best course to follow? It is submitted that we should adopt a pragmatic approach to the problem. It means that the member states of the Hague Conference should make up their minds so as to put on the agenda the matter in question. The next step would be to strive for co-ordination of the work of the both international bodies.

II. Differentiation Between Various Kinds of Contracts

Arts. 2–8 of the EC Draft Convention constitute a sound approach to many problems of contractual obligations. On the one hand, there are general rules dealing with questions common to contractual obligations within the scope of the Draft as delimited by art. 1. On the other hand, there is an attempt to establish specific rules for some situations where particular public interests may be involved (arts. 2 [3], 5 and 7).

It is especially the latter group of rules that deserves to be further elaborated. I may refer to the penetrating analysis of the problem presented by *Lando*[1]. A good basis for discussion can be found in *Lando*'s suggestion to distinguish between on the one hand commercial contracts and on the other hand consumer contracts and other non-commercial contracts.

The problems relating to consumer contracts are being discussed intensely in various countries. Consequently, the progress of protective legislation in this area is rather rapid. Under the circumstances it would be advisable not to leave those questions open when striving for practicable rules of conflict in contracts.

The trend in substantive law is towards mandatory legislation in the field of consumer contracts. This trend is reflected in the view of *Lando* that the parties should not be given the same freedom to choose the applicable law in consumer contracts as they enjoy in commercial contracts. The present writer adheres to the view of *Lando*.

As to the employment contracts there is, in municipal legislation, a trend similar to that in cosumer contracts. However, it is submitted that the need to provide for an exception to the principle of party autonomy in conflict of laws is less urgent in the field of employment contracts than it is in consumer contracts. In order to elucidate my view I make only two points. First, the choice of law by the parties to an employment contract seems to be in practice between two alternatives only, *viz* the law of the country in which the work is carried out, or in which the establishment of the employer is situated (*cf.* art 5). Second, a rigid rule to the effect that the employment contract is governed by the law of the place of work would not cover those cases where the employee does not habitually carry out his work in any one country (*cf.* art. 5 [b] of the Draft Convention). However, this situation may occur frequently in connection with international transactions, *e. g.* erection of plant and machinery abroad.

Consequently, it is submitted that the rules of conflict for employ-

---

[1] *Lando*, RabelsZ 38 (1974) p. 15 ff.

ment contracts can be developed along the lines suggested in the EC Draft Convention. The idea expressed in art. 7 can be further elaborated so as to make it possible for a judge to reach flexible solutions in cases relating to employment contracts. One of the problems here may be how to establish co-ordination between conflicting mandatory rules in the cases in which the contract has been carried out in various countries.

CHOICE OF LAW AND THE EFFECTS OF SILENCE
Comments on arts. 2 (4) and 8 (2) of the EC Draft Convention

By

GUNTHER KÜHNE

Bochum/Bonn

I. The Present Situation

In the course of the negotiations about the EC Draft "Convention on the Law Applicable to Contractual and Non-Contractual Obligations" two alternative proposals for arts. 2 (4) and 8 (2) regarding the effects of silence in the contracting process were put forward, none of which found unanimous approval by the delegations.

According to alternative 1 the effects of silence on the part of one party to an offer concerning the applicable law or the contract itself are to be determined by the law of the place of habitual residence of that party. Irrespective of choice of law considerations silence of one party may be interpreted as consent in cases where this interpretation follows from the previous course of dealing between the parties or from international trade usages of which the parties, by reason of their business activity, were or should have been aware.

According to alternative 2 silence by one of the parties may be interpreted as consent only if that interpretation follows from a previous course of dealing between the parties or from international trade usages.

II. The Necessity of a Special Provision

The questions dealt with in arts. 2 (4) and 8 (2) of the Draft Convention are part of the wider complex relating to the applicable law in the area of formation of contracts. The Draft Convention does not explicitly cover this subject. On the contrary, it is widely assumed that arts. 2 (2) and 8 (1) only mean the validity of the contract as opposed to questions concerning the meeting of the minds. In this respect the choice of law question is left to the *lex fori*. Regardless of whether this policy is to be approved or not it seems advisable to explicitly include in the Draft Convention a choice of law rule on the effects of silence. The problem what legal effects should be given to silence on the part of an offeree is essentially a problem of defining the scope and limits of the pre-contractual standards of care the offeree is held to observe in his own interest. Consequently, it is especially important for the offeree to have as clear an idea as possible about these standards of care. A relatively great extent of legal certainty is, therefore, required not so much at the time of an eventual lawsuit but immediately after reception of an offer.

Neither the *lex-causae* approach nor the *lex-fori* rule sufficiently take into account the certainty aspect. In both alternatives the pre-contractual standards of care very often will be definable only by an *ex-post* evaluation of the whole situation.

III. Critique of the Alternatives

1. Alternative 1 of arts. 2 (4) and 8 (2) contains a combined substantive and choice of law rule. The substantive rule – silence to be regarded as consent under certain conditions – is subject to no objection.

Much more problematical, however, is the selection of the offeree's habitual residence as a relevant connecting factor.

Example: A with habitual residence in state X, goes on a business tour to state Y. He has an accommodation in a hotel for several days. During this period he receives several offers from business partners to which he does not reply.

Under alternative 1 the question what effect A's silence has must be answered according to the laws of state X, if there are no bilateral customs or international trade usages.

This solution certainly takes into account A's interest in having applied a law he is familiar with. On the other hand, it introduces into the pre-contractual relations between A and his partners a law which is totally extraneous to them and which they have no reason to take into account.

2. Alternative 2 only contains a substantive law solution. Its positive scope is essentially the same as that of alternative 1 and does not meet objections.

What is rather doubtful is the negative scope of alternative 2 (... *only* if that interpretation follows ...). What does this mean?

First, this may mean that the requirements for taking silence as consent are exhaustively enumerated to the effect that choice of law rules leading to substantive rules with lower standards for silence to operate as consent are completely inapplicable. Second, this passage can be interpreted as only defining the limits of its scope without ruling out the possibility that silence means consent by way of the application of normal choice of law rules.

Both interpretations are unsatisfactory. The first one has its basic weakness in setting aside the whole choice of law process. There is no justification for not taking silence as consent in case the requirements of alternative 2 are not met, but where according to the choice of law mechanism the applicable national law regards silence as consent. On the other hand, the second interpretation is inadequate as it leaves room for applying the *lex fori*. Under these conditions the offeree will often be in a state of uncertainty about the pre-contractual standards of care imposed on him. This obviously underrates the need for legal certainty in terms of forseeability of the applicable law.

IV. Search for a Solution

1. Alternative 1 of arts. 2 (4) and 8 (2) can be supported insofar as it contains both a substantive and choice of law rule. A choice of law solution as such must, however, select a connection which takes into account the interests and the expectations of the offeror and the offeree alike.

It should, therefore, be seriously taken into consideration whether it seems preferable to select as connecting factor the place where the offeree has received the offer. The "place of reception" can be defined as the place where the offer has entered the offeree's sphere in a way that he can be supposed to have taken knowledge of the offer. Thus, actual knowledge is not the decisive element. There are cases where the offeree has not taken notice of an offer which, nevertheless, had previously entered his sphere of influence (*e.g.* sent to an agent). The "place of reception" then is the place where the offer has entered the offeree's "sphere of influence" (*e. g.* been thrown into the offeree's mail box, handed over to his agent).

2. There may, however, be cases in which the "place of reception" only plays a more or less fortuitous part as compared to other connecting factors.

Example: A and B – both with habitual residence in state X – are on a business tour in state Y. A sends an offer for a contract to B.

In this case the "place of reception" in state Y establishes less important a connection than the habitual residence in state X, common to both parties. Picking the law of state Y would mean to disregard the common factors of both parties.

There may be still other cases which need an exception from the "place of reception" rule, *e. g.* where the offeree has previously sollicited the offer. Or in cases where the choice of the applicable law follows the conclusion of the contract or where the contract is subsequently modified. In the latter category of cases the centre of gravity will generally lie in the state the law of which is applicable to the contract itself.

From this it follows that the exceptions to the "place of reception" rule will have to be formulated in a flexible way in order to cover the variety of possible fact situations. Arts. 2 (4) and 8 (2) should be merged into one rule. To make the structure of the Draft more transparent, the effects of silence should be dealt with in a separate article (art. 2 a).

3. Proposed Article 2 a

(1) The effects of silence on the part of a party regarding a proposal as to the applicable law, made by the other party before or in connection with the conclusion of the contract, and the effects of silence on the part of a party regarding the conclusion of a contract shall be determined in accordance with the law of the place where that party has received the proposal or offer.

(2) If the relation between the parties is characterized by special circumstances and, therefore, more closely connected with another country than that which determines the applicable law according to paragraph 1, the law of that other country shall apply.

(3) Notwithstanding the provisions of the law applicable according to paragraphs 1 and 2 consent to the choice of law or to the contract may be deduced from silence on the part of a party if that interpretation follows from the previous course of dealing between the parties or from international trade usages of which the parties, by reason of their business activity, were or should have been aware.

LES OBLIGATIONS CONTRACTUELLES

Par

OLE LANDO

Copenhague*

Art. 1er: Le champ d'application de la Convention

Limitation à l'ordre international. – D'après l'art. 1er, la Convention ne s'applique qu'aux situations présentant un caractère international. Ainsi le Groupe des Experts a-t-il suivi ce qui est devenu une tradition dans les conventions internationales portant sur les droits patrimoniaux.

Cependant, l'on peut s'interroger sur l'opportunité d'une telle limitation.

En effet, cette condition paraît fondée dans la mesure où elle concerne le droit des parties de choisir librement la loi applicable (v. sur cette question *infra* à propos de l'art. 2). Mais pourquoi limiter l'application des autres dispositions de la Convention aux seules situations présentant un caractère international? La plupart des règles de conflit peuvent tout aussi bien être appliquées à des situations étrangères présentant un caractère purement interne: toute solution contraire pourrait avoir des conséquences inéquitables.

Supposons qu'un citoyen allemand porte atteinte à l'honneur d'un autre citoyen allemand, tous deux étant domiciliés en Allemagne. Par la suite le coupable se rend en Angleterre où il est poursuivi en dommages-intérêts. En Allemagne, la diffamation constitue un délit susceptible de poursuites judiciaires, ce qui n'est pas le cas en Angleterre. Selon le droit international privé anglais, l'action sera déclarée non fondée même si le Royaume-Uni a adhéré à la Convention. La diffamation ne peut faire l'objet de poursuites judiciaires, car elle n'est pas considérée comme un délit selon le droit anglais. La décision

---

* Cet article, traduit de l'anglais par *Marc Fallon,* est un condensé de l'étude parue au RabelsZ 38 (1974) p. 6–55.

anglaise *The Halley*[1a] constitue une application de cette règle. Etant doné que la situation ne présente pas un caractère international, l'art. 10 de la Convention, qui aurait exclu la règle énoncée dans le cas *The Halley,* est inapplicable. Si, de passage en Allemagne, un anglais avait commis le même acte à l'encontre d'un allemand, il aurait pu être attaqué en diffamation d'après l'art. 10 de la Convention, la situation ayant un caractère international. Un tel résultat défie le bon sens le plus élémentaire.

Même en matière de contrats, il ne paraît pas nécessaire – ni justifié – de limiter la Convention aux seules situations internationales lorsqu'aucune référence n'a été faite à la loi d'un pays déterminé.

Néanmoins, ainsi qu'il en fera question *infra* à propos de l'article 2, il convient de restreindre la loi d'autonomie aux seuls contrats internationaux.

C'est pourquoi l'auteur de la présente étude propose de supprimer, à l'article 1er, les mots «dans les situations ayant un caractère international», et de formuler comme suit l'alinéa 1er de l'article 2 relatif à l'autonomie de la volonté: «Le contrat présentant un caractère international est régi par la loi choisie par les parties.»

Toutefois l'auteur estime, en accord avec les autres délégués, que le texte ne doit pas définir ce qu'il entend par les termes «situation ayant un caractère international». En effet l'expérience démontre qu'il est impossible de donner une définition précise du contrat international. Cette question devrait être laissée à l'appréciation du juge.

Clauses d'arbitrage et d'élection de for. – L'exclusion des clauses d'arbitrage et de juridiction semble résulter de l'absence d'un accord, au sein du Groupe des Experts, sur le droit des conflits en cette matière.

Pourtant la Convention de New York de 1958 pour la reconnaissance et l'exécution des sentences arbitrales étrangères réglait déjà le problème de la détermination de la loi applicable à certains aspects de la validité des clauses d'arbitrage (v. les articles 2 et 5 [1 a] de cette Convention). Cette Convention a été signée par la Belgique, le Danemark, la France, l'Italie, le Luxembourg, les Pays-Bas et la République Fédérale d'Allemagne.

Le problème de la loi applicable à la validité d'un accord compromissoire est également réglé par les articles 6[2] et 9[1a] de la Convention européenne sur l'arbitrage commercial international de 1961, signée par la Belgique, le Danemark, la France, l'Italie et la République Fédérale d'Allemagne. La récente Convention de Bruxelles du 27 septembre 1968 concernant la compétence judiciaire et l'exécution des décisions en matière civile et commerciale, traite également de

---

[1a] *The Halley* (1868), L.R. 2 P.C. 193.

certaines questions relatives à la validité des conventions sur la compétence. L'article 17 stipule que «si, par une convention écrite ou par une convention verbale confirmée par écrit, les parties, dont l'une au moins a son domicile sur le territoire d'un Etat contractant, ont désigné un tribunal ou les tribunaux d'un Etat contractant pour connaître des différends nés ou à naître à l'occasion d'un rapport de droit déterminé, ce tribunal ou les tribunaux de cet Etat sont seuls compétents».

Toutefois la Convention de Bruxelles laisse sans solution certaines questions relatives à la validité et à l'interprétation des clauses juridictionelles. De même, certaines limites restreignent les champs d'application respectifs des règles qui sont prévues par les Conventions sur l'arbitrage non encore ratifiées par tous les Etats Membres de la CEE. Beaucoup de contrats internationaux contiennent une clause d'arbitrage ou de juridiction. Leur validité est assez souvent mise en question. Il est souhaitable de régler par une Convention internationale la question de la validité et de l'interprétation de ces clauses; une plus grande prévisibilité en résulterait pour les parties.

L'auteur de la présente étude est conscient des divergences profondes qui existent dans le droit des conflits des divers Etats Membres sur cette matière. Néanmoins la majorité de ceux-ci ont adopté une solution satisfaisante que l'on pourrait insérer dans la Convention, à savoir que la validité et l'interprétation d'une clause d'arbitrage ou de juridiction est soumise à la loi qui régit le contrat.

Art. 2: L'autonomie de la volonté

L'alinéa 1er de l'article 2 du Projet de Convention stipule que «le contrat est régi par la loi choisie par les parties».

Le contrat doit être international. – La majorité des Conventions et la plupart des droits nationaux – de source jurisprudentielle ou législative – s'accordent à limiter le principe de l'autonomie de la volonté aux seuls contrats internationaux. Le Projet de Convention CEE est conforme à cette tendance, ses dispositions ne s'appliquant qu'aux situations présentant un caractère international (v. *supra* à propos de l'article 1er).

Caractère absolu de l'autonomie de la volonté. – Le problème des limites de l'autonomie de la volonté a déjà fait l'objet de bien des controverses: le choix est-il illimité? Est-il soumis à l'existence de points de contact bien précis? Ou bien un lien raisonnable avec le système juridique choisi peut-il suffire? Une autre thèse souvent défendue exige que le choix soit fait de bonne foi ou, en renversant la charge de la preuve, refuse tout effet au choix fait de mauvaise foi ou en fraude à la loi.

L'article 2 du Projet de Convention CEE n'exige aucun point de contact. Le Groupe des Experts s'est montré partisan d'une «règle qui laisse un pouvoir discrétionnaire aux parties». Ainsi le choix de la loi par les parties ne serait-il soumis à aucune limite. Par ailleurs le Groupe des Experts n'a pas envisagé l'hypothèse d'un choix effectué avec légèreté ou opéré en fraude à la loi.

Appréciation critique. – Le principe de l'autonomie de la volonté jouit d'un large crédit dans la plupart des systèmes juridiques. Et l'expérience semble démontrer que cette solution doit prédominer en ce qui concerne les contrats commerciaux internationaux.

Cette règle, si communément admise, paraît toutefois perdre de vue que le choix effectué par les parties peut, même en l'absence de toute intention de fraude à la loi, aller à l'encontre de la politique législative *(fundamental policy)* d'un système juridique étroitement lié au contrat, en ignorant les dispositions impératives qui en sont l'expression. Or, le fondement de l'autonomie de la volonté ne justifie pas toujours la violation de ces «*fundamental policies*». En outre, dans un contrat non commercial, une entreprise pourrait aisément abuser du choix illimité qui est ainsi laissé aux parties en exploitant sa position de force vis-à-vis d'un consommateur ou d'un travailleur dépourvus de toute protection.

Les formes nouvelles de limitations à l'autonomie de la volonté

La législation économique. – Les systèmes juridiques contemporains connaissent divers types de normes impératives, notamment de droit économique: lois prohibant les pratiques qui entravent le jeu de la libre concurrence, législation des prix, lois monétaires et autres mesures destinées à réglementer le marché. L'impact de ce droit nouveau sur les conflits de lois est étudié *infra* à propos de l'article 7.

Inégalités sociales. – Outre ces mesures, il convient de mentionner ce que l'on pourrait appeler une législation protectrice qui trouve sa raison d'être dans l'inégalité régnant, au sein de notre système économique, entre les diverses forces en présence au cours des négociations contractuelles.

En réalité, le véritable contrat international est celui conclu entre sociétés commerciales de dimension internationale. Les négociations y sont menées dans un réel équilibre des forces en présence. Mais il n'en reste pas moins que certains contrats internationaux sont des contrats de consommation, conclus entre une entreprise et un consommateur[1b]. Dans cette hypothèse, l'inégalité règne souvent. En effet, l'entreprise jouit d'une position de force par rapport au consommateur: elle est mieux au courant de tout et apporte plus de soin à l'établissement des conditions du contrat. Les contrats de louage de services entrent dans la même catégorie, tout autant que les accords contractés par de petits argiculteurs ou par de petits producteurs de l'industrie familiale. Tous ces cas ont en commun de mettre en présence une partie plus faible, le travailleur ou le petit producteur, face à une personne plus compétente et économiquement puissante.

La belle idée de la liberté du consentement de toute personne adulte et saine d'esprit est en train de perdre du terrain. L'on commence à réaliser que le consommateur ne bénéficie pas d'une réelle liberté de contracter. C'est ce qui apparaît dans les contrats d'adhésion que l'on retrouve dans tous les pays occidentaux: ceux-ci contiennent des clauses onéreuses pour le consommateur, le travailleur, le petit producteur[2].

Interventions de législateur. – Dans le but de remédier aux abus qui peuvent résulter des inégalités sociales et du déséquilibre des forces en présente dans la négociation des contrats, diverses mesures ont été prises en vue de la protection de la partie la plus faible.

Dans un certain nombre de pays, des dispositions impératives régissent les contrats mettant en présence des parties qui ne se trouvent pas sur un pied d'égalité. Ainsi des conditions particulières règlent-elles la vente à tempérament, le contrat de bail, les prêts de sommes peu importantes, l'assurance sur la vie et l'assurance accident, le contrat de louage de services, etc. Toutes ces mesures sont applicables aussi bien aux contrats d'adhésion qu'à ceux conclus de gré à gré. Quoique la plupart de ceux dont il est question ici soient des contrats de consommation et d'autres du genre, la protection peut parfois être étendue également à des contrats présentant un caractère commercial. Une société qui loue ses bureaux et assure ses biens contre l'incendie bénéficie ordinairement de la protection des règles impératives sur le bail et l'assurance incendie.

[1b] La notion de consommateur doit être prise ici dans son sens le plus large: c'est celui qui, en contractant avec une entreprise, ne cherche que son propre profit ou celui de son entourage. Il achète ou emprunte des biens pour son usage exclusif; il participe à des excursions accompagnées; il touche un salaire modeste; il souscrit à une assurance vie, à une assurance accident, mais à titre privé.

[2] V. *Lando,* Diskussionsbericht, en: Richterliche Kontrolle von Allgemeinen Geschäftsbedingungen (1968) p. 169–171; *id.,* Standard Contracts – A Proposal and a Perspective: Scand. Stud. L. 10 (1966) p. 127–148.

En outre, certains pays comme l'Italie[3], Israël[4] et la Suède[5], ont fait les premiers pas vers la protection de la partie la plus faible dans les contrats d'ahésion, les clauses onéreuses qu'il contiennent faisant l'objet d'une réglementation nouvelle. Dans d'autres pays comme en Allemagne de l'Ouest, aux Etats-Unis et – dans une moindre mesure – en Angleterre, ce sont les tribunaux qui ont pris cette initiative[6]. En Allemagne, la nullité des stipulations onéreuses a été reconnue sur la base des règles générales du Code civil, tout particulièrement des §§ 138. 242 et 315[7]. Aux Etats-Unis, le même résultat fut obtenu en recourant au § 2–302 du *Uniform Commercial Code* pour protéger la personne lêsée par les clauses léonines d'un contrat de vente[8]. Récemment en Angleterre, le *Supply of Goods (Implied Terms) Act* de 1973 octroie à l'acheteur – qu'il s'agisse d'une vente ordinaire ou d'une vente à tempérament – une protection étendue contre les clauses d'exonération qui ont pour effet de libérer le vendeur de toute responsabilité pouvant découler d'une éviction ou d'un défaut du produit. Ainsi la protection de l'acheteur consommateur est-elle devenue beaucoup plus forte que celle de l'acheteur professionnel[9].

Toutes ces mesures traduisent la politique législative fondamentale (*«fundamental policy»*) de l'Etat qui les édicte.

De la nécessité de différencier les divers types de contrats

Les intérêts étatiques en cause. – Des raisons valables justifient certes le principe de l'autonomie de la volonté. La prévisibilité est sou-

---

[3] Code civ. it., art. 1341; v. *Gorla,* Standard Conditions and Form Contracts in Italian Law: Am. J. Comp. L. 11 (1962) p. 1.

[4] V. *Uri Yadin,* Legislative Control of Standard Contracts, en: Richterliche Kontrolle (*supra* note 2) p. 143 et 175.

[5] Décret suédois de 1971 sur les contrats léonins; v. *Grönfors/Sundquist,* Konkurrensen, samhället och lagen (1971) p. 45 et 57; *Adlercreutz,* Avtal (1971) p. 96.

[6] Dans beaucoup de pays, on est arrivé à cette protection de manière fort discrète, en invoquant l'absence d'un consentement réel aux clauses onéreuses, ou en interprétant celles-ci de manière à leur donner une portée plus raisonnable et conforme à l'équité. Généralement, les bénéficiaires de cette jurisprudence sont d'avantage les consommateurs et travailleurs que les sociétés commerciales. V. *G. Raiser,* Die richterliche Kontrolle von Formularbedingungen im amerikanischen und deutschen Recht (1966) p. 14; *Planiol/ Ripert,* Traité pratique de droit civil VI (1952) p. 551; *Auer,* Die richterliche Korrektur von Standardverträgen (1964) p. 71; *Lando,* Udenrigshandelsret[2] I (1973) p. 61 ss.; v. aussi *von Godin,* Kommentar zum HGB[2] III (1953) p. 56.

[7] *Fritz Hauss,* Deutschland, en: Richterliche Kontrolle (*supra* note 2) p. 7.

[8] V. les décisions citées par *Bender,* Uniform Commercial Code Service, Reporter-Digest (1965) note à § 2–302.

[9] Eliz. 2, c. 13 (1973): v. particulièrement les sections 4 et 12.

vent nécessaire aux parties, et les commerçants ont besoin de la liberté de mouvement que leur procure ce principe. Cependant des arguments tout aussi pertinents peuvent être avancés à l'encontre du principe de l'autonomie de la volonté. En effet, dans les négociations contractuelles, le déséquilibre des forces peux détruire cette liberté dans le chef de la partie la plus faible. Celle-ci risque d'être placée devant l'alternative suivante: ou bien renoncer au contrat, ou bien adhérer aux conditions imposées par l'autre partie. De plus, certains contrats intéressent vivement l'ordre public. Ils sont régis par une législation dont le but premier est la protection de la partie la plus faible contre des clauses léonines.

Le pour et le contre de tous les intérêts en présence devra chaque fois être pesé avec minutie, de sorte que la solution obtenue ne sera pas nécessairement la même pour tous les types de contrats.

La différenciation des contrats. – Le droit matériel des contrats présente un visage varié. Le dirigisme du *«welfare state»* a eu un impact considérable sur bon nombre de contrats, surtout non commerciaux. Et la liberté des parties a subi des restrictions très fortes tout en restant plus ou moins intacte en ce qui concerne les contrats commerciaux comme le transport, l'assurance, le contrat d'agence, le prêt et la concession de licence.

En ce qui concerne la détermination du centre de gravité, un certain nombre de contrats se prêtent généralement à une localisation aisée; mais d'autres présentent souvent un grand éparpillement des points de contact, si bien qu'il est difficile de les rattacher à un pays quelconque en se basant uniquement sur des éléments objectifs. Parmi les contrats de la première espèce, on peut citer le bail d'immeubles, le contrat de louage de services; par contre le contrat de vente d'un meuble conclu par correspondance entre deux commerçants qui résident dans des pays différents, appartient à la seconde espèce.

Enfin certains contrats sont internationaux de nature: ce sont la vente commerciale, l'assurance maritime, la réassurance et le crédit commercial. D'autres espèces de contrats, tels que la vente à tempérament et le bail d'immeubles, se retrouvent moins fréquemment dans le commerce international.

Variation des intérêts étatiques selon les divers types de contrats. – Comme on l'a vu plus haut, l'autonomie de la volonté des parties dépendra de l'évaluation des intérêts en cause. D'une part l'intérêt de la collectivité réclame l'application de ses règles impératives de protection. Il est d'autant plus grand et d'autant plus valable que des règles impératives régissent le contrat et que celui-ci présente des liens étroits avec le pays en question. Généralement, cet intérêt public est concerné d'avantage par les contrats de consommation que par les contrats commerciaux. Les intérêts du commerce international exigent une certaine liberté. Celle-ci a une raison d'être toute particulière dans les contrats qui sont internationaux de nature (v. *supra* p. 131). Certains d'entre eux sont souvent difficiles à localiser, et dans ce cas le choix par les parties de la loi du contrat est de nature à assurer la prévisibilité. D'autre part l'application forcée des règles impératives d'un autre Etat aux contrats internationaux pourrait constituer une entrave à la libre circulation des biens et services. Par conséquent, les règles de conflit de l'Etat dont les règles impératives sont écartées par l'effet de la référence à une autre loi, devraient prendre ces intérêts en considération. Il devrait en être de même lorsque ses règles de conflit conduiraient à la désignation d'une loi autre que celle choisie par les parties. Les règles impératives de la loi choisie par les parties trouvent à s'appliquer en toute hypothèse.

On va voir que moins un contrat est soumis au dirigisme étatique et plus il est international par essence et plus la recherche du centre de sa gravité se révélera malaisée, autant plus grande devrait être l'autonomie des parties. Cette liberté est même une nécessité pour les contrats commerciaux, bien plus que pour les contrats de consommation ou de louage de services.

Tout naturellement, l'autonomie de la volonté connue dans le droit des conflits doit être à la mesure de celle que le droit matériel autorise. En effet, elle y puise non seulement son origine et son évolution, mais également ses limites.

Il conviendrait par conséquent de limiter l'autonomie absolue aux seuls contrats commerciaux internationaux. La vente commerciale, le crédit-bail *(leasing)*, le contrat d'agence, le contrat de distribution, l'assurance en matière de transports, la réassurance, le contrat de licence, en sont quelques exemples. Dans ces contrats commerciaux dits «libres», il faudrait permettre aux parties de choisir une loi dépourvue de tout lien de rattachement objectif avec le contrat. Dans la majorité des cas, elles auront d'ailleurs un intérêt légitime à agir de la sorte. La pratique relate peu d'abus, et c'est pourquoi l'on pourrait établir une présomption de bonne foi en faveur du choix effectué. Comme l'a souligné *Martin Wolff*[10], ce choix ne sera pas nécessairement frauduleux pour le seul motif qu'il visait à échapper aux règles impératives d'un système juridique en relation étroite avec le contrat.

Il paraît donc justifié de reconnaître un plein effet au choix effectué par les parties dans le cadre d'un contrat commercial international que l'on peut appeler «libre», sauf preuve de la mauvaise foi, c'est-à-

---

[10] *M. Wolff*, Private International Law [2] (1950) p. 419.

dire d'une intention «*morally impeachable or anomalus and unrea-sonable*» [11].

Par contre il ne faudrait pas reconnaître aux parties une liberté aussi étendue en ce qui concerne les contrats qui échappent au commerce international, tels le bail d'immeubles, le contrat de louage de services, l'assurance vie et l'assurance accident, le prêt de sommes peu importantes, la vente à tempérament, la vente sous condition et autres contrats de consommation. La loi applicable au bail serait celle du lieu où se trouve l'immeuble; le contrat de louage de services serait soumis dans la plupart des cas à la loi du lieu d'exécution; on pourrait appliquer la loi du lieu du domicile de l'assuré au contrat d'assurance sur la vie, et la loi du lieu où le risque peut être localisé – à savoir habituellement le lieu où se trouve l'objet assuré – pour l'assurance incendie. En ce qui concerne la vente au consommateur, le prêt ainsi que la vente à tempérament, le principe serait l'application de la loi de la résidence habituelle du consommateur.

Cependant, il conviendrait de ne pas ôter tout effet aux choix d'une autre loi lorsque celle-ci présente un lieu de rattachement assez fort avec le contrat et que la clause de loi applicable ne constitue pas une charge trop lourde pour la partie la plus faible.

Et même en ce qui concerne les contrats soumis au dirigisme étatique, il faudrait admettre un certain droit des parties au choix d'une loi qui ait une connexion prépondérante avec le contrat, dans l'hypothèse où les négociations peuvent être menées sur un pied d'égalité. Ainsi en est-il de l'assurance groupe sur la vie et de l'assurance incendie contractées par une société commerciale.

Mais si des limites doivent être assignées à l'autonomie de la volonté en ce qui concerne le contrat de louage de services, le contrat de consommation et d'autres contrats non commerciaux où fait défaut un équilibre des forces, il ne faut pas pour autant restreindre le domaine de la loi du contrat au champ étroit que lui donnent quelques tribunaux et une certaine doctrine. Le domaine de la loi du contrat doit être plus étendu lorsque le choix est opéré en fonction d'une politique sociale déterminée qu'en vertu de la volonté discrétionnaire des parties [12] (v. *infra* à propos des articles 5 et 6).

---

[11] M. *Wolff, ibid.*

[12] Pour le contrat d'assurance, v. Restatement of the Law Second, Conflict of Laws 2d (1971) comm. c) et e) du § 192. *Batiffol* estime que la «conception moderne du rôle de l'Etat, luttant contre les inégalités sociales», doit se traduire dans le droit des conflits en matière contractuelle. Il critique cependant la distinction entre les contrats «libres» et les autres, «parce que la limite n'est pas nette». Selon lui, l'application des «lois de police» et autres «règles d'application immédiate» doit être indépendante de celle de la loi contractuelle; *Batiffol/Lagarde,* D. i. p. [5] II (1971) no. 576 et la note 29, et no.

Une distinction doit dès lors être faite entre les contrats dits «libres» et ceux qui ne le sont pas, entre les contrats commerciaux et les contrats non commerciaux. La plupart des systèmes juridiques connaissent probablement de telles distinctions, et ce sont à peu près les mêmes types de contrats qui présenteront un caractère international d'un pays à l'autre, malgré certaines variantes inévitables selon circonstances de temps et de lieu.

Cette perspective de solution se situe dans la ligne de la Convention CEE. L'alinéa 3 de l'article 2 prévoit que le choix fait par les parties dans un contrat de louage de services ne pourra en aucune manière porter atteinte aux règles impératives protectrices du travailleur qui sont en vigueur au lieu où celui-ci fournit habituellement ses prestations. Cette règle doit être rapprochée de celle de l'article 5 (v. *infra* à propos de l'article 5).

Article 2 alinéa 3 a pour but d'éviter «que, par le biais du choix d'une loi dont les dispositions sont moins protectrices du travailleur que celles du pays où il accomplit habituellement son travail, l'employeur puisse se soustraire aux dispositions impératives en vigueur dans ce pays pour la protection des travailleurs. Il va sans dire que si le choix des parties porte sur une loi contenant des dispositions impératives également ou même plus protectrices du travailleur que celles du pays où il accomplit habituellement son travail, la limite à l'autonomie de la volonté du 3ème alinéa de l'article 2 ne joue pas» [13].

L'alinéa 3 de l'article 2 «ne déroge au principe de l'autonomie de la volonté que dans l'hypothèse, la plus fréquente en fait, où le travailleur accomplit habituellement son travail dans un même pays.

Dans l'hypothèse inverse où une règle de rattachement subsidiaire est prévue à l'article 5 b, la liberté des parties de désigner la loi applicable au contrat de travail demeure entière, sous la seule réserve des lois de police mentionnées à l'article 7» [14].

L'alinéa 3 de l'article 2 maintient en principe la validité du choix d'une loi autre que celle du pays où le travailleur accomplit habituellement son travail; il se limite à veiller au respect des dispositions impératives de cette loi qui visent à la protection du travailleur.

---

612. Il convient pourtant de noter que la distinction entre «lois de polices» et d'autres lois impératives qui ne seraient pas d'application immédiate, n'est pas plus facile à faire. L'arrêt *Alnati* de la Cour Suprême des Pays-Bas en constitue un exemple parmi d'autres (HR 13 mai 1966, Ned. Jur 1967 no. 3). Le «dépeçage» résultant de cette approche est de nature à provoquer une incertitude bien plus grande que la distinction entre les contrats «libres» et les autres, entre les contrats commerciaux d'une part, et les contrats de consommation ou autres contrats non commerciaux d'autre part.

[13] Rapport, *infra* p. 265.   [14] Rapport, *infra* p. 265.

Il convient cependant de noter combien délicate peut se révéler une distinction – que les pays de la *common law* n'ont d'ailleurs pas encore assimilée parfaitement – entre les règles impératives (*«mandatory provision»*) et les règles supplétives (*«directory provision»*). A titre d'exemple, l'on peut se demander dans laquelle de ces catégories il faut faire entrer les règles qui gouvernent l'interprétation des contrats – par exemple la règle *in dubio contra stipulatorem* –, ou celles qui concernent la formation des contrats, notamment l'échange des consentements.

L'alinéa 3 de l'article 2 devrait interdire aux parties de choisir une loi autre que celle du lieu où le travailleur fournit habituellement ses prestations. Il n'en serait autrement que dans la mesure où le droit matériel du lieu d'exécution autoriserait ce choix.

D'autre part, on peut se demander pour quelle raison le Groupe des Experts n'a prévu de dispositions particulières que pour le seul contrat de travail. Une semblable protection ne pourrait-elle pas être accordée également au souscripteur d'une assurance vie, d'une assurance incendie, d'une assurance accident ou d'une assurance crédit? Le *Restatement of the Law Second, Conflict of Laws 2 d* (1971), garantit une telle protection à l'assuré (v. §§ 192 et 193). De même, pourquoi la Convention ne prévoit-elle aucune limite à l'autonomie de la volonté pour la vente au consommateur et la vente à tempérament?

Il est intéressant de noter que les sections 3 et 4 du Titre II de la Convention de Bruxelles sur la compétence et l'exécution des décisions prévoient une telle protection en ce qui concerne l'assurance ainsi que la vente à tempérament d'objets mobiliers corporels et le prêt à tempérament lié au financement d'une vente de tels objets. Ces dispositions permettent à l'assuré d'attraire la compagnie d'assurances devant plusieurs tribunaux, tandis que l'assureur ne peut porter son action contre l'assuré que dans l'Etat où ce dernier possède sa résidence habituelle. De plus l'assuré ne peut renoncer à ces droits que par une convention postérieure à la naissance du différend. L'acheteur et l'emprunteur à tempérament bénéficient de règles semblables; elles garantissent à la partie la plus faible un règlement des différends par son propre juge. Si le Groupe des Experts avait du proposer l'application de la loi de la partie la plus faible aux contrats d'assurance vie, de vente et de prêt à tempérament, on aurait pu arriver à une harmonie des solutions. Pourtant, même si le Groupe des Experts avait inséré le contrat d'assurance dans le champ d'application de la Convention, ce contrat eût probablement été soumis à la loi de la résidence habituelle de l'assuré[15]. L'on ignore toutefois si cette règle de conflit eût pu avoir une portée impérative.

---

[15] Rapport, *infra* p. 254.

L'application de la loi de la résidence habituelle du consommateur ne devrait être obligatoire que dans les cas bien précis où celui-ci tire profit du contrat dans son propre pays; il devrait également en être ainsi dans l'hypothèse où c'est l'entreprise commerciale elle-même qui a émis l'offre de contracter dans le pays de la résidence habituelle du consommateur. Par contre, lorsque cette offre a été formulée par le consommateur dans le pays de l'entreprise et qu'il ne tire aucun profit de ce contrat dans son propre pays, l'autonomie de la volonté devrait subsister. Mais si, dans cette hypothèse, le contrat a une connexion prépondérante avec un autre pays, il faudrait appliquer la loi de ce pays, même en l'absence de tout accord entre les parties.

Art. 4: La détermination de la loi contractuelle en l'absence de choix certain des parties

L'article 4 de la Convention CEE stipule:

«A défaut de choix explicite ou implicite, le contrat est régi par la loi du pays avec lequel il présente les liens les plus étroits.
Ce pays est:

a) celui où la partie qui doit fournir la prestation caractéristique a sa résidence habituelle, au moment de la conclusion du contrat;
b) celui où cette partie a son établissement principal au moment de la conclusion du contrat, si la prestation caractéristique doit être fournie en exécution d'un contrat conclu dans l'exercice d'une activité professionnelle;
c) celui où est situé l'établissement secondaire de cette partie, s'il résulte du contrat que la prestation caractéristique sera fournie par cet établissement.
L'application de l'alinéa précédent est écartée lorsque la prestation caractéristique, la résidence habituelle ou l'établissement ne peuvent être déterminés ou qu'il résulte de l'ensemble des circonstances que le contrat présente des liens plus étroits avec un autre pays.»

Le domaine de cette disposition s'étend à tous les contrats, excepté le contrat de louage de services, les contrats portant sur des immeubles (v. *infra* les commentaires des articles 5 et 6) et le contrat d'assurance.

La solution de l'article 4 constitue une certaine innovation dans le droit actuel des divers Etats Membres de la CEE, lesquels n'avaient pu, jusqu'à présent, élaborer de règles de conflits adaptées à l'hypothèse du silence des parties.

Les avantages de la solution de l'article 4. – En utilisant comme règle de principe la méthode de la soumission du contrat à la loi du pays avec lequel il présente les liens les plus étroits (méthode du centre de gravité), le Groupe des Experts a mis en avant une solution de nature à satisfaire les exigences modernes de la circulation des biens et services.

Un dilemme de taille barre le chemin de la réforme du droit des conflits en matière d'obligations contractuelles: faut-il promouvoir avant tout l'équité, la justice dans chaque cas particulier et risquer par le fait même de compromettre toute prévisibilité? Ou bien faut-il satisfaire le besoin de prévisibilité et créer des règles dont l'application trop mécanique pourrait avoir des répercussions préjudiciables?

La règle de droit risquera d'autant plus de porter atteinte à l'équité que sa formulation manquera de souplesse: c'est là une objection sérieuse à un excès de rigidité. Bien plus aujourd'hui que par le passé, le juge se préoccupe de la situation respective des parties. L'argument de la prévisibilité a pour lui bien peu de poids à côté de son sentiment de l'équité et de l'administration de la bonne justice. C'est pourquoi il faut écarter les règles abstraites qui manquent de souplesse.

D'autre part, dans l'étude de la détermination de la loi applicable on ne devrait pas s'inspirer uniquement des contrats qui ont donné lieu à des différends. Certes les contrats posant les conflits de lois difficiles sont d'avantage susceptibles de poursuites judiciaires que ceux qui ne suscitent aucune difficulté. Et les milieux intéressés à l'elaboration du droit s'intéressent d'avantage à ces cas litigieux difficiles qui font l'objet de publications et de maintes discussions, qu'à cette «majorité silencieuse» de contrats qui fonctionnent bien et n'appellent aucune attention particulière. Cependant, lorsque le juge rend une décision dans un cas délicat, c'est rarement avec l'intention de créer un précédent; malgré cela, la jurisprudence constitue la première source du droit dans bon nombre de pays, et l'interprète a tendance à accorder force de loi à des motifs qu'il considère comme déterminants dans l'espèce, même en l'absence d'une volonté du tribunal dans ce sens. Or, les parties ont avant tout besoin de règles de conflit qui leur garantissent une ligne de conduite fixe dans l'élaboration et l'exécution du contrat. Ce besoin de prévisibilité est une donnée d'une importance primordiale.

Mais encore faut-il se demander dans quelle mesure la rigidité de la règle de conflit peut assurer la prévisibilité désirée; et, dans l'affirmative, en vaut-elle vraiment le prix?

Actuellement, aucun pays ne peut établir de règle qui apporterait le haut degré de prévisibilité que désirent les parties. En effet, les solutions conflictuelles en matière de contrats varient considérablement d'un système juridique à l'autre, et d'autre part, un contrat international peut donner lieu à des poursuites dans plus d'un pays.

Pourtant, une convention internationale comme celle en préparation entre les Etats Membres de la CEE peut atteindre un degré de prévisibilité assez satisfaisant.

Mais, à la longue, cela ne vaudrait pas la peine d'introduire dans cette convention des règles rigides et trop générales. En effet, dans la plupart des pays, le droit matériel des contrats connaît actuellement une évolution rapide, tout comme d'ailleurs les conditions du commerce international. Cette évolution affectera sans doute le droit des conflits, sans que les règles générales et abstraites ne puissent toutefois l'assimiler. Par contre un minimum de souplesse facilitera l'évolution des solutions jurisprudentielles en permettant une meilleure adaptation au changement.

La méthode du centre de gravité que le Groupe des Experts a adoptée constitue un moyen terme entre la rigidité formelle de la règle et l'approche extrêmement souple que proposent certains auteurs américains. Ce compromis soumet le contrat à la loi du pays sur le territoire duquel le milieu économique et social dans lequel il s'insère, peut être localisé. D'une part, le juge n'est pas tenu de se référer à un seul et même critère de rattachement pour tous les contrats ou tous ceux d'une même catégorie. Il rassemble les divers facteurs et en pèse l'importance dans chaque cas particulier. D'autre part, la règle de conflit conserve sa structure traditionnelle. Les facteurs de rattachement ne perdent pas leur rôle fondamental. De plus, ce qui est pris en considération, ce ne sont pas les éléments isolés de la question particulière posée au juge, mais bien l'ensemble des points de contact de la relation contractuelle elle-même en tant que phénomène social formant un tout.

La méthode du centre de gravité conduit à la détermination de la loi applicable par une recherche, non pas quantitative, mais qualitative des divers éléments de rattachement. Leur importance respective est fonction de la politique sociale *(general social policies)* qui est à la base des dispositions matérielles; elle dépend également des exigences du commerce international: ainsi en est-il de la nécessité de prendre en considération l'intérêt général des parties.

Le principal établissement comme facteur de rattachement principal. – L'article 4 de l'avant-projet prévoit trois facteurs principaux qui tous se réfèrent à la prestation caractéristique. Lorsque le contrat est conclu hors de l'exercice d'une activité professionelle, le principe est l'application de la loi de la résidence habituelle de la personne qui fournit la prestation caractéristique. Dans les autres cas, la loi applicable est celle du principal établissement, à savoir le centre des activités professionnelles. Si la prestation caractéristique doit être fournie à partir d'une filiale ou d'une agence, le principe est l'application de la loi de cette résidence secondaire.

Il est fort probable que les deux dernières hypothèses visées se présenteront le plus souvent dans la pratique[16].

L'auteur de la présente étude approuve dans son principe la solution de l'article 4.

Arts. 5 et 6: Les exceptions au principe de la prestation caractéristique

Les articles 5 et 6 prévoient deux exceptions importantes au principe de la prestation caractéristique énoncé à l'article 4.

Article 5

A défaut de choix explicite ou implicite, les contrats de travail sont régis par la loi du pays
a) où le travailleur accomplit habituellement son travail,
b) où se trouve l'établissement qui a embauché le travailleur si ce dernier n'accomplit pas habituellement son travail dans un même pays,
a moins qu'il ne résulte de l'ensemble des circonstances que le contrat de travail présente des liens plus étroits avec un autre pays.

Article 6

A défaut de choix explicite ou implicite, les contrats ayant pour objet des immeubles sont régis par la loi du lieu où l'immeuble est situé à moins qu'il ne résulte de l'ensemble des circonstances que le contrat présente des liens plus étroits avec un autre pays.

Comme on pourra le constater, ces deux règles établissent également une présomption. Les dispositions de l'article 5 sont en relative harmonie avec l'état des droits allemand, belge, français et néerlandais. Mais elles s'écartent de la solution rigide que la Commission avait proposée au Conseil le 23 mars 1972[17] (v. *supra* les rapports entre l'article 5 et l'alinéa 3 de l'article 2).

L'article 6 reprend une solution unanimement admise dans les neufs pays de la CEE.

Le contrat de consommation: proposition d'une exception nouvelle au principe. – Nous avons fait état des limites qu'il faudrait assigner, dans le cas des contrats de consommation, à l'autonomie de la volonté pleinement reconnue pour les contrats commerciaux. Ainsi avons nous proposé de soumettre à la loi de la résidence habituelle du consommateur la plupart de ces contrats, tels que la vente au consommateur, la vente à tempérament, le prêt de sommes peu importantes, le bail

---

[16] En ce qui concerne la théorie de la prestation caractéristique, v. *Schnitzer*, Handbuch des IPR[4] I (1957) p. 52, et II (1958) p. 639.

[17] J.O.C.E. 18 mai 1972, no. C 49/26.

d'objets mobiliers, les excursions accompagnées, l'assurance vie et l'assurance maladie-invalidité. En plus la loi du lieu où le risque peut être localisé devrait régir l'assurance incendie et l'assurance accidents; le bail d'immeubles serait soumis à la loi du lieu de la situation de l'immeuble. En principe, il ne faudrait reconnaître aucun effet au choix d'une loi autre par les parties, à moins que les dispositions matérielles du droit désigné ne permettent ce choix.

Dans l'élaboration de tels contrats, l'une des parties exerce souvent une position dominante. Ainsi une société commerciale détient-elle la puissance financière; elle accorde généralement plus d'importance que le consommateur aux conditions du contrat: le plus souvent ce dernier n'y prête aucune attention. En outre l'entreprise est mieux au courant que lui des données commerciales, techniques et juridiques du contrat. Dans le but de rompre ce déséquilibre des forces, certains pays – parmi lesquels ceux de la CEE – ont accompli les premiers pas vers la protection du consommateur (v. *supra* à propos de l'article 2). Une politique législative protectrice se répand à travers le monde, touchant des contrats de plus en plus nombreux: ce sont non seulement des dispositions protectrices gouvernant les contrats de consommation, mais également des règles à portée plus générale destinées à protéger la partie la plus faible dans les contrats d'adhésion.

Dans la majorité des cas, ces normes matérielles se limitent à la réglementation du marché intérieur. Dans l'hypothèse la plus fréquente d'une offre émise par une société commerciale sur le marché du consommateur, les sociétés tant locales qu'étrangères jouissent d'un même régime garantissant de bonnes conditions de concurrence. L'application de la loi de la résidence habituelle du consommateur accordera donc à celui-ci la protection à laquelle il peut légitimement s'attendre, sans qu'il ne soit obligé de s'enquérir des implications particulières que comporte le fait de contracter avec une société étrangère.

D'ailleurs, en ce qui concerne le contrat d'assurance sur la vie, le *Restatement of the Law Second, Conflict of Laws 2 d* (1971) prévoit l'application de la loi de la résidence habituelle de l'assuré (§ 193); le Comité Européen des Assurances a également proposé cette solution dans son rapport de 1968. L'on a déjà souligné plus haut que le Groupe des Experts aurait pu prévoir l'application de cette loi s'il avait décidé l'inclusion des contrats d'assurance dans le champ d'application de l'avant-projet.

Enfin, il faudrait assurer une certaine souplesse à la règle qui prévoit l'application de la loi de la résidence habituelle du consommateur ainsi qu'aux autres règles de conflit impératives dont il est question. S'il résulte des circonstances de la cause que le contrat présente des liens bien plus étroits avec un autre pays, l'on pourrait appliquer la loi de ce pays. Si, par exemple, le consommateur prend contact avec l'entreprise étrangère dans le pays de celle-ci et s'il retire tout le profit du contrat à l'étranger, il paraît plus indiqué d'appliquer la loi de l'entreprise étrangère.

Art. 7 : Les règles d'application «immédiate» ou «nécessaire»

Article 7

Lorsque le contrat présente également des liens avec un pays autre que celui dont la loi est applicable en vertu des articles 2, 4, 5, 6, 16, 17, 18 et 19, 3è alinéa, et que la loi de cet autre pays contient des dispositions réglant impérativement la matière d'une façon qui exclut l'application de toute autre loi, il sera tenu compte de ces dispositions dans la mesure où leur nature ou leur objet particuliers pourraient justifier cette exclusion.

L'article 7 consacre le concept de loi d'application «immédiate» ou «nécessaire». Jusqu'à présent, seules les dispositions appartenant à la loi du for étaient prises en considération comme lois d'application «immédiate». A l'appui de cette prise en considération, les tribunaux invoquaient tour à tour l'exception de l'ordre public, l'objectif législatif ou d'autres principes. En réalité, le tribunal appliquera toujours les règles directement applicables de son propre pays, qu'il s'agisse de lois de droit public comme la législation *anti trust*, la législation sur les prix ou sur le contrôle des changes, ou de lois de droit privé comme les Règles de La Haye relatives à la responsabilité des transporteurs. Et jusqu'à présent, les juges étrangers ont rarement appliqué directement de telles normes, si bien que leur prise en considération dépendait du lieu où l'action était intentée. Cette situation provoquait un *«forum shopping»* qui laissait la place à l'incertitude dans les transactions internationales.

La limitation du domaine de la théorie de l'ordre public à l'article 22 et la consécration des règles d'application immédiate de droit étranger à l'article 7, manifestent un effort louable de la part du Groupe des Experts en vue d'une application uniforme des «lois d'ordre public» *(«laws of public order»)*.

Le Rapport ne contient aucune tentative d'énumération des lois d'application immédiate visées à l'article 7. Leur qualification dépendra de la volonté du législateur qui les édicte, comme le Rapport le souligne fort à propos :

«Il est impossible de dresser une liste de ces lois puisque ... [leur applicabilité immédiate] ne dépend pas de la matière dans laquelle elles interviennent, mais de la volonté du législateur qui les édicte. Telle disposition, imposant par exemple un versement minimum immédiat de l'acheteur dans les ventes à tempérament, pourra être considérée dans un pays comme une loi de police, applicable à tous les contrats conclus sur son territoire, et dans un autre pays comme une simple loi contractuelle, applicable seulement aux contrats régis par la loi de ce dernier. Sous cette réserve, on a encore cité, comme pouvant être couvertes le cas échéant par cet article 7, les lois sur la résiliation de certains contrats (par exemple la loi belge du 27 juillet 1961 sur la résiliation unilatérale des concessions de vente exclusive à durée indéterminée), les lois relatives au contrôle des mouvements de capitaux ou des mouvements de marchandises (interdictions de certains paiements à l'étranger, de certaines importations ou exportations)[18]»

Appréciation critique. – D'après l'auteur de la présente étude, il conviendrait de faire une distinction entre, d'une part, les règles de droit privé qui visent à la protection de la partie la plus faible, et d'autre part les lois dites de droit public, à savoir essentiellement la législation économique et certaines dispositions de droit social qui régissent les rapports contractuels.

Cette distinction entre les lois de droit public et celles de droit privé est fondamentale dans les pays du Code civil. Une grande partie de la doctrine et de la jurisprudence soutiennent encore aujourd'hui que le droit des conflits se limite en principe aux seules règles matérielles de droit privé. Or, les contours de ces catégories n'ont jamais été très nets, et bien des règles ont un caractère à la fois privé et public. C'est pourquoi la distinction opérée a fait l'objet de vives critiques, et certains auteurs souhaitent la suppression pure et simple des deux concepts. Pourtant, tout système juridique connaît des règles matérielles qui relèvent exclusivement de l'une ou l'autre des deux catégories. Et qui oserait prétendre que les périodes de pénombre suffisent à supprimer le contraste de la lumière et de l'obscurité?

Cette distinction, jusqu'à présent inconnue des pays de la *Common Law,* semble pourtant utilisée par certains auteurs. Ainsi *J. H. C. Morris* souligne que, reconnue universellement, sa compréhension ne fait aucune difficulté; de plus elle reste d'une grande utilité malgré l'impossibilité de la cerner de très près et de lui trouver une base assez solide pour résister à l'analyse.

Les règles protectrices de droit privé

Lorsque la situation contractuelle présente des liens étroits avec un pays déterminé, cet Etat a un intérêt prépondérant à l'application, en tant que loi contractuelle, de son propre droit considéré comme un

---

[18] Rapport, *infra* p. 278.

tout, dans la mesure où les règles protectrices de droit privé sont mises en cause. Ainsi l'autonomie de la volonté devrait-elle être exclue pour autant que le lien de rattachement soit suffisamment solide: le contrat devrait alors être soumis aux lois protectrices émanant de l'Etat avec lequel il présente des liens tels que la loi contractuelle devra nécessairement être la loi de cet Etat même (v. l'hypothèse des contrats de travail et de consommation en relation avec les arts. 2, 4, 5 et 6, *supra* p. 133 s.). Les efforts accomplis par le législateur pour faire face aux inégalités sociales ne peuvent aboutir par l'application des seules normes qui présentent un caractère d'impérieuse nécessité, solution pourtant proposée par le Groupe des Experts. D'autre part la nécessité de prévoir des exceptions aux règles des articles 2, 3, 4, 5, 6 etc., comme prescrites dans l'article 7, se ferait moins pressante si la vente au consommateur par exemple, était soumise à la loi de la résidence habituelle de l'acheteur, le contrat de travail à la loi du lieu d'exécution (v. l'art. 5), et si des restrictions d'ordre général étaient apportées à l'autonomie de la volonté pour tous les contrats «non égalitaires» *(weak party contract)*. Les règles impératives qui, eu égard à leur importance, sont exclusives de l'application de toute autre loi, seront alors généralement celles de la loi contractuelle; et les parties seront à même de prévoir leur application. La question de la prise en considération de règles impératives d'un autre droit se posera rarement, à supposer qu'elle puisse jamais se poser. Et même si cette éventualité se présentait, ces règles devraient, en principe, ne pas trouver à s'appliquer, faute pour les parties d'avoir pu prévoir leur prise en considération.

Législation économique et autre règles de droit public

Rattachement à la loi contractuelle. – La législation économique ne devrait-elle être prise en considération que lorsqu'elle fait partie de la loi contractuelle? Certains auteurs l'ont prétendu, et les tribunaux ont parfois soutenu cette thèse dans des pays de *Common Law*. D'après cette jurisprudence, des réglementations de change étrangères ont pu trouver à s'appliquer pour la seule raison qu'elles faisaient partie de la loi contractuelle; et inversément, lorsque la loi du pays dont émanaient ces normes n'était pas la loi contractuelle, leur application était exclue. Dans cette dernière hypothèse, lorsque le contrat présentait un lien assez fort avec le pays d'où émanait la norme réglementaire, c'est sur base de l'interprétation de la volonté des parties que la loi de ce pays était écartée comme ne constituant pas la loi contractuelle[19].

---

[19] En Angleterre: *Rossano* v. *Manufacturers Life Insurance* Co., [1963] 2 Q. B. 352. Au Canada: *Imperial Life Assurance Co. of Canada* v. *Colemenares,*

L'auteur de la présente étude propose, quant à lui, d'appliquer la législation économique qui fait partie de la loi contractuelle. Certes, il est dangereux de laisser aux parties la faculté de décider elles-mêmes de l'applicabilité de la législation économique d'un pays déterminé; cependant, lorsque de telles normes appartiennent effectivement à la loi contractuelle, la question de leur applicabilité ne soulève pas de tels problèmes. Cette proposition ne va pas à l'encontre de l'avant-projet.

Application de la législation économique étrangère ne faisant pas partie de la loi contractuelle. – L'autonomie de la volonté ne devrait évidemment pas permettre aux parties de fixer elles-mêmes le champ d'application territorial de la législation économique étrangère de droit public. Certes, la prévisibilité pour les parties de l'application de ces normes serait assurée s'il ne fallait les prendre en considération que dans l'hypothèse où la loi contractuelle est la loi du pays dont elles émanent. Pourtant dans bien des cas, il faudra – soit par nécessité soit en raison de l'équité – tenir compte des normes étrangères qui ne font pas partie de la loi contractuelle. A vrai dire, il n'est pas aisé de donner une énumération exhaustive de ces cas, et l'incertitude du droit dans la plupart des pays ne permet pas de se fier à la jurisprudence publiée. *L'auteur de la présente étude propose deux principes généraux:*

Premièrement, les mesures d'ordre économique établies par un Etat étranger ne devraient être prises en considération que lorsque la règle étrangère a la volonté d'être appliquée à l'objet du litige. Cette condition paraît bénéficier d'un soutien unanime.

Deuxièmement, la prise en considération des normes économiques étrangères dependerait de l'existence d'un lien assez fort entre le contrat – ou les parties au contrat – et le système juridique en question pour rendre leur application impérieuse ou bien exigée par l'esprit de la coopération internationale.

Cette application sera impérieuse lorsque l'Etat légiférant sera à même de contraindre les parties au respect de ces normes.

D'autre part, la prise en considération des normes étrangères est raisonnable dans la mesure où elle peut renforcer la communauté d'intérêts entre les Etats. Ainsi en est-il des contrats qui affectent directement les intérêts économiques de l'Etat légiférant et qui, dans d'autres pays, sont soumis à des dispositions semblables assurant le respect des mêmes intérêts étatiques. L'auteur de la présente étude se rallie à l'opinion de *Zweigert* qui préconise le respect de la volonté d'application d'une mesure étrangère d'ordre économique lorsque sa prise en

(1967) 62 D.L.R. (2d) 461. Aux Etats-Unis: *In re Sik's Estate,* 129 N.Y.S. 2d 134 (1954); *In re de Gheest's Estate,* 243 S.W. 2d 83 (Mo. 1951).

considération contribue à l'harmonie des solutions sur le plan international[20].

Applications des principes

L'application d'une norme étrangère sera souvent commandée à la fois par une impérieuse nécessité et par les exigences de la coopération internationale.

Premier exemple. – A s'engage vis-à-vis de B à respecter les prix fixés par B pour la vente des produits de B dans le pays X; A possède son principal établissement dans le pays X. D'après la loi du pays X, les clauses de maintien du prix de revente sont illicites et de nul effet. B possède son principal établissement dans le pays Y. Les tribunaux du pays Y ne doivent reconnaître l'efficacité d'une telle clause vis-à-vis de A, même si le droit de l'Etat Y la considère comme licite.

Or, il est plus probable que les autorités de l'Etat X sont à même de supprimer la clause de maintien des prix. Par conséquent, la sagesse commande l'application des dispositions législatives de l'Etat X, la clause en question touchant directement aux intérêts économiques de cet Etat.

Par ailleurs, il se peut que ce soit la seule force des choses qui contraigne le tribunal à prendre en considération une mesure restrictive étrangère même si elle n'est pas raisonnable. Ce peut être le cas d'un décret sur la collaboration avec l'ennemi émanant d'un pays adverse, ou encore de mesures confiscatoires de certains droits contractuels: le respect de ces normes s'impose uniquement en raison du pouvoir de fait dont dispose l'Etat légiférant[21]. Par conséquent, lorsqu'un impératif majeur autre que la coopération internationale pousse le juge à l'application d'une norme étrangère, le domaine de cette application doit être restreint au strict minimum.

Deuxième exemple. – La société Alpha a son principal établissement dans le pays X et fait du commerce dans le pays Y. Elle émet des obligations dans les pays X et Y; celles-ci sont soumises à la loi du pays Y; elles sont remboursables dans le pays Y, et exclusivement en monnaie du pays Y. Par la suite, un décret émanant du pays X impose aux émetteurs résidant dans le pays X de rembourser leurs dettes dans le pays X et en monnaie ayant cours légal dans le pays X, sans que puissent être invoquées les clauses contractuelles relatives au payement.

---

[20] D'après *Zweigert*, Nichterfüllung auf Grund ausländischer Leistungsverbote: RabelsZ 14 (1942) p. 291, la volonté du législateur étranger doit être prise en considération pourvu que son intérêt à voir appliqué son propre droit ait un caractère exclusivement international (*«international-typische Interessen»*).

[21] V. *Kegel*, IPR[3] (1971) p. 52.

Les tribunaux du pays Y ne devraient tenir compte du décret qu'à l'égard des seuls obligataires domiciliés dans l'Etat X; ceux qui ont leur résidence dans d'autres pays et qui réclament le remboursement de leur créance dans la monnaie ayant cours légal dans l'Etat Y, devraient pouvoir échapper au décret.

D'autre part, même si dans certains cas l'Etat légiférant n'est pas en mesure d'assurer l'exécution des normes qu'il édicte, l'esprit de coopération internationale peut néanmoins en exiger le respect[22].

Troisième exemple. – Un certain nombre de sociétés dominent le marché local d'un produit déterminé dans le pays Y; de commun accord, elles refusent de vendre le produit à des coopératives dans le pays X; de telles ententes sont reconnues comme licites par la loi de l'Etat Y. Les tribunaux de l'Etat Y devraient prendre en considération la loi de l'Etat X, laquelle n'admet pas de telles ententes. Par conséquent, le juge de l'Etat Y devrait leur refuser toute efficacité vis-à-vis d'une entreprise résidant dans l'Etat Y et qui n'a pas respecté cet accord.

Dans l'hypothèse voisine d'une entente survenue à l'étranger et visant à perturber le marché de l'Etat Y, les autorités saisies dans l'Etat Y prendraient des mesures à l'encontre d'une telle entente si elles le pouvaient. Cependant, au même titre que les autorités saisies dans l'Etat X, elles risqueraient de se trouver dans l'impossibilité d'anihiler cette entente. C'est pourquoi, l'aide d'une autorité étrangère pourrait leur être souhaitable[23].

Il en irait de même de la réglementation sur le contrôle des changes qui, au contraire des mesures exceptionnelles prises au sujet de l'emission d'obligations (v. *supra* le deuxième exemple), se retrouve dans bien des systèmes juridiques. Il faudrait la prendre en considération non seulement lorsqu'elle appartient à la loi contractuelle, mais également dans l'hypothèse où le contrat met en jeu les restrictions d'ordre monétaire que connaît le système juridique dont elle fait partie (application de la *lex patrimonii*)[24].

---

[22] V. *Zweigert* (*supra* note 20) p. 288 et 291.

[23] Cet exemple a trait aux conditions de fond du contrat. Il faudrait que l'Etat X puisse prévoir des sanctions pénales, quasi-pénales ou administratives contre une telle entente: v. la Résolution du Conseil de l'OCDE, 5 octobre 1957, qui recommande une coopération entre les Etats en matière de législation anti-trust (Doc. L. [67] p. 53, version finale); v. également la proposition de l'*International Law Association* (1972) relative aux droits des Etats de prévoir des sanctions pénales, quasi-pénales et administratives contre les actes de concurrence déloyale (Rapport soumis lors de la Conférence de New York en 1972 par le Comité chargé de l'examen des effets extraterritoriaux de la réglementation sur la circulation des biens).

[24] V. l'art. VIII § 2 b) des Statuts du Fonds Monétaire International (accords de Bretton Woods).

Art. 18: La loi applicable à la forme du contrat

L'article 18 stipule:

«Pour être valable quant à la forme, un acte juridique doit satisfaire aux conditions établies, soit par la loi qui le régit ou le régissait au fond au moment de sa passation, soit par celle du lieu où il est intervenu. Lorsqu'un acte juridique est formé de plusieurs déclarations, la validité quant à la forme de chacune d'elles est appréciée séparément.

Les dispositions du présent article ne s'appliquent pas à la constitution, au transfert et à l'extinction des droits réels portant sur une chose.»

La solution de l'alinéa premier de l'article 18 est conforme à celle que connaissent la majorité des systèmes juridiques, dont la plupart des droits européens qui prévoient l'application facultative de la *lex loci contractus* aux questions relatives à la forme des actes. Ils admettent également l'application de la loi contractuelle lorsqu'elle suffit à valider la forme d'un acte répondant aux prescriptions de la loi du lieu de conclusion. Ainsi le rattachement choisi présente un caractère alternatif dans le sens de l'application de la loi la plus libérale.

Quelles sont les justifications d'un tel principe? Celui-ci mérite-t-il d'être conservé?

Les exigences relatives à la forme des actes visent essentiellement à établir à suffisance l'existence de l'accord intervenu entre les parties ainsi que son contenu; elles assurent également la protection du débiteur de l'obligation. La rédaction des clauses, l'apposition de scellés, l'acte notarié, etc., l'incitent à la réflexion et à la prudence; certains d'eux lui permettent une meilleure compréhension du contrat auquel il consent. Or, l'application exclusive de la loi contractuelle correspond le mieux à cet objectif, très proche de celui des règles protectrices[25]. Comment alors l'application de la *lex loci contractus* aux questions de validité pourrait-elle se justifier?

Certes, l'adage *locus regit formam actus* s'appliquait à l'origine à la plupart des actes juridiques – contrats, testaments, mariages –, et la loi du lieu de conclusion a même continué à s'appliquer aux conditions de forme dans des systèmes juridiques qui en avaient exclu l'application aux conditions de fond[26]. D'autre part, des arguments très pertinents plaidaient en faveur de l'application de la *lex loci contractus* là où l'intervention d'un officier public (notaire ou même juge) se révélait nécessaire[27]. Néanmoins, ces formalités particulières se font rares

---

[25] *Schmitthoff,* The Conflict of Laws[3] (1954) p. 119.

[26] V. *Lando,* Contacts for International Contracts, American and Scandinavian Conflict Rules Compared, dans: Ius privatum gentium, Festschrift Max Rheinstein I (1969) p. 383.

[27] V. *Rabel,* The Conflict of Laws[2] II (1960) p. 487; *von Savigny,* System des

aujourd'hui en ce qui concerne les contrats commerciaux; de plus,
l'application de la *lex loci contractus* a perdu, aujourd'hui, le fondement logique sur lequel elle reposait autrefois.

Hypothèse du contrat conclus «inter presentes». – *Kahn-Freund* explique de la manière suivante l'application de la loi du lieu de conclusion à la question de la validité du contrat *«inter presentes»*[28]: il
est probable qu'au cours des négociations contractuelles, les questions
de fond préoccupent d'avantage les parties que les questions de forme,
moins importantes à leurs yeux. De tels problèmes ne se posent qu'in-
cidemment au moment de la passation même de l'acte et appellent
une issue relativement prompte. A ce stade, il faut que les parties puissent recevoir immédiatement des conseils d'ordre juridique; or, dans
la mesure où ils concernent la forme des actes, ceux-ci ne peuvent
se baser que sur la seule loi locale.

Au terme de l'analyse minutieuse qu'il a faite de la règle *locus regit
actum*, *Zweigert* attribue à la *favor gerentis* le fondement de l'application facultative de la *lex loci contractus*. Il sera plus facile d'obtenir
des informations précises et exactes sur les conditions de forme exi-
gées au lieu où peut être localisée l'obligation contractuelle. Voilà le
fondement réel de la règle, et non pas – comme le pensent certains –
la *favor negotii*[29].

Toutefois, si la *favor gerentis* peut fournir une explication satisfaisante de la règle *locus regit actum*, en constitue-t-elle pour autant
la justification fondamentale? Les questions de fond pouvant se présenter tout aussi inopinément que les questions de forme, certains en
ont déduit que la loi du lieu de conclusion devait également régir les
questions relatives au fond.

L'auteur de la présente étude estime que la *favor negotii* constitue
la justification la plus convaincante de l'application facultative de la
lex loci contractus aux questions relatives à la forme des actes. Les
tribunaux n'apprécient guère le fomalisme rigoureux dont ils savent
l'effet néfaste[30]. En effet, les contestations sont généralement soulevées devant eux pour ôter tout effet à un contrat conclu de bonne

---

heutigen Römischen Rechts VIII (1849) § 382; v. aussi la monographie de *Silz*,
Du domaine d'application de la règle «Locus regit actum» (1933).

[28] V. *Dicey/Morris(-Kahn-Freund)*, Conflict of Laws [8] (1967) p. 750.

[29] *Zweigert*, Zum Abschluß schuldrechtlicher Distanzverträge, dans: Festschrift Ernst Rabel (1954) p. 636. Sur cette question, v. également *Neuhaus*,
Die Grundbegriffe des IPR (1962) p. 114.

[30] V. *Corbin* on Contracts, § 293: «If a court is convinced that the contract
was made as alleged and that there has been no fraud or perjury, it has no
sympathy for a party whose only excuse for repudiation is lack of a statutory
formality» (cité par *Ehrenzweig*, The Conflict of Laws [1962]) p. 470 s.

foi, et elles contribuent rarement à écarter les transactions de mauvaise foi. Tout comme le *Statute of Frauds* anglais, elles frappent à l'aveuglette et, au lieu d'avoir l'effet préventif escompté, suscitent la fraude à la loi[31]. D'autre part, le respect des exigences de forme auxquelles doit satisfaire un contrat international pourrait se révéler bien plus difficile que dans le cas d'un contrat purement interne, car bien souvent l'une ou l'autre règle étrangère aura été ignorée de l'une des parties. Cependant, tant la jurisprudence que le législateur ont remédié à de tels inconvénients en consacrant le principe du rattachement alternatif. C'est là un des rares exemples de la mise en œuvre universelle d'une règle de conflit aux fins de limiter l'application de toute une série de normes restrictives prévoyant des formalités trop sévères. Cet objectif a conduit à l'application de la loi la plus libérale parmi des divers systèmes juridiques intéressés.

L'interprétation que la jurisprudence italienne a donnée de l'article 1341 du Code civil (1942) constitue un bel exemple du souci de restreindre au maximum l'application des conditions de forme. Cette disposition soumet la validité de certaines clauses onéreuses comme les conventions d'exonération ou les clauses compromissoires dans les contrats type, à un écrit signé par la partie adhérante et attestant son consentement spécial: ainsi la partie adhérante doit-elle apposer au moins deux signatures au bas de l'acte[32]. Les tribunaux italiens refusent de considérer l'article 1341 du Code civil comme une disposition d'ordre public[33] et en limitent l'application aux seuls contrats régis par la loi italienne. Les tribunaux ont rattaché l'article 1341 à la règle alternative contenue dans l'article 26 disp. prel.[34]. Mais ils vont encore plus loin en refusant l'application de l'article 1341 à certains contrats internationaux conclus entre des sociétés commerciales dans des cas qui relèvent du domaine de la loi italienne d'après l'article 26 disp. prel.[35].

Par conséquent, l'auteur de la présente étude estime qu'il faut maintenir la règle de la loi la plus libérale. En effet la *favor negotii*, qui a donné naissance à une *favor gerentis,* a reçu un accueil favorable dans la pratique. Elle a même été consacrée par des réformes législatives assez récentes comme l'article 1341 du Code civil italien.

[31] V. *Chitty* on Contracts[23] I (1968) no. 158.

[32] V. *Gorla* (*supra* note 3).

[33] App. Genova 27 juin 1957, Dir. Mar. 1958, p. 499; App. Milano 19 mai 1964, Clunet 93 (1966) p. 702; v. aussi Cass. 2 mars 1964, Riv. Dir. Int. 47 (1964) p. 659 = Clunet 93 (1966) p. 702; 2 mai 1960, Clunet 88 (1961) p. 860; v. également OLG Hamburg 23 mars 1966, IPRspr. 1966–67 no. 279.

[34] Cass. 2 mars 1964 et 2 mai 1960 (*supra* note 33). V. aussi *Angelo Pesce,* NJW 1971, p. 2111.

[35] App. Milano 23 avril 1965, Clunet 93 (1966) p. 702, 704.

L'application universelle de la règle de la loi la plus libérale ajoute
à ses mérites. Les européens tout particulièrement sont sûrs de son
application par leurs propres tribunaux et par ceux des pays limi-
trophes. En tant que règle de conflit uniforme, elle assure la prévisibilité dans le commerce international. C'est pourquoi elle doit être
maintenue.

C'est ce que fait l'article 18 de l'avant-projet CEE en lui donnant
toutefois une autre formulation. Il suffit que le contrat remplisse les
conditions de forme prévues par la loi qui le régit au fond au moment
de la contestation ou qui le régissait au moment de sa conclusion
(hypothèse de conflit mobile). Cette innovation doit être accueillie
favorablement.

Hypothèse du contrat entre absents. – Lorsque les contractants résident dans des Etats différents au moment de la conclusion, celle-ci
ne peut être localisée en un lieu unique. La plupart des systèmes
juridiques ont laissé cette hypothèse sans solution, de sorte que le
problème de la mise en œuvre de la *lex loci contractus* reste posé dans
ce cas [36]. En réalité, la règle *locus regit actum* n'est pas faite pour les
contrats entre absents. En effet, au moment de sa création, c'est-à-dire
avant la moitié du XIXème siècle, la plupart des contrats internationaux étaient conclus sur des foires ou des marchés, ou chez le client
lui-même par des vendeurs itinérants [37].

Quoiqu'aujourd'hui beaucoup, si pas la plupart des contrats internationaux sont conclus entre absents, l'application de la loi du lieu
de conclusion aux questions de fond reste encore la règle dans certains
pays; et un choix y est opéré entre les diverses lois en présence. Certains auteurs ont voulu étendre ces règles aux questions de forme [38].
L'on peut reprocher à cette solution l'incertitude qu'elle engendre. En
effet la question de la localisation de la conclusion du contrat est résolue différemment d'un pays à l'autre [39]. Ainsi en Italie, le contrat par
correspondance est localisé au lieu de la réception de l'acceptation
alors qu'en Angleterre prévaut la solution du lieu d'où l'acceptation
a été envoyée.

Les auteurs allemands contemporains suivent la solution proposée
par *Zweigert*[40]. Celui-ci permet à chacune des parties d'émettre sa
promesse de contracter suivant les formes en vigueur au lieu où la

---

[36] *Zweigert* (*supra* note 29) p. 647–648 donne un éventail de réponses données par certains pays.

[37] *Zweigert* (*supra* note 29) p. 643; *Lando* (*supra* note 26) p. 386.

[38] M. *Wolff* (*supra* note 10) p. 450.

[39] V. *Dicey Morris(-Kahn-Freund)* (*supra* note 28) p. 751; *Zweigert* (*supra*
note 29) p. 634.

[40] *Zweigert* (*supra* note 29) p. 636; *Soergel/Siebert(-Kegel)*, BGB[10] VII
(1970) art. 11 no. 8.

promesse est faite. Selon ces auteurs, cette règle de conflit trouverait à s'appliquer chaque fois que le respect des conditions de forme n'est dû que par un seul des contractants: c'est le cas, en droit allemand, pour l'engagement à se constituer comme sûreté d'une dette dans la forme d'un écrit. Et il en irait de même des contrats où les engagements respectifs des parties nécessitent l'accomplissement de certaines formalités. Ainsi en droit allemand les promesses de contracter émanant des deux parties en vue de la vente d'un bien-fonds doivent être constatées devant notaire. Cette condition n'existe pas en Italie. Dans l'hypothèse d'un contrat régi par la loi allemande, l'offre de contracter envoyée d'Italie par le vendeur ou l'acheteur ne devra pas être constatée devant notaire; d'après *Zweigert*, l'offre envoyée d'Allemagne devra remplir cette condition.

Cette tendance considère la *favor gerentis* comme le fondement de l'application alternative de la *lex loci contractus*. Chacune des parties bénéficie d'une protection suffisante dès lors qu'il lui suffit d'observer les formalités en vigueur au lieu où elle remplit ses obligations contractuelles.

L'avant-projet CEE se situe dans cette tendance: lorsque le contrat est formé de plusieurs déclarations, la validité quant à la forme de chacune d'elles est appréciée séparément.

Pourtant, l'on peut se demander pourquoi pour une partie contractante il ne suffirait pas d'observer les conditions de forme prévues au lieu où le cocontractant remplit ses obligations ou, dans le cas d'un contrat unilateral, celles prévues au lieu où se trouve celui à qui la promesse est faite. Pourquoi *Zweigert* et ses partisans refusent-ils le droit d'invoquer l'application exclusive des règles de forme en vigueur au lieu de la réception de l'offre et – si nécessaire – au point de départ de l'acceptation? D'autre part, dès lors qu'ont été observées les règles de forme en vigueur au lieu où se trouve l'un des contractants, celui-ci ne peut-il vraiment pas être assuré de la validité formelle du contrat même s'il ignore les formalités prévues par la loi contractuelle ou par la loi du lieu où se trouve le cocontractant? Ou bien doit-il encore vérifier le respect des formalités prévues par l'une de ces lois?

Zweigert soutient que l'application facultative des deux lois conduirait à une solution inacceptable qui irait à l'encontre du but même de la règle[41]. Mais de quel but s'agit-il? De la *favor gerentis*? Or, la *favor gerentis*, loin de rendre plus lourde la tâche des parties, est destinée à leur venir en aide: elle n'exclut donc nullement la *favor negotii*.

La règle proposée par *Zweigert* peut trouver des partisans parmi ceux qui croient à la fonction préventive des règles relatives à la forme,

---

[41] *Raape*, IPR[5] (1961) p. 220–221; *Zweigert* (*supra* note 29) p. 636.

parmi ceux qui estiment d'une impérieuse nécessité de permettre à chacune des parties de se demander dans quelle mesure elle doit tenir compte des règles de forme en vigueur au lieu où elle se trouve. Cet objectif de protection obligerait le vendeur ou l'acheteur allemand de recourir aux services d'un notaire pour la vente ou l'achat d'un bien-fonds. Cependant cet objectif ne peut expliquer, dans certains cas, l'application plus libérale de la loi contractuelle. Pourquoi ne pas protéger le contractant allemand lorsque le contrat de vente est régi par la loi italienne?

Au contraire si, comme le propose l'auteur de la présente étude, la justification première du choix des dispositions les plus libérales réside dans la protection du contrat contre les pièges du formalisme et si, comme le croient bien des tribunaux et des législateurs, l'on peut minimiser le rôle préventif des règles relatives à la forme, dans ce cas il suffirait que le contrat, pour être valable, remplisse soit les conditions de la loi contractuelle, soit celles prévues par l'une des lois en vigueur aux lieux où résident les parties. Cette solution permet au contractant désireux de s'assurer de la validité formelle du contrat, de se référer aux seules conditions prévues par la loi du lieu où il se trouve [42].

Art. 20: La capacité

Quoique les questions relatives à la capacité soient exclues du domaine de l'avant-projet CEE, l'article 20 traite d'un problème qui y touche de près.

L'article 20 stipule que:

«Aucune personne physique ne peut invoquer son incapacité contre celui qui, dans un acte juridique, l'aura de bonne foi et sans imprudence, conformément à la loi du lieu de l'acte, considérée comme capable.»

Dans l'arrêt *Lizardi*, la Cour de cassation de France avait établi qu'un étranger incapable selon sa loi personnelle serait néanmoins tenu de respecter les obligations découlant d'un contrat conclu dans le pays du for lorsque la loi de ce pays déclare le contrat valable et à condition que le cocontractant ait agi «de bonne foi et sans imprudence» [43]. L'article 20 trouve son origine dans la solution de l'arrêt *Lizardi*. Cependant la règle *Lizardi* se bornait à protéger un citoyen de l'Etat du for contre un étranger incapable selon sa loi personnelle. Cette solution a trouvé une explication en France dans l'idée de l'«inté-

---

[42] V. *Rabel* (*supra* note 27) p. 518; *Vischer*, Internationales Vertragsrecht (1962) p. 153–154; Code civil argentin, art. 1181.

[43] Cass. req. 13 janvier 1861, S. 1861. 1. 305.

rêt national» destinée à protéger le commerce français. Les intérêts extérieurs à la France ne sont donc nullement garantis tandis que les citoyens français mineurs ou frappés d'incapacité bénéficient de la protection de l'alinéa 3 de l'article 3 du Code civil lorsqu'ils font du commerce à l'étranger. Au contraire, la solution de l'avant-projet conduira à l'application fréquente du droit étranger pour protéger le contractant de bonne foi contre une personne incapable selon sa loi personnelle. Par conséquent le juge français ne pourra pas écarter un contrat conclu au Danemark entre un citoyen français âgé de 20 ans et une personne de bonne foi. Ainsi la loi étrangère jouit-elle d'un domaine d'application aussi large que celui de la *lex fori*.

Appréciation critique. – Dans le XIXème siècle fortement teintée de libéralisme, les règles relatives à la capacité de contracter figurèrent parmi celles qui furent le mieux à même d'assurer la protection de la partie la plus faible contre les effets néfastes de l'inégalité des force au cours de l'élaboration du contrat et qui découle du manque d'expérience, du manque de compétence, de l'ignorance. Or, un peu partout l'on commence maintenant à se rendre compte que le déséquilibre des forces se rencontre non seulement chez les mineurs et les faibles d'esprit, mais dans une portion beaucoup plus importante de la population. C'est pourquoi les contrats de consommation et d'autres contrats du genre ont déjà fait l'objet – et feront encore l'objet – d'une législation protectrice de plus en plus nombreuse.

L'enfant aussi bien que les consommateurs en général ont besoin de la protection que leur assure le système juridique qui y a le plus d'intérêt. Dans la plupart des contrats de consommation, il s'agira de la loi du domicile du consommateur; dans les contrats de travail, ce sera la loi du lieu où le travailleur fournit habituellement ses prestations. Pour tous ces contrats, le système juridique intéressé à une telle protection devrait coïncider avec la loi contractuelle, et les parties ne seraient pas autorisées à choisir une loi autre que celle-là. Par conséquent le contractant qui se trouve dans une position dominante ne pourra pas imposer à la partie la plus faible l'application d'une autre loi; et le choix d'une loi déterminée ne permettra jamais au mineur de s'octroyer la capacité de contracter.

C'est pourquoi il devient pratiquement inutile d'établir des règles de conflit spéciales pour la capacité si l'on applique les principes de rattachement proposés *supra* (p. 134) à propos des articles 5 et 6 concernant les contrats de consommation et autres contrats de ce genre. La loi contractuelle apportera à la partie la plus faible la protection désirée.

Des problèmes peuvent se poser dans les régions qui connaissent des échanges fréquents de biens au-delà des frontières. Il se peut que des mineurs âgés de 18 à 20 ans et dont la loi personnelle n'accorde la majorité qu'à 21 ans, se rendent en grand nombre dans un pays voisin qui reconnaît la capacité dès l'âge de 18 ans, et qu'ils y contractent des engagements en vue de l'acquisition de biens. Il faudrait que de tels contrats soient soumis à la loi du domicile du consommateur, sans prendre en considération la bonne foi du cocontractant. Et si la loi du domicile du consommateur protège celui-ci sous d'autres aspects que la capacité, ces règles protectrices devraient également être appliquées. Pareille solution conflictuelle tient compte des particularités que présentent les situations interterritoriales ou celles qui se localisent à proximité des frontières: dans de telles hypothèses, l'Etat de la résidence a un intérêt tout particulier à assurer la protection du consommateur contre toute tentative considérée comme malencontreuse d'échapper à celle que lui offre sa propre loi.

Dans les contrats commerciaux toutefois, l'incapacité devrait ne pouvoir être soulevée que très rarement, et cette question devrait être soumise à la loi contractuelle. Dans de tels contrats en effet, le besoin de protection ne se fait pas aussi pressant, et l'impératif de la sécurité des transactions et de la prévisibilité devrait le supplanter[44].

Cependant l'application de la loi contractuelle doit recevoir une exception importante. En quel lieu que soit survenue la conclusion du contrat, toute personne restera tenue de ces engagements lorsque la loi de son domicile lui attribue la capacité.

---

[44] V. *Graveson*, The Conflict of Laws[6] (1969) p. 420.

COMMENTS ON ARTS. 1 TO 21 OF THE DRAFT CONVENTION

By

KURT LIPSTEIN

Cambridge[*]

Art. 1: Scope of the Convention[1]

The Convention is rightly restricted to situations of an international character (a), but this character can be determined not only by the quality of the persons to the contract, the objects of the contract and the terms of its performance. Extraneous elements, such as the fact that the insurers reside in a particular country, may be relevant factors which render an agreement international in character[2].

The exceptions (b)–(f) are acceptable, but English lawyers, applying both the common law and the Geneva Conventions on the Execution of Foreign Awards of 26 September 1927 and the Protocol on Arbitration Clauses of 24 September 1923 would be inclined to apply the general principles to the validity of arbitration agreements[3]. It may be that the Draft Convention wishes to keep clear of areas where uniform law can apply, and that it has in mind (c) the existence of the European Convention concerning International Commercial Arbitration of 21 April 1961[4] esp. arts. VI (2), VII (not ratified by the U.K.) supplemented by the Agreement of 17 December 1962[5], and (b) the Geneva Conventions on Bills of Exchange and Cheques. The sentiments expressed in the Report by *Giuliano* are shared by the present writer.

---

[*] *Abbreviated literature: Dicey/Morris,* The Conflict of Laws[9] (1973); *Lando,* The EC Draft Convention on the Law Applicable to Contractual and Non-contractual Obligations, Introduction and Contractual Obligation: RabelsZ 38 (1974) pp. 5–55.

[1] Report, *infra* p. 251–255; *Lando* p. 8–11.

[2] See, as regards art. 2, *Lando* p. 11–12.

[3] *Dicey/Morris* rules 196, 199, 203.

[4] UNTS 484, 349, 364; see the accessions UNTS 510, 341 (Poland), 514, 295 (Germany), 523, 343 (Upper Volta), 544, 376 (Cuba), 584, 260 (France).

[5] UNTS 523, 93.

I also share *Lando*'s doubts[6] as to whether the limitation of the Convention to international situations is too narrow, unless cases such as that set out at the beginning can be included. I believe, however, that a broad interpretation can accommodate these cases; any foreign element attracts the Convention. Even if all the facts have occurred in country A, but the action is brought in country B, it has always been clear that, for the purposes of country B, the situation contains an international element even if it does not in country A. The international character of an obligation is relative. *The Halley*[7] does not deny the international character of the tort, but English Private International Law applies the rule in *Boys v. Chaplin*[8].

Again, to leave out agreements on the choice of a court may cause strange discrepancies, if the question arises whether a void international contract contains a valid jurisdictional clause. If the contract is governed by the Convention and the jurisdictional agreement contained therein is not, conflicting conclusions based on several legal systems may be unavoidable[9]. A multiplicity of rules of Private International Law in the same state dealing with the same subject is undesirable.

This applies to (d) and (e) – contracts of insurance and concerning the formation, and internal management as well. I am not clear about company dissolution which, in English law, will require a winding-up procedure.

Art. 2: Free Choice of Law [10]

The unlimited freedom to select a foreign legal system will be welcomed by English lawyers. If the agreement contains a foreign element (see above and art. 1) the parties are best in a position to determine the question as to what legal system is to apply, and the exercise of a capricious choice is practically unknown (an erroneous choice occurred in the *Vita Food Case*[11]). If the agreement does not contain a foreign element, any reference to foreign law does not affect the applicable law, but serves as an incorporation only of the terms of the foreign law into the agreement (which is *ex hypothesi* governed by some other legal system, which alone applies)[12].

---

[6] *Lando* p. 9.   [7] *The Halley* (1868), L.R. 2 P.C. 193.

[8] *Boys v. Chaplin*, [1968] 2 Q.B. 1 = [1968] 1 All E.R. 283 = [1968] 2 W.L.R. 328 (C.A.); [1971] A.C. 356 = [1969] 2 All E.R. 1085 = [1969] 3 W.L.R. 322 (H.L.).

[9] For a unitary approach see *Dicey/Morris* p. 1060 and note 30; p. 1092 and note 19.

[10] Report, *infra* p. 255–266; *Lando* p. 11–25.

[11] *Vita Food Products, Inc.* v. *Unus Shipping Co.*, [1939] A.C. 277 (P.C.).

[12] See *Dicey/Morris* p. 732–735.

Similarly, English lawyers will approve of the proposal that the validity of consent to the choice of law is to be governed by the law which would be applicable if the choice of law were valid. This rule applies to consent in general, and not only to the choice of law clause contained in the agreement[13].

Similarly, the acceptance of implied consent will be approved[14]. It must be understood, however, that implied consent is not to be confused with tacit consent[15]. The former is a matter of fact, the latter is an inference sanctioned by some legal system (which according to English notions should be the law which would govern the contract, if it were properly concluded, though a good case can be made out in favour of the respective personal laws). Here the effect of silence is an issue of fact.

English lawyers will admit that it is possible to agree that the various aspects of a contract are to be governed by different legal systems[16], but in the absence of unusual and compelling reasons, such a splitting-up of the contract will not be admitted easily[17].

Objections against a free choice based on the argument that the bargaining strength of the parties may be unequal, especially in certain types of international transactions[18], carry perhaps less force in continental Europe than in the United States where the business of insurance and hire purchase transactions is more easily conducted across boundaries. At the same time, the control over branches of foreign companies is well developed in the countries of the EEC.

There will be general agreement that certain rules for the protection of employees which are in force in the country in which he habitually carries out his work cannot be ousted by a free choice of law; only two observations are required. Firstly, the distinction between *jus cogens* and *dispositivum* is not easily administered internationally, but, secondly, it would seem that no question of applying *foreign* compulsory law can arise here. Clearly the compulsory rules of the place where the work is carried out are only safeguarded in that country by the prohibition of an absolutely unfettered choice of law. They are never enforced in any country other than that in which they have been enacted. More thought will have to be given to the nature of such laws of absolute territorial validity; their express claim to operate

---

[13] *Dicey/Morris* rule 148, p. 763–765.
[14] *Dicey/Morris* rule 146 sub-rule 2, p. 735–741.
[15] *Lando* p. 21–25.
[16] *Dicey/Morris* p. 722–723 and note 10.
[17] *Dicey/Morris* p. 722–723 and note 11.
[18] *Lando* p. 15–21.

exclusively and the nature of the claim (vested in a public authority or not directed towards a purely monetary performance) [19].

Art. 3 [20]

The right of the parties to select the law governing their agreement either at the time of the conclusion or later, or to modify it, has been recognised in England [21], subject to the qualification that a subsequent conduct of the parties is not to be relied upon to infer from it that a particular intention to select the law of a specified country existed at the time when the contract was concluded.

The reservation in favour of rights of third parties (who, it is assumed, have garnished a claim or have a charge over it) is novel but acceptable.

Art. 4 [22]

English Private International Law is both objective and very flexible when it comes to determine the applicable law in the absence of an express or implied choice of law [23], and the objective, but rigid formulation of art. 4 II a in particular may cause some reservations to be made, at least at first, especially where maritime contracts are concerned (charterparties, bills of lading). The rigid formulation is, however, mitigated to a certain extent by arts. 4, third para., 5 and 6. Nevertheless, the technique of concentrating on the *lex debitoris primarii* will not easily commend itself, given the subsidiary and perhaps excessively ancillary nature of the provision in art. 4, third para. This objection is less valid where the contract is one concluded in the course of a business activity [art. 4 II (b) and (c)]; here it will have the effect of encouraging the parties to make an express or implied choice in order to exclude the operation of an unwelcome, though predictable, legal system.

Art. 5 [24]

This provision will not cause much controversy, even if the very limited practice in England has followed a different trend [25].

---

[19] *Gamillscheg,* in: Int. Encycl. Comp. L. III Ch. 28 (1973) ss. 44–47, p. 21–22.
[20] Report, *infra* p. 266–268; *Lando* p. 25–26.
[21] *Whitworth Estates Ltd.* v. *Miller,* [1970] A.C. 583 at p. 603 per Lord *Reid.*
[22] Report, *infra* p. 268–275; *Lando* p. 26–32.
[23] *Dicey/Morris* rule 146, sub-rule 3.
[24] Report, *infra* p. 275 s.; *Lando* p. 32–33.
[25] *Gamillscheg (supra* note 19) Ch. 28 s. 27, p. 14–15.

Art. 6[26]

This principle coincides with the corresponding English rule[27].

Art. 7[28]

The aim of this provision is laudable. Whether in its present form it is too vague is another matter. Firstly, it will be difficult to determine whether the foreign rules in issue "govern the matter compulsorily". Will it make any difference whether a choice of law clause is attached to the rule[29]?

Secondly, should it not be necessary and sufficient to show that the particular rule renders a provision of the contract void? If so, the problem is twofold:

(a) Should illegality (or at present the compulsory character of a rule) be taken into account if enshrined in any possible legal system which may show a connection? To my mind the *lex loci contractus* as such is not to be considered. Is it then only the *lex loci solutionis* which counts?

(b) Should the foreign illegality be taken into account so as to render that particular part of the contract illegal, although the contract is governed by another law or is the foreign compulsory rule merely a factor or *datum* which transforms the foreign illegality into a local impossibility?

Art. 8[30]

As was stated above, the effect of silence on the express or implied choice of law is a question of fact. However, the effect of silence on the conclusion of the contract and the validity of consent in general are matters of law. English lawyers would probably incline towards the application of the law which would be applicable, if the agreement were valid[31]. But I have some sympathy with the view that in a contract *inter absentes* the respective laws of the habitual residence of the parties should determine this question.

---

[26] Report, *infra* p. 276 s.; *Lando* p. 32–33.
[27] *Dicey/Morris* rule 80, exception 1 on p. 532.
[28] Report, *infra* p. 277–279; *Lando* p. 33–39.
[29] See *e. g. Morris*, L.Q.Rev. 62 (1946) p. 170; *Nussbaum,* Private International Law (1942) p. 70–73 and the writers cited by *Lipstein*, Rec. des Cours 135 (1972-I) p. 97 ss., at p. 195 notes 3 and 5.
[30] Report, *infra* p. 279 s.; *Lando* p. 39–42.
[31] See *Dicey/Morris* rule 148, p. 763.

Art. 9 [32]

The controversy as to whether *inter partes* the proper law of the contract or the *lex situs* should govern the proprietary effects of a contract, while in regard to third parties the *lex situs* should apply unconditionally, is set out by *Lando*. The Draft Convention seems to leave this question to the law of the Member States, and in the present climate of opinion I would agree.

Art. 15 [33]

While the principle that the law governing an obligation is to determine the rights and obligations thereunder, that is to say the substance of the obligations, and that the mode of performance is determined, in the last resort, by the *lex loci solutionis* are also part of English law [34], English law will also take into consideration any illegality under the *lex loci solutionis* [35]. Some of the details of the proposed rule may cause difficulties, however. Set-off, damages and limitation of actions are governed by the *lex fori* [36]. Nevertheless, there are exceptions.

In the first place, a foreign statute of limitation may destroy the right and not only the remedy. In this case it will apply as part of the *lex causae,* and if the period of time is shorter than that of the *lex fori,* the limitation of the *lex causae* will prevail [37].

Secondly, a set-off attached to the substantive law of the *lex causae* may be taken into account in certain circumstances [38].

Thirdly, no excessive significance should be attached to the alleged difference between English law and continental law inasmuch as the former is said to allow damages for breach of contract and specific performance only in exceptional circumstances, while specific performance is said to be the rule in continental law.

In fact, the substantive duty under a contract is always to perform what is promised. Only the procedure of enforcement is governed by the *lex fori.* Here again, the difference between English and continental law is not as big in practice, as it would appear at first sight, since neither French nor German law can force the unwilling debtor to perform [39].

---

[32] Report, *infra* p. 280; *Lando* p. 43–44.

[33] Report, *infra* p. 294–297; *Lando* p. 44–46.

[34] *Dicey/Morris* rule 153 (1) and (2), p. 792.

[35] *Dicey/Morris* rule 151, exception p. 781.

[36] See *Dicey/Morris* rule 204 (2), (3), (7), p. 1102–1106, 1114–1115.

[37] *Dicey/Morris* p. 1104.   [38] *Dicey/Morris* p. 1114.

[39] See for France the literature on the *astreinte* and see German ZPO §§ 887, 888.

Art. 16[40]

English lawyers will agree[41].

Art. 17[42]

Although the problem of subrogation or statutory assignment has not yet been before English courts, it is believed that the practice adopted in France and Germany will commend itself to English lawyers.

Art. 18[43]

English law agrees[44], but I share *Lando*'s doubts as to whether in dealings *inter absentes* the rigid application of two legal systems is required. The solution of the conflict of laws in time is interesting, but it requires some reflection before I can a comment.

Equally, I am not convinced that a reservation in favour of the mandatory provisions of some other legal system with which the transaction is connected is required here (see art. 7). In matters of form the function of the rules involved is to put the parties on their guard, to provide evidence and to ensure certainty. These purposes should not be frustrated by vague additional requirements.

Art. 19[45]

(1) The discussion of the problem of presumptions, of fact and of law, rebuttable and irrebuttable, in relation to the question whether they constitute rules of substance or of procedure[46], shows that this matter is too complex to be regulated in one sentence. Obviously inferences to be drawn from the behaviour of the parties in conducting the proceedings fall to be determined by the *lex fori,* but there are also inferences concerning legal relationships which, if rebuttable, may fall under the regime of the *lex fori.*

(2) While art. 19 (2) permitting the admissibility of foreign modes of evidence in favour of any formal *favor negotii* would seem, at the face of it, to fly in the face of English law[47] it is believed that it will not do

---

[40] Report, *infra* p. 297–299; *Lando* p. 47.
[41] See *Dicey/Morris* rules 84–85, p. 551–555.
[42] Report, *infra* p. 299 s.; *Lando* p. 47–48.
[43] Report, *infra* p. 300–304; *Lando* p. 48–53.
[44] See *Dicey/Morris* rule 150, p. 771–775.
[45] Report, *infra* p. 304–309; *Lando* p. 33.
[46] See *Dicey/Morris* p. 1110–1111.
[47] See *Dicey/Morris* rule 204 (4) and p. 1106–1112.

so in practice. Art. 19 (2) seems to permit the admissibility of other types of evidence than are admitted by the *lex fori* for the particular type of transaction (evidence in writing only, not witnesses), provided, however, that the additional mode of evidence is not unknown as such, *i. e.,* in other circumstances, by the *lex fori.*

English lawyers will only be concerned with the need to embody contracts for the sale of land in England in a note or memorandum in writing [Law of Property Act 1925, s. 40 (1)]; and for the observance of similar formalities under the Statute of Frauds 1677, in so far as it has not been repealed by the Law Reform (Enforcement of Contracts) Act 1954, *i. e.* for declarations of trust and the disposition of equitable interests in land, agreements between master and seamen, policies of sea insurance, bills of assignment, assignments of copyright, money-lenders' contracts, loans to persons in business when the rate of business is to vary with the profits or the lender is to share the profits and desires not to incur the liabilities of a partner; special agreements between solicitor and client, agreements to submit differences to arbitration; promises to answer for the debt of another.

It is another matter whether the requirement of a deed if a contract is not for consideration would apply here too, but it is believed that in the light of *Re Bonacina*[48] it will be treated as a matter of substance governed, *ex hypothesi* by foreign law.

Clearly the restrictions added in art. 19 (2) in respect of proof of formalities will commend themselves to English lawyers, once the principle enshrined in art. 19 is accepted.

It is not clear to me as yet whether and to what extent art. 19 (3) will cause difficulties, in particular as to the permissible modes of rebuttal. This will depend upon the nature of any presumption which may be involved.

Art. 20[49]

The exceptional rule validating an incapacity to contract under the law generally applicable (and which is not defined by the Convention) has no counterpart in English Private International Law, but is not necessarily contrary to English fundamental notions. However, the need for such a provision appears to exist only if the act is executed *inter praesentes* and not otherwise.

---

[48] *Re Bonacina,* [1912] 2 Ch. 394.
[49] Report, *infra* p. 309 s.; *Lando* p. 53–55.

Art. 21 [50]

Notwithstanding the fact that I expressed some hesitating thoughts on the application of *renvoi* when the parties have failed to make an express or implied choice [51] I concur with the Draft.

Art. 22

No comment.

Arts. 10–14: Torts

It is not possible to examine in detail the provisions on torts (arts. 10–14), but the following general observations must suffice.

Art. 10. – The retention of the criterion that the *lex loci delicti* is to apply commends itself more than the somewhat extravagant American notions. For the same reason even the subsidiary use of such connecting factors as the closer connection is unsatisfactory [52].

It is to be conceded that the general rule is to give way to a *lex communis* of the parties, but many problems remain. Should this exception be restricted to cases where the *lex communis partium* is also the *lex fori* (as *Boys* v. *Chaplin* suggests for the moment [53], as well as the German Decree of 1942 [54])? What is the place where the event occurred? Should a contractual link take precedence over a delictual relationship?

English lawyers will also remember that, at present, they must administer a "double actionability" rule, which would have to be severely modified [55].

Art. 11, not unlike the corresponding provision of the Hague Convention on the Law applicable to Traffic Accidents (art. 8) will cause many difficulties in England. While it may be possible to determine the kinds of damage in accordance with the law governing the tort, the measure of damages cannot be easily determined in accordance with foreign law (as foreign courts will find if they must consider the English rules). The same applies to the form of compensation, since this may be closely bound up with local enforcement procedures. Again, the determination of liability for others may raise a preliminary

---

[50] Report, *infra* p. 310 s.

[51] See *Lipstein*, Camb. L. J. 31 (1972-B) p. 67 ss. at p. 83 note 3.

[52] See most recently *Jayme*, RabelsZ 38 (1974) p. 583 ss. at p. 588.

[53] *Boys* v. *Chaplin* (*supra* note 8).

[54] VO des Ministerrats . . . 12. December 1942, RGBl. I 706.

[55] For the present position see *Lipstein*, Clunet 100 (1973) p. 445–446 (the French version is defective) and the literature cited there.

question[56]. Further, all matters of limitation of actions – as distinct from matters destroying a substantive right – are the concern of the *lex fori*, at least at present, and while it may be advisable to apply the foreign *lex loci* if it provides shorter time limits, the converse will meet with objections. The same applies to measures interrupting the period of limitation from running.

Art. 12 is acceptable[57].

The Report overlooks[58] that, at least in tort, the effect of a substantive destruction of the right to sue is not equal to acquisitive prescription.

Art. 13 may require further refinement in the light of the treatment of this topic by *Zweigert* and *Müller-Gindullis*[59].

Art. 14 requires separate consideration in the light of the novelty of the situation.

---

[56] See *Lipstein*, in: Ius privatum gentium, Festschrift Max Rheinstein I (1969) p. 414 ss., at p. 420–421.

[57] See *The Halley* (*supra* note 7) at p. 203 and *Lipstein* (*supra* note 54) p. 420–421.

[58] Report, *infra* p. 291.

[59] *Zweigert/Müller-Gindullis*, in: Int. Encycl. Comp. L. III Ch. 30 (1973).

LES ACTES ILLICITES DANS L'AVANT-PROJET DE LA CEE

Par

A. E. VON OVERBECK et PAUL VOLKEN

Fribourg et Bern *

I. La notion d'acte illicite

L'avant-projet n'utilise pas la notion de «acte illicite» ou «délit». Il parle des «obligations non contractuelles» parmi lesquelles il distingue celles dérivant d'un «fait dommageable« (arts. 10 et 12) et celles dérivant d'un «fait autre qu'un fait dommageable» (art. 13).

L'emploi de termes nouveaux lors de l'unification du droit international privé correspond presque à une tradition, notamment lors de la rédaction de conventions multilatérales. Il suffit de rappeler les tentatives dans ce sens de la Conférence de La Haye de droit international privé. En remplaçant «domicile» par «résidence habituelle» et «tutelle» par «protection des mineurs», elle a enrichi le vocabulaire du droit international privé[1]. Ces termes ont reçu un accueil positif dans la doctrine et semblent faire leur preuve dans la pratique. L'avant-projet de la CEE a fait une tentative analogue, qu'il convient d'approuver, même si toutes ses conséquences ne sont pas satisfaisantes.

La nouvelle terminologie en matière d'actes illicites a certainement deux avantages. Tout d'abord, elle met en pratique le postulat, souvent énoncé mais rarement suivi, selon lequel les règles de conflit ne doivent pas être trop fortement liées à un langage juridique national, mais devraient, conformément à leur tâche de concilier divers ordres juridiques, se servir de termes autonomes[2]. A cet égard, même la revi-

---

* Version française abrégée de l'article «Das internationale Deliktsrecht im Vorentwurf der EWG»: RabelsZ 38 (1974) pp. 56–78.

[1] Aussi p. ex. la «délivrance» au sens de la loi uniforme sur la vente, art. 19, alinéa premier; v. O. *Riese*, Die Haager Konferenz über die internationale Vereinheitlichung des Kaufrechts vom 2. bis 25. April 1964: RabelsZ 29 (1965) p. 1 ss., p. 32.

[2] V. S. *Braga*, Kodifikationsgrundsätze des IPR: RabelsZ 23 (1958) p. 420 ss., spéc. p. 424.

sion de règles de conflit nationales pourrait s'inspirer de l'avant-projet. D'autre part, la nouvelle terminologie épargnera au juge beaucoup de problèmes épineux de qualification et contribuera à éviter des interprétations divergentes.

Les deux catégories de rattachement (objets du rattachement) utilisées pour les obligations non contractuelles – obligations dérivant d'un fait dommageable (art. 10), d'une part, obligations dérivant d'un fait autre qu'un fait dommageable (art. 13), d'autre part – sont extrêmement larges, extrêmement générales et rédigées de façon très neutre. Lorsque l'on se demande quelles obligations non contractuelles doivent être attribuées à l'une ou l'autre catégorie, l'on constate que la réponse est possible dans certains cas, mais qu'il est extrêmement difficile de tirer une limite précise. De façon générale, on pourra dire que les délits et les quasi-délits tombent sous les arts. 10 ou 12, tandis que les obligations découlant de la loi, telles que l'enrichissement sans cause, la gestion d'affaires, la dette alimentaire légale envers les parents, seraient visées par l'art. 13. Mais au delà, toute tentative de définir l'étendue du rattachement des délits, ou même de faire l'inventaire des états de fait délictuels, rencontre des difficultés considérables. La cause de ces difficultés réside dans la nature du droit des actes illicites, tant au point de vue du droit international privé qu'au point de vue du droit matériel. Les difficultés en droit international privé résultent surtout de la diversité des ordres juridiques nationaux: l'«acte illicite» français ne correspond pas nécessairement au *«delitto»* italien, le *«tort»* britannique n'équivant pas à la *«unerlaubte Handlung»* au sens allemand. Au point de vue du droit matériel, toute classification devient difficile par la diversité presque infinie des règles nationales sur la responsabilité. D'une part, ces dispositions sont éparpillées partout dans de nombreuses lois spéciales, d'autre part, elles instituent un grand nombre de degrés différents de responsabilité, qui vont de la faute grave jusqu'aux responsabilités les plus sévères fondées sur la cause, le danger ou le risque.

La catégorie de rattachement large et neutre de l'art. 10 permet à l'avant-projet d'englober tous les degrés et toutes les formes possibles et imaginables de la responsabilité pour délit, un acte dommageable au sens de l'avant-projet pourrait même être un cas fortuit pour autant que celui-ci soit de nature à donner lieu à une obligation extra-contractuelle. Il conviendra de vérifier si la terminologie de l'avant-projet, pour séduisante qu'elle soit, convient aux besoins de la pratique.

L'avant-projet consacre trois articles aux règles de conflit en matière d'acte illicite. Les règles de conflit proprement dites se trouvent aux premier et deuxième alinéas de l'art. 10, l'alinéa premier contient la règle de principe, l'alinéa 2 la règle d'exception. Le troisième et le quatrième alinéas de l'art. 10, ainsi que l'art. 12 précisent les deux règles de conflit. Enfin, l'art. 11 définit le domaine d'application de la loi délictuelle. Il est complété par quelques règles particulières, telles que l'art. 15 sur les conditions et les modalités d'exécution et les arts. 16 et suivants sur la cession contractuelle et légale.

Les obligations découlant de la loi sont réglées dans le seul art. 13.

1. Le principe (art. 10, alinéa premier)

L'art. 10, alinéa premier, soumet les obligations non contractuelles dérivant d'un fait dommageable à la *lex loci delicti*. L'on peut s'étonner que cette solution se soit imposée si facilement, car rarement elle a été autant contestée qu'à l'heure actuelle. Les propositions de choisir une autre solution de principe ne manquent pas.

Ces propositions ne datent pas d'aujourd'hui, ainsi dans la doctrine plus ancienne, le rattachement au statut personnel[3], à la loi régissant des contrats[4] ou à la *lex fori*[5] ont été proposés. Ces tentatives, peut-être fondées sous certains aspects, ne pouvaient pas apporter de réponse satisfaisante quant à l'ensemble.

Aujourd'hui, ce sont surtout les juristes anglais et américains qui lancent des attaques virulentes contre le principe traditionnel. L'on peut distinguer à cet égard deux courants.

Le premier courant, dont les représentants se rangent dans le groupe des «legal realists» américains *(Cavers, Currie, Ehrenzweig, Leflar et von Mehren/Trautmann)*[6], met en question non seulement la *lex loci delicti*, mais tout le droit international privé classique comme tel. Il se dresse contre le fonctionnement «mécanique» du rattachement a priori, nie que le droit international privé puisse être codifié et veut remplacer les règles de conflit par une argumentation influencée par le résultat matériel *(«result selecting approach»)*. Quant à la voie à suivre pour arriver à la décision la meilleure possible au point de vue

---

[3] *Fiore*, Clunet 27 (1900) p. 449, 717.

[4] *André Weiss*, Traité théorique et pratique de d. i. p.[2] IV (1912) p. 415.

[5] *Von Savigny*, System des heutigen Römischen Rechts VIII (1849; Neudruck 1956) p. 246 et 248; *Wächter*, AcP 24 (1841) p. 230 ss.; 25 (1842) p. 361 ss.; H. *Mazeaud*, Rev. crit. 29 (1934) p. 377 ss. *Mazeaud* paraît avoir abandonné son point de vue entretemps, v. son intervention dans Trav. Com. fr. d. i. p. 25–27:1964–66 (1967) p. 71. Pour un aperçu général des théories plus anciennes, v. *Bourel*, Responsabilité civile, dans: *Dalloz*, Rép. dr. int. II (1969) p. 771 nos. 5 ss.; *Delachaux*, Die Anknüpfung der Obligationen aus Delikt und Quasidelikt im IPR (1960) p. 87 ss.

[6] V. l'aperçu des tendances aux Etats-Unis par *Joerges*, Zum Funktionswandel des Kollisionsrechts (1971) p. 38–82; *Trutmann*, Das IPR der Deliktsobligationen, Ein Beitrag zur Auseinandersetzung mit den neueren amerikanischen kollisionsrechtlichen Theorien (1973), spéc. p. 17–55.

matériel, les «*legal realists*» ne sont d'accord que sur un point. Ils écartent le recours aux règles de conflit en faveur d'un programme sur les méthodes de travail du droit international privé. Sur l'aménagement concret de ce programme, les esprits se séparent. *Currie*[7] veut procéder par la «*governmental interest analysis*», *Cavers*[8] par les «*principles of preference*», *Ehrenzweig*[9] par la priorité de la *lex fori* et *von Mehren/Trautmann*[10] par le «*functional approach*». La jurisprudence ayant repris cette orientation et notamment la doctrine de *Currie* dans quelques décisions largement discutées[11], l'école des «*legal realists*» a notamment gagné d'importance dans le droit des actes illicites.

Le deuxième courant anglo-américain ne vise pas le droit international privé comme tel, mais de manière d'autant plus décidée la portée générale du principe de la *lex loci delicti*. Citons comme représentants de cette tendance, le *Restatement Second* américain[12] et M. *Kahn-Freund* pour le Royaume-Uni[13]. Le paragraphe 145 du *Restatement Second* propose comme principe la loi du lien le plus étroit[14]. La conception de *Kahn-Freund* va dans un sens analogue. Il développe le principe de la «*proper law of the tort*», énoncé par *J. H. C. Morris*[15]

---

[7] *Currie*, Selected Essays on the Conflict of Laws (1963) p. 3 ss.

[8] *Cavers*, The Choice-of-Law Process (1965) p. 1 ss., spéc. p. 63; *id.*, Contemporary Conflicts in American Perspektive; Rec. des Cours 131 (1970-III) p. 75.

[9] *A. Ehrenzweig*, A Treatise on the Conflict of Laws (1962); *id.*, «False Conflicts» and the «Better Rule» – Threat and Promise in Multistate Tort Law: Va. L. Rev. 52 (1966) p. 847.

[10] *Von Mehren/Trautmann*, The Law of Multistate Problems, Cases and Materials on Conflict of Laws (1965) p. 76 s.

[11] V. *Babcock* v. *Jackson*, 191 N.E. 2d 279 (N. Y. 1963), et Comments, Colum. L. Rev. 63 (1963) p. 1212; *Dym* v. *Gordon*, 209 N.E. 2d 792 (N. Y. 1965); *Kell* v. *Henderson*, 270 N.Y.S. 2d 552 (1966); *Heath* v. *Zellmer*, 151 N.W. 2d 664 (Wis. 1967); *Reich* v. *Purcell*, 432 P. 2d 727, 63 Cal. Rptr. 31 (1967), et Comments, U.C.L.A.L. Rev. 15 (1967/68) p. 552.

[12] Restatement of the Law Second, Conflict of Laws 2d (1971) Chap. 7 Torts, Para. 145, p. 414 ss. – V. aussi *F. Vischer*, RabelsZ 38 (1974) p. 128, spéc. p. 145. – Sous l'influence de *Reese*, l'avant-projet de La Haye pour une convention sur la responsabilité des fabricants pour leurs produits partait de la résidence habituelle du lésé, le projet définitif de la Douzième session d'octobre 1972 a cependant, à la demande de beaucoup de gouvernements, donné de nouveau plus de poids à la *lex loci delicti*; v. *Lorenz*, Der Haager Konventionsentwurf über das auf die Produktenhaftpflicht anwendbare Recht: RabelsZ 37 (1973) p. 317 ss., p. 337 ss.

[13] *Kahn-Freund* dans *Dicey/Morris*, The Conflict of Laws[9] (1973) p. 930; *id.*, Delictual Liability and the Conflict of Laws: Rec. des Cours 124 (1968-II) p. 63 ss.

[14] V. *Trutmann* (*supra* note 6) p. 49; *Vischer* (*supra* note 12) p. 146.

[15] *Morris*, The Proper Law of the Tort: Harv. L. Rev. 64 (1951) p. 881.

dans la direction du «*social environment*» du délit[16]. *Kahn-Freund* et le *Restatement* n'acceptent le lieu du délit ni comme règle sans exception ni même comme point de rattachement préféré, ils le considèrent seulement comme une solution possible à côté de laquelle se place, sur le même rang, le statut personnel commun ou la loi commune du contrat, ou encore la *lex fori*[17].

Le droit de l'Europe continentale ne manque pas d'exemples d'exceptions à la *lex loci delicti*, l'on peut citer l'Ordonnance allemande du 7 décembre 1942, l'art. 12 EGBGB ou l'art. 85 de la loi suisse sur la circulation routière. D'autre part, la jurisprudence française[18] et néerlandaise[19] s'est écartée de la loi du lieu du délit dans nombre d'espèces, sans cependant mettre en cause l'application en principe de la *lex loci*.

Malgré les tendances anglo-américaines et les autres tentatives d'assouplir le rattachement des actes illicites, l'on peut constater que les partisans de la *lex loci delicti* – du moins en tant que règle de principe – sont encore nombreux, et cela particulièrement dans les Etats membres de la CEE. Non seulement la plupart des règles de conflit nationales (écrites ou non écrites)[20], mais aussi une série de nouveaux traités ou projets de traité[21] se fondent sur la loi du lieu de délit. MM.

---

[16] *Kahn-Freund* (*supra* note 13) dans *Dicey/Morris* p. 935 et Rec. des Cours p. 63 ss.; *id.*, Ann. Inst. Dr. int. 53 (1969) I, p. 397, 400 s. – Alors que la 8e éd. de *Dicey/Morris* (p. 914) portait le sous-titre «Social environment as a test», le passage correspondant, modifié, figure, dans la 9e éd., sous «*The proper law of the tort*».

[17] *Kahn-Freund* (*supra* note 13) dans *Dicey/Morris* p. 938 et Rec. des Cours p. 63 ss.; Restatement (*supra* note 12) Para. 145 lit. a–d. La 9e éd. de *Dicey/Morris* ajoute ici un second alinéa se référant à la «*most significant relationship*».

[18] Cass. 30 mai 1967 *(Kieger* c. *Amigues)*, Rev. crit. 56 (1967) p. 728; v. aussi Rev. crit. 52 (1963) p. 547; 62 (1973) p. 89. Pour d'autres exemples, v. *Bourel* (*supra* note 5) nos. 29 ss.

[19] *Offerhaus*, Obligations délictuelles, Exposé préliminaire: Ann. Inst. Dr. int. 53 (1969) I, p. 354.

[20] Pour les Etats membres de la CEE, v. Rapport, *infra* p. 281 s. nos. 1–2; pour d'autres Etats, v. *Batiffol/Lagarde*, D. i. p.[5] II (1971) p. 196, no. 7; *Dutoit*, Memorandum, dans: Act. Doc. La Haye 11 (1968) III, p. 9 no. 2; *Essén*, Rapport, *ibid.* p. 205 no. 2 ad art. 3; *Kahn-Freund*, Rec. des Cours (*supra* note 13) p. 12 s.; *Kropholler*, Ein Anknüpfungssystem für das Deliktsstatut: RabelsZ 33 (1969) p. 602 notes 2 et 3; *Vischer*, IPR, dans: Schweizerisches Privatrecht I (1969) p. 688.

[21] Traité Benelux portant loi uniforme au d. i. p. du 3. 7. 1969, art. 14, texte dans: Les législations de d. i. p. (1971) p. 28 = Rev. crit. 57 (1968) p. 814; Convention de La Haye sur la loi applicable en matière d'accidents de la circulation routière du 4. 5. 1971, art. 3, texte dans: Act. Doc. La Haye 11 (1968) III, p. 193 ss. = Rev. crit. 57 (1968) p. 796 s.; Convention de La Haye sur la loi applicable à la responsabilité du fait des produits du 2. 10. 1973, art. 4, texte dans RabelsZ 37 (1973) p. 596 ss. = Rev. crit. 61 (1972) p. 818; v. Convention

Batiffol et *Lagarde* ont démontré récemment les fondements théoriques et logiques de la *lex loci delicti*[22].

Même celui qui conteste à la *lex loci delicti* son caractère absolu traditionnel ne pourra nier que, parmi beaucoup de points de rattachement possibles et incertains, le lieu du délit est relativement le mieux défini. Cela lui donne un titre légitime, mais non absolu, pour s'appliquer. En fin de compte, ce que l'on met en doute actuellement, c'est moins le principe de la *lex loci delicti* que le caractère absolu de celle-ci et les divergences portent sur la question de savoir si, et dans quelle mesure, des dérogations au principe sont admissibles. C'est là que paraît résider l'origine de toute l'insécurité actuelle du droit international privé des délits: d'une part, l'on sent le besoin d'exceptions, mais dans beaucoup de droits, celles-ci ne peuvent dans l'état actuel intervenir que par le truchement de l'ordre public ou de qualifications fictives. L'avant-projet admettant précisément des exceptions, nous accepterons son rattachement de principe à la loi du délit.

2. La circonstance de rattachement

L'art. 10, alinéa premier, soumet les délits et quasi-délits à la loi du pays où le fait s'est produit. La localisation n'offre pas de difficulté lorsque le dommage se produit immédiatement à la suite du fait dommageable. Mais l'on sait que les difficultés commencent lorsque l'acte dommageable et le résultat se produisent en des lieux différents.

L'avant-projet ne donne pas de solution des controverses relatives aux délits à distance. La terminologie choisie dans la version française originale semble plutôt indiquer la loi du résultat, mais selon le rapport, la commission d'experts ne voulait pas prendre position sur ce point[23]. Cela est d'autant plus regrettable que l'avant-projet vise à unifier le droit international privé des Etats contractants pour tous les cas, et non seulement pour les rapports entre eux. Faute de solution claire en matière de délits à distance, l'on appliquera, dans les

---

internationale sur le transport des voyageurs et des bagages par chemin de fer du 25. 2. 1961 (CIV), art. 28, et Convention additionnelle du 26. 2. 1966.

[22] *Batiffol/Lagarde*, D. i. p.[6] I (1974) p. 341 no. 285, partent de la caractéristique essentielle de l'obligation délictuelle. Ils constatent que le délit ne peut être localisé ni par les titulaires de droits et d'obligations (les personnes par hasard impliquées) ni par son objet (une créance qui ne peut pas être localisée) mais uniquement par le «fait juridique qui lui donne naissance», c'est-à-dire l'acte générateur, l'acte dommageable. Ils concluent que, dès lors, le lieu où cet événement est intervenu s'offre comme seul rattachement possible. Sur les problèmes de la *lex loci delicti*, v. aussi *Trutmann* (*supra* note 6) p. 5.

[23] V. Rapport, *infra* p. 282 s. no. 3. – La Convention de La Haye du 2. 10. 1973 sur la responsabilité des fabricants pour leurs produits ne règle pas non plus cette question.

Etats membres de la CEE, malgré l'existence d'un droit des délits prétendument uniforme, des principes divergents. La jurisprudence française, conformément à la doctrine dominante[24], choisira plutôt le rattachement au lieu du résultat, tandis que, en Allemagne, l'on continuera à se fonder sur la théorie de l'ubiquité[25] et l'on appliquera la loi la plus favorable au lésé. Une prise de position nette eût été non seulement désirable, mais possible; elle aurait évidemment nécessité un système différencié de rattachements spéciaux destiné à tenir compte dans certains cas de celui des deux lieux – lieu de l'action ou lieu du résultat – que l'on aurait écarté en principe.

3. La catégorie de rattachement

Nous avons déjà relaté combien la catégorie de rattachement était vaste. Un examen du droit suisse démontre, au point de vue du droit international privé, que l'art. 10, alinéa premier, couvre 70 normes de responsabilité du droit civil et du droit des obligations, auxquelles il faut ajouter les dispositions de plus 30 lois spéciales. Il ne semble pas que la situation soit bien différente dans les Etats membres de la CEE.

Seuls les dommages dus dans le domaine nucléaire et la responsabilité de l'Etat ou d'autres personnes morales de droit public, ainsi que celle de leurs organes ou agents pour leurs actes de fonction, sont exclus de ce vaste ensemble par les arts. premier, lettre f, et 14 de l'avant-projet.

Il est impressionnant de voir le législateur de la CEE saisir, par une seule règle de conflit, des responsabilités que les législateurs nationaux ont dû régler dans des douzaines de lois. Mais l'on se demandera aussi si l'on n'a pas trop simplifié et généralisé.

Il est certain qu'une catégorie de rattachement formulée de façon si générale élimine de nombreux problèmes de qualification. Mais cet avantage paraît plus que compensé par les difficultés auxquelles donnera lieu la description beaucoup trop générale du domaine d'application de la *lex loci delicti*. La catégorie de rattachement de l'avant-projet, avec son aspiration universelle, serait plus facile à défendre si elle était accompagnée de règles différenciées pour des domaines spéciaux. La doctrine récente ne manque pas de suggestions dans ce sens. Ainsi même certains défenseurs de la *lex loci delicti* tendent à soumettre, par exemple la responsabilité civile entre membres d'une famille, à la loi familiale, les délits du travail à la loi du contrat de travail ou les délits de circulation à la loi du domicile commun ou de

---

[24] V. *Batiffol/Lagarde* (*supra* note 20) p. 199 no. 561 et les références.
[25] V. *Kegel* IPR[3] (1971) p. 268.

la résidence habituelle commune[26]. Pour la propriété intellectuelle et dans certains domaines du droit des transports, il existe déjà un système de protection basé sur les conventions multilatérales. Si ces questions étaient englobées par la version définitive de la Convention CEE, des conflits de convention ne manqueraient pas de se produire. Les Conventions de La Haye sur les accidents de la circulation et sur la responsabilité des fabricants pour leurs produits démontrent que, même sur un plan multilatéral, des rattachements spéciaux pour des domaines partiels du droit des délits peuvent être trouvés. Dans le cercle plus homogène de la CEE, de telles solutions devraient rencontrer beaucoup moins de difficultés que dans le cercle étendu des Etats réunis à La Haye.

On ne saurait, d'autre part, contester que les difficultés d'une codification détaillée du droit des délits seraient considérables et qu'à l'époque actuelle, il y a de bons arguments pour se contenter de règles assez générales. L'on pourrait imaginer que celles-ci seraient peu à peu complétées par des règles relatives à des domaines spéciaux dans lesquels les conceptions se seraient clarifiées.

II. Le rattachement exceptionnel

L'art. 10, alinéa 2, permet de s'écarter, dans des cas particuliers, de la *lex loci delicti*. L'on exige à cet effet une condition négative: qu'il n'existe pas de liens significatifs entre la situation résultant du fait dommageable et le pays où se produit ce fait, et une condition positive: que la situation présente une connexion prépondérante avec un autre pays.

L'art. 10 est construit sur des considérations analogues à celles qui ont présidé au rattachement objectif des contrats par l'art. 4 de l'avant-projet. L'art. 10, alinéa premier, prescrit l'application de la *lex loci delicti* en présumant qu'il s'agit de la loi avec laquelle l'acte a les rapports les plus étroits. Mais lorsque la présomption est infirmée, la loi applicable en soi cède la place à la loi la plus appropriée. La loi du délit n'est plus considérée de manière irréfragable comme la loi appropriée, mais il y a seulement en sa faveur une simple présomption. C'est là que l'avant-projet innove de manière fort heureuse.

L'art. 10, alinéa 2, soulève les deux questions de la délimitation entre rattachement principal et rattachement exceptionnel et des critères du lien le plus étroit.

---

[26] Sur le rattachement accessoire, v. *Kropholler* (*supra* note 20) p. 625.

1. Le droit de «l'autre Etat»

Pour déroger à la loi du lieu du délit, l'art. 10, alinéa 2, exige qu'il manque entre le lieu du délit et la situation le lien significatif. Il en sera ainsi dans les catégories de délits où le lieu est tout à fait fortuit, ainsi lors d'accidents du tourisme routier, de dommages causés par une concurrence économique au niveau mondial ou par des actes illicites commis au moyen de mass media ignorant les frontières. Admettons qu'un accident de la circulation ait pu frapper les mêmes personnes n'importe où ailleurs *(«transitory torts»)*, et qu'il n'y ait pas non plus de lien spécial avec un autre ordre juridique, mais plutôt des liens équivalents avec plusieurs législations. En pareil cas, le rattachement exceptionel n'intervient pas encore. Pour abandonner le rattachement principal de l'art. 10, alinéa premier, l'absence de lien significatif entre délit et lieu du délit ne suffit pas, il faut simultanément qu'il y ait «une connexion prépondérante» avec un autre ordre juridique. L'avant-projet retient la primauté de la *lex loci delicti,* celle-ci est applicable, et en principe, et en cas de doute.

2. Le lien plus étroit

Pour que la loi du lieu du délit soit remplacée par une autre loi, il faut qu'il y ait avec celle-ci un lien plus fort, plus typique qu'entre délit et lieu de délit. Quand en est-il ainsi? L'art. 10, alinéa 3, veut que normalement la connexion plus étroite se fonde sur un élément commun à la victime, d'une part, et à l'auteur du dommage ou au tiers responsable, d'autre part. Quels pourraient être ces éléments? Cela n'est pas dit, l'on pourrait songer au domicile commun, à la résidence habituelle commune ou encore à la nationalité commune des parties. Puis on se demanderait si la *lex fori,* un contrat entre parties ou la volonté de celles-ci serait suffisant. Le contexte général paraît indiquer plutôt des éléments objectifs, connexes à la situation délictuelle. Nous hésiterions toutefois à éliminer d'avance les critères que nous avons indiqués en deuxième lieu. Les circonstances d'espèce indiqueront si une dérogation de la *lex loci delicti* est possible, défendable ou nécessaire, et l'appréciation du juge sera en fin de compte déterminante. Cette appréciation devrait se tenir dans les limites des alinéas 2 et 3 de l'art. 10, il est permis de penser que dans ce cadre, les diverses théories, anciennes et nouvelles, sur l'assouplissement du rattachement des délits renaîtront.

Alors que les alinéas 1 et 2 de l'art. 10 se fondent sur le fait du dommage, l'alinéa 3 met au contraire au centre les personnes intéressées, cela tant du côté de la victime que du côté de l'auteur. Le rattachement exceptionnel ne doit pas porter avantage ou préjudice à l'une des parties, mais au contraire doit se fonder sur un élément qui leur soit commun.

3. Règles de sécurité et de police

La règle de l'art. 12, qui prescrit de tenir compte des règles de sécurité et de police du lieu du délit, dans la détermination de la responsabilité, doit également être rangée dans les dispositions sur la loi applicable. Rappelons que les Conventions de La Haye sur les accidents de la circulation routière (art. 7) et la responsabilité des fabricants pour leurs produits (art. 9) contiennent des règles du même ordre.

Dans la mesure où le for est au lieu du délit, la règle de l'art. 12 va de soi. Lorsque, en revanche, le for n'est pas dans l'état du lieu du délit, l'art. 12 intervient tant dans le cadre du rattachement principal qu'en cas de rattachement exceptionnel. Dans cette dernière hypothèse, il résultera de cette disposition que certaines questions de droit, par exemple le degré de précaution à observer, seront néanmoins jugées selon la *lex loci delicti*. Dans le cadre du rattachement principal (art. 10, alinéa premier), l'art. 12 conduit à appliquer non seulement les règles de droit privé étranger sur les actes illicites, mais aussi des règles impératives de l'ordre juridique en question, même lorsqu'elles ont un caractère de droit public. L'art. 12 écarte ainsi la théorie, parfois défendue en droit international privé, de la non-application du droit public étranger. L'art. 12 précise encore que les règles de sécurité et de police à observer sont celles en vigueur au moment du délit. Cette précision n'est pas inutile dans ce contexte, que l'on songe par exemple à la fixation de vitesses maxima, locales ou générales, à la suite de graves accidents de la circulation.

Les règles sur le droit applicable sont enfin complétées par l'art. 10, alinéa 4, qui prescrit qu'en cas de pluralité de victimes, la loi applicable est déterminée séparément à l'egard de chacune d'elles. Une solution analogue, dans l'intérêt du lésé, est contenue à l'art. 4, lettre a, alinéa 2, de la Convention de La Haye sur les accidents de la circulation routière[27].

---

[27] Le cas où il y a plusieurs auteurs du dommage n'est pas réglé. Les experts voulaient laisser cette question ouverte (Rapport, *infra* p. 287 no. 6). Dans ce contexte, il ne faut pas seulement résoudre la question de savoir si tous les auteurs doivent être responsables selon le même droit ou si la loi applicable doit être déterminée séparément pour chacun d'eux. Il faut aussi tenir compte des questions de la solidarité, de recours entre responsables, mais aussi d'institutions de procédure telles que la *litis denuntiatio*.

III. Le domaine de la loi applicable aux actes illicites

En principe, l'avant-projet veut soumettre toutes les questions juridiques se rapportant à la l'obligation délictuelle à la *lex delicti*. Son domaine est précisé surtout par l'art. 11, mais aussi par les arts. 1, 12, 15, alinéa premier, 16, alinéa 2, et 17, alinéa 2.

1. L'art. 11 énumère en huit chiffres les plus importantes questions du droit des délits. Le mot «notamment» indique que ce catalogue n'est pas exhaustif, il ne veut surtout pas exclure d'autres questions du domaine d'application de la loi délictuelle.

2. Parmi les autres dispositions mentionnées, nous devrons notamment envisager les arts. 15, 16 et 17[28]. Nous avons déjà vu que l'art. 12 réservait les règles de sécurité et de police du lieu du délit, nous aurons encore une observation à faire sur l'art. premier.

L'art. 15, alinéa 2, soumet à la loi qui régit une obligation les conditions de l'exécution, les divers modes d'extinction et les conséquences de l'inexécution. Il s'ensuit que la *lex delicti* régit également les questions telles que le moment et le lieu de l'exécution, la monnaie de paiement, l'exécution par des tiers, la divisibilité ou indivisibilité de la prestation, la solidarité, les effets de la demeure du créancier ou du débiteur, la novation, la compensation, la consignation et la prescription, pour ne mentionner que les points les plus importants. En comparant les arts. 11, no. 4, et 15, alinéa 2, l'on pourrait avoir l'impression que ces dispositions se recouvrent puisque l'on parle, d'une part, des «modalités de la réparation» et, d'autre part, des «modalités d'exécution». Or la première disposition vise des questions telles que celle de savoir si la prestation doit être fournie en nature ou en espèces, par acomptes ou par un seul versement. Au contraire, l'art. 15, alinéa 2, est restreint aux modalités de l'exécution proprement dite. Le rapport reconnaît que cette notion n'est pas comprise partout de la même façon, elle sera qualifiée selon la *lex fori*. Les exemples de modalités d'exécution sont le plus souvent tirés du droit des contrats, l'on parle par exemple de l'examen de la marchandise.

Selon les arts. 16 et 17, la loi qui régit l'obligation, donc dans notre cas la loi délictuelle, détermine le caractère transférable de la créance.

3. Conformément à la doctrine dominante et aux solutions des conventions récentes, l'avant-projet veut donc donner un domaine d'application aussi étendu que possible à la loi délictuelle et en concrétiser la définition[29].

---

[28] V. *Lando*, RabelsZ 38 (1974) p. 44 ss.

[29] Pour la doctrine, v. notamment *Batiffol/Lagarde* (*supra* note 20) p. 202

Remarquons que le catalogue de l'art. 11 a été formulé trois fois au cours de ces dernières années et à chaque fois presque dans le même sens. Il se retrouve dans la Résolution d'Edimbourg de l'Institut de Droit international[30], de 1969 (art. 4), dans la Convention de La Haye sur les accidents de la circulation routière, de 1971 (art. 8 que l'avant-projet de la CEE reprend presque textuellement) et dans la Convention de La Haye sur la responsabilité des fabricants pour leurs produits, de 1972 (art. 8)[31]. Etant donné l'unité de doctrine dans ce domaine, nous pouvons renoncer à un examen détaillé des divers chiffres de l'art. 11, pour renvoyer aux exposés de *Essén, Kahn-Freund, Offerhaus* et *Reese*[32].

4. Dans le contexte de l'art. 11, il convient de relever deux points douteux, l'un relatif à l'interruption et la suspension des délais de prescription et de péremption, l'autre relatif à la capacité délictuelle.

a) L'art. 11, chiffre 8, soumet la prescription et la péremption, ainsi que le point de départ, l'interruption et la suspension des délais, à la *lex delicti*. Cela est tout à fait conforme aux conceptions juridiques continentales, puisque nous considérons la prescription et des questions semblables comme appartenant au droit matériel et non à la procédure. Mais en ce qui concerne l'interruption et la suspension des délais, cette disposition pourrait donner lieu à des incertitudes. A propos de l'interruption – et des considérations analogues valent pour la suspension – il convient de distinguer entre les causes d'interruption, les actes interruptifs et les effets de l'interruption. Il appartient certainement au droit matériel de définir quelles mesures sont susceptibles d'interrompre les délais et quelles sont les conséquences de l'interruption. En revanche, la question de savoir comment prendre ces mesures ne peut être régie par le droit matériel que dans les cas où l'acte lui-même est une institution du droit matériel[33]. Mais les formes

---

no. 563; *Kegel* (*supra* note 25) p. 276; *Vischer* (*supra* note 20) p. 698; v. les conventions citées *supra* note 21.

[30] Résolution sur les obligations délictuelles en d. i. p. adoptée par l'Institut de Droit international à la Session d'Edimbourg (4–13 septembre 1969): Ann. Inst. Dr. int. 53 (1969) II, p. 370.

[31] V. *supra* note 21.

[32] Essén, Rapport: Act. Doc. La Haye 12 (1968) III, p. 212; *Kahn-Freund*, Ann. Inst. Dr. int. 53 (1969) II, p. 450 notes 16 ss.; *J. Offerhaus, ibid.* p. 335 ss.; Conférence de La Haye de d. i. p., Les conflits de lois en matière de responsabilité des fabricants pour leurs produits, Avant-projet de Convention adopté par la Commission spéciale et Rapport de M. *W. L. M. Reese:* Doc. prél. no. 5, juillet 1971, p. 12.

[33] Par exemple en cas d'interruption par reconnaissance de la dette, par paiement partiel ou paiement des intérêts, ou par fourniture de sûretés, *cf.* pour la Suisse, art. 136, chiff. 1 CO, pour la République Fédérale d'Allemagne, §§ 202–208 BGB.

de loin les plus fréquentes et les plus importantes d'interruption, telles que la poursuite pour dettes, l'ouverture d'une action ou un autre acte de procédure, appartiennent au droit de procédure et sont réglées par celui-ci. Lorsque par exemple la loi allemande, applicable aux délits, prévoit que le délai peut être interrompu en ouvrant une action judiciaire, mais que le for se trouve en France, l'on peut bien emprunter au droit allemand le motif d'interruption et ses effets. Mais seul le droit de procédure du for peut décider si l'action a été régulièrement ouverte et si, partant, l'interruption s'est vraiment produite. La même chose vaut pour l'interruption par la poursuite pour dettes ou par un acte de procédure. Peut-être faudrait-il trouver pour l'art. 11, chiffre 8, une formule plus nuancée qui tienne compte de ces distinctions.

b) Une deuxième remarque concerne la capacité délictuelle. Elle n'est mentionnée ni dans l'art. 8 de la Convention de La Haye sur la circulation routière, ni dans l'art. 11 qui le reprend. En soi, cette omission n'est pas grave, aucune des deux dispositions ne veut dresser un catalogue exhaustif. L'on peut aussi ranger la capacité délictuelle sous le chiffre 1, puisqu'elle est sans doute une condition de la responsabilité délictuelle. Enfin, la doctrine unanime soumet la capacité délictuelle à la *lex delicti*. Ces considérations s'appliquent sans réserve à la Convention de La Haye, mais peut-être pas à l'avant-projet de la CEE. Car, alors que la Convention de La Haye ne mentionne pas du tout la capacité délictuelle, l'avant-projet exclut expressément, dans son article premier, lettre a, la capacité. Or, il semble que tous les Etats membres de la CEE qui ont participé à l'élaboration de l'avant-projet rangent la capacité délictuelle dans la *lex delicti* et, par conséquent, il est difficile d'admettre que la commission d'experts ait voulu l'exclure à l'art. premier, lettre a. Nous serions tentés de croire qu'il y a là une inadvertance qu'il y aurait lieu de rectifier dans le texte définitif. La pratique ne comprendra pas toujours que, malgré l'art. premier, lettre a, la capacité délictuelle est englobée par l'art. 11, cela d'autant moins que le rapport est muet sur ce point.

L'on ne saurait méconnaître qu'une énumération du genre de l'art. 11 – même si elle est expressément désignée comme exemplative – entraîne toujours le danger d'un argument *a contrario*.

IV. Les obligations non contractuelles dérivant d'un fait autre qu'un fait dommageable (Legalobligationen)

L'art. 13 reprend le système et la terminologie de l'art. 10. A l'instar des arts. 10 et 12, il ne définit pas les obligations «*ex lege*» dont il s'agit ici. L'art. 13 vise la catégorie de rattachement des «obligations non contractuelles qui ne dérivent pas d'un fait dommageable», par exemple l'enrichissement illégitime, la gestion d'affaires, le paiement de l'indu, etc. Par analogie aux rattachements principal et exceptionnel de l'art. 10, alinéas 1 et 2, l'art. 13 soumet ces obligations en principe à la loi de l'Etat dans lequel le fait générateur de l'obligation s'est produit. Mais lorsqu'il y a une connexion plus étroite avec la loi d'un autre pays, celle-ci est applicable.

Le rattachement exceptionnel selon l'art. 13 n'est pas défini exactement comme celui de l'art. 10, alinéas 2 et 3, en matière délictuelle. Il les suit en ce que le rattachement exceptionnel n'intervient que lorsqu'il y a entre le fait générateur de l'obligation et «l'autre droit» une connexion prépondérante commune à toutes les parties.

Mais contrairement à l'art. 10, alinéa 2, l'art. 13 n'exige pas l'absence de lien significatif avec le *lex loci actus,* si bien que le juge a ici une marge d'appréciation plus large et que le rattachement exceptionnel pourra plus facilement être admis.

La formule moins sévère de l'art. 13 n'eût-elle pas été suffisante, également en matière de délits? – Les critères plus sévères eussent été justifiés, si l'on avait complété la règle générale par des règles spéciales pour certains délits.

V. La responsabilité de l'Etat et des fonctionnaires

L'art. 14 de l'avant-projet, en excluant l'application des règles de conflit des arts. 10 à 13 à la responsabilité de l'Etat et de ses organes, définit le champ d'application de l'avant-projet et pourrait trouver sa place aussi bien dans l'art. premier.

Cette disposition traite différemment l'Etat et ses organes et agents: alors que le premier est entièrement soustrait à l'application de l'avant-projet, les organes et agents ne lui échappent que dans la mesure où il s'agit d'actes relevant de la puissance publique et accomplis par eux dans l'exercice de leurs fonctions. Cette inégalité est-elle justifiée?

On peut distinguer les activités de l'Etat *jure imperii* et les activités *jure gestionis.* Pour les actes *jure imperii,* il est clair que le problème des conflits de lois ne se pose pas. Ces actes sont soustraits au droit privé et soumis au droit public interne qui décide en principe lui-même sur la licéité de ces actes, sur les conséquences de leur illicéité et sur les prétentions de l'individu lésé. En revanche, lorsque l'Etat agit *jure gestionis,* il agit comme un particulier, selon le droit privé et peut aussi être actionné par les voies de la procédure civile. Les obligations non contractuelles découlant de cette activité pourraient donc, dans la mesure où il y a un élément international, tomber dans le champ d'application de l'avant-projet. L'exclusion complète de toutes les activités de l'Etat n'est pas justifiée du point de vue du droit privé et du droit des conflits. Il est vrai qu'ici intervient un important point de vue de procédure: même pour les activités *jure gestionis*, l'Etat ne se soumet pas volontiers à une juridiction étrangère. S'il était actionné à l'étranger, il serait douteux qu'il mette sa propre force publique à disposition pour l'exécution contre lui-même[34].

L'activité des organes ou agents peut être subdivisée en activités *jure imperii*, activités *jure gestionis* et activités que l'agent exerce à titre privé. Il n'y a pas de doute que l'art. 14 soustrait à l'avant-projet la première catégorie. Il convient de traiter ce domaine séparément, puisque la responsabilité des fonctionnaires est aujourd'hui le plus souvent, en vertu de la loi ou du droit coutumier[35], construite comme une responsabilité de l'Etat pour ses fonctionnaires (assortie parfois d'un droit de recours) et régie en partie par des lois spéciales de droit public. Des doutes pourraient surgir pour le deuxième domaine, où l'agent exerce des activités étatiques *jure gestionis*. L'art. 14 réserve les actes relevant de la puissance publique accomplis dans l'exercice des fonctions. Puisque dans le domaine commercial, l'Etat lui-même n'agit pas en vertu de son *jus imperii*, l'agent chargé de tâches commerciales de l'Etat ne peut pas non plus exercer la puissance publique. Un tel agent agit souvent envers des tiers comme un particulier. Dans le rapport interne avec l'Etat en revanche, il n'exerce que des tâches lui incombant en vertu de sa fonction. Aussi les nouvelles lois sur la responsabilité de l'Etat pour l'activité de ses agents ne distinguent plus entre l'activité *jure imperii* ou *jure gestionis*, mais prévoient au contraire la responsabilité de l'Etat pour tous les actes commis par l'agent dans l'exercice de ses fonctions. Il ne serait, par conséquent, pas approprié de soumettre, pour ces activités, les fonctionnaires à une responsabilité plus étendue que l'Etat.

En revanche, l'agent qui agit comme particulier, reste soumis au droit privé de la responsabilité et il est juste de lui appliquer à cet égard l'avant-projet.

---

[34] V. toutefois les tentatives du Conseil de l'Europe dans: Projet de Convention européenne sur l'immunité des Etats (Strasbourg 1972).

[35] V. pour la Suisse, la loi fédérale du 14. 3. 1958 sur la responsabilité de la Confédération, des membres de ces autorités et de ses fonctionnaires, RS 170.32; pour la République Fédérale d'Allemagne, art. 34 GG; § 839 BGB; v. *Soergel(-Glaser)*, Kommentar zum BGB[10] III (1969) § 839; pour la France, *Ferid*, Das Französische Zivilrecht I (1971) p. 852 ss.

VI. L'application des règles générales des arts. 21–32 aux obligations non contractuelles

Nous nous bornerons ici à une brève observation sur l'art. 21 de l'avant-projet, qui exclut le renvoi. En matière d'obligations non contractuelles, le bien-fondé de cette solution paraît évident. En revanche, sa motivation dans le rapport n'est peut-être pas tout à fait concluante. Celui-ci invoque le fait que l'application de la *lex loci delicti* est modérée par le rattachement exceptionnel de l'art. 10, alinéa 2, et il ajoute: «L'article lui-même opère donc le renvoi qui pourrait découler de la règle de conflit de la *lex loci delicti*». Or cette dernière pourrait connaître une règle de conflit toute différente de l'art. 10, alinéa 2. L'on voulait exprimer, semble-t-il, que, étant donné la solution différenciée et flexible de l'avant-projet, le correctif du renvoi devient inutile[36].

---

[36] Dans un sens analogue, le Tribunal féderal suisse en matière contractuelle, arrêt du 21. 10. 1955, ATF 81 II 391, spéc. 395; v. aussi *Jagmetti*, Die Anwendung fremden Kollisionsrechtes durch den inländischen Richter (1961) p. 83.

COMMENTS ON ARTS. 10 AND 11 OF THE DRAFT CONVENTION

By

OLE TORLEIF RØED

Oslo

I.

Norway has ratified the International Bills of Exchange Conventions of June 7, 1930, and the International Cheque Conventions of March 19, 1931. Furthermore Norway has adopted the Convention on the Law Applicable to International Sales of Goods of June 15, 1955.

Apart therefrom there are some Nordic Conventions with regard to marriage, adoption, bankruptcy, succession and distribution.

II.

Most of the Norwegian law is therefore case law. In my observations I will confine myself to discussing the law applicable to non-contractual obligations and deal specifically with the draft convention arts. 10 and 11.

I should perhaps think that it would be illustrating to deal with a few of the leading Norwegian cases in this matter.

a) In 1905 there was a collision in the Kieler canal between a Russian and a Norwegian vessel. It was decided by a German Court that the compulsory pilot on board the Norwegian vessel had shown negligence, and that the collision was attributable to this negligence.

The insurance company of the Russian vessel sued the Norwegian vessel's insurance company in Norway for payment of the damage arising out of the collision.

It was held that there was no claim against the Norwegian company as German law should apply, and under German law the vessel is without liability for negligence for a compulsory pilot[1].

---

[1] Norges Høiesteret Dec. 15, 1905, N.D.S. 6 (1905) p. 435.

This is, as will be seen, a clear-cut application of the *lex loci delicti commissi*. The Supreme Court made, however, an express reservation that this always should be the case.

b) Another case of collision between vessels happened in Tynemouth in the estuary of the river Tyne between two Norwegian vessels, the one having a compulsory pilot on board. It was undisputable that the collision was attributable to a fault committed by the compulsory pilot. The only question in dispute was whether the Norwegian vessel was responsible for the negligence shown by a compulsory pilot.

The Supreme Court held that as these two vessels both were Norwegian, the proper law to apply for the dispute at bar would be Norwegian law; under Norwegian law the owner was responsible for the negligence of the compulsory pilot.

It is, however, interesting to note that the Supreme Court stated that the value of the lost vessel should be estimated according to the prices in Norway, with due consideration to the fact that the vessel at the time of the loss was in England[2].

In this context it should be noted that there is a Swedish decision of some interest in this respect. A Swedish and a Danish vessel collided in the Thames estuary. There was a compulsory pilot on board the Swedish vessel, who was at fault.

The Swedish Supreme Court held that English law should apply in deciding if the Swedish vessel was responsible for the fault. This was held to be the case[3].

c) A small Norwegian vessel collided in internal Norwegian waters with a German vessel. Both vessels were damaged. The Court held that both vessels were at fault and determined the fault of the vessels to be $^2/_3$ on the Norwegian vessel and $^1/_3$ on the German vessel.

The question arose which law with regard to limitation of liability should apply with regard to the German vessel. It was held by the Norwegian Supreme Court that German law was applicable as the law of the flag, irrespective of the fact that under the German conflicts of law rule the *lex loci delicti commissi* was applicable. The principle of renvoi is not adopted. Norwegian law limited at that time the liability of the vessel under the ordinary rule of the Hague Convention then in effect to £ 10 per ton plus freight on keel, whereas the German system of limitation was based upon the value of the vessel[4].

d) A Norwegian car collided on a German Autobahn with a German motor-cycle whose driver was injured. The Supreme Court of Norway held that German law would apply, and applying German law, the

---

[2] Norges Høiesteret Sep. 25, 1923, N.D.S. 24 (1923) p. 289.
[3] Högsta Domstolen April 1, 1936, N.D.S. 37 (1936) p. 193.
[4] Norges Høyesterett Jan. 18, 1958, N.D.S. 1958, p. 1.

Norwegian Supreme Court held that the German driver was entitled to compensation for the injury he had sustained[5].

e) A Norwegian bus was hired by a group of Norwegians to bring them down to Gothenburg to watch a soccer-match between Norway and Sweden, and thereafter take them back. While driving on the Swedish road, the bus collided with a Swedish van, and one of the passengers was killed.

It was held that Norwegian law was applicable and not Swedish law. Furthermore the compensation was assessed according to the Norwegian rules as a sum once and for all and not according to Swedish law where the compensation would be given in yearly amounts.

It was contended that this would make the recourse between the Insurance Companies extremely difficult, but this point was disregarded wholly by the Norwegian Supreme Court. The Norwegian Supreme Court underlined that this was a contract of transport from a village in Norway, to Gothenburg and back to Norway. It was specifically emphasized that all persons involved were Norwegian, and that the widow and the children of the killed person did not present any claim against the Swedish van, only against the Norwegian bus owners. The facts that probably the Swedish van also was responsible being at fault and that there would be complications with regard to the recourse claim against the Swedish van, were not taken into consideration[6].

It should be emphasized that a true analysis of the legal questions involved may be split up in at least the following points:

1) *The conditions or basis for a claim.* – This involves establishing that normative provision has been violated or that strict liability provisions exist. This must, however, be connected with a specific system of law which can be no other than that of *delicti commissi.*

To put it more specific: If there is left-hand driving, you should certainly drive on the left hand to avoid a collision, and not on the right hand, even if both drivers belong to a country where they have right-hand driving.

Furthermore a driver has to obey all local signs during driving. It should also be noted that "not driving too fast in the circumstances" must be construed according to the *lex loci delicti commissi* and not according to any other law.

The same applies to other corresponding questions in other areas of life, *e. g.* "taking proper care of the shot-gun" or "using dynamite with the utmost care".

---

[5] Norges Høiesteret Oct. 1, 1938, N.Rt. 1938, p. 691.
[6] Norges Høyesterett March 5, 1957, N.Rt. 122 (1957) p. 246.

As stated by *Martin Wolff:* "To sum up: the orbit within which the lex loci delicti is operative is very limited; it is restricted to the question: is the act that caused the damage justifiable?" [7]

2) The *cause between the violation of the specific normative provision and the damage* – a small bumper collision causes the death of a passenger who has a weak heart. Is the collision the cause or the weak heart?

3) Specific provisions with regard to exoneration as minority, contributory negligence, consent, necessity, insanity, identification.

4) *Rules for measuring the compensation,* what sort of damages to be compensated.

5) *Limitation of liability,* recourse from Insurance Companies etc.

6) *Specific questions with regard to security, lien.*

Contrary to the report and the draft art. 11 I am of the opinion that it is not necessary nor advisable that all these questions should be decided in the same way and according to the same system of law.

It is stated in the French text of the report: "En effet, toutes les délegations ont reconnu l'opportunité de déterminer le domaine de la loi applicable aux obligations visées par l'article 10 de la Convention dans la façon la plus claire et précise que possible" [8].

With deference I cannot subscribe to such an observation. Everything must depend upon the foreign element of the case. Some times the foreign element is preponderent and then, of course, it is only an expression of simple justice that foreign law should be applied. No court, however, is eager to apply foreign law; as a matter of fact they do it reluctantly and only when it is necessary. This is quite understandable, because a foreign court will always have difficulties in arriving at a fair interpretation of a foreign law even with the best of help.

This is illustrated by a decision of the Swedish Supreme Court from 1933 [9], where two Swedish cars collided in Norway, and the passengers in the car which was at fault were injured. The Swedish Supreme Court applied Norwegian law as it thought it was and held that there was no claim against the other car-owner. It applied the identification rule which, even still, is not clear, and definitely was not so in 1933.

The extent of liability depends to a great degree upon the rules in force of the forum (consequential damages *lucrum cessans*).

The assessment of compensation for bodily injury at least should be based upon the cost of living at the place where the victim is resi-

---

[7] *M. Wolff,* Private International Law [2] (1950) p. 493.

[8] Report, *infra* p. 288 s.

[9] Högsta Domstolen Sep. 20, 1933, N.J.A. 1933, p. 364.

dent not where the injury took place. Most courts will apply their own rules for the measure of compensation.

I find that this attitude of the courts should be taken into consideration in drafting a convention like the following.

To sum up my observations:

In deciding whether there is a claim and all the legal consequences derived therefrom, it is not necessary to apply the same law in all respects.

QUELQUES REMARQUES RELATIVES À L'AVANT-PROJET DE CONVENTION SUR LA LOI APPLICABLE AUX OBLIGATIONS CONTRACTUELLES ET NON-CONTRACTUELLES

Par

JEAN GEORGES SAUVEPLANNE

Utrecht

1. Remarques d'ordre général

Le but d'une unification du droit international privé comme celle préconisée par la Communauté européenne est de rendre uniforme dans les pays participants les règles de droit en cause. Par conséquent, l'unification doit produire des règles de droit qui peuvent être appliquées d'une façon uniforme dans les différents pays. Pour atteindre ce but on peut faire usage de deux méthodes. L'une consiste à rédiger des règles très précises et très détaillées qui laissent le moindre doute possible quant à leur interprétation. L'autre méthode consiste à rédiger des règles souples qui laissent assez de liberté au juge, mais à créer en même temps un mécanisme apte à assurer l'uniformité dans l'interprétation desdites règles. La raison en est que l'application des règles uniformes est abandonnée aux juges nationaux et que faute de règles précises et d'un mécanisme unificateur on crée le risque d'interprétations différentes, de sorte que le but de l'unification n'est pas atteint. Toutefois, d'une part la rédaction de règles précises favorise indubitablement la prévisibilité des solutions, mais d'autre part l'application des règles rigides empêche souvent de rendre justice dans le cas individuel. Or, dans le droit international privé moderne on aperçoit une tendance à accentuer la justice dans le cas concret plutôt que la prévisibilité. Bien entendu, la prévisibilité joue toujours un rôle important, notamment par rapport à l'unification. Le but de l'unification est précisément d'assurer la prévisibilité du droit applicable en écartant les divergences entre les règles nationaux. Or, on n'atteint pas ce but en le limitant à édicter des règles vagues, qui laissent à chaque juge une liberté considérable en ce qui concerne leur interprétation. La meilleure solution serait de chercher à créer un équilibre qui laisse assez de souplesse tout en assurant un degré suffisant de prévisibilité. La difficulté de l'unification internationale consiste justement dans le fait que habituellement l'application du droit uniforme doit être abandonnée aux juges nationaux. C'est pourquoi il est difficile de réaliser l'équilibre et qu'il faut choisir entre les deux méthodes. Dans ces conditions le choix porte sur la rédaction de règles précises parce que l'abandon au juge national de l'interprétation des règles vagues signifie en réalité qu'on renonce à l'unification. C'est sur ce point que la situation dans laquelle se trouve la Communauté européenne présente un grand avantage. Dans cette Communauté il existe un mécanisme qui peut assurer l'uniformité de l'interprétation du droit communautaire. Lorsqu'elle est saisie d'un recours ex article 177 du Traité instituant la Communauté économique, la Cour des Communautés peut, par décision préjudicielle, donner une interprétation d'une règle de droit communautaire qui lie le juge devant lequel cette règle venait d'être invoquée. En appliquant une procédure analogue aux règles de droit international privé on a la possibilité de rédiger des règles souples sans toutefois risquer que l'unification préconisée n'aboutisse pratiquement à rien à cause des divergences trop considérables dans l'interprétation desdites règles par les juges nationaux.

De ce point de vue on peut approuver la méthode suivie dans le projet. Le projet contient pour la plus grande partie des règles souples, qui, tout en donnant des indications claires sur les rattachements à appliquer, laissent aux juges la liberté de rendre justice dans le cas individuel. Une telle méthode peut réaliser l'équilibre entre, d'une part, la prévisibilité des solutions et, d'autre part, la justice dans la solution du cas concret, à condition que la Cour puisse exercer un contrôle efficace sur l'interprétation desdites règles. La méthode suivie paraît donc présupposer que les états communautaires se mettent d'accord sur l'application d'une procédure qui permet à la Cour d'exercer un contrôle sur l'interprétation des règles de la Convention. C'est à cette condition seulement que je puis approuver la méthode du projet. Si la possibilité d'un contrôle par la Cour n'est pas réalisée je doute de l'efficacité de la méthode suivie, et je me demande si dans cette hypothèse le seul moyen de réaliser l'unification ne consiste dans l'élaboration des règles précises.

En supposant que la condition que j'ai posée soit remplie, je ferai quelques remarques sur la loi applicable aux contrats, la loi applicable aux actes illicites et la loi applicabe aux transferts d'une créance. Je terminerai par une brève observation sur l'article 20 relative à l'incapacité.

2. La loi applicable aux contrats

Le droit international privé en matière des contrats aux Pays Bas est formé par la jurisprudence. La tentative faite par les pays de Bénélux pour codifier leur droit international privé a échoué. Le projet d'une loi uniforme Bénélux n'est pas entré en vigueur et dans l'état actuel des choses il n'a guère de chances d'être encore adopté. Le projet originaire de 1951 a été révisé en 1966, mais ce projet revisé, qui a depuis subi quelques retouches, a succombé sous les critiques dont il a fait l'objet. Toutefois, certains articles des projets ont influencé la doctrine et la jurisprudence, notamment aux Pays Bas. Ça ne vaut pas pour l'article relatif à la loi applicable aux contrats. Au contraire sur ce point le projet originaire a dû être modifié pour correspondre au droit jurisprudentiel.

La jurisprudence néerlandaise consacre l'autonomie des parties dans le choix de la loi applicable. D'après la Cour de Cassation les parties à un contrat de caractère international peuvent choisir la loi applicable à ce contrat, et le résultat d'un tel choix est que le contrat est entièrement soumis aux dispositions de cette loi, sans qu'il soit tenu compte des dispositions, même impératives de la loi qui serait applicable dans l'absence d'un tel choix[1]. La règle de l'article 2, premier alinéa, de l'avant-projet correspond donc au droit jurisprudentiel néerlandais.

La question se pose de savoir s'il faut néanmoins faire une distinction d'après la nature de contrat et d'exclure le choix de la loi dans certaines catégories de contrats. Il s'agit notamment des contrats dits de consommation où il existe un déséquilibre entre les positions économiques des parties. A cet égard je partage l'opinion de M. *Batiffol* qu'une telle distinction est difficile à appliquer parce que la limite n'est pas nette[2]. Il résulte des exemples donnés par M. *Lando* (dans son commentaire sur les articles du projet relatifs aux obligations contractuelles[3]), qu'en effet le même contrat peut tomber l'une fois dans la catégorie des contrats dits de consommation, et l'autre fois dans la catégorie des contrats libres, selon les positions respectives des parties. La délimitation est donc tellement vague qu'elle ne crée que des incertitudes. Je préfère de résoudre ce problème par le jeu des règles d'application immédiate. L'objection que cela mène à un dépéçage du contrat ne me paraît pas convaincante. En effet, pour autant que je sache, les lois relatives à la protection des consommateurs ne

---

[1] HR 13 mai 1966 *(Alnati)*, Ned. Jur. 1967 no. 3.
[2] *Batiffol/Lagarde*, D. i. p.[5] II (1971) no. 576 note 29.
[3] *Lando*, RabelsZ 38 (1974) p. 6/19.

règlent pas les contrats qu'elles envisagent d'une façon exhaustive, mais n'en règlent que certains aspects. Pour le reste, ces contrats demeurent soumis aux règles de droit commun, notamment en ce qui concerne les règles sur les contrats en général. La législation spéciale en matière de protection du consommateur effectue donc pour ainsi dire un dépéçage dans le droit national, et je ne vois aucune raison pour exclure un tel effet lorsqu'il s'agit d'un contrat de caractère international soumis à une loi autre que celle dont les règles d'application immédiate ont vocation à être appliquées.

A défaut d'un choix explicite ou implicite, la jurisprudence manifeste une tendance de rattacher le contrat d'après le critère de la prestation caractéristique. L'application de ce critère a été sûrtout due à l'influence du regretté professeur *de Winter,* qui en sa qualité de conseiller suppléant à la Cour d'Appel d'Amsterdam a participé à la rédaction des arrêts rendus par cette Cour dans lesquels ledit critère fut appliqué. Ainsi, dans les contrats d'agence commerciale, la prestation caractéristique a été localisée dans le pays où se trouve le centre des activités de l'agent[4]. Dans les contrats de vente internationale les tribunaux ont appliqué la loi du pays de la résidence habituelle ou de l'établissement du vendeur, conformément à la Convention de la Haye de 1955, nonobstant que le gouvernement néerlandais ait refusé de ratifier cette Convention[5]. Les critères appliqués dans l'article 4 de l'avant-projet me semblent être en harmonie avec cette jurisprudence. Par contre, le critère formulé à l'article 5, sous b), pour désigner la loi applicable au contrat de travail dans le cas où le travailleur n'accomplit pas habituellement son travail dans un même pays, n'est pas en harmonie avec la jurisprudence récente. La Cour de Cassation a été d'avis que lorsque le champ des activités du travailleur s'étend sur plusieurs pays, le contrat de travail est régi par la loi du pays où le travailleur a son établissement central. Ce n'est qu'à défaut d'un tel établissement qu'elle a déclaré applicable la loi du pays où se trouve l'établissement qui a embauché le travailleur. La cour a donc intercalé la loi de l'établissement central du travailleur entre la loi du pays où celui-ci accomplit son travail et la loi de l'établissement qui l'a embauché; l'application des deux lois se fait d'ailleurs sous réserve de circonstances particulières qui entraînent l'application de la loi d'un autre pays[6]. Sous la même réserve la Cour a soumis un contrat

---

[4] Hof Amsterdam 1er avril 1970 *(NAP N. V.* c. *Christophery),* Ned. Jur. 1971 no. 115.

[5] Ainsi Arr. Rb. Leeuwarden 4 juin 1964 *(van Nimwegen* c. *John Coombs),* Ned. Jur. 1936 no. 12; Arr. Rb. Amsterdam 4 décembre 1968 *(Wolf* c. *A.I.C.A.),* Ned. Jur. 1969 no. 452.

[6] HR 8 juin 1973 *(Mackay* c. *American Express Co.),* Ned. Jur. 1973 no. 400.

d'agence commerciale à la loi du pays où se trouvait l'établissement de l'agent[7]. Ça pose évidemment la question de savoir quelle loi sera applicable sous le régime de l'article 5, b, lorsqu'un contrat d'agence présente en même temps les caractéristiques d'un contrat de travail.

Il convient de faire observer que la jurisprudence néerlandaise applique en principe toutes les dispositions de la loi applicable, sans faire une distinction entre règles de droit privé et règles de droit public. Ainsi la Cour de Cassation a décidé que l'application de la loi du contrat inclut l'application des règles de cette loi relatives à la réglementation des changes, sous réserve de leur contrariété à l'ordre public international néerlandais[8].

3. La loi applicable aux actes illicites

L'article 14 du projet de la loi uniforme Bénélux est un des rares articles qui a été applaudi comme constituant un véritable progrès dans le développement du droit international privé en matière d'obligations non-contractuelles. L'article a été approuvé par la quasi-totalité de la doctrine néerlandaise et la jurisprudence néerlandaise l'a appliqué à plusieurs reprises. L'article pose en principe que le caractère illicite d'un acte et les obligations qui en résultent sont déterminées par la loi du pays où l'acte a eu lieu.

Le second alinéa fait une exception importante. Lorsque les conséquences de l'acte appartiennent à la sphère juridique d'un pays autre que celui où le fait a eu lieu, les obligations qui en résultent sont déterminées par la loi de cet autre pays. Certes, la disposition est criticable pour autant qu'elle provoque une rupture des liens entre la cause et les effets d'un acte. On a relevé que dans le cas visé dans l'alinéa 2 et la cause et les effets doivent être soumis à la loi du pays de la sphère juridique, sauf à tenir compte des règles de conduite et de sécurité en vigueur dans le pays où le fait s'est produit. Quelque juste que soit cette critique on ne peut nier que c'est grace à cet article que la jurisprudence néerlandaise s'est évoluée dans la direction d'une application souple et nuancée de la règle concernant la loi applicable à l'acte illicite. Ainsi elle a appliqué la loi néerlandaise à un accident survenu en France lorsque et l'auteur et la victime étaient des néerlandais domiciliés aux Pays Bas[9]; de même, elle a appliqué la loi belge aux

---

[7] HR 6 avril 1973 *(Topsøe c. Del Prado)*, Ned. Jur. 1973 no. 371.

[8] HR 17 avril 1964 *(Escomptobank)*, Ned. Jur. 1965 no. 22.

[9] Hof s'Gravenhage 16 juin 1955 *(de Beer c. de Hondt)*, Ned. Jur. 1955 no. 615.

accidents survenus aux Pays Bas lorsque et l'auteur et la victime étaient des belges domiciliés en Belgique [10].

L'article 10 de l'avant-projet fait également une exception à l'application de la loi du lieu du délit. Mais cette exception paraît plus étroite que celle appliquée aux Pays Bas. En effet, pourque la loi du lieu du délit soit écartée une double condition doit être remplie. D'une part il ne doit pas exister un lien significatif avec le pays où le fait s'est produit, d'autre part la situation doit présenter une connexion prépondérante avec un autre pays. Donc, même lorsqu'une telle connexion se présente la loi du lieu du délit demeure applicable s'il existe également un lien significatif avec le pays où ce lieu se trouve situé. La doctrine et la jurisprudence néerlandaises ne semblent pas attacher une telle importance à l'existence de ce lien, mais semblent seulement se demander s'il existe une connexion prépondérante avec un autre pays que celui où le délit s'est produit. Ainsi, dans l'exemple donné dans le rapport explicatif (deux ressortissants italiens qui ont leur résidence habituelle en Allemagne, et dont l'un est l'auteur et l'autre la victime d'un accident survenu en Italie) il serait possible que le juge néerlandais préférât l'application de la loi allemande. Sur ce point le projet ne semble donc pas être en harmonie avec le développement du droit jurisprudentiel néerlandais.

J'approuve cette jurisprudence qui est conforme aux tendances doctrinales actuelles en faveur d'un assouplissement de la règle de conflit en matière d'actes illicites, et je donne une réponse nettement affirmative à la question posée par MM. *von Overbeck* et *Volken* dans leur commentaire sur les articles du projet relatifs aux obligations délictuelles [11], à savoir si la formule moins stricte de l'article 13 qui exige seulement une connexion prépondérante avec un autre pays que celui du lieu de l'acte, n'aurait pas été suffisante également dans le droit des délits.

En ce qui concerne l'exigence que la connexion doit se fonder normalément sur un élément de rattachement commun, la jurisprudence néerlandaise est en harmonie avec le projet. Ainsi elle a refusé d'écarter l'application de la loi du lieu où le fait dommageable s'était produit dans le cas d'un accident de circulation survenue en Allemagne entre une personne domiciliée en Belgique et une personne domiciliée aux Pays Bas [12].

---

[10] Arr. Rb. Breda 2 octobre 1962 *(Backx c. Fransen)*, Ned. Jur. 1963 no. 109.

[11] *von Overbeck/Volken*, RabelsZ 38 (1974) p. 56/73.

[12] Arr. Rb. Roermond 27 juin 1968 (*Generale Transport c. Maco*), Ned. Jur. 1969 no. 422.

4. La loi applicable aux transferts des créances

L'article 17 du projet de loi uniforme Bénélux prévoit l'application de la loi qui régit l'obligation à la question de savoir si l'obligation peut faire l'objet d'un transfert et dans quelles conditions. Cet article régit toutes les espèces de transfert, tant volontaire que par l'effet de la loi. Le second alinéa exige l'observation des règles qui sont prescrites par la loi du domicile du débiteur dans l'intérêt de celui-ci ou dans l'intérêt des tiers, lorsque le transfert a lieu sans le concours du débiteur. La Cour de Cassation a presque textuellement repris cet article en déterminant la loi applicable à la cession d'une créance[13].

Cet article a fait l'objet de sévères critiques dans la doctrine.

On a notamment reproché à ces auteurs de ne pas avoir fait une distinction entre le transfert volontaire d'une créance et la transmission d'une créance par l'effet de la loi. En ce qui concerne cette dernière, la quasi-totalité des auteurs a préféré l'application de la loi régissant le rapport juridique qui est à la base de la transmission. Ainsi on a voulu déterminer la subrogation légale de l'assureur par la loi qui régit le contrat d'assurance. C'est de nouveau le regretté professeur *de Winter* qui a engagé la jurisprudence de la Cour d'Appel d'Amsterdam dans cette voie. Après une certaine hésitation cette Cour a nettement pris position en faveur de l'application de la loi de l'institution juridique pour laquelle la subrogation a été créée en s'inspirant des formules employées par les Cours de Cassation belge et française[14]. D'autres juridictions ont suivi cet exemple, de sorte qu'on peut maintenant constater que la décision précitée de la Cour de Cassation n'est plus suivie en matière de subrogation légale et qu'une règle jurisprudentielle vient d'être formée, qui est en harmonie avec l'article 17, premier alinéa, de l'avant-projet de convention. La loi qui régit la créance demeure seulement applicable pour déterminer le caractère transférable de celle-ci; les droits et obligations du débiteur sont également déterminés conformément à cette loi.

En ce qui concerne la cession d'une créance la jurisprudence n'est pas uniforme, mais dans la majorité des décisions on semble faire la même distinction qui est faite à l'article 16 du projet. Toutefois, en s'inspirant de l'alinéa 2 de l'article 17 du projet Bénélux, la loi du domicile du débiteur est prise en considération pour déterminer l'observation des règles prescrites dans l'intérêt de celui-ci, comme les règles concernant la signification de l'acte. Récemment, certains auteurs ont

---

[13] HR 17 avril 1964 (*supra* note 8).

[14] Hof Amsterdam 21 janvier 1972 (*Vogels* c. *Van Loon*), Ned. Jur. 1972 no. 280.

mis en doute le bien-fondé de cette jurisprudence. Ils se sont demandés s'il est justifié de faire une distinction entre, d'une part, le transfert volontaire, et d'autre part, le transfert involontaire de la créance. Ils ont fait observer que dans les deux cas le transfert a la même fonction, à savoir de transmettre une créance à un autre créancier. Lorsqu'il s'agit d'une cession volontaire, le transfert de la créance présente une connexion aussi étroite avec le rapport entre les créanciers successifs que dans l'hypothèse d'une transmission par l'effet de la loi. En plus, la cession volontaire remplit souvent la fonction d'une subrogation légale. Ainsi, dans les systèmes qui ne connaissent pas la subrogation ou ne la connaissent qu'imparfaitement, il est d'usage, dans les contrats d'assurance, d'obliger l'assuré de céder les créances qui naîtront à son profit du chef d'un dommage couvert par l'assurance. De même, dans certains systèmes d'assurance sociale, l'assureur a le droit de subordonner le paiement de l'indemnisation à la cession de la créance de la part de l'assuré. D'après lesdits auteurs tous ces arguments militent en faveur d'abolir en droit international privé la distinction entre le transfert volontaire et la transmission involontaire d'une créance, et de soumettre tous les deux à une même règle de conflits. Et le transfert volontaire et la transmission involontaire d'une créance devraient être régis par la loi qui détermine les rapports entre créanciers successifs. On pourrait à la rigueur faire une distinction d'après la nature de la créance, et appliquer des règles différentes à, d'une part, le transfert d'une créance contractuelle et, d'autre part, celui d'une créance extra-contractuelle; on a même mis en doute l'utilité d'une telle distinction, vu que les raisons d'un transfert peuvent bien être les mêmes dans l'une et l'autre hypothèse. Moi-même je me suis laissé convaincre du bien-fondé de cette opinion et je serais donc partisan d'une règle unique, conforme à la règle contenue à l'article 17, pour tout transfert de toute créance ou, subsidiairement, de la limitation de l'article 16 aux seuls transferts de créances contractuelles, et de l'application de l'article 17 à tous les transferts, tant volontaires qu'involontaires, des créances extra-contractuelles.

5. La question de l'incapacité

En droit international privé néerlandais la capacité d'une personne physique ressort du statut personnel et est déterminée par la loi nationale de la personne en question. L'article 2 du projet Bénélux consacre cette règle. Le second alinéa y fait exception. C'est la même exception qui figure à l'article 20 de l'avant-projet. En général, la doctrine néerlandaise a approuvé cette exception. Les auteurs sont d'avis que cette disposition fournit une protection raisonnable à celui qui, de bonne foi, traite avec un étranger dont il ignore l'incapacité. Contrairement à la jurisprudence française, les auteurs du projet n'ont pas voulu limiter cette protection à des personnes qui agissent dans le pays du for, mais ils ont bilatéralisé la règle. Ça aussi a reçu l'approbation de la doctrine qui est d'avis que ladite règle, au lieu de favoriser le commerce national, doit protéger toutes les personnes qui traitent avec des incapables, sans discriminer d'après le lieu où ils agissent. Je partage cette opinion et par conséquent je ne partage pas les critiques soulevées à l'encontre de l'article 20, notamment par M. *Lando*[15].

[15] *Lando* (*supra* note 3) p. 54.

CERTAIN PROBLEMS RELATING TO THE APPLICATION OF THE EEC DRAFT IN THE FIELD OF INTERNATIONAL MARITIME LAW

By

ERLING SELVIG

Oslo

I. Introduction

According to art. 1 the EEC Draft is intended to apply also to conflict-of-law questions arising in the field of international maritime law.
The purpose of this paper is to draw attention to certain problems
which may result therefrom, particularly in view of the fact that international maritime law has for a long time been a field of extensive
international unification of law. This unification has affected to a great
– although somewhat varying – extent the law of the several members
of EEC as well as most other European shipping countries.

The EEC Draft is based on a distinction between contractual and
non-contractual obligations. The problems which this Draft may raise
in the field of maritime law shall here be discussed with reference to
two subjects: contracts for the carriage of goods *(infra sub* II) and
maritime liabilities arising out of collision *(infra sub* III) falling within
each of the two categories mentioned. In passing I should like to
observe, however, that the distinction between contractual and non-
contractual liabilities is not one easily applied in transportation law,
where the most important liability problems relate to cases of damage
to persons or property. It is a question of some doubt in many jurisdictions, for instance, whether personal injury to a passenger results in
a contractual or in a tortious liability or, perhaps, in both *(Anspruchs-
konkurrenz)*. The same question may also arise in cases of damage
to cargo. Unless the qualification be the same in the various jurisdictions, the EEC Draft will not bring about the degree of uniformity
envisaged.

From a practical view the main purpose of establishing uniform conflict-of-law rules within the EEC would be to provide for greater legal security in commercial matters and to prevent forum shopping[1]. The question may be raised whether choice-of-law rules of the very flexible nature established in the Draft are likely to achieve these goals. No doubt, much will depend on the extent to which the rules are uniformly interpreted and applied by the courts of the EEC countries when exercising the great measure of discretion given them by the Draft (*cf.* art. 23). With respect to matters of international maritime law one should take into account that forum shopping frequently depends on many other factors than just applicable law, *e. g.* the convenience and costs of going to a particular forum, and traditional approaches to the evaluation of facts and legal issues and to the application of legal standards. Moreover, for many matters of international maritime law there have been developed specific and well recognized choice-of-law rules, and in such areas the EEC Draft may introduce new elements of uncertainty. If this be the case, the Draft may, with respect to maritime matters, prove to encourage litigation and forum shopping, the amount involved in a maritime dispute being such as justifying the exploration of even a small chance of a more favourable forum.

II. Contracts for the Carriage of Goods by Sea

1. When considering the questions relating to the application of the EEC Draft to contracts for carriage of goods by sea, one would have to distinguish between contracts evidenced by *bills of lading* and contracts evidenced by *charterparties.*

2. The first question is whether the EEC Draft art. 1 (b) should read so as to exclude *bills of lading.* This provision deals with "commercial bills, such as bills of exchange, cheques and promissory notes" (*"Handelspapiere"*). The reason for this exclusion is that such papers "are governed by Conventions on the broadest international scale"[2]. The bills of lading are not specifically referred to, but it would seem that the reason stated and even other reasons justify the exclusion also of bills of lading. Bills of lading play a rôle in international trade equivalent to that of bills of exchange, to which the bills of lading are often attached.

Bills of lading are governed by the rules of the 1924 Bills of Lading Convention which have obtained world wide implementation and are

---

[1] Report ch. I para. 2, *infra* p. 243.
[2] Report art. 1 no. 3, *infra* p. 252.

in force in most shipping countries, including the EEC Members States. This Convention applies "to all bills of lading issued in any of the Contracting States" [3]. In other words, it is the place of the issue of the bill of lading which is the decisive factor for the application of the Convention. This Convention does not deal with all matters relating to bills of lading, notably not with questions relating to the transfer of the bill of lading or its character as a negotiable document. However, such matters are not dealt with in the EEC Draft (*cf.* art. 9); I assume that art. 16 only applies to the assignment of non-negotiable debts. In other words, the provisions of EEC Draft would govern the same contractual matters as are dealt with in the 1924 Convention. This being so, the view quoted above from the Report would also apply to bills of lading.

In addition it should be observed that the contracts referred to in EEC Draft art. 4 would probably not work satisfactorily within the international law on bills of lading. Of course, the center-of-gravity approach of art. 4 paras. 1 and 3 would not cause difficulties if it would always be interpreted to refer to the place of the issue of the bill of lading or to some other contact which would mean that a bill of lading issued in a Contracting State would be governed by the rules of the 1924 Convention. However, this cannot be taken for granted, notably because the presumption as to the meaning of the center-of-gravity approach contained in art. 4 para. 2 creates considerable uncertainty in this respect.

In matters of bills of lading art. 4 para. 2 would as a rule lead to the application of *the law of the State in which the carrier has his principal place of business, i. e.* in most cases *the law of the flag of the ship.* Admittedly, many bills of lading contain choice-of-law-clauses referring to the law of the carrier or of the flag, but it is generally recognized that in international shipping this is not a satisfactory solution. The law of the carrier or of the flag will frequently be the law of a distant country not linked in any way with the particular transport. In order to meet the need for such a link one has in maritime transportation as well as other transportation relied, generally speaking, on factors for the applicable law such as the place of departure and/or the place of destination. It would seem, therefore, that the EEC Draft art. 4 is not well suited to deal with choice-of-law problems relating to bills of lading.

Furthermore it should be recognized that the 1924 Convention contains *international mandatory rules* relating to bills of lading [see art. 3

---

[3] The scope of application is somewhat enlarged by art. 5 of the Brussels Protocol February 23, 1968, but this protocol has not yet entered into force.

(8) of the Convention]. In view of this, the principle of freedom for
the parties to provide in the contract for the law applicable established
in the EEC Draft art. 2 would create difficulties if applied to bills of
lading. Such a rule could make it possible to evade the rules of the
Convention; this is clearly demonstrated by *Vita Food Products* v.
Unus Shipping Co.[4] As this case also shows, the risk of evasion is
particularly relevant when, as provided in art. 2 para. 2, the validity
of the choice-of-law clause shall be determined according to the law
therein referred to. The provisions of art. 7 – designed to meet such
objection to some extent[5] – leaves a too great measure of flexibility
to be satisfactory in the context of bills of lading. Whether the art. 7
refers to the mandatory rule of the forum State or of some other State
is here immaterial – in any event it is left to the discretion of the court
to take account of the mandatory rules. It appears from the exampli-
fication given in the Report[6] that art. 7 is drafted with reference to
special mandatory rules of a particular State[7]. The position is obviously
different where the mandatory rules have their basis in an international
Convention such as the 1924 Convention, acceded to by all EEC countries and most other shipping countries in the world. The somewhat
cautious approach of the Draft art. 7 would not then seem justified.

If such a mandatory regime shall be implemented effectively, it is
required that courts and legislators of Contracting States apply choice-
of-law criteria based on such links as would make the rules of the Convention applicable within its scope of application, *viz.* with respect
to the 1924 Convention, to any bill of lading issued in a Contracting
State[8]. If not, the State concerned cannot be said to fulfil its obligation
as a party to the Convention. Furthermore, the implementation of the
mandatory regime would require certain limitations on the validity
of choice-of-law clauses so as to ensure that such a clause does not
take a bill of lading issued in a Contracting State out of the scope
of application of the mandatory rules contained in the Convention.
The EEC Drafts arts. 2 and 7 do not meet the requirements mentioned
above, and this is another reason why the Draft should not apply to
bills of lading.

It is no answer to this objection to refer to the EEC Draft art. 27,
which preserves the obligations of EEC members as parties to the 1924
Convention. Admittedly, in France the Convention will be applied in

---

[4] *Vita Foods Products, Inc.* v. *Unus Shipping Co.*, [1939] A.C. 277 (P.C.).
[5] *Cf. Lando,* RabelsZ 38 (1974) p. 6 ss., especially p. 21 ss. and 33 ss.
[6] Report art. 7 no. 1, *infra* p. 278.
[7] *Cf.* also *Lando (supra* note 5) p. 16–19 and 35–39.
[8] *Cf. Selvig,* Am. J. Comp. L. 13 (1964) p. 482 s. and *id.,* Ark. f. Sjørett 6
(1963–66) p. 558 ss., especially p. 564 s.

all cases covered by art. 10 of the Convention, but, for instance, in Belgium, Germany or United Kingdom the national enactment of the 1924 Convention apply only to trade to and/or from the country concerned. Only by means of appropriate conflict-of-law rules would a court in any such country be able to make the Convention applicable to bills of lading issued in a Contracting State in a trade other than to and/or from the State to which the court belongs. If such rules are not established forum shopping is bound to take place.

3. There exist no internationally uniform rules relating to contracts of carriage evidenced by *charterparties*. As far as I can see, the EEC Draft arts. 2 and 4 are on the whole not likely to cause great difficulty if applied to charterparties.

Charterparties contain frequently choice-of-law clauses and art. 2 will recognize this practice. In cases where there is no express or implied choice-of-law by the parties, art. 4 para. 1 and 3 may provide satisfactory guidance. The presumption as to the content of the center-of-gravity rule contained in art. 4 para. 2, however, would to some extent be subject to the same objection as that made above with reference to bills of lading. It is probable that in this context one must distinguish between voyage charterparties and time charterparties, the latter being more suited to the application of the law of the shipowner or of the flag. Even in other respects the rules of art. 4 para. 2 may raise some problems if applied to charterparties. One question is how the provision should be applied in cases where the operation of the ship is divided between the shipowner and the charterer. Another relates to the application of sub-para (b) in cases of performance of carriage by a ship. Likewise there are cases where the shipowner has his actual place of business in one State while his ship is registered in another.

With respect to charterparties it is important that the choice-of-law may be made by the parties explicitly as well as implicitly[9]. Charterparties not directly stating the applicable law, contain very often arbitration clauses or jurisdiction clauses. It is a prevailing view in maritime circles that, as a rule, such clauses also amount to a choice of the law of the forum State[10]. It does not appear that the EEC Draft art. 4 may, or is intended to, disturb this rule.

---

[9] Report art. 2 no. 3, *infra* p. 259 s.

[10] Cf. *Carver/Colinvaux*, Carriage by Sea[12] I (1971) no. 575; *Collins*, J. Marit. L. Comm. 2 (1970/71) p. 363 ss.; *Rodière*, Traité général de droit maritime I (1967) no. 24; *Schaps/Abraham*, Das deutsche Seerecht[3] II (1962) pre-note 31 to § 556; *Philip*, Dansk international privat- og processret (1971) p. 299 s. and 412 s.

III. Maritime Torts

1. The EEC Draft art. 10 provides that "Non-contractual liability which results from an event entailing damage shall be governed by the law of the State in which such event occurred" (para. 1). If, however, the situation resulting from the event has no significant link with such State, but, on the other hand, a predominant link with another State, the law of the latter shall apply (para. 2). The law applicable according to art. 10 determines not only the basis and extent of liability, but also a number of other matters, including any limitation of liability (art. 11).

The provisions of arts. 10–11 may raise certain problems and difficulties if applied to cases of maritime liabilities. In order to show this it is here sufficient to deal with liabilities arising out of *collision* between ships, but in a discussion thereof a distinction has to be made between the basis for liability (*infra* 2) and the limitation of liability (*infra* 3 and 4).

2. Internationally uniform rules relating to *liability for collision* are contained in a Convention of September 23, 1910 which has been ratified by most shipping countries (except the United States of America), including all EEC States. These rules govern the liability of one ship towards the other ship (including any person or cargo on board), and they apply "as regards all persons interested when all the vessels concerned in any action belong to States of the High Contracting Parties, and in any other cases for which the national law provides" (art. 12). However, the national law may be applicable as *lex fori* if all interested persons belong to the *forum* State (art. 12 no. 2).

The Collision Convention art. 12 means that no true choice-of-law question as regards the basis of liability should arise in cases of collisions between *ships from different Contracting States.* The question would here be one of choosing between different national enactments of the rules of the Convention, and in principle the choice should be immaterial, whether based on the *lex loci delicti* rule of EEC Draft art. 10 or on any other rules. However, the position is quite different if the substantive law chosen shall also govern any limitation of liability – a rule laid down in EEC Draft art. 11. Whether EEC Draft art. 10 is an appropriate rule in such a context is discussed below 3 and 4.

A true choice-of-law question relating to the basis for liability may arise in cases of collision between *ships of the same State.* The EEC Draft art. 10 para. 2 would here seem to provide an adequate solution, making the law of the common-flag State applicable regardless of where the collision took place [11].

---

[11] *Cf.* art. 10 no. 4, *infra* p. 284.

A choice-of-law question arises also in cases of collision between *ships of different States of which at least one is a non-contracting State,* because such a collision is not one to which the Collision Convention applies. As regards such collisions on the high sea the EEC Draft art. 10 gives no guidance[12], and the applicable law would have to be determined according to existing conflicts of law rules (as a rule, the law of the flag or *lex fori*)[13]. In cases of collisions in the territorial waters of a Contracting State art. 10 would make the rules of the Collision Convention apply and thus cause no problem. If, however, a collision took place in the waters of a non-contracting State, the law of that State and not the rules of the Convention would apply. This may be justified if one of the ships belongs to that State, but in other cases[14] a more suitable choice-of-law rule would probably be one making the rules of the Convention applicable. This would extend the scope of the internationally uniform rules as envisaged in the Convention art. 12 para 1 *in fine*.

3. A shipowner's liability for damage caused by collision to another ship, including property or persons on board, would be subject to rules on the *limitation of shipowner's liability* contained in legislation of most shipping countries. In a number of countries, including most West-European States, such legislation incorporates the provisions of the *1957 Limitation Convention*. According to its art. 7 this Convention applies whenever a shipowner seeks to limit his liability before the courts of a Contracting State (the *lex fori* principle), but a Contracting State may provide for the exclusion of shipowners or ships not belonging to Contracting States and make such shipowners or ships subject to a different regime of limitation of liability. The Convention applies regardless of applicable law as to the basis of any liability subject to limitation.

In EEC countries being parties to the 1957 Convention, consequently, the rules of the Convention as *lex fori* and not the *lex loci delicti* of the Draft arts. 10–11 would govern the limitation of shipowners' liability, *cf.* the Draft art. 27. In this connection the law applicable as to the basis of liability is immaterial. This would, for instance, be the position in France or the United Kingdom which have ratified the Convention without excluding ships or shipowners belonging to non-contracting

---

[12] Report art. 10 no. 7, *infra* p. 287 s.

[13] *Cf. Sundström,* Foreign Ships and Foreign Waters (1971) = Ark. f. Sjørett 11 (1971–72) p. 1 ss.; *Rodière,* Traité (*supra* note 10) IV (1972) no. 108; *Schaps/ Abraham* (*supra* note 10) pre-note 25 to § 734.

[14] For instance, a collision between a German (Contracting State) ship and a Canadian (Non-contracting State) ship in US waters.

States[15]. In the Federal Republic of Germany, on the other hand, the rules of the Convention as incorporated in HGB §§ 486 ss. (*Seerechts-änderungsgesetz* of June 21, 1972, art. 1) are meant to apply only to *"alle nach deutschem Recht begründeten Ansprüche"*[16]; according to art. 3 of that Act the Convention itself shall apply to *"Ansprüche . . ., die nicht nach den deutschen Gesetzen zu beurteilen sind"*, provided that the shipowner seeking limitation before a German court is *"Angehöriger eines Vertragsstaats"*. According to the new German legislation, consequently, the EEC Draft arts. 10–11 would apply to determine applicable law if limitation were sought by a *shipowner from a State not party to the 1957 Convention.* The choice would then depend on the rules discussed *supra sub* III, 2 and neither in theory nor in practice would this be satisfactory.

First, in the case of such a shipowner the choice-of-law rule to be applied by a German court would be different from that applied, *e. g.,* by a French or English court, and in particular cases this could have significant implications for the extent to which he could limit his liability. In this area, consequently, the EEC Draft will not achieve its object of preventing forum shopping among EEC Member States.

Second, the rules on the applicable law would be rather complicated, the choice-of-law as regards limitation of liability depending on the three or more criteria mentioned *supra sub* III, 2. The resulting solutions may also appear to be rather arbitrary. In cases of collision on the high sea the law of the forum or of the flag of either ship would probably apply[17], but if the same collision took place in territorial waters, *lex loci delicti* would apply.

Third, the rule in EEC Draft art. 11 that *lex causae* shall determine questions of limitation of liability would cause great difficulties for the implementation of the system of *global* limitation contained in the 1957 Convention or of any similar systems contained in national laws (*infra* 4).

4. Limitation of shipowners' liability take the form of *global* limitation, *viz.* the limit applies to *the aggregate of all claims arising against the shipowner on a distinct occasion.* In a collision case, for instance, limitable claims may arise in respect of non-contractual liability towards the other ship, including property or persons on board, as well as in respect of contractual liability towards members of the crew,

---

[15] Cf. *Sundström* (*supra* note 13) p. 66–68; *Rodière*, Droit maritime[5] (1971) § 147; *Légendre*, D.M.F. 20 (1968) p. 382 s.

[16] This is stated in the preparatory works in the comments to art. 3 no. 1, reference being made to BGH Jan. 29, 1959, BGHZ 29, 237 ss. Cf. also *Schaps/ Abraham* (*supra* note 10) § 486 note 41.

[17] *Schaps/Abraham* (*supra* note 10) pre-note 25 to § 734, cf. § 486 note 41.

passengers or cargo on board the ship responsible for the collision. It should be noted that in such cases it is very unlikely that the basis for liability in respect of all the different claims be the same substantive law. In such circumstances it is not possible to maintain the principle that the substantive law for each of the claims should also determine any limitation of the liability. This would most likely mean that in one and the same case several different and irreconcilable limits of liability or systems for global limitation would be involved, and adequate aggregation of claims within a system of global limitation would not then seem possible. *To achieve such aggregation of claims one would have to choose one system of global limitation despite the fact that the basis for the claims may be different substantive laws.*

If the EEC Draft arts. 10–11 should be applied when making this choice, the law applicable to determine the non-contractual liabilities involved would also govern global limitation. In cases of collisions in territorial waters the *lex loci delicti* would apply to global limitation. However, this solution may not be justified as regards the contractual claims arising from the accident – claims which incidently may not be governed by the law of one and the same country. A solution will have to be found taking into account the fact that contractual as well as non-contractual liabilities have arisen. Choice-of-law rules other than those of Draft arts. 10–11 may consequently be preferable, *e. g.* the *lex fori* (of the 1957 Convention) or the *law of the flag*, both recognized by courts and writers in many countries [18]. In other words, *the choice-of-law as regards global limitation is a question both different and separate from that of choosing applicable substantive law as regards the basis of liability in respect of particular claims.* The position may be different in other fields of the law where limitation of liability is provided for in the form of *a limit for each particular claim* and not as global limitation.

The difficulties here pointed out are also inherent in the new legislation of the Federal Republic of Germany. According to the preparatory works, this Act is to some extent based on the same *(lex causae)* principle as EEC Draft arts. 10–11, that *"auf einen Anspruch, der materiellrechtlich nach deutschem Recht zu beurteilen ist, auch die deutschen Regeln über die Haftungsbeschränkung anzuwenden* [sind]*"* [19].

---

[18] *Cf. Rodière (supra* note 15) § 165; *Sundström (supra* note 13) p. 182 ss. (Scandinavian law prior to the enactment of the 1957 Convention); Norges Høyesterett Jan. 18, 1958, N.D.S. 1958, no. 1 (German law as the law of the flag); Stockholm rådhusrätt Feb. 17, 1958, N.D.S. 1958, no. 50; for a survey of the choice-of-law rules applied in a number of West-European countries, *cf. Siesby,* Söretlige lovkonflikter (1965) p. 149 ss., especially p. 225 ss.

[19] BT-Drucks. VI/2225. – This principle was well established in pre-1972 German law according to which global limitation was enforced in the form

As mentioned *supra sub* III,3, HGB §§ 486 ss. shall apply to all claims based on German law while the 1957 Convention shall apply as *lex fori* to claims based on foreign law where the shipowner is domiciled in a State party to the Convention. This system seems to imply that there shall be *separate limits and separate aggregation for claims governed by German law and for claims governed by some other law even if the claims concerned have arisen on the same occasion.* Whether this be the true intention of the legislator or how German courts should solve the resulting difficulties are questions for which no certain answer can be provided.

To this writer the observations above suggest that the principle that the law applicable to the basis of liability shall also govern the limitation of liability (EEC Draft art. 11) is irreconcilable with the system of global limitation recognized in the 1957 Convention or similar national legislation. Nor is it justified always to apply the *lex loci delicti* rule or other rules of EEC Draft art. 10 to determine applicable law as regards global limitation; as pointed out, the *lex fori* or the *law of the flag* has usually been held to govern questions of shipowners' limitation of liability. Consequently, an exception should be inserted in the EEC Draft to make it clear that the Draft does not apply to limitation of shipowners' liability. It is no answer to refer to the Draft art. 27 as preserving the *lex fori* rule of the Convention of 1957, because, as we have seen, that principle has not been fully implemented, for instance, in the legislation of the Federal Republic of Germany.

IV. The EEC Draft and International Unification of Maritime Law

1. The numerous Conventions in the field of international maritime law have brought about a large measure of unification of law at least in the European area. The EEC members as well as other European States are parties to the most or at any rate the most important of these Conventions. The great measure of unification of law has reduced the need for uniform choice-of-law rules as well as the possible scope

---

that the liability of the shipowner for maritime claims could only be asserted against the ship and its freight; he had no personal responsibility for the claims *(Schiffsvermögenshaftung)*. Under this system, as a rule, it was not possible to distinguish the question whether the shipowner was liable from the question of the extent of his liability, and the rule that *lex causae* governed limitation of liability would seem to be the only feasible one. However, it is difficult to see the reasons for retaining this principle in the global limitation system established by the German Act of 1972.

of application of such rules. Unification of choice-of-law rules may be considered as a substitute for unification of substantive law, and it is obvious that they must be drafted with particular regard to the many areas in the law where greater differences exist between the various national laws than in the field of maritime law. Such uniform choice-of-law rules may not, however, constitute a suitable supplementary component in the field of international maritime law, and it would seem to be preferable to exclude altogether maritime contracts and torts from the scope of the EEC Draft.

In this connection it should be born in mind that the various Conventions contain provisions relating to the scope of application of the uniform rules which by and large are based on other contacts than those reflected in the main provisions of the EEC Draft (arts. 4 and 10–11), for instance the forum, the nationality of the ship, the place of the contract, etc.

If applicable to maritime matters, the rules of the EEC Draft may consequently prove to be a foreign element in international maritime law, creating complexity and disharmony rather than simplicity and acceptable solutions.

2. It is likely that the work on unification of international maritime law will continue in the years to come, also in the form of modernization of already existing Conventions. The question may be posed whether the EEC Draft will create any difficulties for EEC members wanting to become parties to such new Conventions or protocols. This question has reference to the provisions of EEC Draft arts. 26 and 28, establishing a consultation machinery in certain cases where a member wishes to adopt measures inconsistent with the EEC Draft.

It is probable that the accession to a Convention purporting to unify certain aspects of maritime law would not be covered by art. 28, dealing with Conventions, the principal aim of which is to lay down rules of private international law. It is more likely that such accession would amount to the derogation of the EEC Draft "in a special field" within the meaning of art. 26. If, however, this provision is interpreted restrictively as referring only to unilateral, national measures, it would be difficult to state with certainty what would be the right of a State ratifying the EEC Draft to acceed independently to a multilateral Convention unifying matters of maritime law. Would such accession amount to a breach of its obligation as a party to the EEC Draft?

3. The observations above would, generally speaking, seem to apply analogously to other fields of transportation law which have been the subject of extensive international unification, for instance air law.

PARTY AUTONOMY AND THE EC DRAFT CONVENTION

By

ERIK SIESBY

Copenhagen

The Main Features of the Draft's Treatment of Party Autonomy

The Draft Convention treats the choice-of-law clause as a connecting factor. If a contract contains a choice-of-law clause referring to the law of a certain country that law is the *lex contractus.*

With respect to the scope of the *lex contractus* it makes no difference whether the *lex contractus* is the law of the closest connection according to art. 4 or the law chosen by the parties in accordance with art. 2.

The validity and the formation of a choice-of-law agreement is subject to special rules [art. 2 (2) and Annex art. 2 (4)] different from those governing the validity and formation of contracts without choice-of-law clauses.

If the contract in question does not have an international character the Convention does not deal with the choice-of-law clause. Presumably a choice-of-law clause in such a "national" contract should be considered invalid as a connecting factor.

The authors of the Draft Convention apparently have had in mind only one type of choice-of-law clause: the normal general choice-of-law clause, whereby the parties intend to remove the uncertainty as to what law governs the contract. The following questions will be discussed in connection with these features of the Draft Convention:

I. What legal effects should be, given to a normal choice-of-law clause which cannot be given effect as a connecting factor a) because the contract is not "international" or b) because the choice-of-law clause is invalid according to art. 2 (2) or Annex art. 2 (4)?

II. Should special rules govern the validity and formation of choice-of-law agreements?

III. What legal effects should be given to choice-of-law clauses in order to realize the intentions of the parties?

IV. The limits of party autonomy.

I.

The Report refers to the well-known distinction between *"kollisionsrechtliche"* and *"materiellrechtliche"* choice-of-law clauses[1]. These two concepts may be defined as follows: *"Kollisionsrechtliche"* choice-of-law clauses derive their validity from a special conflict rule. The chosen law supersedes the otherwise applicable law including its mandatory rules. The mandatory rules of the chosen law apply to the contract so as to invalidate provisions in the contract which are inconsistent with those rules. The reference to the chosen law is understood as a reference to the law (including its intertemporal rules) at the time of the judgment.

"Materiellrechtliche" choice-of-law clauses derive their validity from the law governing the contract and are to be understood as clauses incorporating the chosen law into the contract with the effect that the chosen law forms part of the contract just as any other non-legal rules or provisions which may have been incorporated in the contract by a reference clause. Therefore the mandatory rules of the law which apart from the choice-of-law clause governs the contract are not superseded by the clause. Presumably the mandatory rules of the chosen law would not normally invalidate provisions in the contract.

Although the concepts of *"kollisionsrechtliche"* and *"materiellrechtliche"* choice-of-law clauses are hardly adequate instruments for the description of the manifold types of choice-of-law clauses we may for the sake of argument apply these concepts in discussing the effect of choice-of-law clauses which do not fulfill the conditions for having effect as connecting factors.

a) National contracts. – If the contract is not an international one I suppose the authors of the Report would not consider a choice-of-law clause as a connecting factor which makes the chosen law the law governing the contract. In other words such a choice-of-law clause should not be given *"kollisionsrechtlichen"* effect. Would it not, however, be reasonable to let such a clause have *"materiellrechtlichen"* effect – in case the clause forms part of a contract which is valid according to the *lex contractus?* The difference between the two types

---

[1] Report, *infra* p. 258.

of choice-of-law clauses is minimal and in most cases of no actual importance because no mandatory rules "in the otherwise applicable law" are involved. The parties to the contract will at the time of contracting very rarely have had any clear idea of the character of the choice-of-law clause as either *"kollisionsrechtlich"* or *"materiellrecht-lich"*.

b) *International contracts.* – If the choice-of-law clause is invalid according to the chosen law [art. 2 (2)] whereas the contract is valid according to the otherwise applicable law (art. 4) should not the choice-of-law clause be given "materiellrechtlichen" effect?

If on the other hand the choice-of-law clause is valid according to the chosen law it should be of no consequence that the clause would have been invalid if the law of the closest connection applied.

Choice-of-law clauses in international contracts will consequently be upheld as valid in more cases than other clauses in international contracts.

II.

I doubt that it is reasonable to favour choice-of-law clauses by lowering the usual standards for validity and formation of contracts. In a great many cases choice-of-law clauses are found among the printed provisions in contract formulas. The parties – and especially the adhering party to an adhesion contract – may not have been able to realize the significance and all the consequences of the choice-of-law clause at the time of contracting. In many cases only a legal master mind would be able to evaluate the consequences of the choice-of-law clause. It may therefore involve hardship to one of the parties to the contract if he is deprived of the protection which follows from the rules concerning validity and formation of contracts in the law of the closest connection.

I fear that art. 2 (2) will create more problems than it solves.

In the normal cases the validity of choice-of-law clauses is not in dispute. In the very rare cases where the question is brought up it would presumably be fairly simple to judge the validity and formation of the clause in accordance with the law of the closest connection ("the otherwise applicable law"). Art. 4 and the following articles of the Convention provide a fairly high degree of certainty with respect to the law of the closest connection.

If special rules concerning the validity and formation of choice-of-law clauses are found to be desirable I would recommend that such rules should be of a substantive nature such as Annex art. 2 (4), 2nd variant, 1st period. The rules should provide the adhering party with a reasonable protection against a choice-of-law clause which would radically weaken his legal position according to the otherwise applicable law.

III.

Choice-of-law clauses may be phrased in various ways and may have different meanings. The Report mentions that the parties to a contract may wish to split the contract and to apply different laws to each part of the contract[2]. The question whether such stipulations should be accepted or not is, however, left open.

There can be no doubt that the parties to a contract may choose one law to govern the contract in general and in addition incorporate a special statute from another legal system into the contract. It may, however, be questioned whether this incorporated statute should be given superseding effect in relation to mandatory rules in the otherwise applicable law.

The various attitudes of contracting parties to the choice-of-law problems may be described (a) by the rules to which the parties refer by the choice-of-law clause and (b) by the effect the parties intend these rules to have in relation to other provisions of the contract as well as in relation to the otherwise applicable law (especially the mandatory rules of that law).

The normal *general choice-of-law clause* does not specify any particular rules but refers in a general way to the law of a certain country. The text of the Draft Convention presupposes that the choice-of-law clause contains a reference to those substantive rules concerning contracts which would apply if the chosen law had been the law applicable according to art. 4.

Certain questions which are kept outside the scope of *lex contractus* and made subject to special conflict rules may be suitable to be subject to the parties' choice of law. Examples are: the formal validity of the contract (arts. 18–19), transfer of property in so far as only the relations between the parties are involved (*e. g.* the passage of risk). Unless such special conflict rules have a mandatory character there appears to be no objection against interpreting the choice-of-law clause as a reference to such substantive rules.

Differences of wording and the various circumstances under which choice-of-law clauses are being used may indicate that the clauses are not always meant to function in the same way:

A contract formula may contain the clause "This Contract shall be

---

[2] Report, *infra* p. 265 s.

governed by English Law". It may be presumed that the draftsman meant that contract to be interpreted in the light of English law and that should be obvious to the parties who use this formula.

In other cases the choice-of-law clause in a contract formula is clearly not meant to give the draftsman any guidance whatsoever.

A charter party formula contains the clause: "This Contract shall be governed by the laws of the Flag of the vessel carrying the goods..." It would be very unpractical if internationally applied shipping contract formulas would have to be interpreted differently depending upon the nationality of the ship. It may therefore be argued that the law of the flag should not be applied so as to interfere with the internationally accepted meaning of the contract. (A similar line of reasoning is found in a decision by the German Supreme Court. The interpretation of a typical Anglo-American contract clause followed Anglo-American law even though the contract was governed by German law[3].)

The choice-of-law clause should, however, be understood as a reference to rules of interpretation which do not deal with the determination of the meaning of the text of the contract (*e. g.* the Anglo-American "parol evidence rule").

The effect of the chosen law. – It is probably correct that the parties to a general choice-of-law agreement normally intend the chosen law to supersede all rules in the otherwise applicable law – although this intention may be due to ignorance on the part of one of the parties or both. There may, however, be cases where a general choice-of-law clause should be denied superseding effect in relation to an otherwise applicable mandatory law which protects one of the parties.

It seems unrealistic to assume that the parties intended the mandatory rules of the chosen law to invalidate express stipulations in their contract. This effect of the choice-of-law clause can be conceived as a consequence of the law regarding choice-of-law clauses rather than a realization of the intentions of the parties.

Clauses which split the contract[4] are not infrequent in maritime contracts where, for example, disputes concerning the loading and unloading of the ship are referred to be decided according to "the laws and customs of the port". As the adjudication of such questions does not involve the application of mandatory rules the problem whether such clauses have "a choice-of-law effect" or merely an "incorporating effect" has not arisen.

---

[3] RG May 22, 1897, RGZ 39, p. 65.
[4] Report, *infra* p. 265 s.

Clauses which refer special types of disputes to be decided according to a certain law should probably not influence the choice of law respecting other parts of the contractual relationship[5].

Clauses referring to special statutes are usually understood as "merely incorporating" the statute into the contract. Such incorporating clauses are not usually given superseding effect in relation to otherwise applicable mandatory rules.

In case of inconsistency between the incorporated statute and other provisions in the contract the problem is treated as a matter of contractual interpretation and the statute is not – simply because it has the force of law – given an absolutely overriding effect in relation to the rest of the contract.

References to mandatory bill of lading statutes on the other hand usually expressly state that "if any term of this Bill of Lading be repugnant to any extent to the statute by this clause incorporated, such term shall be void to that extent but no further ..."

These so-called paramount clauses are frequently by the courts given the effect that the bill-of-lading statute to which the clause refers is applied instead of the otherwise applicable mandatory bill-of-lading statute. To that extent the clause appears to have a superseding effect.

IV.

The most frequently used arguments in favour of party autonomy in the conflict of laws are:

(a) Party autonomy enables parties to an international contract to remove the uncertainty as to what law governs the contract.

(b) The parties to international contracts have a special need for freedom of contracting. (The parties may, for instance, prefer to submit the contract to a "neutral" law with which they both are acquainted, or in which they have confidence, rather than relying on a law of which one of the parties has no knowledge.)

It is obvious that argument (a) refers to contracts which because of their international character give rise to doubt as to the governing law, while argument (b) refers to a much broader conception of the term international contracts.

The most important reasons for limiting party autonomy are:

1) The enforcement of the mandatory regulations of contracts.

2) Protection of the parties against harmful consequences of the choice-of-law clause which the party had not foreseen and could not reasonably be expected to foresee at the time of contracting.

---

[5] *Cf.* BGH April 14, 1953, BGHZ 9, p. 221 = NJW 1953, p. 1140.

14 *

Argument 1) applies only to choice-of-law clauses which have a superseding effect in relation to mandatory law – typically choice-of-law clauses which have effect as connecting factors. Argument 2) applies to all types of choice-of-law clauses.

The limits of party autonomy may be drawn on the basis of a weighing of these conflicting considerations. The following remarks are concerned only with the limitation of party autonomy which should serve the proper enforcement of mandatory regulations.

Certain distinctions should be made among the various groups of mandatory rules.

First of all there is an important group of mandatory rules which exclusively or mainly deal with international contractual relations. In the field of shipping, mandatory rules provide for protection of seamen, passengers, holders of bills of lading. International transportation of goods by road as well as international air transport have been made subject to mandatory regulation.

Several international conventions regulate these contracts in a mandatory way. The mandatory rules, therefore, serve not only the protection of certain "weak" parties to these contracts but also international uniformity.

In these fields the legislators could not without contradicting themselves let the parties supersede the mandatory rules by means of choice-of-law clauses.

The legislation containing mandatory regulation which is meant to apply to international contracts usually contains special conflict rules delimiting the field of application of the mandatory rules. It seems desirable that such mandatory conflict rules should be respected – within reasonable limits – by other countries. Art. 7 of the Draft Convention might be phrased so as to serve this purpose.

The need for regulation of international commercial activities, especially those of the multinational corporations, has been emphasized from many quarters recently. International agreements "in restraint of trade", the international movements of currency are subject to mandatory legislation, and further development of such legislation is likely. The arguments in favour of party autonomy in the conflict of laws can hardly outweigh the interests in mandatory regulation of such activities.

Another group of mandatory rules are those which are not directed especially towards international contracts. In relation to such rules international contracts may be considered of marginal interest in the sense that from the point of view of the legislator the mandatory regulation of such contracts is far from being of such great importance as the regulation of purely internal contracts.

In relation to such rules the choice of law by the parties should be respected within certain limits. The Draft Convention might be more specific in this regard.

Art. 1 delimits the scope of the Convention. Some of these provisions are suitable as conditions for the superseding effect of the choice-of-law clause. Especially the condition that the obligation must be of an international character. "International" ought to be defined. It is of importance that the parties should not be able at their discretion to give the contract an international character, *e. g.* by inserting a forum clause or by choosing a place of contracting on the other side of the national border.

Matters of status and capacity ought not to depend on the parties' choice of law whereas matters of matrimonial property, testaments or gifts are suitable for choice-of-law clauses if these matters have an international character. Also some commercial papers forum agreements and insurance contracts are clearly suitable for choice-of-law clauses.

As a safety valve to prevent misuse of choice-of-law clauses the requirement known in English law that the choice of law shall be *bona fide* would be useful.

COMMENT ON THE PROVISIONS ON EXTRA-CONTRACTUAL LIABILITY OF THE DRAFT CONVENTION

By

G. O. ZACHARIAS SUNDSTRÖM

Turku[1]

Introduction

The development of Finnish law in the field of private international law has by and large followed trends identifiable in other Nordic countries. However, Finnish court practice is relatively sparse which makes it difficult to state authoritatively in all instances what the law is. Referring to Nordic trends, it is necessary to also mention the differences that exist between, on the one hand, Danish/Norwegian law and on the other Finnish/Swedish law.

In particular in the field of private international law this dualism in the Nordic law is easily identified. To take but one example Denmark and Norway follow the domicile principle while Finland and Sweden adhere to the nationality principle in matters of personal status. Both principles are furthermore uniquely combined in internordic convention law. Thus when looking at the Finnish private international law relating to torts and delicts it is natural to do so in the context of the general Nordic development in the field but in instances of difference it will be safer to let oneself be guided by Swedish than by Danish/Norwegian practice.

---

[1] The author has commented fully on an earlier version of the English text of the EEC Convention. See Report to the Commission of the EC, April 1973, on harmonization of Law in the EC in respect of Company Law, Taxation, Patents and Private International Law in Comparison with Scandinavian – in Particular Danish and Norwegian – Law and Practice.

The Finnish Doctrine

That the applicable law in cases of extra-contractual liability is determined by the use of the *lex loci delicti commissi* is without doubt the principal rule in Finland. Difficulties arise when it is impossible to apply the *lex loci delicti commissi,* or when its application would lead to manifestly absurd results. The Community Draft Convention specifically deals with a number of instances in which a Finnish court may find it difficult to apply a strict *lex loci delicti commissi* rule. It is for this reason both difficult and challenging to attempt to relate the Convention's solutions in these areas to Finnish doctrine.

The EEC Convention Related to Finnish Law

Art. 10 of the Convention prescribes that the *lex loci delicti commissi* shall be determinative in the selection of applicable law for non-contractual obligations. As explained above this is also the basic Finnish position in regard to extra-contractual liability. Unlike Finnish law, however, the Convention contains specific secondary rules, as well as saving provisions for the event that the *lex loci delicti commissi* should lead to the application of a law with which the parties have no other connection than that the accident or event happened to take place within this particular jurisdiction. In such an event the Convention prescribes that the law common to the parties should apply. Leaving aside the finer points inherent in this provision of the Convention[2] since we have no corresponding refinements in Finnish law, one must now observe that in so far as Finnish law has at all moved away from the rigidity of the *lex loci delicti commissi* it has been on the basis of the individualising principle (or method) or as it is better known in the Anglo-American world "the proper law" method or "the center of gravity" method. Whereas in Sweden this principle has found expression in the *Saivo-Windward Island* case and also is suggested as a possibility by *Karlgren,* corresponding concrete expressions in favour of the use of the individualising method have come to light in Finland only in legal writings[3]. An additional difficulty is the almost French style of the Finnish judicial decision. Whereas in some instances one therefore could perhaps suspect that a method close to the

---

[2] For details see Report, *infra* p. 283 ss.

[3] See *Sundström,* Om normkollision vid fartygs sammanstötning (1965); *id.,* Foreign Ships and Foreign Waters (1971) = Ark. f. Sjørett 11 (1971/72) p. 1–243.

individualising method has been used by a court, it will not generally be possible to state so with definiteness.

Thus we have available to us only the analogy, often used, of relating Finnish legal development to corresponding Swedish development, and to take whatever support one in this case may be able to find for a less rigid *lex loci delicti commissi* application in Finland from the fact that the principle in Sweden has been modified in actual court practice.

I am thus suggesting that the type of intermediate solution as it has been adapted in the Community Draft Convention, could well have a strong appeal also in Finland. Obviously one has not been ready to abandon the old *lex loci delicti commissi* in favour of an unrestrained individualising method, at least not yet, but just as clearly it has been felt that some flexibility must be introduced in this otherwise rigid formula.

The only difficulty with art. 10 would appear to be in the final section where it is suggested that a different legal regime may in the case of several victims have to be applied to each one of them. This would appear to be a difficulty in so far as one generally has preferred to create rules which would result in a unitary statute if at all possible. Nor is this it would seem a matter only for Finnish private international law but applies to Nordic law and practice in the field in general. In this as in other matters not yet definitely settled in Nordic private international law it is from Finnish points of view of the greatest significance that the Nordic countries follow like principles. Already the existence of an inter-Nordic private international convention based law dictates such a course, but as indicated above other considerations of Nordic unity will tend to reinforce this to the point of a need. It is for this reason extremely difficult to take a position on the applicability of any rule as specific as the one now in question, beyond noting that at present nothing in Finnish law would seem to dictate against the adoption of such a rule[4].

In respect of art. 11 and the enumeration made there, I shall not comment on all aspects in as much as Finnish law contains very little on the subject. I shall only touch upon a specific difficulty, which again is not peculiar to Finland but of general scope.

It would appear that the factors important to the determination of the extent of damages must not be rigidly tied to the *lex loci* as art. 11 no. 4 of the Convention envisages. It may, for instance, be necessary to take into account the factual price level in the country from which the injured person comes. It may be necessary to take account of fiscal

---

[4] See further the comments under the heading "Additional remarks ..." below.

regimes, or to pay attention to currency considerations and to the level of the bank rates, etc., all of which may influence the actual level of damages that would seem reasonable to the injured party. A factual equivalence to the level of compensation a correspondingly injured person would benefit from in the forum country should be attempted, not an equivalence in absolute amount of money. Similarly, it would seem that under item 5, which concerns the extent to which the victim's heirs may have a right to damages, should not be tied to the *lex loci delicti* as a normal rule, but should be left to separate consideration. Here again too many factors may be influential and so cause factual differences on account of variances in legal, social and economic levels. In short, in some of its aspects art. 11 of the Convention may cause difficulties which Finnish law in its present state of development does not necessarily now experience. More importantly, it would seem that in the name of predictability art. 11 of the Convention will impart to the private international law precisely that rigidity which one has taken care to avoid in the principal choice-of-law rule of art. 10[5].

Finally, art. 12 of the Community Convention expresses a principle which in practice has been applied by all the Scandinavian courts. In later doctrine this problem of the applicability of local rules has become known as the *datum* problem. In Scandinavian doctrine it has now been recognised that *datum* questions must be treated differently from the other choice-of-law complexities, and that it would lead to unacceptable results to treat *data* by any other legal regime than that of the local law[6].

Additional Remarks Relating to Product Liability

If we leave aside other specialised areas of extra-contractual liability, a few words should be said on the subject of product liability although the Convention leaves this area aside. As a choice-of-law problem it will appear most often within the export/import trade and therefore assumes an ever increasing importance in international commerce. The problem is complex, and I shall in this context be able only to indicate briefly the direction in which the thinking appears to have moved. Danish accession to the European Market is accompanied by

---

[5] Predictability is furthered also through the fact that the Convention is intended to be applicable also in relation to third countries, *i. e.*, to replace the current rules on private international law in the Member States.

[6] See in particular *Sundström*, Three Discussions on the Conflict of Laws (1970), and *id.*, Foreign Ships (*supra* note 3).

changes in industrial patterns and in, above all, the pattern of sub-
suppliers and marketing generally which may move away from the
relatively uniform Nordic legal pattern, in which the differences in
legal responsibility have remained fairly small and where legal action
across the borders poses fairly minor problems in terms of language
and technicalities. Thus the change of orientation towards European
markets will put greater pressure on the need for developing choice-of-
law doctrines in this area.

The problem is akin to the classic one regarding the consequence
of an act occurring in a different country from the act itself. In other
words, should it always be the law of the producing country that determines product liability, or should the consumer have the protection
that his own law affords him when he buys products in his own
country? And what about products exported to third countries and
when used there causing damage in some manner or another?

Most considerations will be satisfied by using the law of the country
of sale. This will exclude the law of a country where the goods might
be found for reasons other than sale.

Hence the foreseeability requirement of the manufacturer is at least
to some extent satisfied in that he must normally be able to foresee
where his products shall be for sale. The problem has been observed
internationally and has been made the object of deliberations at the
Hague Conference, the preliminary results of which are in line with
the above conclusions.

Apart from the choice-of-law aspects, actionability in the country
where the damage occurred is an important part of the problem dealt
with in the Community Convention on Jurisdiction (§ 5: 3) where the
possibility of suing the manufacturer in the country where the tortious
consequence occurred has been introduced. As this is a possibility not
normally open to a plaintiff unless the defendant agrees to be sued
or has property or business in the country, much of the problem relating
to product liability will automatically also be taken care of through
this relatively simple device. However, it is only within a geographically relatively well-defined community that one can contemplate such
a solution. One must also take note of the current attempts to stream-
line product safety standards, such as electrical, pharmaceutical, etc.,
safety regulations throughout the Community. Application on a global
scale of the principle that one will be able to sue wherever the tortious
consequence took place may lead to unacceptable results. For example,
the product might have caused damage or injury in some remote corner
of the globe in which the manufacturer had not intended sale of the
product and where possibly local conditions may have been unsuitable
for its use.

It should be clear already from the above summary remarks on the subject that the formulation of choice-of-law rules in the areas of product liability will have grave implications not only for the trade pattern in inter-Scandinavian trade, but also for legal orientation generally in this area of the law. It is for this reason perhaps desirable to consider once more inclusion of suitable rules also in the present Convention.

COMMISSION DES COMMUNAUTÉS EUROPÉENNES

Avant-projet de Convention sur la loi applicable
aux obligations contractuelles et non contractuelles [1]

Préambule

Les Hautes parties contractantes [au traité instituant la Communauté Economique Européenne].

Soucieuses de poursuivre, dans le domaine du droit international privé, l'œuvre d'unification juridique entreprise au sein de la Communauté,

désirant établir des règles uniformes concernant la loi applicable aux obligations contractuelles et non contractuelles,

ont décidé de conclure la présente Convention et ont désigné à cet effet comme plénipotentiaires:

. . .

Titre Premier

Champ d'application

Article premier

Les règles de droit international privé de la présente convention sont applicables, dans les situations ayant un caractère international, aux obligations contractuelles et non contractuelles.

Elles ne s'appliquent pas:

a) en matière d'état et de capacité des personnes physiques, sous

---

[1] Commission des Communautés Européennes Document no. XIV/398/72 Rev.: 1. – Publié aussi dans: Am. J. Comp. L. 21 (1973) p. 587–593 (anglais); Nord. T. Int. R. 42 (1972) p. 220–227 (anglais); RabelsZ 38 (1974) p. 211–219 (allemand); Rev. crit. 62 (1973) p. 209–216 (français); Riv. Dir. Int. Priv. Proc. 9 (1973) p. 189–197 (français); W.P.N.R. 1973, p. 227–230; 1974, p. 417–420 (néerlandais).

réserve de l'article 20, ni en matière de régimes matrimoniaux, de successions, de testaments et de donations,

b) aux effets de commerce, tels que lettre de change, chèque et billet à ordre,

c) aux conventions d'arbitrage et d'élection de for,

d) [aux contrats d'assurance],

e) à la constitution, au fonctionnement interne et à la dissolution des sociétés et personnes morales,

f) en matière de dommage dans le domaine nucléaire*.

Titre Second

Règles uniformes

Article 2

Le contrat est régi par la loi choisie par les parties.

Les conditions relatives à la validité du consentement des parties quant à la loi applicable sont déterminées par cette loi.

[Toutefois, dans les relations de travail, le choix des parties ne peut en aucun cas porter atteinte aux dispositions impératives protectrices du travailleur, en vigueur dans le pays où il accomplit habituellement son travail.]

Article 3

Le choix des parties quant à la loi applicable peut intervenir aussi bien au moment de la conclusion du contrat qu'à une date ultérieure. Ce choix peut être modifié à tout moment par un accord entre les parties. Toute modification quant à la détermination de la loi applicable, intervenue postérieurement à la conclusion du contrat, ne porte pas atteinte aux droits des tiers.

Article 4

A défaut de choix explicite ou implicite, le contrat est régi par la loi du pays avec lequel il présente les liens les plus étroits.

Ce pays est:

a) celui où la partie qui doit fournir la prestation caractéristique a sa résidence habituelle, au moment de la conclusion du contrat;

b) celui où cette partie a son établissement principal au moment de la conclusion du contrat, si la prestation caractéristique doit être fournie en exécution d'un contrat conclu dans l'exercice d'une activité professionnelle;

---

* La question de la loi applicable aux ententes n'a pas été tranchée.

c) celui où est situé l'établissement secondaire de cette partie, s'il résulte du contrat que la prestation caractéristique sera fournie par cet établissement.

L'application de l'alinéa précédent est écartée lorsque la prestation caractéristique, la résidence habituelle ou l'établissement ne peuvent être déterminés ou qu'il résulte de l'ensemble des circonstances que le contrat présente des liens plus étroits avec un autre pays.

Article 5

A défaut de choix explicite ou implicite, les contrats de travail sont régis par la loi du pays
a) où le travailleur accomplit habituellement son travail,
b) où se trouve l'établissement qui a embauché le travailleur si ce dernier n'accomplit pas habituellement son travail dans un même pays,
à moins qu'il ne résulte de l'ensemble des circonstances que le contrat de travail présente des liens plus étroits avec un autre pays.

Article 6

A défaut de choix explicite ou implicite, les contrats ayant pour objet des immeubles sont régis par la loi du lieu où l'immeuble est situé, à moins qu'il ne résulte de l'ensemble des circonstances que le contrat présente des liens plus étroits avec un autre pays.

Article 7

Lorsque le contrat présente également des liens avec un pays autre que celui dont la loi est applicable en vertu des articles 2, 4, 5, 6, 16, 17, 18 et 19, 3ème alinéa, et que la loi de cet autre pays contient des dispositions réglant impérativement la matière d'une façon qui exclut l'application de toute autre loi, il sera tenu compte de ces dispositions dans la mesure où leur nature ou leur objet particuliers pourraient justifier cette exclusion.

Article 8

Les conditions relatives à la validité du consentement des parties au contrat sont déterminées par la loi qui est applicable en vertu des articles précédents.

Article 9

Les dispositions des articles 2 à 8 ne s'appliquent pas au transfert de propriété ni aux effets réels du contrat.

Article 10

Les obligations non contractuelles dérivant d'un fait dommageable sont régies par la loi du pays où ce fait s'est produit.

Toutefois, lorsque d'une part, il n'existe pas de lien significatif entre la situation résultant du fait dommageable et le pays où s'est produit ce fait et que, d'autre part, cette situation présente une connexion prépondérante avec un autre pays, il est fait application de la loi de ce pays.

Cette connexion doit se fonder normalement sur un élément de rattachement commun à la victime et à l'auteur du dommage et, si la responsabilité d'un tiers pour l'auteur est mise en cause, commun à la victime et à ce tiers.

En cas de pluralité de victimes la loi applicable est déterminée séparément à l'égard de chacune d'entre elles.

Article 11

La loi applicable aux obligations non contractuelles aux termes de l'article 10 détermine notamment:

1. les conditions et l'étendue de la responsabilité;
2. les causes d'exonération, ainsi que toute limitation et tout partage de responsabilité;
3. l'existence et la nature des dommages susceptibles de réparation;
4. les modalités et l'étendue de la réparation;
5. la mesure dans laquelle le droit de la victime à réparation peut être exercée par ses héritiers;
6. les personnes ayant droit à réparation du dommage qu'elles ont personnellement subi;
7. la responsabilité du fait d'autrui;
8. les prescriptions et les déchéances fondées sur l'expiration d'un délai, y compris le point de départ, l'interruption et la suspension des délais.

Article 12

Quelle que soit la loi applicable aux termes de l'article 10, il sera tenu compte, dans la détermination de la responsabilité, des règles de sécurité et de police en vigueur au lieu et au moment où le fait dommageable s'est produit.

Article 13

Les obligations non contractuelles dérivant d'un fait autre qu'un fait dommageable sont régies par la loi du pays où il s'est produit.

Toutefois si, en raison d'un élément de rattachement commun aux parties intéressées, il existe une connexion prépondérante avec la loi d'un autre pays, cette loi est applicable.

Article 14

Les dispositions des articles 10 à 13 ne s'appliquent pas à la responsabilité de l'Etat ou d'autres personnes morales de droit public ainsi qu'à celle de leurs organes ou agents pour les actes relevant de la puissance publique et accomplis par eux dans l'exercice de leurs fonctions.

Article 15

La loi qui régit une obligation détermine également les conditions de son exécution, les divers modes de son extinction et les conséquences de son inexécution.

En ce qui concerne les modalités d'exécution, on aura égard à la loi du pays où l'exécution a lieu.

Article 16

Les obligations entre le cédant et le cessionnaire d'une créance sont régies par la loi applicable en vertu des articles 2 à 8.

La loi qui régit la créance originaire détermine le caractère transférable de celle-ci, ainsi que les rapports entre cessionnaire et débiteur et les conditions d'opposabilité de la cession au débiteur et aux tiers.

Article 17

Le transfert d'une créance par l'effet de la loi est régi par la loi de l'institution juridique pour laquelle il a été créé.

La loi qui régit la créance originaire détermine néanmoins le caractère transférable de celle-ci ainsi que les droits et les obligations du débiteur.

Article 18

Pour être valable quant à la forme, un acte juridique doit satisfaire aux conditions établies, soit par la loi qui le régit ou le régissait au fond au moment de sa passation, soit par celle du lieu où il est intervenu. Lorsqu'un acte juridique est formé de plusieurs déclarations, la validité quant à la forme de chacune d'elles est appréciée séparément.

Les dispositions du présent article ne s'appliquent pas à la constitution, au transfert et à l'extinction des droits réels portant sur une chose.

Article 19

L'existence et la force des présomptions légales ainsi que la charge de la preuve sont régies par la loi applicable au rapport juridique. Toutefois, les conséquences à déduire de l'attitude des parties au cours du procès sont régies par la loi du for.

Les modes de preuve des actes juridiques sont déterminés, quant à leur admissibilité, par la loi du for. Toutefois, les parties peuvent également se prévaloir des modes de preuve admis par toute loi, visée à l'article 18, selon laquelle l'acte est valable quant à la forme, pour autant que ces modes de preuve ne soient pas incompatibles avec la loi du for.

La mesure dans laquelle un document écrit sous seing privé, constatant des obligations à la charge de son ou de ses signataires, fait preuve suffisante de ces obligations, ainsi que les modes de preuve admis outre ou contre le contenu de ce document sont déterminés par la loi qui régit la validité en la forme de l'acte selon l'article 18. Si ce document vaut comme instrument de preuve tant selon la loi qui régit l'acte au fond que selon celle du lieu où il a été établi, la première de ces deux lois est seule applicable.

Article 20

Aucune personne physique ne peut invoquer son incapacité contre celui qui, dans un acte juridique, l'aura de bonne foi et sans imprudence, conformément à la loi du lieu de l'acte, considérée comme capable.

Article 21

Au sens des dispositions qui précèdent, la loi d'un pays s'entend les règles de droit en vigueur dans ce pays, à l'exclusion des règles de droit international privé.

Article 22

L'application de l'une des lois désignées par les dispositions qui précèdent ne peut être écartée que si elle est manifestement incompatible avec l'ordre public.

Article 23

Aux fins de l'interprétation et de l'application des règles uniformes qui précèdent, il sera tenu compte de leur caractère international et de l'opportunité de parvenir à l'uniformité dans la façon dont elles sont interprétées et appliquées.

Titre Troisième

Dispositions finales

Article 24

L'application des articles 1 à 23 de la présente Convention est indépendante de toute condition de réciprocité. La Convention s'applique même si la loi applicable n'est pas celle d'un Etat contractant.

Article 25

La présente Convention ne préjuge pas de l'application des dispositions de droit international privé relatives à des matières spéciales et contenues dans des actes normatifs émanant des institutions des Communautés européennes ainsi que dans le droit national harmonisé en exécution de ces actes.

La présente Convention ne déroge pas aux dispositions de droit international privé contenues dans les conventions auxquelles les Etats contractants sont ou seront parties dans le cadre des traités instituant les Communautés européennes.

Article 26

Si après la date d'entrée en vigueur de la présente Convention à son égard, un Etat contractant désire, soit déroger dans une matière spéciale aux dispositions du titre précédent, soit leur apporter un complément, il communique son intention aux autres Etats signataires par l'intermédiaire du Secrétaire Général.

Dans un délai de six mois à partir de la communication faite au Secrétaire Général, tout Etat peut demander à celui-ci d'organiser des consultations entre Etats signataires en vue d'arriver à un accord.

Si, dans ce délai, aucun Etat n'a demandé la consultation ou si, dans les deux ans qui suivent la communication faite au Secrétaire Général, aucun accord n'est intervenu à la suite des consultations, l'Etat peut modifier sa législation dans le sens qu'il avait indiqué. La mesure prise par cet Etat est portée à la connaissance des autres Etats signataires.

Article 27

La présente Convention ne porte pas atteinte à l'application dans un Etat contractant des conventions bilatérales ou multilatérales entrées antérieurement en vigueur à son égard.

Article 28

Si après la date d'entrée en vigueur de la présente Convention à son égard, un Etat contractant désire devenir partie à une convention multilatérale dont l'objet principal ou l'un des objets principaux est un règlement de droit international privé dans l'une des matières régies par la présente Convention ou dénoncer une telle convention, il est fait application de la procédure prévue à l'article 26. Toutefois le délai de deux ans, prévu au paragraphe 3 de l'article 26, est ramené à un an.

Article 29

Lorsqu'un Etat contractant considère que l'unification réalisée par la présente Convention est compromise par la conclusion d'accords non prévus à l'article précédent, cet Etat peut demander au Secrétaire Général du Conseil des Communautés européennes d'organiser une consultation entre les Etats signataires de la présente Convention.

Article 30

Chaque Etat contractant, après consultation des autres Etats signataires par l'intermédiaire du Secrétaire Général du Conseil des Communautés européennes, peut demander la révision de la présente Convention. Dans ce cas, une conférence de révision est convoquée par le Président du Conseil des Communautés européennes.

Article 31

La présente Convention s'applique au territoire européen des Etats contractants, aux départements français d'outre-mer ainsi qu'aux territoires français d'outre-mer.

Le Royaume des Pays-Bas peut déclarer au moment de la signature ou de la ratification de la présente Convention ou à tout moment ultérieur, par voie de notification au Secrétaire Général du Conseil des Communautés européennes, que la présente Convention sera applicable au Surinam et aux Antilles néerlandaises.

Article 32

La présente Convention sera ratifiée par les Etats signataires. Les instruments de ratification seront déposés auprès du Secrétaire Général du Conseil des Communautés européennes.

15 *

Article 33

La présente Convention entrera en vigueur le premier jour du troisième mois suivant le dépôt du cinquième instrument de ratification. La Convention entrera en vigueur pour chaque Etat signataire ratifiant postérieurement, le premier jour du troisième mois suivant le dépôt de son instrument de ratification.

Article 34

Le Secrétaire Général du Conseil des Communautés européennes notifiera aux Etats signataires:
a) le dépôt de tout instrument de ratification;
b) la date d'entrée en vigueur de la présente Convention;
c) les communications faites en application des articles 26, 28, 29, 30 et 31.

Article 35

La présente Convention est conclue pour une durée illimitée.

Article 36

La présente Convention, rédigée en un exemplaire unique en langue allemande, en langue française, en langue italienne, en langue néerlandaise, en langue ... et en langue ... ces textes faisant également foi, sera déposée dans les archives du Secrétariat du Conseil des Communautés européennes. Le Secrétaire Général en remettra une copie certifiée conforme à chacun des Gouvernements des Etats signataires.

Annexe

Article 2, alinéa 4

Première variante

[La portée du silence d'une partie sur une proposition de la loi applicable, faite par l'autre partie avant la formation du contrat ou en connexion avec elle, est appréciée selon la loi de la résidence habituelle de cette partie. Toutefois, nonobstant les dispositions de cette loi, l'accord sur le choix de la loi applicable pourra être déduit du silence d'une des parties si cette interprétation résulte des habitudes précédemment établies entre les parties ou des usages du commerce international dont les parties ont ou devraient avoir connaissance en raison de leur profession.]

Deuxième variante

[L'accord sur le choix de la loi applicable ne peut être déduit du silence d'une des parties que si cette interprétation résulte des habitudes précédemment établies entre les parties ou des usages pratiqués dans le commerce international. Toutefois, si le contrat est déjà formé, la loi qui le régit déterminera si le silence comporte ou non choix de la loi applicable.]

Article 8, alinéa 2

Première variante

[La portée du silence d'une partie quant à la formation du contrat est appréciée selon la loi de la résidence habituelle de cette partie. Toutefois, nonobstant les dispositions de cette loi, le consentement au contrat pourra être déduit du silence d'une des parties si cette interprétation résulte des habitudes précédemment établies entre les parties ou des usages du commerce international dont les parties ont ou devraient avoir connaissance en raison de leur profession.]

Deuxième variante

[La formation du contrat ne peut être déduite du silence d'une des parties que si cette interprétation résulte des habitudes précédemment établies entre les parties ou des usages pratiqués dans le commerce international.]

Declaration Commune

Au moment de procéder à la signature de la présente Convention, les Gouvernements ...

– soucieux d'éviter dans toute la mesure du possible la dispersion des règles de conflit de lois entre de multiples instruments et les divergences entre ces règles,

– souhaient que les Institutions des Communautés européennes, dans l'exercice de leurs compétences sur la base des Traités qui les ont instituées, s'efforcent, lorsqu'il y a lieu, d'adopter des règles de conflit qui, autant que possible, soient en harmonie avec celles de la présente Convention,

– souhaitent que ces Institutions, pour la préparation des actes communautaires comportant des règles de conflit de lois, s'assurent de l'avis d'experts gouvernementaux de droit international privé et recherchent tous moyens propres à donner sa pleine efficacité au concours de ces experts.

COMMISSION OF THE EUROPEAN COMMUNITIES

Preliminary Draft Convention on the Law Applicable to Contractual and Non-Contractual Obligations [1]

Preamble

The High Contracting Parties (to the Treaty establishing the European Economic Community),

Anxious to pursue, in the field of private international law, the work on the unification of laws undertaken within the Community;

Desiring to establish uniform rules concerning the law applicable to contractual and non-contractual obligations;

Have decided to conclude this Convention and to this end have designated as their plenipotentiaries:

. . .

Title One

Scope of the Convention

Article 1

The rules of private international law laid down in this Convention shall apply, in situations of an international character, to contractual and non-contractual obligations.

They shall not apply:

(a) to questions involving the status or capacity of natural persons, without prejudice however to Article 20; nor to questions involving the application of rules governing rights in property between husband and wife, wills, testate or intestate succession or gifts;

---

[1] Commission of the European Communities Document No. XIV/398/72 Rev.: 1. – Also published in: Am. J. Comp. L. 21 (1973) p. 587–593 (English); Nord. T. Int. R. 42 (1972) p. 220–227 (English); RabelsZ 38 (1974) p. 211–219 (German); Rev. crit. 62 (1973) p. 209–216 (French); Riv. Dir. Int. Priv. Proc. 9 (1973) p. 189–197 (French); W.P.N.R. 1973, p. 227–230; 1974, p. 417–420 (in Dutch).

(b) to negotiable instruments, such as bills of exchange, cheques and promissory notes;

(c) to arbitration agreements and agreements on the choice of court;

(d) (to insurance contracts);

(e) to the formation, internal organisation or dissolution of companies or other legal persons or associations of natural or legal persons;

(f) to questions relating to damage or injury in the nuclear field*.

Title Two

Uniform Rules

Article 2

A contract shall be governed by the law chosen by the parties.

Conditions governing the validity of the consent of the parties as to the applicable law shall be determined according to that law.

(However, in relations between employer and employee, the choice of law made by the parties shall in no case prejudice the operation of those compulsory rules for the protection of the employee which are in force in the country in which he habitually carries out his work.)

Article 3

The choice of the applicable law may be made by the parties either at the time of conclusion of the contract or at a later date. The choice may be changed at any time by agreement between the parties. Any change in the choice of the applicable law which is made after the conclusion of the contract shall be without prejudice to the rights of third parties.

Article 4

In the absence of an express or implied choice of law, the contract shall be governed by the law of the country with which it is most closely connected.

This country shall be:

(a) the country in which the party who is to carry out the obligation which is characteristic of the contract has his habitual residence at the time of conclusion of the contract;

(b) the country in which that party has his principal establishment at the time of conclusion of the contract, if the characteristic obligation

---

* The question of the law applicable to agreements which restrict competition has not been examined.

is to be carried out in performance of a contract concluded in the course of a business activity;

(c) the country in which that party's subsidiary establishment is situated, if it follows from the terms of the contract that the characteristic obligation is to be carried out by that establishment.

The preceding paragraph shall not apply if either the characteristic obligation, the habitual residence or the establishment cannot be determined or if in all the circumstances it is clear that the contract is more closely connected with another country.

Article 5

In the absence of an express or implied choice of law, contracts of employment shall be governed by the law of the country

(a) in which the employee habitually carries out his work;

(b) in which the establishment which engaged the employee is situated, if the employee does not habitually carry out his work in any one country;

unless in all the circumstances it is clear that the contract of employment is more closely connected with another country.

Article 6

In the absence of an express or implied choice of law, contracts whose subject matter is immovable property shall, unless in all the circumstances it is clear that the contract is more closely connected with another country, be governed by the law of the place where the immovable property is situated.

Article 7

Where the contract is also connected with a country other than the country whose law is applicable under Articles 2, 4, 5, 6, 16, 17, 18 and 19, paragraph 3, and the law of that other country contains rules which govern the matter compulsorily in such a way that they exclude the application of every other law, these rules shall be taken into account to the extent that the exclusion is justifiable by the particular character and purpose of the rules.

Article 8

Conditions governing the validity of the consent of the parties to the contract shall be determined according to the law which is applicable pursuant to the preceding Articles.

Article 9

Articles 2 to 8 shall not apply to the transfer of property or to effects *in rem* arising out of the contract.

Article 10

Non-contractual obligations arising out of an event which has resulted in damage or injury shall be governed by the law of the country in which that event occurred.

However, if, on the one hand, there is no significant link between the situation resulting from the event which has resulted in damage or injury and the country in which that event occurred and, on the other hand, the situation has a closer connection with another country, then the law of that other country shall apply.

Such a connection must normally be based on a connecting factor common to the victim and the author of the damage but, if the question in issue is the liability of a third party for the acts of the author, it must normally be based on one which is common to the victim and the third party.

Where there are two or more victims, the applicable law shall be determined separately for each of them.

Article 11

Alternative A

The law applicable to non-contractual obligations under Article 10 shall determine in particular:

(1) the conditions and extent of liability;

(2) the grounds for exemption from liability, any limitation of liability and any apportionment of liability;

(3) the existence and kind of damage or injury for which compensation may be made;

(4) the form and extent of compensation;

(5) the extent to which the victim's heirs may avail themselves of his right to compensation;

(6) the persons who are entitled to compensation for damage or injury which they have personally suffered;

(7) liability for the acts of others;

(8) whether a right is extinguished, or an action is barred, by lapse of time, as well as the date from which time is to run and any interruption or suspension of the running of time.

Alternative B **

The law applicable to non-contractual obligations under Article 10 shall determine in particular:

(1) the basis and extent of liability;

(2) the grounds for exemption from liability, any limitation of liability, and any division of liability;

(3) the existence and kinds of injury or damage which may have to be compensated;

(4) the kinds and extent of damages;

(5) the extent to which the victim's heirs may avail themselves of his right to compensation;

(6) the persons who have suffered damage and who may claim damages in their own right;

(7) liability for the acts of others;

(8) rules of prescription or limitation, including rules relating to the commencement of a period of prescription or limitation and the interruption and suspension of this period.

Article 12

Irrespective of which law is applicable under Article 10, in the determination of liability account shall be taken of such rules issued on the grounds of security or in the public interest as were in force at the place and time of occurrence of the event which resulted in damage or injury.

Article 13

Non-contractual obligations arising from an event which does not result in damage or injury shall be governed by the law of the country in which that event occurs. However, if, by reason of a connecting factor common to the interested parties, there is a closer connection with the law of another country, that law shall apply.

Article 14

The provisions of Articles 10 to 13 shall not apply to the liability of the State or of other legal persons governed by public law or to the liability of their organs or agents for acts of public authority performed by the organs or agents in the exercise of their official functions.

** Subparagraphs 1 to 4, 6 and 8 of this Article are in French identical with the corresponding subparagraphs of Article 8 of the Hague Convention on the Law applicable to Traffic Accidents. Alternative B reproduces English version in the Hague Convention.

Article 15

The law governing an obligation shall also determine the conditions of its performance, the various ways in which it may be extinguished and the consequences of its non-performance.

As regards the manner of performance, the law of the country in which performance takes place must be taken into account.

Article 16

Obligations between the assignor and the assignee of a claim shall be governed by the law applicable under Articles 2 to 8.

The law governing the original claim shall determine its assignability and the relationship between the assignee and the debtor, as well as the conditions under which the assignment may be invoked against the debtor and third parties.

Article 17

The assignment of a claim by operation of law shall be governed by the law to which the body of rules appertains for which that form of assignment was created.

The law governing the original claim shall nevertheless determine its assignability, as well as the rights and obligations of the debtor.

Article 18

An act having effects in law shall be formally valid if it is done in accordance with the conditions prescribed either by the law which governs the material validity of the act or which governed its material validity at the time when it was done, or by the law of the place where it was done. The formal validity of the declarations in an act consisting of several declarations shall be determined separately for each of them.

The preceding paragraph does not apply to the creation, assignment or extinction of rights *in rem.*

Article 19

The existence and force of presumptions of law, together with the burden of proof, shall be determined by the law which is applicable to the legal relationship. However, the consequences arising from the conduct of a party to proceedings shall be determined by the law of the forum.

The law of the forum shall determine the admissibility of the modes of evidence of acts having effects in law. However, a party may also rely on a mode of evidence which is admissible under any law referred to in Article 18 under which the act is formally valid, provided that the use of such mode of evidence is not incompatible with the law of the forum.

The law which in accordance with Article 18 governs the formal validity of an act shall determine both how far a private document which establishes obligations on the part of its signatory or signatories, but is drawn up and signed without any special formality, shall be sufficient proof of these obligations and also what modes of evidence shall be admissible to add to, or to contradict, the contents of the document. Where the document has probative value both according to the law governing the material validity of the act and according to the law of the place where it was executed, only the former of those two laws shall apply.

Article 20

No natural person may invoke his incapacity against a person who, in relation to an act having effects in law, in good faith and without acting imprudently, considered him to have capacity under the law of the place where the act was executed.

Article 21

For the purposes of the preceding provisions, the law of a country means the rules of law in force in that country, other than the rules of private international law.

Article 22

Alternative A

The application of any law indicated by the preceding provisions may be excluded only if it is manifestly incompatible with public policy.

Alternative B***

The application of any law indicated by the preceding provisions may be refused only when it is manifestly contrary to public policy ('ordre public').

*** The text of this Article in French is very similar to Article 7 of the Hague Convention on the Conflicts of Laws relating to the Form of Testamentary Dispositions and Article 10 of the Hague Convention on the Law Applicable to Traffic Accidents. Alternative B follows in the main the English version of the Hague Conventions.

Article 23

In the interpretation and application of the preceeding uniform rules, regard shall be had to their international character and to the desirability of achieving uniformity in their interpretation and application.

Title Three

Final Provisions

Article 24

The application of Articles 1 to 23 of this Convention shall be independent of any requirement of reciprocity. The Convention shall apply even if the applicable law is not that of a Contracting State.

Article 25

This Convention shall be without prejudice to the application of provisions of private international law which relate to special subject matters and are contained in normative acts adopted by institutions of the European Communities or in national laws which have been harmonised in implementation of such acts.

This Convention shall not derogate from provisions of private international law contained in conventions to which the Contracting States are or will be parties within the framework of the Treaties establishing the European Communities.

Article 26

If, after the date on which this Convention has entered into force with respect to a Contracting State, that State wishes either to derogate from the provisions of the preceding Title in a special field, or to supplement them in any way, it shall communicate its intention to the other signatory States through the intermediary of the Secretary-General.

Any State may request the Secretary-General, within six months from the date of the communication made to him to arrange consultations between signatory States so that an agreement may be reached.

If no State has requested consultations within the period or if within two years following the communication made to the Secretary-General no agreement is reached in the course of consultations, the State concerned may modify its legislation in the manner indicated. The measures taken by that State shall be brought to the knowledge of the other signatory States.

Article 27

This Convention shall be without prejudice to the application in a Contracting State of bilateral or multilateral Conventions which, with respect to that State, have already entered into force.

Article 28

If, after the date on which this Convention has entered into force with respect to a Contracting State, that State wishes to become a party to a multilateral convention, whose principal aim or one of whose principal aims is to lay down rules of private international law concerning one of the matters governed by this Convention, or if that State wishes to denounce such a convention, the procedure set out in Article 26 shall apply. However, the period of two years, referred to in the third paragraph of Article 26, shall be reduced to one year.

Article 29

If a Contracting State considers that the unification achieved by this Convention is prejudiced by the conclusion of agreements not covered by the preceding Article, that State may request the Secretary-General of the Council of the European Communities to arrange consultations between the signatory States of this Convention.

Article 30

Any Contracting State may, after consulting the other signatory States through the intermediary of the Secretary-General of the Council of the European Communities, request a revision of this Convention. In such a case, a conference of revision shall be convened by the President of the Council of the European Communities.

Article 31

This Convention shall apply to the European territories of the Contracting States, to the French overseas departments and to the French overseas territories.

The Kingdom of the Netherlands may declare at the time of signature or ratification of this Convention or at any time by notifying the Secretary-General of the Council of the European Communities that this Convention shall apply to Surinam and the Netherlands Antilles.

Article 32

This Convention shall be ratified by the signatory States. The instruments of ratification shall be deposited with the Secretary-General of the Council of the European Communities.

Article 33

This Convention shall enter into force on the first day of the third month following the deposit of the fifth instrument of ratification. This Convention shall enter into force for each signatory State ratifying at a later date on the first day of the third month following the deposit of its instrument of ratification.

Article 34

The Secretary-General of the Council of the European Communities shall notify the signatory States of:
(a) the deposit of each instrument of ratification;
(b) the date of entry into force of this Convention;
(c) communications made in pursuance of Articles 26, 28, 29, 30 and 31.

Article 35

This Convention is concluded for an unlimited period.

Article 36

This Convention, drawn up in a single original in the Dutch, French, German, and Italian, ... and ... languages, these texts being equally authentic, shall be deposited in the archives of the Secretariat of the Council of the European Communities. The Secretary-General shall supply a certified copy thereof to the Government of each signatory State.

Annex

Article 2, fourth paragraph

First variant

[The effect of silence on the part of a party regarding a proposal as to the applicable law, made by the other party before or in connection with the conclusion of the contract, shall be determined in accordance with the law of the place of habitual residence of that party. However, notwithstanding the provisions of that law, an agreement as to the choice of the applicable law may be deduced from silence on the part of a party if that interpretation follows from the previous course of dealing between the parties or from international trade usages of which the parties, by reason of their business activity, were or should have been aware.]

Second variant

[An agreement as to the choice of applicable law may be deduced from silence on the part of a party only if that interpretation follows from a previous course of dealing between the parties or from international trade usages. However, if the contract has already been concluded, the law which governs it shall determine whether silence has the effect of a choice of applicable law.]

Article 8, second paragraph

First variant

[The effect of silence on the part of a party regarding to the conclusion of a contract shall be determined in accordance with the law of the place of habitual residence of that party. However, notwithstanding the provisions of that law, consent to the contract may be deduced from silence on the part of a party if that interpretation follows from the previous course of dealing between the parties or from international trade usages of which the parties, by reason of their business activity, were or should have been aware.]

Second variant

[The conclusion of a contract may not be deduced from silence on the part of a party unless that interpretation follows from the previous course of dealing between the parties or from international trade usages.]

Joint declaration

At the time of the signature of this Convention, the Governments ...
– anxious, as far as possible, to avoid dispersion of conflict rules among several instruments and differences between these rules;
– express the wish that the Institutions of the European Communities, in the exercise of their powers under the Treaties by which they were established, will, where the need arises, endeavour to adopt conflict rules which are as far as possible consistent with those of this Convention;
– express the wish that those Institutions will, in the drawing up of Community acts containing rules on the conflict of laws, obtain the opinion of governmental experts on private international law and use all appropriate means to ensure that the contribution of those experts is made fully effective.

RAPPORT

concernant l'avant-projet de convention sur la loi
applicable aux obligations contractuelles et non-contractuelles *

établi par

Mario Giuliano, Milan

(pour les chapitres I et II et pour le commentaire des articles 2 à 17)

Paul Lagarde, Paris

(pour le commentaire des articles 18 et 19)

Th. van Sasse van Ysselt, La Haye

(pour le commentaire des articles 20 à 36)

Chapitre I: Considérations introductives

1. La proposition des gouvernements des pays du Benelux à la Commission des Communautés Européennes

Le 8 septembre 1967, le Représentant permanent de la Belgique adressait à la Commission, au nom de son Gouvernement et de ceux du Royaume des Pays-Bas et du Grand-Duché de Luxembourg, une invitation à réaliser avec les experts des Etats membres et sur la base du projet de convention belgo-luxemburgo-néerlandais, l'unification du droit international privé et la codification des règles de conflit de lois au sein de la Communauté.

---

* Commission des Communautés Européennes Documents XIV/408/72 et XIV/579/72. – Publié aussi dans: Riv. Dir. Int. Priv. Proc. 9 (1973) p. 198–260 (français); W.P.N.R. 1974, p. 420–440 (néerlandais, sans notes).
Œuvres abrégées: Batiffol/Lagarde, D. i. p.[5] I–II (1970–71); *Kegel*, IPR[3] (1971); *Morelli*, Elementi di d. i. p. italiano[10] (1971); *Rigaux*, D. i. p. (1968); *Soergel/Siebert(-Kegel)*, BGB[10] VII: Einführungsgesetz (1970).

Cette suggestion procédait du souci de supprimer les inconvénients qui résultent de la diversité des règles de conflit, notamment dans le domaine du droit des contrats. Il s'y ajoutait «un certain élément d'urgence», compte tenu des réformes susceptibles d'intervenir dans certains Etats membres et, en conséquence, du «risque de figer plus nettement les divergences existantes».

Selon M. *Th. Vogelaar,* Directeur général du marché intérieur et du rapprochement des législations, dans l'allocution d'ouverture qu'il adressa, en tant que Président, aux experts gouvernementaux réunis du 26 au 28 février 1969: «C'est à une unification complète des règles de conflit que cette proposition devrait normalement aboutir. Ainsi, dans chacun de nos six pays, à la place des règles de conflit actuelles et en dehors des cas d'application des conventions internationales liant tel ou tel Etat membre, ce seraient des règles de conflit identiques qui entreraient en vigueur tant dans les relations intéressant les Etats membres entre eux que dans les relations affectant les Etats n'appartenant pas à la Communauté. Cette solution conduirait à la création d'un corps commun des règles juridiques unifiées couvrant le territoire des Etats membres de la Communauté. Le grand avantage de cette proposition c'est, sans nul doute, que le niveau de la sécurité juridique en serait élevé, la confiance dans la stabilité des relations juridiques renforcée, les accords sur la compétence en fonction du droit applicable facilités, et la protection des droits acquis pour l'ensemble du droit privé accrue. Par rapport à l'unification du droit substantiel, l'unification des règles de conflit de lois apparaît plus facilement réalisable, surtout dans le domaine du droit patrimonial, parce que les règles de conflit ne concernent que les relations juridiques qui comportent un élément international»[1].

2. L'examen de la proposition par la Commission et ses suites

Dans l'examen de la proposition des gouvernements des pays du Benelux, la Commission arriva à la conclusion qu'au moins dans quelques domaines particuliers du droit international privé, l'harmonisation des règles de conflit serait de nature à faciliter le fonctionnement du Marché Commun.

L'allocution précitée de M. *Vogelaar* nous offre un aperçu des considérations qui ont amené la Commission à cette conclusion. On peut ainsi les résumer.

Selon la lettre et l'esprit du Traité instituant la C.E.E. l'harmonisation s'est vu reconnaître la fonction de rendre possible ou de faciliter, dans

---

[1] Doc. Comm. C.E. 4.365/XIV/69, p. 1 ss.

le domaine économique, la création des conditions juridiques semblables à celles qui caractérisent un marché intérieur. Certes, on peut diverger d'opinion quant à la délimitation précise des disparités qui produisent directement leurs effets sur le fonctionnement du Marché Commun et celles qui ne le produisent qu'indirectement. Toujours est-il qu'il existe des domaines juridiques dans lesquels les différences entre les ordres juridiques nationaux et l'absence de règles de conflit unifiées entravent certainement entre les Etats membres la circulation des personnes, des marchandises, des services et des capitaux.

D'aucuns préféreront à l'harmonisation des règles de conflit l'harmonisation ou l'unification du droit substantiel. Celle-ci est déjà intervenue comme on sait dans divers domaines. Cependant, l'harmonisation du droit substantiel n'arrive pas toujours à suivre le rythme de l'abolition des frontières économiques. Dès lors, aussi longtemps que le droit substantiel n'est pas unifié, on rencontrera toujours le problème du droit national à appliquer. Avec l'accroissement des relations de droit privé par-dessus les frontières augmente le nombre des litiges dans lesquels la question du droit à appliquer doit être résolue.

En même temps augmente le nombre des cas dans lesquels les tribunaux ont à appliquer un droit étranger. La Convention signée le 27 septembre 1968 sur la compétence judiciaire et l'exécution des décisions en matière civile et commerciale règle d'une manière uniforme la compétence internationale des tribunaux au sein de la Communauté. Elle doit permettre de faciliter et d'accélérer le déroulement de nombre de procès civils et de procédures d'exécution. D'autre part, elle permet aussi aux parties dans beaucoup de matières de conclure des conventions attributives de compétence et de choisir entre plusieurs tribunaux. Ceci peut conduire à ce que la préférence soit donnée au tribunal d'un Etat dont le droit paraît devoir offrir une meilleure issue au procès. Pour prévenir ce «forum shopping», renforcer la sécurité juridique et prévoir plus facilement le droit qui sera appliqué, il serait souhaitable que les règles de conflit soient unifiées dans les domaines d'importance économique particulière, de telle manière que le même droit trouve application quel que soit l'Etat où la décision est rendue...

En résumé, trois considérations dominantes dictent la proposition d'harmoniser les règles de conflit pour quelques types bien définis de rapports juridiques. La première est donnée par l'histoire du droit international privé: vouloir tout unifier est une entreprise trop hardie et de trop longue durée. La seconde est la nécessité de renforcer rapidement la sécurité juridique dans certains secteurs de grande importance économique. La troisième c'est le souci de prévenir une aggravation des disparités entre les règles de droit international privé des divers Etats membres[2].

C'est justement en s'inspirant de ces considérations que la Commission adressa aux Etats membres l'invitation pour une réunion d'experts afin de permettre de se faire une idée complète de l'état actuel du droit en la matière et de décider si et dans quelle mesure une harmonisation ou une unification du droit international privé au sein de la Communauté aurait dû être entreprise. L'invitation était accompagnée d'un questionnaire tendant à faciliter la discussion[3].

3. Attitude favorable des Etats-membres à la recherche de règles uniformes de conflit, détermination des priorités dans cette recherche et constitution du groupe de travail pour l'étude et l'élaboration de ces règles

La réunion à laquelle nous venons de faire allusion s'est tenue du 26 au 28 février 1969. Elle permit de faire un premier bilan de la situation quant aux perspectives et à l'intérêt éventuel d'entreprendre des travaux dans le domaine de l'unification des règles de conflit des Etats membres des Communautés Européennes[4].

Ce n'est pourtant que dans la réunion suivante, du 20 au 22 octobre 1969, que les experts gouvernementaux purent se prononcer d'une façon précise tant sur l'opportunité et le domaine de l'harmonisation à réaliser que sur la procédure et l'organisation des travaux à entreprendre.

En ce qui concerne l'opportunité, les délégations des Etats membres, à la seule exception de la délégation allemande, se déclarèrent fondamentalement d'accord sur leur utilité pour renforcer la sécurité juridique dans la Communauté. La délégation allemande de son côté tout en faisant part de quelques hésitations qui s'étaient manifestées dans les milieux scientifiques et d'affaires à ce sujet, déclara que cette divergence de vues n'était pas telle qu'elle doive dès maintenant influencer la suite des travaux.

En ce qui concerne le domaine de l'harmonisation, on reconnut que, sans préjudice de développements ultérieurs, il était opportun de se consacrer d'abord aux matières les plus liées au bon fonctionnement du Marché Commun en attribuant plus spécifiquement ce caractère: 1) à la loi applicable aux biens corporels et incorporels; 2) à la loi applicable aux obligations contractuelles et extra-contractuelles; 3) à la loi applicable à la forme des actes juridiques et à la preuve; 4) aux questions générales sur les rubriques précédentes (renvoi, qualifica-

---

[2] Doc. Comm. C.E. 4.365/XIV/69, p. 3, 4 et 9.

[3] Doc. Comm. C.E. 12.665/XIV/68.

[4] Pour le compte rendu de cette réunion v. Doc. Comm. C.E. 6.686/XIV/69.

tion, application de la loi étrangère, droits acquis, ordre public, capacité, représentation).

Quant à la base juridique des travaux, à l'unanimité les délégations ont estimé que l'harmonisation envisagée, sans se rattacher expréssément aux dispositions de l'article 220 du traité C.E.E., serait le prolongement naturel de la convention sur la compétence judiciaire et l'exécution des jugements.

Enfin, quant à la procédure à suivre, toutes les délégations ont considéré qu'il était opportun de suivre la même procédure que celle suivie lors des travaux concernant les conventions de l'article 220, déjà signées ou encore en cours d'élaboration, et de rechercher les moyens les plus appropriés pour accélerer le cours des travaux [5].

Les résultats de cette réunion furent soumis, par la Direction générale du marché intérieur et du rapprochement des législations à la Commission, lui proposant de solliciter l'accord des Etats membres pour la poursuite des travaux et la préparation d'un avant-projet de convention portant loi uniforme sur certaines matières relevant du droit international privé.

La Commision se conforma à ladite proposition. Et le Comité des Représentants permanents des Etats membres, lors de sa réunion du 15 janvier 1970, conféra expressément au Groupe le mandat de poursuivre ses travaux en matière d'harmonisation des règles de droit international privé, étant entendu que l'avant-projet ou les avant-projets à élaborer seraient consacrés en priorité aux quatre secteurs indiqués précédemment.

Faisant suite à la décision susmentionnée du Comité des Représentants permanents, le Groupe, dans sa réunion du 2 et 3 février 1970, procéda à l'élection de son Président dans la personne de M. *P. Jenard,* Directeur d'administration au Ministère des Affaires Etrangères et du Commerce Extérieur de la Belgique, ainsi que de son Vice-président dans la personne de M. le Professeur *Miccio,* Conseiller à la Cour de cassation italienne.

Quant aux rapporteurs, compte tenu de la décision déjà prise dans le courant de la réunion précédente au sujet de la répartition en quatre secteurs des matières à examiner par priorité, le Groupe adopta le principe que, afin d'accélérer les travaux, chacun des quatre secteurs aurait son rapporteur et qu'ils seraient désignés comme suit: 1) en ce qui concerne la loi applicable aux biens corporels et incorporels, par la *délégation allemande;* 2) en ce qui concerne la loi applicable aux obligations contractuelles et extra-contractuelles, par la *délégation italienne;* 3) en ce qui concerne la loi applicable à la forme des actes juridiques et à la preuve, par la *délégation française;* 4) en ce qui con-

---

[5] V. le compte rendu de la réunion dans Doc. Comm. C.E. 21.177/XIV/69.

cerne les questions générales, par la *délégation néerlandaise en accord avec les délégations de la Belgique et du Luxembourg.* Par l'effet de ces désignations, le Groupe procéda ensuite à la nomination des rapporteurs dans les personnes de M. le Professeur *K. Arndt,* Oberlandesgerichtspräsident a. D.; de M. le Professeur *M. Giuliano,* de la Faculté de Droit de Milan; de M. le Professeur *P. Lagarde,* de l'Université de Paris I; de M. *Th. van Sasse van Ysselt,* Directeur au Ministère de la Justice des Pays-Bas.

Au cours de la même réunion on aborda également d'autres problèmes. On examina notamment: la nature de la convention à élaborer, au sujet de laquelle la grande majorité des délégués se sont prononcés en faveur d'une convention à vocation universelle, non liée à la réciprocité; la méthode de travail; la participation aux travaux d'observateurs de la Conférence de droit international privé de La Haye et de la Commission Benelux pour l'unification du droit[6].

4. *Organisation, progression et premiers résultats des travaux du Groupe*

Le point de départ des travaux du Groupe remonte à l'examen et à la discussion des questionnaires établis par les rapporteurs M. *Giuliano,* M. *Lagarde* et M. *van Sasse van Ysselt* dans leurs domaines respectifs. Cette discussion eut lieu dans une réunion des rapporteurs tenus, sous la présidence de M. *Jenard,* du 1er au 4 juin 1970. Au cours de cette réunion les trois questionnaires firent l'objet d'une analyse assez large, portant non seulement sur les règles de conflit (nationales ou conventionnelles) en vigueur dans les Etats membres de la Communauté, mais aussi sur les tendances évolutives qui s'étaient déjà manifestées dans la jurisprudence et la doctrine de certains pays ou qu'il aurait été opportun de prendre en considération par rapport à certaines exigences contemporaines de la vie internationale. L'analyse orale dont on vient de parler a été intégrée, d'ailleurs, par les réponses écrites que chaque rapporteur a données, sur la base de la loi, de la jurisprudence et de la doctrine de son propre pays (dans le cas particulier de M. *van Sasse,* des trois pays du Benelux) aux questionnaires établis par ses collègues et par lui même[7].

C'est en fonction de ce travail préparatoire et du matériel ainsi acquis que chacun des rapporteurs a été à même de présenter un rap-

---

[6] V. le compte rendu de la réunion dans Doc. Comm. C.E. 3.189/XIV/70.

[7] V. les documents suivants de la Commission: 12.153/XIV/70 (questionnaire établi par M. *Giuliano* et réponses des rapporteurs); 6. 975/XIV/70 (questionnaire établi par M. *van Sasse van Ysselt* et réponses des rapporteurs); 15. 393/XIV/70 (questionnaire établi par M. *Lagarde* et réponses des rapporteurs).

port intermédiaire, accompagné d'une proposition d'articles relatifs à la matière considérée, qui avait pour but de fournir les bases de travail des réunions du Groupe. Il a été convenu que ces réunions seraient consacrées à l'examen du rapport de M. *Giuliano* sur la loi applicable aux obligations contractuelles et non contractuelles ainsi qu'aux questions faisant l'objet des rapports de M. *Lagarde* et de M. *van Sasse van Ysselt* dans la mesure où ces questions se seraient rattachées à la matière traitée par M. *Giuliano*.

Quant au rapport de M. *Arndt* sur la loi applicable aux biens corporels et incorporels, il a été convenu que ce rapport serait discuté ultérieurement, du fait que M. *Arndt* a expliqué qu'une étude comparative des principaux droits de sûretés devrait précéder son rapport et que la nécessité d'une telle étude a été en principe reconnue.

En faisant abstraction de la réunion des rapporteurs du mois de juin 1970, le déroulement des travaux a absorbé entièrement et intensément onze réunions plénières du Groupe, chaque réunion ayant la durée moyenne de 5 jours[8].

Au cours de sa réunion du mois de juin 1972, le Groupe a terminé l'élaboration de l'avant-projet de convention sur la loi applicable aux obligations contractuelles et non contractuelles et a pris la décision de soumettre le texte du projet de convention, de même que les rapports qui ont été mis au point lors d'une réunion des rapporteurs tenue le 27–28 septembre 1972, au Comité des Representants permanents en vue de leur transmission aux gouvernements des pays membres de la Communauté[9].

5. *Aperçu des sources internes et du caractère des règles en vigueur dans les Etats membres de la C.E.E. en matière de loi applicable aux obligations contractuelles et non contractuelles*

Le but essentiel de l'avant-projet de convention est d'introduire dans le droit national des Etats membres de la C.E.E. un ensemble de règles uniformes sur la loi applicable aux obligations contractuelles et non contractuelles ainsi que sur certaines questions générales de droit international privé dans la mesure où ces questions se rattachent à la matière des obligations.

Sans entrer dans les détails du droit positif, et en nous réservant d'y revenir dans le commentaire des règles uniformes, il est opportun

---

[8] La liste des experts gouvernementaux qui ont participé aux travaux du Groupe ainsi que le calendrier des réunions sont annexés au présent rapport (*infra* p. 315 ss.). Toutes les réunions ont été tenues à Bruxelles, à l'exception de la réunion du mois d'octobre 1971 qui a eu lieu à Rome.

[9] Compte rendu de la réunion du mois de juin 1972, p. 29 ss.

de donner dès maintenant un bref aperçu des sources internes et du caractère des règles de conflit qui sont actuellement en vigueur dans les pays de la Communauté dans le domaine couvert par la convention. Cet aperçu permet de se rendre compte aussi bien de l'intérêt que des difficultés de l'œuvre d'unification entreprise par le Groupe et dont le présent avant-projet n'est qu'un premier résultat.

Parmi les Etats membres de la Communauté (au moment où les travaux du Groupe ont débuté), ce n'est qu'en Italie qu'on relève la présence d'un ensemble de règles de conflit édictées par le législateur et couvrant presqu'entièrement la matière visée par la convention. Il s'agit essentiellement des articles 17, deuxième alinéa, 25, 26, 27, 28, 30 et 31 des Dispositions sur la loi en général, constituant l'introduction au Code civil de 1942, ainsi que des articles 9 et 10 du Code de la navigation de 1942 [10].

Considérablement moins étendue, au contraire, est l'incidence en droit allemand de dispositions législatives ayant trait à la matière visée par la convention. Il n'y a que les articles 7, 11, 12 et 30 de la loi d'introduction du Code civil allemand de 1896 ainsi que le décret du 7 décembre 1942 concernant le droit applicable aux dommages causés et subis par des ressortissants allemands en dehors du territoire du Reich, qui peuvent être mentionnés à ce propos [11]. Le droit international privé des obligations contractuelles et non contractuelles trouve, en effet, presqu'entièrement sa source dans le droit coutumier, développé par la jurisprudence et la doctrine allemandes.

En France et en Belgique aussi, les sources législatives en ce domaine sont très minces [12]. L'article 3 du Code Napoléon, ainsi que nous le verrons dans les commentaires des articles 6 et 9 de la présente convention, y joue indubitablement un certain rôle. En faisant abstraction de quelques interventions législatives récentes en des matières particulières, l'ensemble des règles de conflit sur la loi applicable aux obligations contractuelles et non contractuelles n'est fondé pourtant que sur des règles coutumières ou sur des règles d'origine jurisprudentielle, que la doctrine a grandement contribué à développer et à harmoniser entre elles.

Egalement dans le système de droit international privé des Pays-Bas, notamment en ce qui concerne la matière visée par les règles uniformes de la présente convention, la loi ne joue qu'un rôle tout à fait secondaire par rapport à la jurisprudence [13]. Celle-ci a formulé librement

---

[10] Pour les textes *cf.* T.M.C. Asser Instituut: Les législations de d. i. p., Conflits dès lois et conflits des juridictions (Oslo 1971) p. 121–129.

[11] Pour les textes *cf.* T.M.C. Asser Instituut (note précédente) p. 71–77.

[12] Pour les textes *cf.* T.M.C. Asser Instituut (*supra* note 10) p. 55–60 et 43–46.

[13] Pour les textes *cf.* T.M.C. Asser Instituut (*supra* note 10) p. 23 ss., 30 ss.

des règles de conflit, en s'inspirant souvent de la tradition et de la doctrine, mais en élargissant parfois ses sources d'inspiration et ses recherches d'une solution appropriée au droit comparé et aux solutions retenues en d'autres pays.

La situation, telle qu'on vient de l'exposer, n'a pas été substantiellement modifiée, ni par le projet de loi français complétant le Code civil en matière de droit international privé (de 1967), ni par le traité Benelux portant loi uniforme relative au droit international privé, signé à Bruxelles le 3 juillet 1969[14]. Sans aucun doute ces deux textes constituent un effort intéressant de codification des règles de conflit et, dans le cas des pays du Benelux, également d'uniformisation de ces règles sur le plan interétatique et le Groupe n'a pas manqué de tenir compte, au cours de ses travaux, des résultats de cet effort. Le Traité Benelux n'est cependant pas encore entré en vigueur et il ne semble pas que le projet de loi français doive aboutir dans un prochain avenir.

6. Vocation universelle des règles uniformes

Le Groupe s'est déclaré en faveur de règles uniformes qui s'appliqueraient aussi bien aux ressortissants des Etats membres et aux personnes domiciliées ou résidant à l'intérieur de la Communauté qu'aux ressortissants des Etats tiers et aux personnes qui y sont domiciliées ou qui y résident. Les dispositions de l'article 24 concrétisent cette vocation universelle de la Convention.

Il est apparu au Groupe que l'objet des travaux devrait essentiellement être de formuler des règles générales comme il en existe dans les dispositions législatives actuellement en Italie et en Allemagne, ainsi que dans le traité Benelux et dans le projet français. Dans une telle perspective, ces règles générales qui deviendraient le droit commun de chacun des Etats membres pour le règlement des conflits de lois ne porteraient pas atteinte à la réglementation détaillée de questions bien délimitées issues d'autres travaux, en particulier de ceux de la Conférence de La Haye de droit international privé. Selon le cas, la réserve de l'application de ces conventions particulières est assurée par les dispositions de l'article 27 ou de l'article 29.

7. Sur le caractère normalement général
des règles uniformes de la Convention

Dès le début de ses travaux en matière de loi applicable aux obligation contractuelles, le Groupe a été amené à se prononcer sur le caractère et la portée des règles uniformes de conflit à élaborer en ce do-

---

[14] Pour les textes *cf.* T.M.C. Asser Instituut (*supra* note 10) p. 25–29 et 60–66.

maine. Ces règles devaient-elles être des règles de caractère général, déstinées à s'appliquer indifféremment à tous les contrats ou était-il préférable de scinder la réglementation concernant les obligations contractuelles en une série de règles spécifiques pour les différentes catégories de contrats, ou encore était-il opportun de s'en tenir à une solution intermédiaire, en adoptant des règles générales et en les complétant par quelques règles spécifiques pour *certaines* catégories de contrats?

La solution initialement préconisée par le rapporteur s'inspirait de la dernière alternative. Elle prévoyait qu'à défaut de choix explicite ou implicite des parties, le contrat serait régi, sous réserve des dispositions réglant spécifiquement certaines catégories de contrats, par la loi du lieu de son exécution. Les dispositions faisant exception à la règle générale visaient les contrats suivants: la vente d'objets mobiliers corporels, la commission de bourse sur valeurs ou marchandises, la vente aux enchères, les contrats ayant pour objet des immeubles, les contrats bancaires, les contrats d'assurance, le prêt d'argent.

Lorsque le Groupe a abordé la question de savoir s'il était opportun ou non de compléter les règles générales sur la détermination de la loi applicable au contrat par quelques règles spécifiques au sujet de certaines catégories de contrats, il est apparu clairement que la question ne présentait plus l'intérêt qu'elle avait dans le cadre des propositions initiales du rapporteur. La formulation du texte de l'article 4, tel qu'il a été finalement retenu par le Groupe, notamment en raison de sa souplesse permettait en effet de donner des solutions satisfaisantes pour la plupart des contrats dont la loi applicable formait l'objet de règles spécifiques de conflit dans les propositions du rapporteur. C'est pour cela que le Groupe n'a assorti la règle de l'article 4 que de deux seules exceptions: celles des articles 5 et 6 concernant, à défaut de choix explicite ou implicite des parties, respectivement la loi applicable aux contrats de travail et la loi applicable aux contrats ayant pour objet des immeubles.

Ce caractère normalement général des règles uniformes, qui caractérise également la réglementation en matière d'obligations non contractuelles, a comporté la nécessité d'accompagner les règles de quelques exceptions et de laisser au juge une certaine marge d'appréciation quant à l'application de ces exceptions dans chaque cas d'espèce. Nous reviendrons sur cet aspect dans le commentaire de plusieurs articles qui va suivre dans le Chapitre III du présent rapport.

Chapitre II: Champ d'application des règles uniformes de la Convention

Article premier

1. Ainsi que le prévoit l'alinéa premier de l'article premier, en principe les règles uniformes de la présente convention sont applicables, dans les situations ayant un caractère international, aux obligations contractuelles et non contractuelles.

Il importe de souligner que les règles uniformes de la convention ne sont applicables aux obligations susmentionnées que «dans les situations ayant un caractère international». Cette précision a pour conséquence que restent en dehors du champ d'application des règles uniformes, les situations résultant d'un contrat ou d'un fait générateur d'obligations non contractuelles dépourvus de tout élément d'extranéité; c'est-à-dire, les situations ayant un caractère purement interne. Il s'agit d'une précision qui revient souvent dans les conventions internationales qui ont pour objet l'unification ou l'harmonisation de tel ou tel secteur du droit international privé [15] et qu'il était opportun de l'insérer également dans la présente convention, car il est évident que l'exigence, et même l'urgence, d'une unification des règles de conflit en matière de loi applicable aux obligations contractuelles et non contractuelles ne s'imposent que dans les situations caractérisées par un élément d'internationalité.

La convention ne donne pas une définition de ce qu'on doit entendre par «situations ayant un caractère international». Il s'agit, en principe, de situations qui comportent un ou plusieurs éléments d'extranéité donnant à plusieurs lois vocation de s'y appliquer. L'existence, dans chaque situation concrète, d'éléments d'extranéité susceptibles de lui conférer un caractère international est nécessairement appréciée par le juge. Ce n'est en effet que par rapport au tribunal saisi d'un litige qu'il est possible de déterminer si la situation résultant d'un contrat ou d'un fait générateur d'obligations extracontractuelles présente un caractère international ou, au contraire, un caractère purement interne. On se reportera, pour l'application de cette notion, en matière de contrats, au commentaire de l'article 2, page 260 ss., au point 4.

---

[15] V., par ex., l'article premier de la Convention sur la loi applicable aux ventes à caractère international d'objets mobiliers corporels, conclue à La Haye le 15 juin 1955.

Dans la mesure où il s'agit de contrats rentrant dans la sphère du droit privé, les règles uniformes de la convention sont applicables également aux contrats intervenus entre un Etat et une personne, physique ou morale.

2. Le principe consacré à l'alinéa premier subit pourtant les restrictions énumérées dans l'alinéa 2 de l'article premier.

Tout d'abord, le Groupe s'est trouvé unanimement d'accord pour exclure du champ d'application des règles uniformes certaines obligations en raison de leurs connexions avec des branches du droit privé autres que le droit des obligations *stricto sensu* (littera *a* de l'alinéa 2).

Il en est ainsi, sous réserve de la disposition de l'article 20 de la convention, en matière d'état et de capacité des personnes physiques.

Il en est encore ainsi pour les régimes matrimoniaux, les successions et testaments ainsi que les donations.

3. En second lieu, le Groupe a jugé opportun de soustraire au champ d'application des règles uniformes les obligations dérivant de l'émission et de la circulation d'effets de commerce (tels que lettres de change, chèques et billets à ordre) ainsi que les obligations découlant de dommages dans le domaine nucléaire (litterae *b* et *f* de l'alinéa 2).

Leur réglementation relève en effet de conventions conclues sur un plan international le plus large et dont certaines sont en cours de modification.

4. En troisième lieu, sont exclus du champ d'application des règles uniformes les accords d'élection de for et les conventions d'arbitrages (compromis et clauses compromissoires; littera *c* de l'alinéa 2).

En ce qui concerne les accords d'élection de for, d'une part, certaines délégations ont fait remarquer la difficulté qu'il y aurait à faire jouer l'autonomie de la volonté et même à établir une règle de conflit satisfaisante en ce domaine; d'autre part, certains membres du Groupe, en soulignant les effets de nature principalement procédurale de ces accords, ont insisté sur la nécessité de donner à la règle de conflit qui devrait les régir un caractère de réciprocité. Dans ces conditions, compte tenu de ce que les règles uniformes consacrées dans la présente convention sont des règles de conflit à vocation universelle, le Groupe a estimé qu'il était préférable d'exclure les accords d'élection de for du champ d'application de la convention. Cependant la discussion n'a pas manqué de mettre en évidence l'intérêt du problème et l'utilité qu'il y aurait à trouver une solution en liaison avec la Convention sur la compétence judiciaire et l'exécution des jugements, signée à Bruxelles le 27 septembre 1968.

En ce qui concerne les conventions d'arbitrage, la majorité des délégations s'est prononcée pour leur exclusion du champ d'application des règles uniformes, soit du fait que la matière est étroitement liée à la procédure arbitrale et devrait donc être traitée en même temps que cette dernière, soit en raison du développement du réseau conventionnel (international) en la matière.

5. La littera *e* de l'alinéa 2 de l'article premier exclut du champ d'application de la convention la matière relative à la constitution, au fonctionnement interne et à la dissolution des sociétés et personnes morales.

Cette exclusion n'implique aucunement une sous-évaluation de l'importance de cette matière dans la vie économique des pays membres de la Communauté. Il s'agit en effet d'une matière qui, en raison de son lien très étroit avec les activités économiques et de la place qu'elle tient dans plusieurs dispositions du traité C.E.E., semble bien présenter tous les titres pour ne pas être écartée des travaux communautaires dans le domaine uniforme du droit international privé, notamment dans le domaine des conflits de lois ayant trait aux relations économiques. Selon l'avis de plusieurs délégations, étant donné, que la mission du Groupe était celle d'élaborer des solutions uniformes pour les principales questions d'ordre économique dans le domaine des conflits de lois, cette mission aurait du s'étendre également à la matière de sociétés.

Nonobstant les considérations qui précèdent, le Groupe n'a pas cru qu'il entrait dans son mandat de proposer une réglementation de cette matière en raison des travaux actuellement en cours dans le cadre des Communautés Européennes [16].

---

[16] Trois catégories de travaux sont menés dans le cadre des Communautés Européennes en matière de droit des sociétés. Il s'agit d'abord des *directives* prévues par l'article 54, 3, g du Traité CEE: la première de ces directives est entrée en vigueur, c'est celle du 9 mars 1968 (J.O. des C.E. du 14 mars 1968); elle concerne la publicité, la validité des engagements et la nullité de la société dans les sociétés par actions et dans les sociétés à responsabilité limitée. Quatre autres directives sont actuellement proposées par la Commission au Conseil: elles concernent la constitution de la société anonyme, le maintien et les modifications de son capital (J.O. des C.E. du 24 avril 1970), les fusions (J.O. des C.E. du 14 juillet 1970), la structure et le contenu des comptes annuels (J.O. des C.E. du 28 janvier 1972), la structure de la société anonyme ainsi que les pouvoirs et obligations de leurs organes (non encore publiée). Il s'agit ensuite des *conventions* prévues par l'article 220 du Traité CEE. L'une de ces conventions concerne la reconnaissance mutuelle des sociétés et des personnes morales. Elle a été signée à Bruxelles le 29 février 1968 (le texte a été publié dans le Supplément au Bulletin des C.E. no. 2 de 1969). Le projet d'une seconde convention va être soumis au Conseil: cette convention concernera les fusions internationales. Enfin, des travaux ont été menés en vue de la création d'un statut de sociétés européennes. Ils ont abouti à la proposition d'un *règlement* portant statut des sociétés anonymes européennes, en date du 30 juin 1970 (J.O. des C.E. du 10 octobre 1970).

6. Ce n'est qu'avec beaucoup d'hésitations que le Groupe a pris la décision d'exclure du champ d'application de la Convention les contrats d'assurance figurant entre crochets à la littera *d* de l'alinéa 2 de l'article premier. Ces contrats, qui ne sont souvent qu'un complément précieux d'autres activités économiques (industrielles, commerciales, de transport, etc.), ont sans aucun doute une grande importance dans la vie des pays de la Communauté. Cette importance aurait dû amener à l'inclusion des contrats d'assurance dans le champ d'application, non pas à leur exclusion. Plusieurs dispositions générales, notamment les articles 2 à 4 et éventuellement les articles 6 et 7, semblaient par ailleurs fournir une réglementation satisfaisante pour les contrats d'assurance couvrant les risques de transports et les risques industriels et commerciaux. En ce qui concerne les autres assurances, notamment l'assurance-vie, on aurait pu envisager une règle spécifique donnant compétence à la loi du pays de la résidence habituelle de l'assuré.

Toutefois, l'attention du Groupe a été attirée également sur les travaux communautaires actuellement en cours dans le domaine du rapprochement des législations en matière d'assurances. Et toutes les délégations ont estimé qu'il était opportun d'attendre l'évolution de ces travaux avant de prendre position au sujet de la loi applicable aux contrats d'assurance. L'exclusion de ces contrats du champ d'application de la convention ne constitue donc qu'une solution d'attente.

7. Les matières indiquées dans les six paragraphes qui précèdent ne sont pas les seules matières qui ont soulevé quelques problèmes au moment de la détermination du champ d'application des règles uniformes. Aussi bien les contrats de sécurité sociale que les contrats de transport ont été examinés dans cette optique; mais on est arrivé à la conclusion qu'il n'existait pas des raisons valables pour les exclure du champ d'application de la présente convention.

Quant aux contrats de sécurité sociale, il n'a pas été jugé opportun de les exclure expressément. En effet, on a considéré qu'il pourrait s'agir soit de contrats d'ordre purement privé, auquel cas l'exclusion ne s'impose pas, soit de conventions relevant du droit administratif qui n'entreraient pas par nature dans le champ des obligations contractuelles relevant du droit privé qui sont seules prises en considération par la présente convention en tant qu'obligations contractuelles.

Quant aux contrats de transport, on a considéré que les remarquables résultats atteints jusqu'à présent dans l'œuvre d'unification internationale de la réglementation juridique des contrats ayant pour objet les transports maritimes, aériens, ferroviaires et routiers, avaient réduit certainement l'exigence de règles de conflit en ce domaine; mais ils n'avaient pas entièrement éliminé cette exigence. D'abord, l'ensemble imposant d'instruments internationaux à caractère multilatéral qui sont en vigueur à l'heure actuelle a eu principalement pour effet la création de règles *substantielles* (ou matérielles) uniformes en la matière. En second lieu, l'unification du droit matériel dans le domaine des transports n'a jamais prétendu être exhaustive; elle a été et elle est limitée uniquement à «certaines règles», concernant quelques aspects du rapport contractuel. L'unification du droit matériel en matière de transports laisse donc subsister plusieurs «lacunes». Et, s'il est vrai qu'une partie de ces lacunes sont parfois comblées par l'insertion dans les conventions internationales de quelques règles sur la loi applicable, il est vrai aussi que la portée et la valeur de la plupart de ces règles sont souvent difficiles à préciser et que par conséquent la nécessité de recourir aux règles nationales de conflit n'est pas entièrement éliminée par ces conventions.

C'est pour ces motifs que le Groupe, après un examen approfondi du problème, a décidé de ne pas exclure les contrats de transport du champ d'application de la convention. En ce qui concerne la question de savoir s'il ne conviendrait pas de formuler des règles spécifiques de conflit en matière de contrats de transport, le Groupe a estimé, d'autre part, que les solutions de caractère général qu'il avait retenu pour les contrats, notamment des articles 2, 4 et 7 des règles uniformes, étaient suffisament souples pour permettre au juge, dans chaque cas d'espèce, de faire application de la loi la plus appropriée, compte tenu des indications plus précises qui figurent à ce sujet au commentaire de l'article 4, page 275.

8. Quant aux *ententes,* le Groupe ne s'est pronocé ni sur leur inclusion dans le champ d'application, ni dans l'affirmative, sur la loi qui leur serait applicable.

Chapitre III: Les règles uniformes

Article 2 (Autonomie de la volonté des parties)

1. Principe du pouvoir des parties ou de l'autonomie de la volonté des parties

La règle énoncée dans l'alinéa premier de l'article 2, d'après laquelle le contrat est régi par la loi choisie par les parties, ne constitue que la réaffirmation d'une règle consacrée à l'heure actuelle dans le droit international privé des Etats membres de la Communauté ainsi que dans la plupart des droits des autres pays.

En droit français, la règle qui confère aux parties ce pouvoir (ou cette «autonomie de la volonté» selon l'expression courante) est fondée sur une jurisprudence remontant à l'arrêt rendu le 5 décembre 1910 par la Cour de cassation de l'affaire *American Trading Company* c. *Quebec Steamship Company, Limited*[17a]. L'avant-projet français déjà cité de 1967, ne fait que confirmer l'état du droit international privé français en la matière, lorsqu'il établit, dans le premier alinéa de l'article 2313: «Le contrat de caractère international et les obligations qui en résultent, sont soumis à la loi sous l'empire de laquelle les parties ont entendu se placer».

L'affermissement de la règle dans la jurisprudence française a été accompagné par une évolution correspondante de la doctrine. Les auteurs contemporains les plus éminents se déclarent fondamentalement en faveur du principe de l'autonomie de la volonté des parties quant à la détermination de la loi applicable au contrat ou quant à la «localisation» du contrat dans une sphère juridique déterminée, selon l'opinion d'une partie de la doctrine[17b].

Il en est de même en ce qui concerne le droit allemand, où la matière des obligations contractuelles n'a pas été réglée par le législateur lors de la rédaction définitive de la «loi d'introduction» de 1896. Le règle conférant aux parties le pouvoir de désigner la loi applicable à leur contrat est pourtant fondée sur une jurisprudence qui s'est développée et fermie au cours des dernières décennies, nonobstant l'opposition de la grande majorité de la doctrine allemande antérieure. La doctrine contemporaine, de toute façon, partage entièrement la solution retenue par la jurisprudence[18].

A la différence de ce qui est arrivé en France et en Allemagne, le principe de l'autonomie de la volonté des contractants a été, dès 1865, expressément consacré par le législateur italien dans les dispositions préliminaires du Code civil. Il trouve actuellement son fondement dans le premier alinéa de l'article 25 des dispositions préliminaires du Code civil de 1942, où l'autonomie de la volonté des parties quant au choix de la loi applicable à leur contrat est formellement admise ainsi que dans les articles 9 et 10 du Code de la navigation, où il est prévu que le pouvoir des parties quant à la désignation de la loi applicable peut s'exercer aussi dans les contrats de travail du personnel navigant et dans les contrats d'utilisation de navires, de bateaux ou d'aéronefs.

[17a] Cass. fr. 5 décembre 1910 (*American Trading Co.* v. *Quebec Steamship Co., Ltd.*), Rev. crit. 7 (1911) p. 395 = Clunet 39 (1912) p. 1156.

[17b] *Batiffol/Lagarde* II nos. 567 ss., p. 207 ss.

[18] *Kegel*, IPR p. 253 ss.; *Soergel/Siebert(-Kegel)*, Art. 7 nos. 220–226; *Raape*, IPR[5] (1961) para. 40; *Reithmann*, Internationales Vertragsrecht, Das IPR der Schuldverträge[2] (1972) p. 4 ss.

Selon l'opinion prépondérante en doctrine[19] et selon la jurisprudence constante de la Cour de cassation italienne, la loi applicable au contrat doit être déterminée, d'abord sur la base de la volonté manifestée par les parties à cet égard; ce n'est qu'à défaut d'une telle désignation, que la loi du contrat sera déterminée par les autres éléments de rattachement prévus dans les dispositions susmentionnées.

En ce qui concerne la Belgique, le Luxembourg et les Pays-Bas, la règle de l'autonomie de la volonté des contractants quant au choix de la loi applicable a été également sanctionnée par la pratique judiciaire et la doctrine contemporaine.

Dans son arrêt du 24 février 1938 dans l'affaire *S. A. Antwerpia* c. *Ville d'Anvers*[20], la Cour de cassation de Belgique, en les termes manifestement inspirés de l'arrêt français du 5 décembre 1910[20a], a affirmé pour la première fois que: «la loi applicable aux contrats, tant pour leur formation que pour leurs conditions et effets, (est) celle que les parties ont adopté». De leur côté, plusieurs auteurs belges ont contribué à l'affermissement théorique et pratique de la règle[21].

Aux Pays-Bas, c'est avec l'arrêt du 13 mai 1966 dans l'affaire *Alnati*[22] que le Hoge Raad a donné, pour ainsi dire, la dernière touche à l'évolution de la jurisprudence en la matière. En effet, les arrêts précédents de la Cour suprême ainsi que les divergences existantes en doctrine quant à la portée précise de la règle de l'autonomie de la volonté, n'auraient pas encore permis de caractériser avec suffisamment de certitude l'état du droit néerlandais en la matière[23].

De toute façon, le traité Benelux portant loi uniforme relative au droit international privé, même s'il n'a pas encore été ratifié par les Etats signataires, constitue une manifestation significative de leur présente attitude en ce domaine. Dans le premier alinéa de l'article 13 de la loi uniforme il est statué en effet que: «Les contrats sont régis par

---

[19] *Morelli* nos. 97 s., p. 154 s.

[20] Cass. belge 24 février 1938 *(S.A. Antwerpia* c. *Ville d'Anvers)*, Rev. crit. 33 (1938) p. 661.

[20a] *Cf. supra* note 17 a.

[21] *Frédéricq*, La vente en d. i. p.: Rec. des Cours 93 (1958-I) p. 8 ss., spéc. p. 30 ss.; *Rigaux* nos. 348 ss., p. 414 ss.

[22] HR 13 mai 1966 *(Alnati)*, Rev. crit. 56 (1967) p. 522.

[23] *Kosters/Dubbink*, Algemeen Deel van het nederlandse IPR (1962) p. 222 ss.; *Deelen*, Rechtkeuze in het nederlandse internationaal Contractenrecht, Een jurisprudentie-onderzoek (1965); *Struycken*, note sur l'arrêt Alnati: Rev. crit. 56 (1967) p. 523; *Kokkini-Iatridou*, Topica van IPR (1969) p. 56 ss. – Pour quelques indications de la pratique judiciaire du Luxembourg v. *Bernecker*, Internationales Privat- und Prozeßrecht im Großherzogtum Luxemburg: RabelsZ 27 (1962/63) p. 299–301; *Huss*, Chronique de jurisprudence luxembourgeoise (1960 à 1970): Clunet 98 (1971) p. 147 s.

la loi choisie par les parties, tant en ce qui concerne les dispositions impératives que les dispositions supplétives».

Enfin, il est opportun de rappeler que la règle de l'autonomie de la volonté a été retenue aussi dans la Convention sur la loi applicable aux ventes à caractère international d'objets mobiliers corporels, conclue à La Haye le 15 juin 1955, entrée en vigueur le 1er septembre 1964. L'article 2 de cette convention, qui est en vigueur entre onze pays européens dont plusieurs sont membres des Communautés Européennes[24] dispose que: «La vente est régie par la loi interne du pays désigné par les parties contractantes.»

2. Etendue du principe

On peut se demander s'il n'aurait pas été opportun de préciser, au premier alinéa de l'article 2, que le pouvoir des parties quant au choix de la loi applicable, porte non seulement sur les dispositions supplétives, mais également sur les dispositions impératives de cette loi. Une précision de ce genre, en effet, est formulée dans le premier alinéa de l'article 13 de la loi uniforme Benelux. Ainsi qu'il est dit dans l'exposé des motifs de la loi uniforme[25], les Etats contractants ont voulu écarter, par cette précision, «l'ancienne théorie, aujourd'hui abandonnée, selon laquelle les parties ne pouvaient choisir la loi applicable que dans la matière des règles supplétives et interprétatives de volonté».

La même évolution s'est produite dans les autres pays de la Communauté. C'est justement pour mieux caractériser cette diversité de rôles joués par la volonté des parties dans les deux cas, que la doctrine allemande a l'habitude de distinguer la *kollisionsrechtliche Verweisung* de la *materiellrechtliche Verweisung*[26] et que la doctrine italienne juxtapose un *riferimento al diritto straniero per la determinazione della legge regolatrice* à un *riferimento al diritto straniero in funzione di recezione negoziale*[27]. Des distinctions de ce genre sont d'ailleurs faites également par la doctrine d'autres pays[28].

C'est pour ces raisons que le Groupe n'a pas estimé indispensable de préciser que le choix des parties quant à la loi applicable s'étend aussi bien aux dispositions impératives qu'aux dispositions supplétives.

---

[24] A la date du 1 octobre 1972 entre les huit pays européens suivants: Belgique, Danemark, Finlande, France, Italie, Norvège, Suède, Suisse. Le Niger a également adhéré à la Convention.

[25] Texte officiel du Traité et de la Loi Uniforme reproduit dans le Bull. Benelux 1969 no. 10, p. 51.

[26] *Kegel*, IPR p. 256.

[27] *Perassi*, Riv. Dir. Int. 20 (1928) p. 516 ss.; *Morelli* no. 33, p. 59.

[28] *Rigaux* no. 87, p. 125 s.

Ce n'est qu'après que la loi applicable au contrat a été déterminée (par la désignation des parties ou autrement), que se pose le problème d'établir dans quelle mesure les dispositions de cette loi n'ont qu'un caractère purement supplétif.

La distinction entre l'autonomie de la volonté des parties quant à la détermination de la loi applicable à leur contrat et l'autonomie de la volonté des parties quant à la réglementation «matérielle» de leur rapport contractuel, est en effet désormais acquise dans la jurisprudence et la doctrine de nos pays.

3. Manifestation de la volonté

Dès maintenant il est important de préciser que le choix des parties quant à la loi applicable peut résulter aussi bien d'une manifestation expresse que d'une manifestation implicite (ou tacite) de leur volonté. Cette possibilité se déduit clairement de la coordination de l'article 2, premier alinéa, avec le premier membre de phrase des articles 4, 5 et 6, où sont prévus les rattachements subsidiaires pour la détermination de la loi applicable au contrat «à défaut de choix explicite ou implicite» des parties.

Il s'agit, d'ailleurs, d'une précision qui ne fait que refléter la situation existante dans les pays membres de la C.E.E.

Tant en Allemagne qu'en France, en effet, la jurisprudence ne requiert pas de forme solennelle pour la désignation de la loi applicable. Aussi cette désignation peut-elle être et est-elle souvent simplement implicite [29].

Il en est de même en Italie, où l'admissibilité d'un choix implicite de la loi applicable est fondée sur l'intention du législateur, ce qui résulte du rapport du Garde des Sceaux au sujet de l'article 25 disp. prél. Code civil, ainsi que de l'interprétation et de l'application de cet article par la jurisprudence et la doctrine [30].

En ce qui concerne les pays du Benelux, le troisième alinéa de l'article 13 de la loi uniforme prévoit également que la désignation de la loi applicable peut résulter d'un choix «explicite ou implicite mais certain» des parties.

---

[29] *Soergel/Siebert(-Kegel)*, Art. 7 nos 233–239; *Batiffol/Lagarde* II no. 570, p. 210 s., note 12.

[30] Il suffit de mentionner en ce sens, parmi les décisions les plus récentes et les plus significatives: Cass. it. 28 mars 1953 no. 827 *(Vidale c. Istituto Nazionale Assicurazioni)*, Giur. Compl. Cass. Civ. 32 (1953) p. 46 ss.; App. Genova 12 juillet 1964 *(Assael Nissim c. Crespi)*, Riv. Dir. Int. Priv. Proc. 3 (1967) p. 126 ss. en note; Cass. (Chambres réunies) 28 juin 1966 no. 1680 *(Assael Nissim c. Crespi)*, Riv. Dir. Int. Priv. Proc. 3 (1967) p. 126 ss. En ce qui concerne la doctrine, voir dans le même sens *Morelli* no. 347, p. 61.

Dans cette dernière disposition il est exigé que le choix implicite
des parties quant à la loi applicable soit *certain*. Et cette exigence de
«certitude» paraît figurer aussi dans le deuxième alinéa de l'article 2
de la convention de La Haye de 1955 sur la loi applicable aux ventes
à caractère international, où il est dit que la désignation des parties
«doit faire l'objet d'une clause expresse, ou résulter *indubitablement*
des dispositions du contrat».

Mais il est évident que, par l'emploi de ces termes (certain, indubitable), les auteurs des textes précités n'ont entendu que souligner
l'exigence de ne pas confondre la volonté implicite avec la volonté
hypothétique (ou présumée) des parties. Même si elle n'est qu'implicite,
la volonté des parties quant aux choix de la loi applicable doit être *réelle*,
qui puisse se déduire d'éléments concordants et concluants du contrat et
des circonstances de la cause; il ne faut pas qu'il s'agisse d'une volonté
purement hypothétique. Ainsi que le fait très bien remarquer l'exposé
des motifs de la loi uniforme Benelux[31], «le juge ne peut substituer sa
volonté à celle des parties en leur attribuant un choix qu'elles n'ont
pas fait et auquel elles n'ont peut-être pas pensé».

C'est justement pour ces raisons que le Groupe n'a pas estimé nécessaire de faire allusion au caractère «certain» ou «indubitable» du choix
implicite des parties quant à la loi applicable. Ce qu'on appelle la
volonté hypothétique (ou présumée) des parties n'est pas, à proprement
parler, la volonté de celles-ci, mais bien la volonté de l'interprète (du
juge). Et puisque le libellé du premier alinéa de l'article 2 fait clairement mention de la «loi choisie par les parties», il a paru superflu
d'accentuer ce caractère.

4. *Caractère international du contrat*

Le choix des parties quant à la loi applicable est souvent subordonné
à la condition qu'il s'agisse d'un contrat de caractère «international»;
ou, si l'on préfère une formulation négative de la condition, qu'il ne
s'agisse pas d'un contrat de caractère purement interne, dépourvu de
tout élément d'extranéité.

Pour n'envisager que quelques exemples tirés de la pratique d'ordre
interne et d'ordre conventionnel des Etats membres de la Communauté,
on rappelera que le «caractère international» du contrat est expressément évoqué, dès son intitulé, dans la convention de La Haye de 1955
sur la loi applicable aux ventes à caractère international d'objets mobiliers corporels et qu'il constitue la condition à laquelle est subordonnée

---

[31] Texte officiel (*supra* note 25) p. 52. *Cf.* également à ce propos *Huss*, Les
modes non formels d'expression de la volonté en droit privé luxembourgeois,
en: Trav. Ass. Capitant 20 (1968) p. 65 ss., 203 ss.

l'application des règles uniformes de conflit résultant de cette convention. Il mérite d'être rappelé, en outre qu'aux termes du dernier alinéa de l'article premier de ladite convention: «La seule déclaration des parties, relative à l'application d'une loi ou à la compétence d'un juge ou d'un arbitre, ne suffit pas à donner à la vente le caractère international au sens de l'alinéa premier du présent article».

Une référence formelle au «caractère international» du contrat ne résulte pas textuellement de l'article 13 de la loi uniforme Benelux. Il est aisé pourtant de se rendre compte que, même dans ce cas, le caractère international du contrat constitue la condition à laquelle est subordonnée l'application de la règle de l'autonomie de la volonté. En effet, dans l'exposé des motifs de la loi uniforme il est précisé que: «Contrairement au texte de la loi uniforme de 1951, qui pouvait prêter à équivoque sur ce point, l'art. 13 nouveau consacre expressément la règle traditionnelle et fondamentale de l'autonomie de la volonté: dans un *contrat international,* c'est-à-dire un contrat qui comporte des éléments d'extranéité donnant à plusieurs lois vocation de s'y appliquer, les parties ont la faculté de choisir la loi qui le régira» [32].

Plusieurs importantes manifestations de la doctrine [33] et de la jurisprudence [34] font clairement ressortir, d'ailleurs, qu'en Belgique et aux Pays-Bas le principe de l'autonomie de la volonté est conditionné par l'existence d'un élément «international» dans le contrat; elles nous confirment en ce sens sur la portée qu'il faut attribuer à la précision donnée dans l'exposé des motifs de la loi uniforme.

Bien que la jurisprudence française ne se soit que rarement prononcée sur le problème, en France le pouvoir des parties de désigner la loi applicable paraît également subordonnée à l'existence d'un élément international dans le contrat. La solution a été principalement fondée sur l'arrêt de la Cour de cassation du 28 mai 1963 dans l'affaire *Société Les Films Richebé* c. *Société Roy Export et Charlie Chaplin* [35]. De toute façon la doctrine française paraît nettement orientée en ce sens [36]. Cette orientation de la doctrine – cela vaut d'être noté – a trouvé une expression significative dans l'article 2313 du projet français, où le «caractère international» du contrat constitue expressément la condition pour la soumission du contrat à la loi choisie par les parties.

---

[32] Texte officiel (*supra* note 25) p. 50 s.

[33] *Kosters/Dubbink* (*supra* note 23) p. 228; *Rigaux* no. 352, p. 418.

[34] HR 12 décembre 1947 (*Solbandera S.A.* c. *Blue Star Line),* Clunet 77 (1950) p. 924; HR 13 mai 1966 (*supra* note 22).

[35] Cass. fr. 28 mai 1963 (*Soc. Les Films Richebé* c. *Soc. Roy Export et Charlie Chaplin),* D. 1963 J. 677 = Clunet 90 (1963) p. 1004 = Rev. crit. 53 (1964) p. 513.

[36] *Batiffol/Lagarde* II no. 575, p. 221 s.; *Batiffol,* Contrats et conventions, en: Rép. dr. int. I (1968) nos. 4 s.

En ce qui concerne l'Allemagne, la doctrine de ce pays paraît, elle aussi, pencher pour l'application de la règle de l'autonomie de la volonté aux seuls contrats caractérisés par un élément d'extranéité [37]. Bien que la jurisprudence allemande ne se soit pas encore prononcée spécifiquement en la matière, l'arrêt rendu par le Bundesgerichtshof le 17 décembre 1957, où il est fait application de la règle de l'autonomie de la volonté dans une affaire relative à «einem schuldrechtlichen Vertrag zwischen einem Inländer und einem Ausländer» [38], ainsi que l'arrêt rendu par la même Cour le 30 janvier 1961, où l'on affirme que la soumission d'un contrat à la loi étrangère présuppose qu'un rapport existe entre la loi déclarée applicable, d'une part, et les parties ou le contrat d'autre part [39], semblent bien accentuer l'exigence d'un élément d'extranéité dans le contrat.

Par contre, en Italie, du fait que l'autonomie de la volonté des parties n'est pas expressément limitée par le texte des articles 25 disp. prél. Code civil et 10 Code nav., on a tiré souvent la conséquence que les parties peuvent désigner la loi applicable à leur contrat même si ce contrat est dépourvu de tout élément d'extranéité, même s'il ne s'agit que d'un contrat de caractère purement interne [40]. Cette interprétation semble avoir été retenue, ne serait ce qu'implicitement, par la Cour de cassation dans ses arrêts du 28 mars 1953 no. 827 (affaire *Vidale* c. *Istituto Nazionale Assicurazioni*) et du 2 décembre 1960 no. 3173 (affaire *Agenzia Marittima Mantacos* c. *Soc. Zuest Ambrosetti*) [41]. Mais il est indispensable de souligner que, tant dans l'une que dans l'autre de ces affaires, il ne s'agissait que de rapports contractuels dotés d'un élément d'extranéité. Il paraît imprudent, dans ces conditions, de tirer de ces arrêts la conséquence que la Cour aboutirait aux mêmes conclusions dans le cas de contrats de caractère purement interne.

Dans l'examen de cet aspect des règles de conflit des obligations contractuelles, le Groupe est arrivé à la conclusion qu'il était opportun de subordonner le pouvoir des parties de désigner la loi applicable à leur contrat à la condition que le contrat ne soit pas dépourvu de tout élément d'extranéité. Cette précision, toutefois, ne pouvait pas

---

[37] *Gamillscheg*, Rechtswahl, Schwerpunkt und mutmaßlicher Parteiwille im internationalen Vertragsrecht: AcP 157 (1958/59) p. 313, qui exclut l'application de la règle dans le cas de «reiner Inlandsfall»; *Soergel/Siebert(-Kegel)*, Art. 7 no. 228; *Raape (supra* note 18) para. 40, p. 460 ss.

[38] BGH 17 décembre 1957, IPRspr. 1956–57, no. 23, p. 93.

[39] BGH 30 janvier 1961, IPRspr. 1960–61, no. 39, p. 132 ss. V. aussi HansOLG Hamburg 2 juin 1965, IPRspr. 1964–65, no. 46, p. 153 ss.

[40] *Morelli* no. 34, p. 60 s.

[41] Cass. it. 28 mars 1953 no. 827 (*supra* note 30); 2 décembre 1960 no. 3173 (*Agenzia Marittima Mantacos* c. *Soc. Zuest Ambrosetti*), Riv. Dir. Int. 44 (1961) p. 677.

être limitée au seul choix par les parties de la loi applicable. Elle devait englober nécessairement, d'une part, toute la réglementation de droit international privé portant sur les obligations contractuelles; d'autre part, non seulement les obligations contractuelles, mais également non contractuelles. C'est pour cela que le Groupe a estimé préférable d'insérer la précision dont il est question dans l'article premier, où il est dit que les règles uniformes de la Convention «sont applicables, *dans les situations ayant un caractère international*, aux obligations contractuelles et non contractuelles».

5. *Lien avec la loi choisie*

La liberté des parties quant au choix de la loi applicable à leur contrat n'est aucunement limitée par l'article 2. Les parties peuvent désigner n'importe quelle loi comme loi applicable à leur rapport contractuel, même s'il s'agissait d'une loi qui ne présente apparemment aucun lien avec ce rapport. Il serait en effet imprudent de tenir un tel choix pour «capricieux», comme cela a été parfois considéré par la jurisprudence de certains pays. Le choix des parties est toujours l'expression de leur intérêt commun.

6. *Loi relative à la validité du consentement*

Le 2ème alinéa de l'article 2 dispose que les conditions relatives à la validité du consentement des parties quant à la loi applicable sont déterminées par cette loi.

Cette disposition – qui ne vise que les vices du consentement des parties dans la désignation de la loi applicable – s'inspire de l'article 2 (3ème alinéa) de la convention de La Haye de 1955 sur la loi applicable aux ventes à caractère international d'objets mobiliers corporels.

Il s'agit d'une disposition qui veut répondre à des exigences d'ordre pratique plutôt qu'à des exigences d'ordre théorique. Il s'agit de toute façon d'une disposition qui ne soulève aucune difficulté d'ordre logique. Il n'y a rien de contradictoire ou d'illogique, en effet, dans la soumission des conditions relatives à la validité du consentement, plus exactement des vices du consentement des parties quant au choix de la loi applicable, à la même loi que celle désignée par celles-ci, car c'est la volonté du législateur, non pas la volonté des parties, qui en dispose ainsi.

La solution retenue dans le 2ème alinéa de l'art. 2 permet d'éviter que les conditions relatives à la validité du consentement des parties soient soumises à des lois différentes selon qu'elles ont trait à la désignation de loi applicable ou à la formation du contrat dans son ensemble.

Elle est, au demeurant, la solution résultant à l'heure actuelle des systèmes de droit international privé des Etats qui ont ratifié la convention de La Haye de 1955.

Lors de la réunion des rapporteurs, deux solutions présentant le caractère d'une alternative avaient été prises également en considération.

Selon la première branche de l'alternative, les conditions relatives à la validité du consentement des parties quant à la loi applicable devraient être déterminées par la *lex fori*. C'est la solution retenue par la grande majorité de la doctrine italienne [42].

D'après la seconde branche de l'alternative, les conditions relatives à la validité du consentement des parties quant à la loi applicable devraient être soumises à la loi du lieu où le consentement est intervenu. C'est la solution proposée par un spécialiste belge dans un essai paru en 1966 [43] et présentée de nouveau par son auteur au cours de la réunion des rapporteurs.

Toutefois, le Groupe a écarté tant l'une que l'autre des ces solutions en estimant que les inconvénients que leur adoption pourrait comporter étaient supérieurs à leurs avantages.

7. *Cas du silence de l'une de parties*

Est-ce que le principe consacré dans l'alinéa 2 de l'article 2 doit trouver également application en ce qui concerne la portée du silence d'une partie quant à la loi applicable ou bien cette question doit-elle être réglée différemment? C'est au sujet de cette question ainsi qu'au sujet de la question de la portée du silence d'une partie quant à la formation du contrat, qu'une divergence assez marquée d'opinions s'est manifestée au sein du Groupe.

Selon l'opinion d'une délégation, il serait préférable de ne pas régler ces questions dans la Convention. Ces questions devraient trouver leur solution, non pas dans les règles uniformes de la Convention, mais dans les règles (de conflit ou matérielles) du droit national.

Par contre, les autres délégations se sont déclarées en faveur d'une solution expresse de ces questions, qui devrait trouver sa place, respectivement, dans l'alinéa 4 de l'article 2 et dans un alinéa 2 de l'article 8. Toutefois, un accord n'a pu être réalisé sur un texte unique de ces deux alinéas, en raison du partage des délégations entre partisans d'une règle de conflit et partisans d'une règle matérielle.

Dans ces conditions, le Groupe a décidé de supprimer, dans le texte de l'article 2, l'alinéa 4 et de reproduire cet alinéa, dans les deux

---

[42] *Morelli* no. 34, p. 61.
[43] *Vander Elst,* L'autonomie de la volonté en d. i. p. français et belge, dans: Liber Amicorum L. Frédéricq II (1966) p. 990 ss.

variantes entre lesquelles se partagèrent les délégations, en annexe à la convention. La même décision a été adoptée en ce qui concerne l'alinéa 2 de l'article 8, qui vise la portée du silence d'une partie quant à la formation du contrat[44].

8. Limite à la volonté des parties

La liberté des parties quant au choix de la loi applicable à leur contrat ne subit qu'une seule limite. C'est la limite prévue par le troisième alinéa de l'article 2. D'après cet alinéa, dans les relations de travail, le choix des parties ne peut en aucun cas porter atteinte aux dispositions impératives protectrices du travailleur en vigueur dans le pays où il accomplit habituellement son travail.

Le sens et la portée de cette disposition, qui se rattache évidemment à la règle spéciale pour les contrats de travail résultant de l'article 5, sont tout à fait clairs. Elle a pour but d'éviter que, par le biais du choix d'une loi dont les dispositions sont moins protectrices du travailleur que celles du pays où il accomplit habituellement son travail, l'employeur puisse se soustraire aux dispositions impératives en vigueur dans ce pays pour la protection des travailleurs. Il va sans dire que si le choix des parties porte sur une loi contenant des dispositions impératives également ou même plus protectrices du travailleur que celles du pays où il accomplit habituellement son travail, la limite à l'autonomie de la volonté du 3ème alinéa de l'article 2 ne joue pas.

L'alinéa figure entre crochets, car une délégation n'a pas été en mesure d'accepter ce texte qui, à son avis, ne tiendrait pas compte de la distinction qui devrait être faite entre les dispositions impératives de droit public et les dispositions impératives de droit privé.

Le texte de l'alinéa 3 ne déroge au principe de l'autonomie de la volonté que dans l'hypothèse, la plus fréquente en fait, où le travailleur accomplit habituellement son travail dans un même pays.

Dans l'hypothèse inverse, où une règle de rattachement subsidiaire est prévue à l'article 5 b, la liberté des parties de désigner la loi applicable au contrat de travail demeure entière, sous la seule réserve des lois de police mentionnées à l'article 7.

9. Unité ou pluralité des lois choisies

La question de savoir si les parties doivent ne choisir qu'une seule loi en tant que loi applicable à leur contrat ou si elles peuvent en désigner plusieurs, a été largement traitée par le Groupe. La discussion a porté également sur l'autre volet du problème dit du «dépeçage» du

---

[44] V. *infra* le commentaire de l'article 8, para. 2.

contrat, précisement sur la question de savoir si, en l'absence d'une désignation des parties, le juge appelé à déterminer la loi applicable au contrat a la faculté de morceler le contrat et de faire application de lois différentes aux différentes parties du contrat.

Nous ferons ici abstraction de ce dernier aspect du problème[45]. En ce qui concerne le premier aspect, après avoir constaté qu'il n'y avait pas de décisions de justice ayant eu à appliquer simultanément à un même contrat plusieurs lois déclarées applicables par les parties et après avoir examiné les arguments pour et contre le dépeçage[46], le Groupe en est arrivé à la conclusion que, s'il n'y avait pas de raisons valables pour interdire d'une façon absolue le dépeçage, il n'y avait pas, non plus, de motifs pour l'encourager. Dans ces conditions, le Groupe a jugé préférable de ne pas trancher expressément la question dans la présente convention. La question reste donc ouverte.

Article 3 (Moment du choix)

1. Le premier membre de phrase de l'article 3 reconnaît aux parties la plus grande liberté quant au moment où le choix de la loi applicable peut intervenir. Ce choix peut intervenir aussi bien au moment de la conclusion du contrat qu'à une date ultérieure. La possibilité que le choix de la loi applicable intervienne *antérieurement* à la conclusion d'un contrat n'avait pas besoin d'être prévue séparément, car dans ce cas ce n'est évidemment qu'au moment de la conclusion du contrat que la désignation des parties produira ses effets.

Le deuxième membre de la phrase de l'article 3, de son côté, reconnaît également aux parties la plus grande liberté quant à la modification du choix de la loi applicable qu'elles auraient effectué précédemment. Ce choix peut être modifié à tout moment par un accord entre les parties.

La solution retenue par le Groupe dans l'article 3 ne correspond que partiellement à ce qui semble être l'état actuel du droit des Etats membres de la Communauté en la matière.

Tant en Allemagne qu'en France, en effet, le choix par les parties de la loi applicable paraît bien pouvoir intervenir même après la conclusion du contrat et les tribunaux déduisent parfois la loi applicable de l'attitude des parties au cours de la procédure, lorsqu'elles se réfèrent d'un commun accord apparent à une loi déterminée. Le pouvoir

---

[45] V. *infra* le commentaire de l'article 4, para. 5.

[46] Une synthèse de ces arguments avait été soumise au Groupe sous forme de note par M. *Lagarde*. Comp. aussi *Batiffol/Lagarde* II no. 595, p. 246 s.

des parties de modifier la désignation de la loi applicable à leur contrat paraît également et très largement admis[47].

A ce qu'il paraît, la jurisprudence néerlandaise serait, elle aussi, orientée dans le même sens[48].

Par contre, en Italie, dans son arrêt du 28 juin 1966 no. 1680 dans l'affaire *Assael Nissim* c. *Crespi,* la Cour de cassation (en Chambres réunies) a déclaré que «le choix des parties quant à la loi applicable n'est pas admissible, dans le cas où il aurait été effectué postérieurement à la stipulation du contrat»[49].

D'après cette conclusion, qui n'est pas partagée par une partie de la doctrine italienne[50], le choix des parties ne pourrait intervenir qu'au moment de la conclusion du contrat. Une fois que la loi applicable a été choisie, les parties n'auraient plus la possibilité de se mettre d'accord sur la désignation d'une loi autre que celle qu'elles avaient désignée au moment de la conclusion du contrat.

2. La solution libérale adoptée finalement par le Groupe paraît bien correspondre à une exigence de cohérence. Une fois accepté le principe de l'autonomie de la volonté, et compte tenu de ce que l'exigence d'une désignation par les parties de la loi applicable peut s'imposer aussi bien au moment qu'après la conclusion du contrat, il apparaît tout à fait logique que le pouvoir des parties ne soit pas limité au seul moment de la conclusion du contrat. Il en est de même en ce qui concerne la modification, par un nouvel accord entre les parties, de la loi qu'elles auraient précédemment choisie.

Quant à la manière selon laquelle la modification du choix de la loi applicable pourrait se faire, il est tout à fait compréhensible que cette modification soit soumise aux mêmes règles que le choix initial.

Si le choix ou le changement de la loi applicable intervient au cours de la procédure, la question se pose de savoir dans quelles limites ce choix ou cette modification pourront utilement intervenir.

Cette question relève, toutefois, du droit national de la procédure; et c'est uniquement en conformité de ce droit qu'elle devra être tranchée.

3. Le troisième membre de phrase de l'article 3 a pour but de protéger les droits des tiers toutes les fois qu'une modification de la loi applicable intervient postérieurement à la conclusion du contrat. Cette

---

[47] *Soergel/Siebert(-Kegel),* Art. 7 nos. 269–273 et notes 1 et 3; *Batiffol/ Lagarde* II no. 592, p. 243; *Batiffol (supra* note 36) no. 50; Cass. fr. 18 novembre 1959 *(Soc. Deckardt c. Etabl. Moatti),* Rev. crit. 49 (1960) p. 83.

[48] Comp. *Gamillscheg (supra* note 37) p. 315, note 50.

[49] Cass. 28 juin 1966 *(supra* note 30).

[50] V. *Treves,* Sulla volontà delle parti di cui all'art. 25 delle preleggi e sul momento del suo sorgere: Riv. Dir. Int. Priv. Proc. 3 (1967) p. 315 ss.

réserve du droit des tiers présente également un intérêt en matière de forme des actes. On se reportera sur ce point au commentaire de l'article 18 (*infra* p. 302 s.).

Article 4 (Règle subsidiaire)

1. Examen des solutions du droit positif

A défaut de choix explicite ou implicite des parties, la détermination de la loi applicable au contrat ne s'opère pas à l'heure actuelle d'une façon uniforme dans les droits des Etats membres de la Communauté[51].

En droit français et en droit belge, il n'y a pas lieu de faire de différence entre volonté implicite et volonté hypothétique (ou présumée) des parties. En l'absence d'un choix exprès de la loi applicable, les tribunaux recherchent les divers «indices» susceptibles de faire ressortir la localisation du contrat dans tel ou tel pays. Cette localisation est entendue tantôt d'une façon *subjective* comme l'équivalent de ce qu'aurait été probablement la volonté des parties si elle s'était déclarée, tantôt d'une façon *objective* comme l'équivalent du pays avec lequel l'opération présente le lien le plus étroit[52].

La conception *objective* paraît rencontrer de plus en plus l'appui de la doctrine et de la jurisprudence. En s'inspirant de cette conception, dans son arrêt du 27 janvier 1955 *(Soc. Jansen c. Soc. Heurtey)*, la Cour de Paris affirmait qu'à défaut de manifestation de la volonté des parties, la loi applicable «est déterminée de façon objective par la circonstance que le contrat se trouve, de par sa contexture et son économie, localisé dans un certain pays, ce lien avec lequel l'opération conventionnelle entretient le rapport le plus étroit étant celui où doit s'accomplir la prestation spécifique du contrat en question, en exécution de l'obligation caractéristique de sa nature»[53].

Et c'est toujours cette façon de concevoir la localisation du contrat qui est évoquée, en des termes manifestement inspirés de l'arrêt précité, au deuxième alinéa de l'article 2313 du projet français, où il est dit qu'à défaut de volonté manifestée par les parties, «le contrat est régi par la loi avec laquelle il présente, par son économie, et notamment par le lieu principal de son exécution, le lien le plus étroit».

De même, en droit allemand, la solution retenue par les tribunaux sur la détermination de la loi du contrat en l'absence de choix des par-

[51] Pour un aperçu comparatif *cf. Rabel*, The Conflict of Laws, A Comparative Study[2] II (1960) Ch. 30, p. 432–486.

[52] *Batiffol/Lagarde* II nos. 572 s., p. 214 s.; *Batiffol*, Contrats et conventions (*supra* note 36) nos. 47–91; *Rigaux* nos. 355–359, p. 421 ss.

[53] Paris 27 janvier 1955 *(Soc. Jansen c. Soc. Heurtey)*, Rev. crit. 44 (1955) p. 330.

ties, se base largement sur la recherche des «indices» susceptibles de faire ressortir la «*hypothetischer Parteiwille*», la volonté présumée des parties, en tenant compte des intérêts généraux en jeu dans chaque cas d'espèce[54]. Si cette n'aboutit pas à un résultat, la loi applicable au contrat, d'après la jurisprudence allemande, est déterminée par le lieu de son exécution: plus exactement, par le lieu de l'exécution de chacune des obligations résultant du contrat, car les tribunaux allemands estiment que, si les diverses obligations d'un contrat sont à exécuter dans des pays différents, chaque obligation est régie par la loi du pays de son exécution[55].

En droit italien, où la volonté présumée des parties ne joue aucun rôle[56], la solution du problème qui nous occupe a été donnée expressément et directement par le législateur. A défaut de loi choisie par les parties, les obligations résultant du contrat sont régies par les lois suivantes: a) les contrats de travail à bord de navires ou d'aéronefs *étrangers,* par la *loi nationale du navire ou de l'aéronef* (art. 9 Code nav.); b) les contrats de louage, d'affrètement et de transport dans la navigation maritime, intérieure et aérienne, par la *loi nationale du navire ou de l'aéronef* (art. 10 Code nav.); c) tous les autres contrats, par la *loi nationale des contractants,* si elle leur est commune; autrement, par la *loi du lieu où le contrat a été conclu* (art. 25, 1er alinéa, disp. prél. Code civ.).

---

[54] BGH 14 avril 1953, IPRspr. 1952–53 no. 40, p. 151 ss.: D'après la jurisprudence allemande par «hypothetischer Parteiwille» on n'entend pas la recherche des intentions supposées des parties, mais, en vue de déterminer le droit applicable, une appréciation raisonnable et équitable des intérêts en cause sur une base objective. Selon un autre arrêt «lors de cette appréciation des intérêts en cause, la question essentielle est celle de savoir où se trouve le centre de gravité du rapport contractuel considérée»: BGH 14 juillet 1955, IPRspr., 1954–55, no. 67, p. 206 ss.

[55] On peut consulter sur cette notion *Kegel,* IPR p. 257 ss.; *Soergel/Siebert (-Kegel),* Art. 7 nos. 240–268, ainsi que les nombreuses références à la pratique judiciaire figurant dans les notes; *Reithmann* (*supra* note 18) p. 17 ss., 57 ss.

[56] Le projet préliminaire du Code civil italien, en effet, n'attribuait qu'a la volonté des parties, expresse, implicite ou *présumée,* le rôle d'élément de rattachement pour la détermination de la loi applicable en matière d'obligations contractuelles. Dans le projet définitif, pourtant, toute référence à la volonté présumée des parties fut abandonnée et la nouvelle rédaction de l'art. 25 fut intégrée par la prévision des lois applicables à défaut de volonté manifestée par les parties. Ainsi qu'il est précisé dans le rapport du Garde des Sceaux sur ce projet, «personne ne doute de l'opportunité du principe de l'autonomie de la volonté, lorsque les parties ont manifesté expressément ou tacitement leur volonté; mais à défaut de volonté manifestée par les parties, même tacitement, j'ai estimé que la recherche d'une volonté présumée n'aurait signifié que l'attribution, plus ou moins arbitraire, aux parties d'une volonté inexistante» (Relazione del Guardasigilli al progetto definitivo, no. 13).

Les lois susmentionnées ne s'appliquent qu'à titre subsidiaire; elles ne s'appliquent qu'à défaut de volonté manifestée par les parties quant à la loi applicable. C'est justement en ce sens que se prononce la jurisprudence italienne[57]. Et c'est toujours dans le même sens que se prononce la doctrine[58].

Pour terminer ce bref aperçu, il ne nous reste qu'à rappeler les dispositions du troisième et du quatrième alinéa de l'article 13 de la loi uniforme Benelux. D'après le troisième alinéa, à défaut de choix par les parties, «Le contrat est régi par la loi du pays avec lequel il présente les rapports les plus étroits». D'après le quatrième alinéa, «lorsqu'il est impossible de déterminer ce pays, le contrat est régi par la loi du pays où il a été conclu»[59].

En faisant abstraction de l'Italie, les solutions nationales se rapprochent, dans une certaine mesure, les unes des autres; elles manifestent également, certaines analogies avec les conceptions de la «proper law of contract» des pays anglo-saxons[60], ainsi qu'avec les positions les plus récentes de la jurisprudence d'autres pays[61].

Par ailleurs, même les solutions retenues en Italie en ce qui concerne la loi applicable au contrat à défaut de choix explicite ou implicite des parties ne sont que l'expression d'une connexion, que le législateur italien a jugé prépondérante, entre le contrat et la loi de tel ou tel pays. La seule différence – mais il s'agit évidemment d'une différence essentielle – qui existe entre le droit italien et les systèmes des autres pays de la Communauté est la suivante: tandis que le législateur italien a estimé qu'à défaut de choix par les parties, la loi applicable pouvait être déterminée une fois pour toutes par certains rattachements fixes et rigides, dans les autres pays de la Communauté on a préféré et on préfère s'en tenir à une solution plus souple, laissant à l'interprète (au juge) la tâche d'individualiser dans chaque cas d'espèce, parmi les divers éléments du contrat, le rattachement décisif pour la détermination de la loi applicable ou, si l'on préfère le pays avec lequel le contrat présente les liens les plus étroits.

---

[57] Dans ce sens cf. Cass. it. 28 mars 1953 no. 827 et 28 juin 1966 no. 1680 (supra note 30); Cass. it. 30 avril 1969 no. 1403 (Officina Musso c. Société Sevplant), Riv. Dir. Int. Priv. Proc. 6 (1970) p. 332 ss.

[58] Morelli no. 97, p. 155.

[59] Texte officiel (supra note 25) p. 53.

[60] Graveson, The Conflict of Laws[6] (1969) Ch. 12, p. 419 ss.; Cheshire, Private International Law[8] (1970) Ch. VIII, p. 197 ss.; Morris, The Conflict of Laws (1971) p. 219 ss.

[61] Cf. Schnitzer, Les contrats internationaux en d. i. p. suisse: Rec. des Cours 123 (1968-I) p. 558 ss.; Rabel (supra note 51) p. 438 s.; Lando, The Proper Law of the Contract, en: Scand. Stud. L. 8 (1964) p. 107–202.

2. *Examen des solutions du droit positif (suite)*

Le Groupe a examiné le pour et le contre des solutions actuellement retenues par le législateur ou par la jurisprudence des pays membres de la Communauté.

En ce qui concerne les éléments de rattachement de caractère général retenus en Italie, le Groupe a estimé que le lieu de conclusion du contrat de même que la nationalité commune des contractants n'étaient pas des rattachements suffisamment importants pour la détermination de la loi applicable. De fait, il arrive trop souvent que l'endroit de la conclusion du contrat est tout à fait accidentel par rapport aux intérêts à régir. La détermination de la loi du contrat en fonction du lieu de sa conclusion engendre, d'autre part, plusieurs inconvénients, que la doctrine italienne contemporaine n'a pas manqué de mettre en lumière lorsqu'elle a dû aborder les délicats problèmes pratiques soulevés par l'exécution de certaines obligations contractuelles (par exemple, les obligations résultant du contrat de travail, les obligations de nature pécuniaire, etc.). La nationalité commune des parties, elle aussi, ne se présente normalement que comme un élément tout à fait accidentel par rapport à l'économie du contrat ou à son centre de gravité *(Schwerpunkt)*. Sans doute, les rattachements spécifiques de la nationalité du navire et de l'aéronef relativement à certaines catégories de contrats de la navigation maritime, fluviale et aérienne présentent une valeur et un caractère plus significatifs que les rattachements généraux. Mais la détermination rigide de la loi applicable sur la base exclusive de ces rattachements ne manque pas à son tour de donner lieu à certains inconvénients. Les problèmes soulevés dans la navigation maritime par les navires battant des «pavillons de complaisance» en sont un exemple.

En ce qui concerne les solutions retenues dans les autres pays de la Communauté, le Groupe a estimé que leur souplesse, au cas où elle n'aurait pas été tempérée par des correctifs appropriés, pouvait aller à l'encontre des exigences de la sécurité juridique: exigences essentielles dans le cadre de règles uniformes de conflit des obligations au sein de la Communauté. En effet, la détermination de la loi du contrat sur la base d'un rattachement si vague que celui du pays avec lequel le «contrat présente le lien le plus étroit» ou avec lequel «le contrat présente les rapports les plus étroits» pourrait pratiquement se traduire dans l'abandon pur et simple de la détermination de la loi applicable aussi bien à la sagesse qu'à l'arbitraire des juges [62]. Et cette solu-

---

[62] V. à cet égard le commentaire fort symptomatique du troisième alinéa de l'article 13 de la loi uniforme, tel qu'il résulte de l'exposé des motifs (Texte officiel [*supra* note 25] p. 52 s.).

tion ne serait pas facilement acceptable pour des pays, comme l'Italie, où la tradition est en faveur de rattachements suffisamment rigides.

C'est en partant de ces considérations que le Groupe, après avoir analysé tout un éventail de notions et de formulations alternatives présentées tant par le rapporteur que par plusieurs délégués, a pu se mettre d'accord sur la règle uniforme qui est consacrée dans l'article 4.

3. Choix du critère des liens les plus étroits et de la prestation caractéristique

Selon le premier alinéa de l'article 4, à défaut de choix explicite ou implicite des parties le contrat est régi par la loi du pays avec lequel il presente les liens les plus étroits.

La souplesse du principe général ainsi posé est, pourtant, considérablement tempérée par l'alinéa 2 de l'article 4, où la signification normale du dit rattachement est définie.

Le pays avec lequel le contrat présente les liens les plus étroits est celui dans lequel la partie qui doit fournir la prestation caractéristique du contrat a sa résidence habituelle ou bien son établissement principal, suivant qu'il s'agit d'une prestation à fournir en dehors de l'exercice d'une activité professionnelle ou, au contraire, dans l'exercice de celle-ci (alinéa 2, litterae *a* et *b*). Dans ce dernier cas, s'il résulte du contrat que la prestation caractéristique sera fournie par un établissement secondaire, c'est le pays où est situé cet établissement qui doit être considéré comme le pays avec lequel le contrat présente les liens les plus étroits (alinéa 2, littera *c*).

L'ordre d'idées dont la disposition de l'alinéa 2 s'inspire n'est certes pas inconnu des spécialistes. Il constitue l'expression d'une tendance qui s'est développée et affermie de plus en plus aussi bien dans la doctrine que dans la jurisprudence de nombre de pays au cours des dernières décennies[63]. La soumission du contrat, en l'absence de choix des parties, à la loi de la prestation caractéristique, permet en effet de concrétiser le rattachement du contrat de l'intérieur et non de l'extérieur par des éléments de rattachement qui ne sont pas en relation avec l'essence de l'obligation, tels que la nationalité des parties ou le lieu de conclusion. Il est possible de faire remonter la conception de la loi de la prestation caractéristique à une idée plus générale, à savoir l'idée que cette prestation vise la *fonction* que le rapport juridique en cause exerce dans la vie économique et sociale d'un pays déterminé.

---

[63] V. notamment *Vischer*, Internationales Vertragsrecht (1962) spéc. p. 89–144; *Schnitzer* (*supra* note 61) p. 566–595; *Reithmann* (*supra* note 18) p. 51–55. Aux ouvrages précités nous renvoyons également pour un tableau de la jurisprudence qui a retenu ce rattachement. *Adde* Hof Amsterdam 1er avril 1970 *(NAP N.V. c. Christophery)*, Ned. Jur. 1971 no. 115.

La conception de la prestation caractéristique, permet de rattacher le contrat au milieu économique dans lequel il s'insère.

L'individualisation de la prestation caractéristique d'un contrat ne soulève évidemment aucun problème en cas de contrats unilatéraux. En ce qui concerne les contrats bilatéraux (synallagmatiques) par lesquels les contractants se chargent mutuellement de prestations réciproques, la contre-prestation d'une des parties, dans l'économie moderne, consiste normalement en monnaie. Cette prestation n'est donc pas caractéristique de ces contrats. C'est la prestation pour laquelle le paiement est dû, c'est à dire, selon les catégories de contrats, le transfert de la propriété, la livraison d'objects mobiliers corporels, l'attribution de l'usage d'une chose, la mise à disposition du service, du transport, de l'assurance, de l'activité bancaire, la caution, etc., – qui constitue le centre de gravité et la fonction socio-économique de l'opération contractuelle.

Quant à la localisation dans l'espace de la prestation caractéristique du contrat, il est tout à fait naturel que le pays où la partie qui doit fournir cette prestation a son établissement ou sa résidence habituelle (suivant qu'il s'agit d'une prestation fournie dans l'exercise ou en dehors de l'exercise d'une activité professionnelle) l'emporte sur le pays de l'exécution, bien entendu au cas où ce dernier est un pays autre que celui de l'établissement ou de la résidence habituelle. En effet, dans la perspective qui est à la base de la solution retenue par le Groupe, c'est seulement le lieu de la résidence habituelle ou, respectivement, de l'établissement de la partie fournissant la prestation caractéristique qui apparaît décisif pour la localisation du contrat.

C'est ainsi, par exemple, que dans un contrat bancaire c'est la loi du pays de l'établissement bancaire avec lequel l'opération s'effectue qui régira le contrat. C'est encore ainsi, pour donner un autre exemple, que dans un contrat de représentation conclu en France entre un agent commercial belge et une société française, la prestation caractéristique étant celle fournie par l'agent, ce contrat sera régi par la loi belge, si c'est en Belgique que cet agent a son établissement ou sa résidence habituelle[64].

En conclusion, la disposition de l'alinéa 2 de l'article 4 concrétise et objective la notion trop vague de «liens les plus étroits». Elle apporte en même temps une considérable simplification dans la détermination de la loi applicable au contrat en l'absence de choix des parties. Le lieu où l'acte a été accompli devient sans importance. On n'a plus besoin de déterminer le lieu de conclusion du contrat, avec toutes les

---

[64] C'est la solution retenue par App. Limoges 10 novembre 1970 *(Noblesse c. Soc. Haviland)* ainsi que par Trib. comm. Paris 4 décembre 1970 *(Bilogan c. Soc. Daniel Hechter)*, Rev. crit. 60 (1971) p. 703 ss.

difficultés et les problèmes de qualification que cette détermination soulève dans la pratique. La recherche des différents lieux d'exécution et de leur qualification devient superflue.

Pour chaque catégorie de contrats, c'est la prestation caractéristique qui compte et qui est seule décisive pour la détermination de la loi applicable, même dans les situations particulières de certains contrats (par exemple, dans le contrat de cautionnement où la prestation caractéristique est toujours celle de la caution, qu'il s'agisse de son rapport avec le débiteur principal ou avec le créancier).

Pour parer à l'éventualité de «conflits mobiles» dans l'application de l'alinéa 2, il a été précisé que le pays de la résidence habituelle ou de l'établissement principal de la partie qui doit fournir la prestation caractéristique est le pays où cette partie a sa résidence habituelle ou son établissement «au moment de la conclusion du contrat».

L'alinéa 2 de l'article 4 est applicable non seulement aux personnes physiques, mais aussi aux sociétés et personnes morales qui tomberont normalement sous le chef de la disposition des litterae *b)* et *c)*. A ce propos, la question a été soulevée d'instituer pour les sociétés et personnes morales une présomption en faveur du siège statutaire. Le Groupe n'a pas jugé, toutefois, qu'une telle présomption serait souhaitable et a laissé par conséquent la question ouverte.

4. Marge d'appréciation du juge

Dans le cas où la prestation caractéristique, la résidence habituelle ou l'établissement ne peuvent pas être déterminés, la disposition de l'alinéa 2 de l'article 4 devient inapplicable. Dans ce cas, on retombe sous le chef de l'alinéa premier: c'est à dire, le contrat sera régi par la loi du pays avec lequel il présente les liens les plus étroits.

L'alinéa 3 de l'article 4 en dispose justement ainsi. Mais cet alinéa prévoit également la possibilité de s'écarter de la disposition de l'alinéa 2 dans le cas où il résulte de l'ensemble des circonstances que le contrat présente des liens plus étroits avec un autre pays. Dans ce cas, même si la prestation caractéristique, la résidence habituelle ou l'établissement peuvent être déterminés, il est fait application de la loi de cet autre pays.

La raison d'être de cette dernière disposition est la suivante. Etant donné le caractère général de la règle de conflit consacrée dans l'article 4, qui ne subit d'exceptions qu'en matière de contrats de travail et de contrats ayant pour objet des immeubles, il a paru indispensable d'envisager la possibilité d'appliquer une loi autre que celle visée à l'alinéa 2 toutes les fois qu'il résulte de l'ensemble des circonstances que le contrat présente de liens plus étroits avec un autre pays.

C'est ainsi, à titre d'exemple, que dans un contrat de transport maritime ou fluvial, à défaut de choix explicite ou implicite par les parties, la loi applicable, au lieu d'être celle de la résidence habituelle où de l'établissement de la partie qui effectue l'opération de transport par voie d'eau des marchandises ou des personnes, pourra être celle de la nationalité du navire ou du bateau, s'il résulte de l'ensemble des circonstances que c'est avec le pays de la nationalité que le contrat présente des liens plus étroits. D'autre part lorsqu'en matière de transport maritime et fluvial, le lieu de conclusion du contrat et le lieu du chargement coïncident, cette coïncidence semble bien pouvoir être considérée comme un exemple de liens plus étroits qui pourrait amener le juge, selon l'usage dominant dans plusieurs pays maritimes, à s'écarter de la disposition de l'alinéa 2 pour faire application de la loi du lieu de conclusion et de chargement.

La disposition de l'alinéa 3 de l'article 4 laisse au juge une certaine marge d'appréciation quant à la présence, dans chaque cas d'espèce, de cet ensemble de circonstances qui, seule, peut justifier qu'on s'écarte de la loi applicable en vertu de l'alinéa 2. Mais il s'agit là, comme il l'a déjà été remarqué tout à l'heure, de l'inévitable contrepartie d'une règle de conflit à caractère général et destinée à trouver application pour presque toutes les catégories de contrats.

5. Exclusion du «dépeçage»

Il paraît bien résulter de la formulation adoptée pour l'article 4 qu'à défaut de choix explicite ou implicite, c'est «le contrat», c'est-à-dire l'ensemble du contrat, aussi bien ses conditions de formation que les diverses obligations auxquelles il a donné naissance, qui est régi par la loi du pays avec lequel il présente les liens les plus étroits. Cette interprétation a été défendue par certaines délégations qui ont fait observer que de toute façon l'article 7 maintenait ouverte une soupape de sûreté en permettant au juge, dans les cas les plus graves, de tenir compte des lois de police autres que celles édictées par le pays dont la loi est applicable au contrat. Il convient toutefois de mentionner que le Groupe n'a pu se mettre d'accord pour exclure formellement et de manière absolue la possibilité pour le juge de «dépecer» le contrat en soumettant ses différents éléments à des lois différentes.

Article 5 (Contrats de travail)

La disposition de l'article 5 détermine, à défaut de choix explicite ou implicite des parties, la loi applicable aux contrats de travail.

18 *

Une disposition spécifique de conflit en la matière a été insérée par le Groupe dans la convention non seulement en raison de l'importance des relations de travail dans la vie économique de la Communauté, mais surtout du fait que la règle générale de l'article 4 ne donnait pas une solution satisfaisante pour cette catégorie de contrats.

Après un examen approfondi des différentes questions soulevées par les contrats de travail en droit international privé, et au cours duquel ont été particulièrement pris en considération aussi bien le projet de réglement établi à ce sujet par la Commission C.E.E. que les tendances les plus modernes de la doctrine et de la jurisprudence de nos pays, la solution finalement retenue par le Groupe a été la suivante. Si le travailleur accomplit habituellement son travail dans un même pays, le contrat de travail est régi par la loi de ce pays. C'est la règle qui figure sous le *a)*. Par contre, si le travailleur n'accomplit pas habituellement son travail dans un même pays, le contrat de travail est régi par la loi du pays où se trouve l'établissement qui a embauché le travailleur. C'est le règle qui figure sous le *b)*. Il s'agit évidemment de solutions qui s'écartent sensiblement de celles qui seraient résultées de l'article 4.

Les deux hypothèses dont on vient de parler sont formulées avec suffisamment de souplesse pour couvrir la grande majorité des situations qui peuvent se présenter en matière de relations de travail. Il semble bien, à titre d'exemple, qu'en cas de détachement temporaire et exceptionnel d'un travailleur dans un pays autre que celui où il accomplit habituellement son travail, il n'y ait pas lieu de déroger à la règle du *a)*. Ce n'est que dans les cas où le travailleur est soumis à de fréquents – et presque habituels – changements de pays, que la règle du *b)* est applicable. D'autre part, dans le cas où l'employeur a son siège dans un Etat mais a son établissement (ou ses établissements) dans un autre Etat (ou dans des autres Etats) et où le travailleur est transféré d'une façon permanente du siège à l'établissement ou vice-versa, il semble bien que la loi applicable au contrat de travail doive changer conformément à la règle du *a)*.

La dernière phrase de l'article 5, qui reprend la disposition de l'alinéa 3 de l'article 4, prévoit cependant que s'il résulte de l'ensemble des circonstances que le contrat présente des liens plus étroits avec un autre pays, il est fait application de la loi de ce dernier.

Article 6 (Contrats sur biens immobiliers)

La disposition de l'article 6, toujours à défaut de choix des parties, détermine la loi applicable aux contrats ayant pour objet des immeubles. Cette loi est en principe celle du lieu où l'immeuble est situé, à moins qu'il ne résulte de l'ensemble des circonstances que le contrat présente des liens plus étroits avec un autre pays.

En ce qui concerne le principe qu'elle consacre, la règle n'a pas besoin de commentaire, s'agissant d'un principe qui est retenu dans la plupart des systèmes nationaux de droit international privé et qui satisfait à des exigences tout à fait apparentes. Il n'est pas apparu possible de retenir une formule plus précise. La formule utilisée semble bien se référer non seulement à la vente ou à la cession, mais aussi au bail d'immeubles et au *leasing* immobilier.

Pour le reste, la disposition de l'article 6 ne fait que reprendre la disposition de l'alinéa 3 de l'article 4 lorsqu'elle prévoit que, de l'ensemble des circonstances, peut résulter que le contrat présente des liens plus étroits avec un autre pays. Dans ce cas, il est fait application de la loi de cet autre pays.

Article 7 (Lois de police)

1. Qu'il s'agisse de loi choisie par les parties ou qu'il s'agisse, à défaut de choix des parties, de la loi applicable en vertu des articles 4, 5 et 6, la loi du contrat étend en principe son empire tant à la formation qu'aux effets du contrat.

Ce principe subit pourtant quelques restrictions et la première de ces restrictions est justement celle visée à l'article 7.

D'après cet article, lorsque le contrat présente également des liens avec un pays autre que celui dont la loi est applicable en vertu des articles 2, 4, 5 et 6 et que la loi de cet autre pays contient des dispositions réglant impérativement la matière d'une façon qui exclut l'application de toute autre loi, il sera tenu compte de ces dispositions dans la mesure où leur nature ou leur objet particulier pourraient justifier cette exclusion.

L'incidence des lois de police sur la réglementation juridique de plusieurs rapports contractuels constitue à l'heure actuelle, pratiquement dans tous les pays, un aspect suffisamment connu de la vie économique pour qu'il soit nécessaire d'en souligner les manifestations les plus importantes. Non sans raison, la doctrine a pu parler d'une véritable police du contrat, – certains auteurs ont parlé de lois d'application immédiate ou de lois d'application nécessaire – trouvant son titre d'application, pour les pays où le Code Napoléon est en vigueur, dans l'article 3, premier alinéa, de ce Code, qui vise notamment les lois de police.

Il est impossible de dresser une liste de ces lois de police, puisque

ce caractère ne dépend pas de la matière dans laquelle elles interviennent, mais de la volonté de législateur qui les édicte. Telle disposition,
imposant par exemple un versement minimum immédiat de l'acheteur
dans les ventes à tempérament, pourra être considérée dans un pays
comme une loi de police, applicable à tous les contrats conclus sur son
territoire, et dans un autre pays comme une simple loi contractuelle,
applicable seulement aux contrats régis par la loi de ce dernier. Sous
cette réserve, on a encore cité, comme pouvant être couvertes le cas
échéant par cet article 7, les lois sur la résiliation de certains contrats
(par exemple la loi belge du 27 juillet 1961 sur la résiliation unilatérale
des concessions de vente exclusive à durée indéterminée), les lois relatives au contrôle des mouvements de capitaux ou des mouvements de
marchandises (interdictions de certains paiements à l'étranger, de certaines importations ou exportations).

Est-il opportun, et dans quelle mesure, de tenir compte de ces lois,
lorsqu'elles règlent impérativement certains effets ou certains éléments du contrat dans un pays avec lequel le contrat présente des
liens, mais qui n'est pas le pays dont la loi est applicable? Voilà le
problème auquel la règle de l'article 7 a voulu donner une solution
uniforme.

Toutefois, à la différence de ce qui se passe en d'autres cas (par
exemple en vertu de l'article 15, alinéa 2, pour les modalités d'exécution), l'exclusion de la loi normalement applicable au contrat en
vertu des articles 2, 4, 5 et 6 n'est pas ici *automatique*. La règle est
suffisamment souple pour laisser au juge une certaine marge d'appréciation. Une fois qu'il constate que le contrat présente également des
liens avec un pays autre que celui dont la loi est applicable et que la
loi de cet autre pays contient des dispositions réglant impérativement
la matière d'une façon qui exclut l'application de toute autre loi, le
juge devra en effet apprécier dans quelle mesure la nature ou l'objet
particulier de ces dispositions pourrait justifier l'exclusion de la loi
normalement applicable.

Ce n'est donc que dans la mesure où le contrat présente également
des liens avec un pays autre que celui dont la loi est applicable et à
la condition qu'il estime que la nature ou l'objet particulier des lois
de police en vigueur dans ce pays peut justifier l'exclusion de la loi
autrement applicable, que le juge tiendra compte de leurs dispositions
impératives en les coordonnant avec les dispositions de la loi applicable en vertu des articles 2, 4, 5 et 6.

La règle que nous venons de commenter confère aux juges de nos
pays une tâche sans aucun doute délicate et il se peut que son application par nos tribunaux n'aboutira pas toujours aux mêmes résultats.
Mais l'opportunité de cette règle paraît de toute façon incontestable.

Il s'agit de pouvoir résoudre, d'une façon satisfaisante, les situations extrèmement complexes qui caractérisent souvent les contrats à caractère international, notamment l'exécution de certaines obligations résultant de ces contrats.

2. La loi qui régit le contrat en vertu des articles 2, 4, 5 et 6 régit également sous plusieurs aspects, aux termes des articles 16 et 17, la cession volontaire ainsi que le transfert par l'effet de la loi des créances résultant du contrat.

Il est est de même pour les articles 18 et 19, 3ème alinéa, concernant la validité de la forme d'un acte juridique ainsi que la valeur comme instrument de preuve d'un document écrit sous seins privé[65].

C'est pour ce motif que l'article 7 est complété par l'adjonction des articles 16, 17, 18, 19, 3ème alinéa, dans l'énumération des articles auxquel il fait référence.

Article 8 (Consentement au contrat)

1. On a eu déjà l'occasion de faire remarquer que, dans le système de la présente Convention, le domaine de la loi du contrat s'étend en principe aussi bien à sa formation qu'à ses effets[66].

L'article 8 ne fait qu'expliciter le principe en matière de formation du contrat. Selon cet article, les conditions relatives à la validité du consentement des parties au contrat sont déterminées par la loi qui est applicable en vertu des articles précédents, notamment des articles 2, 4, 5 et 6.

2. Est-ce que le principe doit trouver également application en ce qui concerne la portée du silence d'une partie quant à la formation du contrat? Ou bien cette question doit-elle être réglée différemment?

C'est essentiellement autour de cette question qu'une divergence assez marquée d'opinions s'est manifestée au sein du Groupe.

D'après l'opinion d'une délégation, il serait préférable de ne pas régler cette question ainsi que la question de la portée du silence d'une partie quant à la loi applicable[67]. Ces questions, en d'autres termes, devraient trouver leur solution non pas dans les règles uniformes de la convention, mais dans les règles (de conflit ou matérielles) du droit national.

Par contre, les autres délégations se sont déclarées en faveur d'une réglementation expresse de la question dans la Convention. Cette

---

[65] V. *infra* le commentaire des articles 18 et 19.
[66] Cf. *supra* le commentaire de l'article 7, para. 1.
[67] Cf. le commentaire de l'article 2, para. 7.

réglementation devrait trouver sa place dans l'article 8; plus spécifiquement, elle devrait résulter du texte d'un 2ème alinéa à ajouter à cet article. Toutefois, du fait que les opinions des délégués se partagèrent entre partisans d'une règle de conflit et partisans d'une règle matérielle, aucun accord n'a pu être réalisé sur un texte unique de l'alinéa 2.

Dans ces conditions, le Groupe a décidé de supprimer, dans le texte de l'article 8, l'alinéa 2 et de reproduire en annexe cet alinéa dans les deux variantes entre lesquelles se sont partagées les délégations. La même décision a été adoptée en ce qui concerne la portée du silence d'une partie sur la loi applicable [68].

Dans le cas où l'introduction d'une règle de conflit devrait être retenue, l'alinéa 2 de l'article 8 constituerait une restriction ultérieure au domaine de la loi du contrat tel qu'il est déterminé par la Convention [69].

Article 9 (Transfert de la propriété)

En décidant que les dispositions des articles 2 à 8 ne s'appliquent pas au transfert de propriété et aux effets réels du contrat, l'article 9 établit une restriction nouvelle au principe d'après lequel le domaine de la loi du contrat s'étend tant à sa formation qu'à ses effets [70].

La raison d'être de cette restriction ne requiert qu'une justification très brève. En effet, il s'agit d'une restriction au domaine de la loi du contrat généralement acquise dans la doctrine, la jurisprudence et la pratique conventionnelle des Etats membres de la Communauté et pas seulement de ceux-ci [71]. C'est la loi applicable aux biens corporels et incorporels, non pas la loi du contrat, qui étend généralement son empire au transfert de propriété (par contrat) et aux effets réels du contrat. Et c'est justement dans ce cadre que ces questions trouveront leur solution, lorsque le Groupe, ainsi qu'il est prévu, s'engagera dans la recherche et l'élaboration de règles uniformes de conflit en matière de loi applicable à ces biens [72].

---

[68] *Cf.* le commentaire de l'article 2, para. 7.

[69] La première restriction a été examinée *supra* dans le commentaire de l'article 7.

[70] La première restriction a été examinée *supra* dans le commentaire de l'article 7.

[71] Pour quelques indications en la matière *cf. Batiffol/Lagarde* II nos. 524–525, p. 153 ss.

[72] V. à ce propos *supra* le paragraphe 4 du chapitre I.

Article 10 (Obligations délictuelles)

1. Principe de la lex loci delicti

En édictant que les obligations non contractuelles dérivant d'un fait dommageable sont régies par la loi du pays où ce fait s'est produit, le premier alinéa de l'article 10 se conforme à une règle traditionnelle dans le droit international privé de nos pays.

En effet, dans tous les Etats membres de la Communauté, les obligations nées d'un fait (action ou omission) illicite sont régies en principe par la loi du lieu où est survenu le fait dont elles résultent.

En France, une règle jurisprudentielle que l'on rattache souvent à l'article 3, alinéa premier, du Code civil, s'est justement établie en ce sens. Le projet français de loi complétant le Code civil en matière de droit international privé, dans son article 2312, se conforme à la même règle lorsqu'il statue que «les obligations non contractuelles sont régies par la loi du lieu où est survenu le fait dont elles résultent». Cet article, ainsi qu'il est précisé dans l'exposé des motifs du projet de loi, «étend à l'ensemble des obligations non contractuelles la solution donnée par la jurisprudence en matière de responsabilité délictuelle».

De leur côté, la plupart des auteurs se déclarent en faveur de la compétence de la «loi locale» *(lex loci delicti commissi)* par des considérations souvent pertinentes au sujet de sa raison d'être et par la critique d'autres rattachements proposés en la matière [73].

Aux termes de l'article 25, alinéa 2, des disp. prél. du Code civil italien, les obligations qui relèvent d'un fait illicite sont aussi soumises à la loi du lieu où est survenu le fait dont elle résultent, s'agissant justement de la catégorie la plus importante parmi les obligations non contractuelles visées par ladite disposition [74].

Malgré la limite établie dans l'article 12 de la loi d'introduction au Code civil, c'est le principe de la *lex loci delicti* qui régit également en Allemagne les obligations dérivant d'un fait illicite [75].

En ce qui concerne la Belgique, les Pays-Bas et le Luxembourg, le premier alinéa de l'article 14 de la loi uniforme Benelux dit que «la loi du pays où un fait a lieu, détermine si ce fait constitue un acte illicite, ainsi que les obligations qui en résultent». Comme il est précisé dans l'exposé des motifs de la loi [76], «en soumettant les obligations nées

---

[73] *Batiffol/Lagarde* I no. 285, p. 341 s.; et II nos. 556–559, p. 191 ss.; *Bourel,* Responsabilité civile, en Rép. dr. int. II (1969) nos. 4–34.

[74] *Morelli* no. 100, p. 160 s.

[75] *Kegel,* IPR p. 265 ss.; *Soergel/Siebert (-Kegel),* Art. 12 nos. 1 ss.

[76] Texte officiel *(supra* note 25) p. 54.

d'un fait illicite à la loi du pays où il a eu lieu, la loi uniforme se conforme à la jurisprudence et à la doctrine belges, néerlandaises, luxembourgeoises et françaises» [77].

2. Notion de fait dommageable

Le texte de l'article 10 utilise la formule de «fait dommageable» à la place de celle, plus courante, de «fait illicite» et il est opportun d'en préciser la raison.

Lors de la discussion du libellé originaire de la proposition du rapporteur en la matière, plusieurs experts ont fait remarquer que l'expression «fait illicite» pourrait soulever des problèmes de qualification, compte tenu de ce que la notion de fait illicite n'aurait pas le même contenu dans les droits des pays membres de la Communauté et qu'elle pourrait, dans quelques pays, ne pas englober certains cas de responsabilité objective (non fondée sur la faute).

C'est pour résoudre ces difficultés que le Groupe a estimé qu'il était préférable d'utiliser l'expression «fait dommageable». La même expression avait été d'ailleurs utilisée dans l'article 5, 3°, de la Convention C.E.E. concernant la compétence judiciaire et l'exécution des décisions en matière civile et commerciale; il a paru sage de s'inspirer d'une formule déjà retenue dans le cadre de la C.E.E.

Pourvu qu'il s'agisse de faits générateurs de dommage, l'article 10 vise indistinctement tous les faits dommageables susceptibles d'engendrer la naissance, à la charge de leurs auteurs, de l'obligation de réparer et, en faveur des victimes, du droit à réparation. C'est pour cela, par exemple, qu'en conformité avec des tendances bien assises dans la doctrine et dans la jurisprudence de nos pays, les obligations non contractuelles découlant de faits de concurrence déloyale ou illicite sont régies, elles aussi, par la loi applicable en vertu de l'article 10 [78].

3. Notion de fait dommageable (suite)

Quel est le pays où le fait dommageable s'est produit lorsque le fait générateur du dommage est survenu dans un pays autre que celui où les conséquences dommageables se sont manifestées? Quel est, par exemple, le pays dont la loi est applicable en vertu du premier alinéa de l'article 10 dans le cas d'une lettre injurieuse adressée à un destinataire à l'étranger?

---

[77] Pour quelques indications sur la jurisprudence de ces pays cf. *Rigaux* no. 423, p. 489 ss.; *Kokkini-Iatridou* (*supra* note 23) p. 60; *Huss* (*supra* note 23) p. 148 ss.

[78] *Wengler*, Die Gesetze über den unlauteren Wettbewerb und das internationale Privatrecht: RabelsZ 19 (1954) p. 401 ss.

La loi uniforme ne règle pas cette question. Afin de ne pas entraver les développements qui sont en cours dans la jurisprudence de nos pays, le Groupe a estimé qu'il était préférable de laisser la question ouverte.

4. Exceptions à la règle

Dès le début de ses travaux en matière de loi applicable aux obligations non contractuelles dérivant d'un fait dommageable, le Groupe a envisagé l'opportunité de ne pas attribuer à la *lex loci delicti* un caractère exclusif quant à la détermination de la loi applicable à ces obligations. La loi du lieu où le fait dommageable est survenu est certainement, et doit rester, la loi compétente à titre principal pour la réglementation juridique de ces obligations. Après avoir ainsi posé la règle principale il est apparu toutefois opportun d'envisager également la possibilité de s'en écarter dans certains cas où il n'existerait pas de lien suffisamment significatif entre la situation résultant du fait dommageable et le pays où ce fait s'est produit.

Une évolution intéressante s'est manifestée à cet égard dans la doctrine, la jurisprudence et la pratique de plusieurs pays dans le courant des dernières décennies. Selon certains auteurs, en effet, la solution traditionnelle retenue en matière de loi applicable à la responsabilité civile délictuelle ne serait pas la solution la meilleure et la plus appropriée dans toutes les situations. Le lieu où le fait illicite est survenu constitue sans aucun doute, dans un grand nombre de cas de responsabilité délictuelle, le rattachement le plus solide, souvent le seul rattachement utilisable pour la détermination de la loi applicable au délit. Mais il n'en est pas toujours ainsi. Les circonstances caractérisant ou accompagnant certains faits dommageables peuvent solliciter la recherche de solutions plus appropriées à ces situations; elles peuvent exiger que la loi applicable soit déterminée sur la base d'éléments de rattachement autres que celui du pays où le fait dommageable s'est produit. Parmi les manifestations importantes de ces tendances, il faut ranger également la résolution récemment adoptée à ce sujet par l'Institut de Droit International[79].

---

[79] Pour la résolution de l'Institut v. Conférence de d. i. p. de La Haye, Actes et documents de la Onzième Session III: Accidents de la circulation routière (1970) p. 219 s. En doctrine voir aussi entre autres *Binder*, Zur Auflockerung des Deliktsstatuts: RabelsZ 20 (1955) p. 401 ss.; *Ferrari Bravo*, Aspetti generali della disciplina della responsabilità per fatto illecito nel d. i. p.: Annali Fac. Giur. Univ. Bari 1962; *Beitzke*, Les obligations délictuelles en d. i. p.: Rec. des Cours 115 (1965-II) p. 67 ss.; *Kropholler*, Ein Anknüpfungssystem für das Deliktsstatut: RabelsZ 33 (1969) p. 601 ss.

D'autre part, ce n'est pas uniquement dans la doctrine, mais aussi dans la pratique que ces tendances se sont fait jour.

En droit allemand, un décret de 1942 opéra une première déviation de la règle générale de conflit en matière de responsabilité délictuelle en disposant que, si l'auteur et la victime d'un fait illicite survenu à l'étranger sont, tous les deux, des ressortissants allemands, les obligations résultant de ce fait seront été régies par la loi allemande. Bien qu'il soit controversé si ce décret est encore en vigueur, la jurisprudence allemande a continué et continue à faire application de son principe directeur. En effet, lorsque l'auteur et la victime d'un fait illicite ont la nationalité du même pays, il est fait parfois application de la loi nationale commune, non pas de la *lex loci delicti,* pour déterminer la responsabilité délictuelle[80].

Une seconde importante manifestation de cette évolution est celle de l'article 14 de la loi uniforme Benelux. Après avoir établi la compétence de la loi du lieu où le fait illicite est survenu, l'alinéa 2 de cet article dit que: «Toutefois, si les conséquences de l'acte illicite appartiennent à la sphère juridique d'un pays autre que celui où le fait a eu lieu, les obligations qui en résultent sont déterminées par la loi de cet autre pays.»

D'après l'exposé des motifs[81], la raison d'être de cette exception est la suivante: «Il arrive fréquemment, dans les relations internationales modernes, que les conséquences d'un fait illicite n'aient aucun lien avec le pays où il a eu lieu. Que l'on songe spécialement aux accidents de roulage, où l'auteur et les victimes sont tous ressortissants d'un pays et domiciliés dans un pays autre que celui où a lieu l'accident. De même l'assurance obligatoire pour les dommages aux tiers influence déjà, dans certains pays, l'étendue de la responsabilité et la détermination des personnes responsables.»

Quant à la question de savoir dans quelles conditions les conséquences d'un fait illicite appartiendraient à la «sphère juridique» d'un pays autre que celui où est survenu le fait dont elles résultent, l'exposé des motifs ne donne pas une réponse précise. Il se borne à indiquer que cela «dépend entièrement des circonstances» et que l' «on tiendra compte, par exemple, de la nationalité et du domicile de l'auteur et des victimes, du lieu où les conséquences dommageables se sont révélées pour la première fois, ou encore de la nationalité et du domicile du propriétaire du moyen de transport, cause de l'accident».

Enfin, en matière d'accidents de la circulation routière, plusieurs exceptions à la règle, d'après laquelle «la loi applicable est la loi de

---

[80] *Kegel,* IPR p. 271 ss.; *Soergel/Siebert(-Kegel),* Art. 12 nos. 22–30.
[81] Texte officiel (*supra* note 25) p. 55.

l'Etat sur le territoire duquel l'accident est survenu» (article 3), ont été prévues dans les articles 4 et 6 de la convention de La Haye du 4 mai 1971 sur la loi applicable à la dite catégorie d'accidents.

Les dispositions des alinéas 2 et 3 de l'article 10 ont justement pour but d'aller au-devant de ces tendances et de préciser, d'une façon aussi claire que possible, les limites dans lesquelles la loi applicable aux obligations non contractuelles dérivant d'un fait dommageable peut être celle d'un pays autre que celui où ce fait s'est produit.

5. Exceptions à la règle (suite)

En vertu de l'alinéa 2 de l'article 10 il est fait exception à la *lex loci delicti* lorsque, d'une part, il n'existe pas le lien significatif entre la situation résultant du fait dommageable et le pays où ce fait s'est produit et que, d'autre part, cette situation présente une connexion prépondérante avec un autre pays. Dans ces cas, à la place de la *lex loci delicti,* il est fait application de la loi de cet autre pays.

La disposition est suffisamment souple pour laisser au juge une certaine marge d'appréciation des circonstances pouvant justifier, dans chaque cas concret, l'application d'une loi autre que la *lex loci delicti.* Mais il s'agit d'une marge d'appréciation qui est limitée par des critères aussi clairs et précis que possible. Ce sont justement ces critères qui confèrent à la règle résultant des alinéas 2 et 3 de l'article 10 le caractère d'une exception par rapport à la règle principale consacrée dans le premier alinéa de l'article.

Quels sont ces critères?

D'abord, il est important de souligner que les deux circonstances dont on vient de parler ne sont, pour ainsi dire, que la face et le revers de la même médaille. La seule circonstance qu'il n'existe pas de lien significatif entre la situation résultant du fait dommageable et le pays où ce fait est survenu, pas plus que la seule circonstance que ladite situation présente une connexion prépondérante avec un pays autre que celui du fait dommageable, ne suffisent pas, indépendamment l'une de l'autre, pour faire jouer l'exception. Pour qu'il soit fait application de l'exception et que la *lex loci delicti* soit écartée en faveur de la loi d'un autre pays, il est nécessaire que les deux circonstances dont il est question s'accompagnent – et, pour ainsi dire, se complètent – l'une l'autre. Le libellé de l'alinéa 2 de l'article 10 est tout à fait clair en ce sens. La disposition réalise un équilibre entre l'absence d'un lien significatif et la présence d'une connexion prépondérante. Au demeurant, la connexion d'une situation avec un pays autre que celui du fait dommageable ne saurait être considérée comme prépondérante que si le lien avec le pays où ce fait s'est produit n'est pas significatif. Une dérogation à la loi du pays du fait dommageable n'est donc admise que dans des situations caractérisées en même temps tant par l'absence d'un lien significatif avec le pays où ce fait est survenu que par la présence d'une connexion prépondérante avec un autre pays.

En second lieu, la portée de l'exception est encore précisée par l'alinéa 3 de l'article 10. D'après cet alinéa, en effet, la connexion avec un pays autre que celui du fait dommageable doit se fonder normalement sur un élément de rattachement commun à la victime et à l'auteur du fait dommageable. Dans le cas où la responsabilité d'un tiers pour l'auteur est mise en cause, la connexion avec un pays autre que celui du fait dommageable doit se fonder normalement sur un élément de rattachement commun à la victime et à ce tiers.

En ce qui concerne les éléments de rattachement susceptibles de faire jouer l'exception, il serait évidemment impossible d'en établir ici un inventaire exhaustif. Il pourra s'agir parfois de la résidence habituelle commune des personnes impliquées dans la situation résultant du fait dommageable. En d'autres cas, il pourra s'agir d'un rapport juridique, contractuel ou légal, préexistant entre ces mêmes personnes et régi par la loi d'un pays autre que celui où le fait dommageable s'est produit.

De toute façon, il est opportun de souligner une fois de plus que la connexion dont il est ici question ne fera jouer l'exception que dans les cas où il s'agira d'une connexion «prépondérante» par rapport aux autres éléments de la situation, notamment par rapport au lien, qui ne doit pas être significatif, entre cette situation et le pays où le fait dommageable est survenu. C'est pour cela, à titre d'exemple, que dans le cas de deux ressortissants italiens, ayant leur résidence habituelle en Allemagne et dont l'un est la victime et l'autre l'auteur d'un accident de roulage survenu en Italie au cours de leur villégiature en ce pays, l'application de la *lex loci delicti* ne saurait normalement être écartée en faveur de la loi du pays de la résidence habituelle commune. Dans ce cas, en effet, il sera difficile de constater l'absence d'un lien significatif entre le pays où le fait dommageable s'est produit et la situation qui en est résultée.

Enfin, une dernière remarque sur la terminologie. Au lieu de parler de «conséquences» du fait dommageable, le Groupe a estimé préférable de se référer dans la disposition de l'alinéa 2 de l'article 10, à la «situation résultant du fait dommagéable». Cette dernière expression fait mieux ressortir le caractère purement matériel de la situation envisagée par la disposition. Dans le langage courant des juristes, en effet, le terme *conséquences* a le plus souvent ou, tout au moins, a aussi le sens de *conséquences juridiques* d'un fait ou d'un acte. L'expression utilisée par le Groupe souligne au contraire, au moins indirectement, que, dans l'optique des règles de conflit, ce n'est qu'après que la loi applicable a été déterminée, et seulement dans le cadre de cette loi, qu'on peut parler de conséquences juridiques d'un fait ou d'un acte.

6. *Pluralité de victimes, pluralité d'auteurs*

L'alinéa 4 de l'article 10 reprend la disposition figurant au second alinéa de l'article 4 de la convention sur la loi applicable en matière d'accidents de la circulation routière de La Haye[82].

D'après cet alinéa, en cas de pluralité de victimes, la loi applicable est déterminée séparément à l'égard de chacune d'entre elles. Etant donné que la *lex loci delicti* n'est pas toujours et nécessairement la loi applicable aux obligations délictuelles, le Groupe a estimé que cette disposition apparaîssait tout à fait logique et satisfaisait à l'exigence d'individualiser, en cas de pluralité de victimes, la loi la plus appropriée pour régir les différentes situations résultant du fait dommageable.

Par contre, en ce qui concerne le cas de pluralité d'auteurs, le Groupe a examiné le pour et le contre de la thèse favorable à l'unicité et de celle favorable à la multiplicité éventuelle des lois applicables. Cet examen a mis en lumière, cependant, que le problème n'avait pas encore atteint un dégré suffisant de maturité dans la doctrine et dans la jurisprudence de nos pays; il a donc été décidé de laisser la question ouverte.

7. *Localisation impossible*

Compte tenu de la valeur qu'il attribue à l'endroit où le fait dommageable s'est produit, l'article 10 n'est à même de remplir sa fonction que si cet endroit est connu et s'il s'agit d'un endroit faisant partie du territoire d'un Etat[83]. La règle de l'alinéa premier est tout à fait claire en ce sens. Mais également la règle consacrée dans les alinéas 2 et 3, en raison de son caractère d'exception par rapport à la règle principale du premier alinéa, est manifestement subordonnée à la même condition[84]. L'article 10, aussi bien dans son alinéa premier que dans ses alinéas 2 et 3, ne se propose pas de donner, et ne donne pas, une solution à la question de savoir quelle est la loi applicable aux obligations non contractuelles lorsqu'il s'avère impossible d'individualiser l'en-

---

[82] Sur les motifs qui ont amené la Conference de La Haye à l'adoption de cette disposition v. Actes et documents (*supra* note 79) p. 114 s., 116 s., 209 ss.

[83] L'hypothèse ici examinée est distincte de celle où le fait dommageable et ses conséquences se sont produits en deux pays différents, mais connus. V. *supra* le commentaire de ce même article au para. 3.

[84] V. *supra* le commentaire de ce même article au para. 5.

droit où le fait dommageable s'est produit (par exemple: délit commis dans un train au cours du passage de la frontière entre deux pays) ou lorsque cet endroit est en dehors de la compétence territoriale de tout Etat (par exemple: abordage de navires en haute mer). Au demeurant, ce n'est que par une disposition spéciale que ces questions auraient pu être réglées dans la convention.

Le Groupe s'est demandé s'il était opportun d'insérer dans les règles uniformes une disposition spéciale à ce sujet; il n'a pas manqué d'examiner, même brièvement, quelques solutions qui pouvaient être envisagées en la matière: entre autres, la possibilité de faire dépendre la détermination de la loi applicable, dans les situations dont on vient de parler, de l'autonomie de la volonté des parties intéressées. Toutefois, à la suite de cet échange de vues, le Groupe a estimé qu'il était préférable de ne pas régler la question, qui reste donc entièrement ouverte.

Article 11 (Domaine de la loi désignée par l'article 10)

1. Tandis que l'article 10 est consacré à la détermination de la loi applicable en matière d'obligations non contractuelles dérivant d'un fait dommageable, l'article 11 est consacré au domaine de la loi applicable en la matière. Dès maintenant, toutefois, il est important de signaler que l'article 11 n'est pas le seul article de la convention ayant une incidence sur le domaine de la loi applicable aux obligations non contractuelles. Il faut également tenir compte à ce sujet des prescriptions de l'article 12 ainsi que de celles des articles 14 et 15 de la convention: dans la mesure où ces dispositions, en raison de leur caractère tout à fait général, sont applicables également aux obligations non contractuelles.

En adoptant l'article 11 le Groupe n'a pas voulu faire une énumération exhaustive de toutes les questions couverts par la loi applicable à la responsabilité civile, mais s'est contenté d'une énumération énonciative (marquée dans le texte par l'emploi de l'adverbe *notamment*), afin de ne pas exclure involontairement une question importante. L'article ne mentionne donc que les principales questions qui sont régies par la loi applicable à la responsabilité civile découlent de faits dommageables.

L'article 11 reprend, avec quelques modifications, le texte de l'article 8 de la Convention sur la loi applicable en matière d'accidents de la circulation routière de La Haye. En effet, toutes les délégations ont reconnu l'opportunité de déterminer le domaine de la loi applicable aux obligations visées par l'article 10 de la Convention dans la façon la plus claire et précise que possible. En même temps, toutes les délégations ont été de l'avis que l'article 8 de la convention susmentionnée répondait très bien, dans son ensemble, à cette exigence et pouvait, dès lors, être pris comme modèle pour la formulation de la règle à insérer dans la présente convention.

C'est pour cela qu'en procédant dans les deux paragraphes qui vont suivre à quelques observations sur les divers points envisagés par l'article 11, il sera nécessairement et largement tenu compte des remarques de M. *Eric W. Essén,* développées dans son rapport explicatif de la convention de La Haye, au sujet de l'article 8 de cette convention[85].

2. Le numéro 1 de l'article 11 mentionne *les conditions et l'étendue de la responsabilité.* Il s'agit des éléments intrinsèques de la responsabilité à savoir les conditions positives de celle-ci.

Par conditions de la responsabilité, on entend par exemple si la responsabilité est basée sur la faute ou s'il s'agit d'une responsabilité objective, la définition de la faute, y compris le problème de savoir si l'omission peut, au même titre que l'action, constituer une faute, l'existence d'un fait générateur de responsabilité, les présomptions de responsabilité, le rapport de causalité entre le fait dommageable et le dommage, les personnes responsables, etc.

La référence à l'étendue de la responsabilité vise, entre autres, les limitations légales de celle-ci et indique que le plafond de la responsabilité, s'il en existe un, est régi par la loi déclarée applicable à la responsabilité en vertu de l'article 10. Tombe sous ce chef notamment la question des intérêts compensatoires.

Selon le numéro 2 de l'article 11, la loi déclarée applicable détermine également les *causes d'exonération, ainsi que toute limitation et tout partage de responsabilité.* Cette disposition se réfère aux éléments extrinsèques de la responsabilité, à savoir les conditions d'exonération.

Parmi les causes d'exonérations, on classe par exemple la force majeure, y compris l'état de nécessité et le fait d'un tiers, ainsi que la faute exclusive de la victime.

Quant à la notion de partage de la responsabilité, elle peut se référer au cas où il y a faute concomitante de la victime et d'un tiers; dans ce cas, la responsabilité du dommage est partagée entre l'auteur et la victime, éventuellement suivant les proportions variables d'après la gravité respective des fautes commises.

En vertu du numéro 3 de l'article 11, la loi déclarée applicable détermine *l'existence et la nature des dommages susceptible de réparation.*

C'est selon cette loi qu'on déterminera donc s'il existe un préjudice

---

[85] Actes et documents (*supra* note 79) p. 212 ss.

qui peut engendrer la responsabilité civile ainsi que l'ordre des préjudices réparables, tel que le dommage corporel, matériel, moral. La loi déclarée applicable détermine également les divers éléments du dommage dont la victime peut demander réparation, comme les pertes subies et les gains manqués par la victime *(damnum emergens, lucrum cessans),* ainsi que, comme cela résulte du numéro 4, l'évaluation de ces divers éléments.

Le numéro 4 de l'article 11 vise les *modalités et l'étendue de la réparation.* Il s'est avéré nécessaire de mentionner expressément ce point, étant donné que la question de la mesure de la réparation est actuellement réglée dans certains pays, comme le Royaume-Uni, par la *lex fori.*

La loi applicable détermine aussi le mode de réparation, à savoir si le préjudice doit être réparé en nature ou par équivalent, sous forme de dommages-intérêts, ainsi que l'évaluation du montant de la réparation. ʹ

3. Le numéro 5 de l'article 11 a trait à la *mesure dans laquelle le droit de la victime à réparation peut être exercé par ses héritiers.*

Cette disposition modifie partiellement la disposition du numéro 5 de l'article 8 de la convention de La Haye. Cette dernière disposition parle de la «transmissibilité du droit à réparation» et couvre, ainsi qu'il ressort clairement du texte anglais [86], la transmission tant par acte de cession que par voie successorale. Etant donné que dans la présente convention la cession de créances forme l'objet d'une règle spécifique de conflit, il était évidemment nécessaire de limiter le contenu du numéro 5 de l'article 11 à la seule hypothèse de transmission par voie successorale.

Dans ce dernier cas, il s'agit de savoir si une action peut être intentée par un ayant cause de la victime – non pas à titre personnel aux fins d'obtenir réparation du dommage qu'il a subi «par ricochet» à la suite du décès de la victime – mais à titre d'héritier en vue d'obtenir réparation du dommage initial subi par la victime dans son corps ou dans ses biens. Le texte adopté ne règle pas la question de la loi applicable à la détermination de la qualité d'héritier, qui est abandonnée à la règle de conflit du juge saisi.

Quant à l'exercice par les héritiers du droit de la victime à réparation, il fallait choisir entre deux tendances: l'une en faveur de l'application en la matière de la loi successoriale, l'autre estimant que la transmissibilité relève plûtot de la loi applicable à la responsabilité. Le Groupe a préféré cette seconde solution. Elle présente un intérêt particulier en raison des divergences qui existent entre les pays de *Common Law* et les pays continentaux sur la question de la transmis-

---

[86] Qui est formulé de la façon suivante: «The question whether a right to damages may be assigned or inherited».

sibilité du droit à réparation. Bien que l'opposition des premiers à la recevabilité de l'action héréditaire ait subi de nombreux aménagements, des divergences subsistent encore en ce qui concerne les conditions d'exercice de l'action des héritiers.

Enfin il y a lieu de signaler que le problème de la transmissibilité passive aux héritiers de l'obligation de réparer incombant au défunt ne peut dépendre que de la loi de la succession.

D'après le numéro 6 de l'article 11, la loi applicable détermine aussi *les personnes ayant droit à réparation du dommage qu'elles ont personnellement subi.* Cette disposition vise en particulier la question de savoir si une personne autre que la «victime directe» peut obtenir réparation du dommage qui lui est causé «par ricochet», à la suite du préjudice qui a frappé la victime. Il arrive très souvent que le dommage moral soit l'un de ces préjudices, qui sont la conséquence d'un premier dommage subi par autrui: par exemple, le décès accidentiel d'une personne cause de l'affliction à une autre personne. Mais une telle situation se rencontre également dans le domaine du dommage matériel. Quand le texte dit que le préjudice doit être personnel à celui qui en demande réparation, cela ne veut pas dire qu'une personne morale, constituée par un groupement d'individus, ne puisse pas se faire indemniser du préjudice qui atteint l'ensemble des intérêts qu'elle représente. Le problème de savoir si une action en réparation intentée par une personne morale sera recevable dépend, lui aussi, de la loi déclarée applicable à la responsabilité.

Aux termes du numéro 7 de l'article 11, la loi applicable aux obligations non contractuelles dérivant d'un fait dommageable détermine la *responsabilité du fait d'autrui.* La disposition modifie, en l'élargissant, le texte de la disposition contenue dans le numéro 7 de l'article 8 de la convention de La Haye, qui ne vise que la responsabilité du commettant du fait de son préposé.

En vertu du numéro 8 de l'article 11, la loi applicable à la responsabilité détermine *les prescriptions et les déchéances fondées sur l'expiration d'un délai, y compris le point de départ, l'interruption et la suspension des délais.* Par prescription, l'article 11 vise la prescription extinctive, par opposition à la prescription acquisitive, et qui d'une manière générale peut être décrite comme un mode d'extinction d'un droit à la suite du non-exercice de celui-ci avant l'expiration d'une période de temps déterminée par la loi. Elle doit être prise au sens large couvrant les courtes prescriptions. Pour renforcer ce sens large, l'article se réfère en outre aux déchéances. La notion de déchéance, connue dans les systèmes juridiques continentaux, se réfère à la perte d'un droit ou d'une action faute de l'exercer dans le délai prévu et sous les conditions requises. En procédure, les déchéances sont généralement dénommées forclusions. Le texte ne vise que les déchéances fondées sur l'expiration d'un délai et les cas où l'on peut être déchu d'un droit autrement que par l'expiration d'un délai ne sont pas couverts par l'article 11, numéro 8.

Le principe de soumettre la prescription à la loi applicable à la responsabilité est d'une utilité certaine. Il apporte une certitude en la matière, en mettant fin à l'opposition ancienne entre partisans de l'application à cette question de la loi du for, pour le motif qu'elle concerne la procédure, et partisans de l'application de la loi régissant la responsabilité, pour le motif qu'il s'agit là d'une question touchant au fond de la responsabilité.

4. Ainsi qu'il ressort assez clairement des considérations qui précèdent, l'article 11, même si son énumération n'est pas exhaustive, confère à la loi applicable à la responsabilité civile le plus large domaine d'application possible. Il eût été en effet inutile de dégager une loi régissant en principe la responsabilité civile de faits dommageables si l'on avait par la suite soustrait à son empire une foule de questions relevant de la responsabilité. Tout ce que le droit civil soumet à la responsabilité délictuelle, sauf les matières expressément exclues dans l'article premier de la convention, entrera donc dans ce domaine.

Au cours des travaux du Groupe, la question a été soulevée de savoir si le droit d'agir directement contre l'assureur du responsable civil devrait rentrer dans le domaine de la loi applicable en vertu de l'article 10 ou s'il conviendrait d'insérer dans le convention une disposition particulière à ce sujet.

A la suite d'une discussion assez approfondie, le Groupe, en raison de la divergence de conceptions des droits nationaux sur l'action directe, n'a pas jugé possible de présenter une solution uniforme en la matière, et, à la différence de la convention de La Haye du 4 mai 1971, a laissé la question ouverte.

Article 12 (Règles de sécurité et de police)

Nonobstant sa formulation très générale, cet article vise essentiellement les situations où la loi applicable aux obligations non contractuelles dérivant d'un fait dommageable n'est pas la *lex loci delicti*. C'est justement dans ces situations, en effet, qu'il peut se révéler utile et même indispensable de tenir compte, dans la détermination de la responsabilité, des règles de sécurité et de police en vigueur au lieu et au moment où le fait dommageable s'est produit.

L'article 12 est pour ainsi dire le pendant de l'article 7 de la présente convention en matière d'obligations contractuelles. Il reprend une disposition de la convention de La Haye sur la loi applicable en matière d'accidents de la circulation routière (article 7).

Les termes utilisés dans l'article 12 laissent une certaine marge d'appréciation à l'égard des diverses réglementations qui sont à prendre en considération dans un cas donné.

Article 13 (Autres obligations non contractuelles)

Cet article étend, dans une large mesure, aux obligations non contractuelles dérivant d'un fait autre qu'un fait dommageable, la règle et l'exception retenues dans l'article 10 de la présente Convention.

La disposition vise essentiellement les quasi-contrats (gestion d'affaires, enrichissement sans cause; paiement de l'indû) ainsi que les autres obligations qui peuvent être ramenées, d'une façon ou de l'autre, à la même catégorie. Un exemple de ces dernières est celui des obligations dérivant de l'assistance et du sauvetage maritimes (intervenus sans l'accord, exprès ou tacite, de l'assisté ou du propriétaire éventuel): à la condition que ces opérations aient lieu dans les eaux internes ou dans les eaux territoriales d'un Etat. S'il en était autrement, à savoir s'il s'agissait de faits d'assistance et sauvetage maritimes survenus (toujours sans l'accord de l'assisté ou du propriétaire éventuel) en haute mer, l'article 13 serait évidemment inapplicable. En effet, tant l'article 13 que l'article 10 de la Convention présupposent que les faits générateurs d'obligations se soient produits dans le territoire d'un Etat donné et ils ne sont plus à même de remplir leur fonction lorsque l'endroit où ces faits sont survenus n'est pas connu ou est en dehors de la compétence territoriale de tout Etat. Quant à la question de savoir quelle loi serait applicable dans ces derniers cas, le Groupe a estimé qu'il était préférable de la laisser ouverte[87].

Pour terminer, il est nécessaire de faire remarquer que l'exception à la règle d'après laquelle les obligations visées par l'article 13 sont, elles aussi, régies par la loi du pays où s'est produit le fait dont elles résultent, est plus souple que l'exception correspondante des alinéas 2 et 3 de l'article 10. L'exception de l'article 13 n'exige pas, en effet, que la connexion prépondérante de ces obligations avec un autre pays s'accompagne – et, pour ainsi dire, se complète – avec l'absence d'un lien significatif avec le pays où s'est produit le fait dont elles découlent. L'article 13 laisse donc au juge une marge plus large d'appréciation quant à la présence de circonstances pouvant justifier l'application d'une loi autre que celle du pays où le fait générateur d'obligations quasi-contractuelles est survenu.

---

[87] *Cf.* aussi le commentaire de l'article 10, para. 7.

Article 14 (Responsabilité de l'Etat)

Le domaine de la loi applicable aux obligations non contractuelles n'étend pas son empire à la responsabilité de l'Etat ou d'autres personnes morales de droit public ainsi qu'à celle de leurs organes ou agents pour les actes relevant de la puissance publique et accomplis par eux dans l'exercice de leurs fonctions. L'article 14 en dispose justement ainsi, en déclarant que les dispositions des articles 10 à 13 ne s'appliquent pas à la matière dont nous venons de parler.

Le but et la portée de cette restriction au domaine aussi bien de la loi du délit que de la loi applicable aux autres obligations non contractuelles sont évidents. Une délégation aurait préféré préciser que l'exclusion vise les actes accomplis non seulement dans l'exercice, mais aussi dans la limite des fonctions des organes de la puissance publique. Cependant, une précision en ce sens n'est pas apparue strictement indispensable.

Dans les conditions indiquées dans l'article 14, et dans les situations ayant un caractère international, la responsabilité de l'Etat, des personnes morales de droit public et de leurs organes, ne saurait être appréciée que dans le cadre de la loi et devant les tribunaux de l'Etat dont la responsabilité est mise en cause. A la rigueur, cette responsabilité ne soulève pas de problèmes de droit international privé *stricto sensu*, mais éventuellement des problèmes de compétence judiciaire, plus spécifiquement d'immunité de juridiction.

De ce point de vue on aurait pu même se passer de fixer expressément la restriction consacrée dans l'article 14. Mais le Groupe a estimé qu'il était préférable de donner une solution expresse à la question pour éviter toute incertitude et tenir compte des particularités du droit allemand en ce domaine.

Article 15 (Exécution, extinction, inexécution)

1. Aux termes de l'alinéa premier de l'article 15, la loi qui régit une obligation en vertu des articles 2 à 6, 10 et 13, étend en principe son empire également aux conditions de son exécution, aux divers modes de son extinction et aux conséquences de son inexécution.

Quel est le sens des expressions utilisées dans cet alinéa?

En ce qui concerne les «conditions d'exécution» de l'obligation, cette expression semble bien se référer à l'ensemble des conditions résultant de la loi ou du contrat suivant lesquelles la prestation qui caractérise toute obligation doit être exécutée, à l'exclusion tant des modalites d'exécution (visées spécifiquement par l'alinéa 2 de l'article 15), que des conditions relatives à la capacité des personnes impliquées dans l'exécution de la prestation (s'agissant d'une manière exclue, sous réserve de l'article 20, du champ d'application des règles uniformes) ainsi que des conditions relatives à la forme de l'acte juridique éventuellement à accomplir pour l'exécution de la prestation (visées spécifiquement par l'article 18 de la convention). Tombent sous le chef de la disposition de l'alinéa premier de l'article 15: la question de la diligence avec laquelle la prestation doit être exécutée; les conditions relatives au lieu et au temps de l'exécution de la prestation; la mesure dans laquelle l'obligation peut être exécutée par une personne autre que le débiteur; les conditions concernant l'exécution de l'obligation tant en général que par rapport à certaines catégories d'obligations (obligations solidaires, obligations alternatives, obligations divisibles et indivisibles, obligations pécuniaires); dans le cas où la prestation consiste dans le paiement d'une somme d'argent, les conditions relatives à la libération du débiteur qui a effectué le paiement, à l'imputation des paiements, à la quittance; etc.

Quant à l'expression «modes d'extinction» elle s'entend des différents modes d'extinction de l'obligation, à l'exclusion de son exécution. Plus spécifiquement, l'expression vise la novation, la compensation, la confusion, la remise de dettes et la prescription extinctive ou libératoire. Dans le cas de la compensation, il faut envisager l'hypothèse que les obligations à compenser sont soumises à deux lois différentes. Dans cette hypothèse, il semble bien que la compensation ne se réalise que dans la mesure où elle est admise par la loi régissant chacune des obligations à compenser[88].

Enfin, l'expression «conséquences de l'inexécution» a trait aux conséquences que la loi ou le contrat font découler de l'inéxecution d'une obligation contractuelle ou non contractuelle, qu'il s'agisse de la responsabilité de la partie à laquelle l'inexécution est imputable ou qu'il s'agisse de l'exception d'inexécution et de la résolution du contrat pour inexécution. La nécessité (éventuelle) d'une mise en demeure du débiteur pour que la responsabilité de celui-ci soit engagée rentre également dans ce contexte.

Cependant, la portée plus précise de la disposition ne saurait se dégager qu'à la suite de sa coordination avec les autres dispositions ayant trait au domaine de la loi du contrat, et, respectivement, de la loi du fait dommageable. Or, c'est justement cette coordination qui permet de se rendre compte que la portée de l'article 15 est plus large en matière d'obligations contractuelles qu'elle l'est en matière d'obligations non contractuelles.

---

[88] En ce sens *Batiffol/Lagarde* II no. 614, p. 272; *Morelli* no. 107, p. 170.

En ce qui concerne ces dernières obligations, en effet, l'article 11 des règles uniformes précise d'une façon détaillée – ainsi que nous l'avons constaté précédemment – les questions rentrant dans la domaine de la loi applicable au fait dommageable. L'article 11 paraît bien, d'ailleurs, pouvoir s'appliquer par analogie aux obligations non contractuelles découlant d'un fait autre qu'un fait dommageable. Il est vrai que l'énumération de ces questions, telle qu'elle résulte de l'article 11, n'est pas exhaustive. Mais il est vrai également que, même si elle est énonciative, cette énumération couvre sans aucun doute la plupart des questions qui peuvent se présenter en la matière et vise expressément plusieurs questions qui, s'il n'y avait pas l'article 11, tomberaient sous le chef de l'alinéa premier de l'article 15[89].

Par contre, dans la convention il n'y a pas de disposition comparable à celle de l'article 11 en ce qui concerne le domaine de la loi applicable aux obligations contractuelles. Les dispositions des articles 7, 8 et 9 ont certes une incidence, positive ou négative – ainsi que nous l'avons souligné dans les commentaires respectifs – sur le domaine de la loi du contrat. Mais, mises à part ces dispositions, le Groupe n'a pas jugé indispensable de préciser d'une façon générale que le domaine de la loi du contrat s'étend en principe à tous ses effets. Une précision de ce genre n'est pas apparue strictement nécessaire du fait que les plus importants effets du contrat consistent essentiellement dans l'exécution, ou dans les conséquences de l'inexécution, de l'obligation qu'une partie contractante (ou chacune des parties contractantes) a pris l'engagement d'accomplir par rapport à l'autre partie; par ailleurs, l'extension à ces effets du domaine de la loi du contrat est couverte dans une large mesure par l'article qu'on est en train de commenter.

En ce qui concerne les obligations contractuelles, la portée de l'alinéa premier de l'article 15 est donc plus large qu'elle ne l'est en matière d'obligations non contractuelles découlant d'un fait dommageable. L'adverbe «également», qui est inséré dans le texte de l'article 15 précise, au demeurant, que cet article n'est pas le seul qu'il faut prendre en considération pour la détermination du domaine de la loi applicable aux obligations contractuelles et non contractuelles.

2. Une restriction à l'alinéa premier de l'article 15 est établie dans l'alinéa 2. D'après cet alinéa, en ce qui concerne les «modalités d'exécution» de l'obligation, on aura égard à la loi du pays où l'exécution a lieu.

Il s'agit d'une restriction qui est souvent évoquée dans le droit national de certains pays[90] ainsi que dans quelques conventions inter-

---

[89] V. notamment les nos. 1, 4 et 8 de l'article 11.

[90] Par exemple en Italie, où la majorité de la doctrine, malgré l'absence d'une disposition expresse de la loi, se prononce en faveur de la restriction

nationales[91]. Plusieurs auteurs se sont prononcés et se prononcent également en faveur de cette restriction au domaine de la loi applicable aux obligations contractuelles et non contractuelles: bien entendu, lorsque l'exécution de l'obligation a lieu dans un pays autre que celui dont la loi est applicable[92].

Que faut-il entendre, toutefois, par «modalités d'exécution» d'une obligation? La notion ne paraît pas avoir, en effet, un contenu uniforme et précis dans les divers droits et dans les diverses conceptions doctrinales[93]. De son côté, le Groupe n'a pas voulu donner une définition rigoureuse de cette notion. La qualification de la notion de «modalités d'exécution» d'une obligation sera, par conséquent, opérée en conformité de la *lex fori*. Parmi les dispositions rentrant normalement dans la catégorie des modalités d'exécution, il semble bien, de toute façon, qu'on puisse mentionner la réglementation des jours fériés, celle des modalités d'examen de la marchandise ainsi que les mesures à prendre en cas de refus de celle-ci[94].

Article 16 (Cession de créance)

1. Les opinions sont partagées en droit international privé sur la question de savoir quelle loi doit régir le transfert de créances[96]. Après une discussion approfondie de la question, au cours de laquelle le pour et le contre de plusieurs propositions du rapporteur et des délégations a été soigneusement examiné, le Groupe en est arrivé à la conclusion qu'il était opportun de ne pas englober dans un seul article les solutions finalement retenues en matière de loi applicable au transfert de créances, mais de formuler séparément ces solutions suivant que le transfert

---

dont il est question. En ce sens *Conforti*, L'esecuzione delle obbligazioni nel d. i. p. (1962) p. 27 ss., 204 ss.

[91] *Cf.* les indications données ci-après dans la note 94.

[92] *Batiffol*, Obligations, en: Rép. dr. int. II (1969) nos. 59–65, p. 497; *Vitta*, Prospettive del d. i. p. (1968) p. 154 ss.

[93] V. à ce propos l'intéressante analyse de M. *Broggini*, Le modalità d'esecuzione dei contratti in d. i. p. (1951).

[94] V. à ce sujet l'article 4 de la convention de La Haye de 1955 sur la loi applicable aux ventes à caractère international, ainsi que l'article 38, 4 de la convention de La Haye de 1964 portant loi uniforme sur la vente internationale des objets mobiliers corporels.

[96] *Batiffol/Lagarde* II no. 611, p. 264 ss.; *Zweigert*, Das Statut der Vertragsübernahme: RabelsZ 23 (1958) p. 643 ss.; *Vischer* (*supra* note 63) p. 238 ss.; *Reithmann* (*supra* note 18) p. 386 ss.; *Holleaux*, Cession de créance, dans: Rép. dr. int. (1968) p. 283 ss.; *Beuttner*, La cession de créance en d. i. p. (1971).

d'une créance est l'effet d'une convention ou qu'il est l'effet (direct) de la loi.

C'est pour cela que l'article 16, dont nous allons traiter maintenant ne vise que la cession faite par le créancier (cession volontaire ou cession proprement dite); tandis qu'au transfert de créances par l'effet de la loi (subrogation légale) est consacré l'article 17.

2. L'alinéa premier de l'article 16 dispose que les obligations entre cédant et cessionnaire d'une créance sont régies par la loi applicable en vertu des articles 2 à 8 qui précèdent.

L'interprétation de cette disposition ne donne lieu à aucune difficulté. Il est évident que, d'après le premier alinéa de l'article 16, le rapport entre cédant et cessionnaire d'une créance est régi par la loi applicable à la convention de la cession, qui est justement la loi applicable «en vertu des articles 2 à 8».

Bien que l'objet et le sens de la disposition ne soulèvent guère de doute, on pourrait se demander pourquoi le Groupe n'a pas rédigé cette disposition d'une façon plus simple et, probablement, plus élégante du point de vue de la technique législative. Pourquoi ne pas dire, par exemple, que le «transfert d'une créance par convention est régi dans les rapports entre cédant et cessionnaire par la loi applicable à cette convention»?

Une formulation de ce genre, en effet, avait rencontré le consentement de la majorité des membres du Groupe au début de l'élaboration du texte de l'article 16. Mais elle a été ensuite abandonnée en raison des difficultés d'interprétation qu'elle aurait pu engendrer en droit allemand, où l'expression «transfert» d'une créance par convention englobe les effets de la cession vis-à-vis du débiteur: ce qui était au contraire expressément exclu par l'alinéa 2 de l'article 16.

C'est pour éviter une formulation qui permettrait de penser que la loi applicable à la convention de cession, dans les systèmes de droit où elle est entendue comme *Kausalgeschäft,* détermine également les conditions de validité de la cession au regard du débiteur, que le texte actuel a été finalement adopté.

3. Aux termes de l'alinéa 2 de l'article 16, c'est au contraire la loi qui régit la créance originaire – qui est applicable en ce qui concerne tous les autres problèmes ici soulevés par la cession de créances. Dans un souci de clarté le Groupe a jugé utile de préciser que le domaine de la loi applicable à la créance originaire s'étend non seulement au caractère transférable (ou cessible) de celle-ci, mais également aux rapports entre cessionaire et débiteur ainsi qu'aux conditions d'opposabilité de la cession au débiteur et aux tiers. Cette dernière précision se réfère aux mesures prescrites par la loi interne de certains pays (signification de la cession, remise d'une copie de l'acte de cession,

etc.), qui sont considérées comme une *conditio sine qua non* pour que la cession puisse être valablement opposée au débiteur et aux tiers.

4. L'article 16 s'étend à toute cession volontaire de créance et notamment aux cessions de créances effectuées dans le cadre de cette opération très répandue à l'heure actuelle et sans doute importante dans la vie économique de nos pays qu'est le *factoring*.

Article 17 (Transfert de créance par l'effet de la loi)

1. Ainsi qu'on a eu déjà l'occasion de le faire remarquer [97] cet article ne vise que le transfert d'une créance par l'effet de la loi. Il est opportun de souligner que l'expression «transfert d'une créance par l'effet de la loi» a été jugée préférable à celle, plus courante, de «subrogation légale» pour éviter les problèmes de qualification et indiquer que l'article 17 vise toute espèce de transfert d'une créance par effet de la loi, même si elle devait être qualifiée en droit interne par une expression autre que celle de subrogation légale (par exemple: cession légale, etc.).

D'après l'alinéa premier de l'article 17, ce transfert est régi par la loi de l'institution juridique dans le fonctionnement de laquelle il intervient. La règle se conforme aux manifestations les plus récentes de la jurisprudence de quelques Etats membres de la Communauté, notamment de l'Allemagne, de la Belgique et de la France, en la matière. C'est justement en ce sens que s'est prononcée la Cour de cassation française dans son arrêt du 17 mars 1970 dans l'affaire *Reyes et autres* c. *Etats-Unis d'Amérique,* en déclarant que «la subrogation légale est régie par la loi de l'institution pour le fonctionnement de laquelle elle a été créée» [98]. Et c'est toujours à une solution quasi-identique qu'-étaient parvenues la Cour de cassation de Belgique dans son arrêt du 23 octobre 1969 sur l'affaire *République Fédérale d'Allemagne* c. *Bureau belge des assureurs automobiles* [99a] ainsi que la Cour fédérale d'Allemagne dans son arrêt du 26 avril 1966 concernant une espèce identique [99b].

En application de la règle susmentionnée, à titre d'exemple: la subrogation légale de l'assureur de dommages aux droits de l'assuré contre l'auteur du dommagé sera régie par la loi qui régit le contrat d'as-

---

[97] V. *supra* le commentaire de l'article 16, para. 1.

[98] Cass. fr. 17 mars 1970 *(Reyes et autres c. Etats-Unis d'Amérique),* Rev. crit. 59 (1970) p. 688 s. (avec note de M. *Lagarde).*

[99a] Cass. belge 23 octobre 1969 *(République Fédérale d'Allemagne c. Bureau belge des assureurs automobiles),* Rev. crit. 59 (1970) p. 690 s. = J. Trib. 1970, p. 28 s.

[99b] BGH 26 avril 1966, IPRspr. 1966–67 no. 31 b, p. 100 s.

surance; la subrogation légale de la sécurité sociale aux droits de celui qu'elle indemnise contre le tiers responsable sera soumise à la loi dont le mécanisme de cette institution relève; la subrogation légale au profit de celui qui, étant tenu avec d'autres au paiement de la dette, avait intérêt à l'acquitter (telle qu'elle est prévue par les articles 1251-3° du Code civil français et 1203-3° du Code civil italien) – qui concerne les codébiteurs solidaires, ou d'une obligation indivisible, et la caution – sera soumise à la loi régissant l'obligation, contractuelle ou non contractuelle, dont elle dérive, etc.

2. Il est fait exception à la règle de l'alinéa premier en ce qui concerne le caractère transférable de la créance ainsi que les droits et les obligations du débiteur. Ce caractère, comme les droits et obligations du débiteur, doivent être déterminés selon la loi qui régit la créance originaire. C'est la précision qui donne à juste titre l'alinéa 2 de l'article 17.

Dans le transfert d'une créance par l'effet de la loi, en effet, c'est la créance originaire qui continue sa vie dans la personne du subrogé légal. Il est donc tout à fait logique que la position du débiteur vis-à-vis du subrogé légal ne soit pas aggravée par rapport à la position qu'il avait vis-à-vis du créancier originaire.

La mention des droits et obligations du débiteur englobe et présuppose nécessairement l'existence de la créance qui est l'objet du transfert par l'effet de la loi, ou, si l'on préfère, englobe et présuppose nécessairement l'existence de l'obligation dont la créance originaire relève. L'existence, de même que la non-extinction de la créance originaire, sont donc, elles aussi, soumises à la loi qui régit la créance originaire.

Article 18 (Forme des actes juridiques)

1. L'article 18 a trait à la forme des actes. Il convient d'en préciser le domaine, avant d'indiquer les diverses lois qu'il déclare applicables.

A. Domaine de l'article 18

2. *Actes visés.* – L'article 18 est applicable aux *actes* juridiques, *lato sensu*. Le terme retenu est plus large que celui de contrat et englobe les actes unilatéraux qui entrent dans le champ d'application de la convention, et notamment les reconnaissances de dette et certaines renonciations.

Aucune disposition ne vise expressément les *actes publics*. Cette omission est volontaire. Tout d'abord, la notion d'acte public n'est pas connue de toutes les législations et elle pourrait poser de délicats problèmes de qualification.

D'autre part, une disposition spéciale n'aurait pu que consacrer la règle, admise par tous les Etats contractants, selon laquelle un officier public instrumente selon la loi dont il tient ses pouvoirs. Or une telle disposition est apparue inutile, car le texte adopté ne fait nullement échec à ladite règle. En effet, sauf dans le cas des actes dressés par des consuls, la loi dont l'officier public tient ses pouvoirs est celle du pays dans lequel il instrumente, donc celle du pays où l'acte est passé et ce cas est visé par l'article 18. Et, pour ce qui est des actes établis par des consuls, la validité de l'acte dressé selon la loi de l'Etat d'envoi du consul résulte des conventions consulaires dont la présente convention réserve l'application (article 27).

Enfin l'absence de mention dans l'article 18 des actes publics permet, par application de la règle générale, de valider les actes dressés par un officier public qui aurait jugé utile, comme cela arrive aux Pays-Bas, de suivre les formes prévues par la loi étrangère qui régit l'acte quant au fond.

L'article 18, dans son second alinéa, exclut de son champ d'application la constitution, le transfert et l'extinction des *droits réels* portant sur une chose. Cette exclusion s'explique, non seulement parce que les formes requises pour ces opérations (par exemple la tradition réelle) relèvent généralement de la loi de situation de la chose, mais surtout parce qu'une autre convention est prévue pour régler les conflits de lois en matière de droits réels et qu'il n'appartenait pas à la présente de préjuger les solutions qui seront alors retenues[100].

L'exclusion ne concerne que les formes de la constitution, du transfert ou de l'extinction des droits réels – le partage étant inclus implicitement dans cette énumération –, mais non celles du contrat qui aurait pour objet l'une de ces opérations. Ainsi les formes d'un contrat de vente d'une chose sont soumises à l'article 18 en tant qu'il s'agit d'un acte créateur d'obligations, mais les effets «réels» de ce contrat ne sont pas réglés par ledit article.

A cette exclusion, prévue à l'article 18, s'ajoute bien entendu celle des formes des actes exclus par l'article premier du domaine général de la convention et qu'il est inutile d'énumérer à nouveau.

3. Notion de forme. – L'article 18 ne définit pas ce qu'il faut comprendre par «forme» des actes. Il a paru plus réaliste de ne pas prendre position sur ce redoutable problème de qualification dont l'importance est d'ailleurs quelque peu réduite par les solutions apportées au problème de rattachement, qui rapprochent dans une assez large mesure la forme et le fond.

---

[100] *Cf.* en Allemagne, art. 11, al. 2 EGBGB; en Italie, art. 26 al. 2 Disp. prél. C. civ.; au Benelux, art. 19 *in fine* projet 1969.

B. Lois applicables

4. *Le principe de l'application alternative de la lex causae et de la lex loci actus.* – Le système retenu par l'article 18 est un compromis entre la *favor negotii*, qui pousse à un certain libéralisme en matière de forme des actes, et le respect dû à la forme qui, le plus souvent, ne fait que mettre en œuvre des exigences de fond.

Il n'a pas paru possible de suivre, dans la première direction, l'exemple de la Convention de La Haye du 5 octobre 1961 sur les conflits de lois en matière de forme des dispositions testamentaires. La *favor testamenti* se justifie par le fait que le testament est un acte de dernière volonté qui, par hypothèse, ne pourra pas être refait lorsque sa validité, après le décès du testateur, sera mise en cause. Cette considération ne vaut pas pour les autres actes juridiques pour lesquels une trop grande liberté en matière de forme reviendrait à priver de tout effet les exigences formulées en ce domaine par les diverses législations, dans un but souvent très légitime. Au surplus, les liens entre les questions de forme et les questions de preuve (article 19) rendent souhaitable une limitation des lois applicables à la forme.

En revanche, afin d'éviter que les parties ne soient surprises par une annulation de leur acte pour un vice de forme inattendu, l'article 18 a tout de même prévu un système assez souple, reposant sur l'application alternative de la loi du lieu de conclusion de l'acte et de celle qui le régit au fond.

Cet éventail de lois applicables a paru suffisant et c'est pourquoi a été écartée l'application éventuelle de la loi de la nationalité ou de la résidence habituelle communes des parties[101]. En revanche, aucune hiérarchie n'a été établie entre la *lex causae et la lex loci actus*. Il suffit que l'acte soit valable selon l'une de ces deux lois pour que soient écartées les causes de nullité en la forme de l'autre[102].

Le renvoi doit être écarté en matière de forme, comme en toute autre matière réglée par la convention (*cf.* article 21).

5. *Problèmes posés par l'application à la forme de la loi qui régit l'acte au fond.* – L'application à la forme de la *lex causae* est déjà admise, à titre principal ou à titre subsidiaire, par le droit des six Etats contractants et se justifie amplement par les liens rationnels unissant le fond et la forme[103].

---

[101] L'application éventuelle de la loi nationale commune est prévue expressément par l'article 26 des Dispositions préliminaires au Code civil italien. V. aussi art. 2315 du projet français de 1967.

[102] La solution retenue s'inspire de celle qui a été consacrée, mais dans un cadre plus large, par Cass. it. 30 avril 1969 (*supra* note 57).

[103] Solution retenue à titre principal en Allemagne, art. 11 EGBGB; à titre subsidiaire en Italie (art. 26 disp. prél.) et en France (Cass. 28 mai 1963 [*supra*

La détermination de la *lex causae* doit se faire, lorsqu'il s'agit d'un contrat, par application des articles 2 à 6 de la convention. L'article 18 règle spécialement l'hypothèse du conflit mobile, dans laquelle, conformément, à l'article 3, la *lex causae* a changé depuis la date de conclusion du contrat. La solution retenue est la plus libérale, puisqu'elle prévoit, en faveur de la validité, l'application alternative de la loi qui régissait le fond de l'acte au moment de sa passation ou de celle qui le régit au moment de la contestation.

Toutefois, l'application à la forme de la *lex causae* la plus récente – lorsqu'elle est la plus favorable à la validité de l'acte – ne doit pas préjudicier aux tiers qui avaient pu de bonne foi compter sur l'application de la *lex causae* initiale selon laquelle l'acte était nul en la forme. Cette réserve du droit des tiers est mentionnée dans l'article 3 et sa portée est assez générale pour couvrir le changement corrélatif de la loi applicable à la forme.

6. *Problèmes posés par l'application à la forme de l'acte de la loi du lieu où il est intervenu.* – L'application à la forme de la loi du lieu de passation de l'acte résulte de la maxime multiséculaire «*locus regit actum*», également admise, le plus souvent à titre principal, par le droit des six Etats contractants[104].

Toutefois la détermination du pays où l'acte «est intervenu» donne lieu à une difficulté classique lorsque l'acte est formé de plusieurs déclarations, par exemple dans l'hypothèse du contrat par correspondance. Plutôt que de choisir ici, plus au moins artificiellement, entre le lieu de l'émission de l'offre et celui de l'émission de l'acceptation, comme le font certaines codifications récentes[105], l'article 18 de la convention retient une solution plus originale et apparemment plus réaliste, inspirée directement de l'article 43 du projet Frankenstein d'un code européen de droit international privé, selon laquelle la validité quant à la forme de chacune des déclarations est appréciée séparément. Cette solution est conforme à la justification actuelle de la règle *locus regit actum* qui repose sur la commodité des parties. Il suffit donc que chacune des parties ait respecté les exigences de forme du lieu où elle a fait la déclaration qui lui incombait pour que l'acte soit valable.

Toutefois, si la loi du pays où l'une des déclarations a été faite pose une exigence de forme qu'on peut qualifier de «bilatérale» en ce sens qu'elle doit être remplie par l'acte tout entier (par exemple l'exigence du «double» en matière de contrats synallagmatiques, article 1325 Code

---

note 35] et projet de 1967, art. 2315); admise implicitement par art. 19 projet Benelux.

[104] V. les références à la note précédente.

[105] *Cf.* art. 13, al. 4 du traité Benelux.

Napoléon, ou encore l'exigence d'une double signature pour la validité de l'acte), cette exigence doit être suivie, même si elle est inconnue de la loi du pays où intervient l'autre déclaration.

7. *Réserve des lois de police.* – La mention de l'article 18 figurant dans l'article 7 implique que le système d'application alternative de la *lex causae* et de la *lex loci actus* peut être écarté au profit de la loi de police d'un pays avec lequel l'acte juridique présente également des liens étroits.

Il est en effet apparu que certaines règles de forme avaient un caractère impératif si marqué qu'elles devaient recevoir application même si leurs exigences n'étaient pas formulées par l'une des lois normalement applicables à la forme aux termes de l'article 18.

Ont été citées, comme pouvant éventuellement tomber sous le coup de cette réserve: – les règles de forme édictées par la loi de situation d'un immeuble pour les contrats non translatifs de propriété portant sur cet immeuble et conclus dans un pays étranger; – les règles de forme édictées par le pays d'exécution d'un contrat de travail, notamment la forme écrite de la clause de non concurrence, même si la forme orale est admise par la loi du lieu de conclusion ou par la loi choisie par les parties; – les règles de forme en matière de vente à tempérament.

Bien entendu, conformément au système établi par l'article 7, il appartiendra dans chaque cas au juge saisi d'apprécier si la «nature ou l'objet particuliers» de ces lois de police peut justifier l'exclusion des règles prévues à l'article 18.

Article 19 (Preuve)

1. L'article 19 règle les conflits de lois concernant la preuve des obligations.

Aucune règle de principe ne vise la preuve en général. Cette omission tient à ce que le Groupe de travail a estimé ne pas devoir prendre parti sur la nature juridique du droit de la preuve, situé aux confins du droit de la procédure et du droit substantiel. Il a cru préférable de ne régler que certaines questions soulevées par le droit des preuves et de ne pas lier l'interprète, par une disposition d'ordre général, sur les questions non tranchées par la convention, comme par exemple l'obtention des preuves à l'étranger et notamment les *commissions rogatoires*.

Trois grandes questions ont été réglées, qui font chacune l'objet d'un alinéa distinct. Il s'agit de l'objet et de la charge de la preuve, de l'admissibilité des modes de preuve des actes juridiques et enfin de quelques questions concernant la force probante des documents écrits, au sens donné à cette expression dans les pays de droit latin.

2. Objet et charge de la preuve

L'alinéa premier de l'article 19 soumet à la loi applicable au rapport juridique «l'existence et la force des présomptions légales ainsi que la charge de la preuve»[106]. Cette solution ne soulève guère de difficultés, les matières visées touchant au fond du droit et ne pouvant être dissociées de la loi qui le régit. A titre d'exemple, la présomption de faute qui pèse dans certaines législations sur le gardien d'une chose qui a causé un dommage peut, selon les cas, tomber devant la preuve, soit de l'absence de faute, soit de la cause étrangère, soit seulement de la faute de la victime, soit être irréfragable. Il est clair que l'organisation d'une telle présomption est une question de fond qui ne peut dépendre que de la loi qui régit la responsabilité civile.

La seconde phrase du premier alinéa apporte un tempérament à la règle en disposant que «les conséquences à déduire de l'attitude des parties en cours du procès sont régies par la loi du for». Ce texte vise certaines dispositions qui existent dans le droit procédural de certains Etats, notamment de l'Allemagne, et qui, même qualifiées de présomptions légales, se rattachent étroitement à la procédure et ne peuvent dépendre que de la loi du for. Il en est ainsi, à titre d'exemple, de la règle qui, en cas de défaut d'une partie, présume bien fondée l'allégation de la partie qui comparaît, ou encore de celle qui présume que le silence gardé par une partie au procès sur les faits allégués par l'autre partie vaut accord de celle-ci sur leur existence.

3. Admissibilité des modes de preuve des actes juridiques

Le second alinéa de l'article 19 concerne exclusivement l'admissibilité des modes de preuve des *actes* juridiques (au sens d'acte de volonté, *negotium*). Le texte ne prend pas position sur les faits juridiques proprement dits (accident, décès) dont la preuve est très généralement soumise à la loi du for.

En ce qui concerne les actes juridiques, le texte consacre l'application alternative de la loi du for et de celle qui régit la forme de l'acte. Cette solution libérale, très favorable à la preuve de l'acte, est déjà admise en France et dans les pays du Benelux[107]. Elle paraît être la

[106] Rédaction inspirée de celle de l'article 20, al. 2 traité Benelux.

[107] V. art. 20 al. 3 du traité Benelux et, en France, Cass. 24 février 1959 *(Isaac)*, D. 1959 J. 485; 12 février 1963 *(Ruffini* c. *Sylvestre)*, Rev. crit. 53 (1964) p. 121 s.

seule qui puisse concilier les exigences de la loi du for et le souci de respecter les prévisions légitimes des parties lors de la conclusion de leur acte.

La loi du for détermine normalement les modes de preuve de l'acte juridique (1° phrase de l'alinéa 2). Si cette loi admet la preuve par témoins d'un contrat, elle doit être suivie, quelles que soient sur ce point les dispositions plus sévères de la loi qui régit l'acte quant au fond ou quant à la forme.

En revanche, dans le cas inverse, si la loi qui régit la forme de l'acte se contente d'un accord verbal et admet que cet accord puisse être prouvé par témoins, les prévisions des parties qui ont fait confiance à cette loi seraient déjouées si cette preuve leur était refusée au seul motif que la loi du tribunal saisi exige la preuve par écrit de tous les actes juridiques. Il faut donc permettre aux parties de se prévaloir, devant le tribunal saisi, des modes de preuve admis par la loi de la forme et tel est le sens de la seconde phrase de l'alinéa.

Toutefois, ce libéralisme ne doit pas conduire à imposer au juge saisi des modes de preuve qui seraient incompatibles avec sa loi de procédure. Ainsi s'explique la précision qui figure dans le dernier membre de phrase de l'alinéa 2, qui permet au juge, sans même avoir recours à l'ordre public, d'écarter les modes de preuve qu'il ignorerait, comme le témoignage de l'une des parties ou la commune renommée. On a également considéré le cas des droits soumis à une inscription sur un registre public, pour estimer que l'autorité chargée de la tenue de ce registre pourrait, grâce à cette disposition, n'admettre que les modes de preuve prévus par sa propre loi.

Tel étant le système général adopté, une précision a dû être apportée quant à la loi de la forme, applicable alternativement avec la loi du for.

Le texte se réfère à «toute loi, visée à l'article 18, selon laquelle l'acte est valable quant à la forme». Cette formule signifie que si, par exemple, l'acte est valable en la forme selon la loi qui le régit au fond mais ne l'est pas selon la loi du lieu où il a été passé, les parties pourront se prévaloir seulement des modes de preuve prévus par la première de ces deux lois, même si la seconde est plus libérale en matière de preuve. La place faite en matière de preuve à la loi de la forme suppose d'évidence que cette loi de forme ait été respectée. En revanche si l'acte est valable en la forme selon les deux lois *(lex causae* et *lex loci actus)* visées à l'article 18, les parties pourront se prévaloir des modes de preuve prévus par l'une ou l'autre de ces lois.

4. Force probante

Le troisième alinéa de l'article 19 règle certaines questions qui relèvent, dans les pays de droit latin, de la notion de force probante.

Il eût sans doute été plus élégant de poser une règle générale sur la loi applicable à la force probante, comme le fait, par exemple, l'article 20, alinéa 4, du projet Benelux. Mais il est très vite apparu que cette notion n'était pas comprise de la même façon dans le droit des divers Etats membres et il a semblé plus expédient de se borner à apporter quelques solutions particulières aux problèmes les plus urgents.

La méthode suivie oblige à préciser le domaine des règles posées par l'alinéa 3 de l'article 19, avant d'analyser les solutions qu'il retient.

Domaine

Ce domaine doit être précisé quant aux actes visés et quant aux questions tranchées.

5. Actes visés

Le texte vise «un document écrit sous seing privé, constatant des obligations à la charge de son ou de ses signataires». Cette rédaction très précise appelle plusieurs observations.

– L'acte visé est un document écrit. Cette précision montre bien que le texte envisage ici l'acte instrumentaire et non l'opération juridique que cet instrument constate.

– Ce document écrit constate des obligations à la charge de son ou de ses signataires. Il s'agit donc d'un écrit au sens strict du terme, revêtu de la signature de celui ou de ceux qu'il engage. On a voulu par là éliminer des documents douteux, tels que des copies ou des témoignages écrits par des tiers, ou la lettre d'une partie faisant allusion aux obligations de l'autre.

– Enfin et surtout, le texte ne vise que les documents sous seing privé. L'article 19 ne comporte aucune règle concernant la force probante des actes publics.

Les raisons de cette exclusion sont d'abord, pour une part, celles qui ont été mentionnées sous l'article 18, et principalement la difficulté de donner une définition de l'acte public qui soit acceptable par tous les Etats membres. En outre, il est apparu qu'une disposition sur la force probante des actes publics – qui aurait évidemment prévu l'application de la loi de l'Etat dont l'officier public tient ses pouvoirs – aurait dû être complétée par une règle attribuant compétence exclusive aux tribunaux de cet Etat pour se prononcer sur la force probante dudit acte. Il a semblé qu'une telle règle ne serait pas à sa place dans une convention concernant seulement les conflits de lois en matière d'obligations.

6. Questions tranchées

L'article 19, alinéa 3, retient seulement deux questions, étroitement liées entre elles.

La première question est celle de «la mesure dans laquelle un document écrit ... fait preuve suffisante [des] obligations [qu'il constate]». Soit un document écrit, signé des parties et constatant un contrat. Ce document écrit est par hypothèse admis comme mode de preuve du contrat. Mais il se peut que, selon la loi applicable, ce document vaille preuve légale du contrat, en ce sens que le juge est obligé, sur production de ce document, de tenir le contrat pour prouvé. Il se peut au contraire que la loi applicable permette au juge d'estimer insuffisante cette preuve par le document et l'autorise à réclamer des preuves additionnelles. D'où la nécessité de préciser la loi applicable.

La seconde question est celle des «modes de preuve admis outre et contre le contenu [du] document», selon la vieille terminologie du Code Napoléon (article 1341), reprise par l'article 19. La question est de savoir si le juge a l'obligation de s'en tenir aux dispositions figurant sur le document écrit qui lui est produit, ou s'il peut accepter, par d'autres modes de preuve tels que le témoignage, la preuve que des compléments ou des modifications ont été apportées par les parties à ces dispositions écrites.

Les autres questions entrant généralement sous le concept de force probante n'ont pas été tranchées par la convention. Il en est ainsi, par exemple, de la vérification de la sincérité de la signature, ou de la détermination du caractère public ou privé de l'acte.

Dans un ordre d'idées assez voisin, il est bien certain que la convention ne concerne aucunement la *légalisation,* les problèmes de force probante et ceux de légalisation étant tout à fait distincts.

7. *Lois applicables*

L'alinéa 3 soumet les deux questions susmentionnées à «la loi qui régit la validité en la forme de l'acte selon l'article 18».

Cette solution, comme celle qui, dans l'alinéa précédent, concerne l'admissibilité des modes de preuve, est la seule qui assure aux parties le respect de leurs prévisions légitimes. Si les parties se sont ménagées, conformément à la loi qui régit la forme de l'acte, une preuve préconstituée et si elles se sont assurées que, selon cette loi, ce document écrit faisait preuve suffisante de leur contrat, c'est à bon droit qu'elles ne se sont ménagées aucune preuve complémentaire et leurs prévisions seraient trompées si, par application de la loi du for, une preuve additionnelle leur était demandée. De même, si la loi de la forme exclut toute preuve non écrite outre ou contre le contenu aux actes instrumentaires, les parties sont assurées qu'aucune modification non écrite ne peut leur être opposée et elles seraient donc trompées si la loi du for, autorisant que cette «contrepreuve» fût rapportée par témoins, leur était appliquée.

Inversement, si la loi de la forme prévoit que des modifications au contenu de l'acte écrit peuvent être prouvées par témoins, la partie qui se serait ménagée cette preuve testimoniale serait trompée si la loi du for lui interdisait de la produire.

Tel étant la justification de la règle, et compte tenu de ce que l'article 18 prévoit que deux lois peuvent s'appliquer, alternativement, à la forme de l'acte, il a fallu préciser laquelle de ces deux lois s'appliquerait aux questions réglées par l'alinéa 3 de l'article 19.

Le texte retient en principe la loi selon laquelle le document vaut comme instrument de preuve. Il est possible en effet que, selon l'une des deux lois visées à l'article 18, le document (par exemple une lettre missive) vaille seulement comme commencement de preuve par écrit et que, selon l'autre, moins exigeante pour ce qui est de la rédaction des actes instrumentaires, il vaille preuve écrite. C'est alors la seconde de ces lois qui s'appliquera.

Mais si le document vaut preuve écrite selon les deux lois visées à l'article 18, et si ces deux lois règlent de façon contradictoire les problèmes ici envisagés, un choix est nécessaire. La convention a donné la préférence à la loi qui régit l'acte au fond.

Il faut enfin mentionner la réserve des lois de police, qui résulte de la mention à l'article 7 du troisième alinéa de l'article 19.

L'hypothèse envisagée est celle où les parties ont rédigé un écrit qui n'était pas exigé pour la validité de l'acte par la *lex loci actus,* ni même peut-être par la loi régissant l'acte au fond, mais qui était exigé par la loi de police d'un Etat avec lequel le contrat présente des liens étroits (par exemple en matière de contrat de travail ou de vente à tempérament). Le sens de la mention de l'article 19, al. 3, dans l'article 7 est que la force probante de cet écrit doit être appréciée par référence à la loi qui l'exige et non, comme il est prévu à l'article 19, al. 3, par référence à celle qui régit la validité en la forme de l'acte.

Article 20 (Incapacité d'une partie)

La convention ne contient pas de règle générale sur la loi qui régit la capacité. Une règle aurait pu être formulée puisque dans les six Etats fondateurs de la C.E.E. la capacité (et l'incapacité) d'une personne sont régies par sa loi nationale. Mais étant donné que le rôle de la nationalité en matière de statut personnel semble s'affaiblir et qu'il est possible que la convention soit mise en vigueur dans des Etats, comme le Royaume Uni, l'article 20 se borne à régler le cas où l'incapacité, qu'elle soit régie par la loi nationale ou par la loi du domicile, ne pourra être invoquée. Des dispositions analogues, tendant à protéger la partie qui a cru contracter avec une personne apparemment capable, se trouvent dans la loi uniforme Benelux (article 2), l'article 2291 du projet français, dans les dispositions générales précédant au Code civil italien (article 17) et dans la loi introductive du Code civil allemand (article 7).

Il est à signaler que les dispositions de l'article s'appliquent même si les parties ne sont pas de nationalité différente. Un Français mineur qui a contracté en Belgique avec un compatriote majeur ne pourra donc invoquer avec fruit son incapacité contre son cocontractant si celui-ci l'a considéré, de bonne foi et conformément à la loi du lieu de l'acte, comme capable. C'est à la partie, qui défend le contrat, de prouver qu'elle était de bonne foi et qu'elle n'a pas agi imprudemment en supposant que l'autre partie était capable.

Article 21 (Exclusion du renvoi)

Cet article exclut le renvoi.

Il est évident qu'en matière d'obligations contractuelles, le renvoi ne doit jouer aucun rôle si les parties ont choisi la loi applicable à leur contrat. Si elles l'ont fait c'est bien avec l'intention que cette loi soit applicable dans ses dispositions matérielles; leur choix exclut alors tout renvoi à une autre loi[108].

L'exclusion du renvoi s'impose aussi lorsque les parties n'ont pas (explicitement ou implicitement) choisi une loi. Dans ce cas le contrat est régi, en vertu de l'article 4, al. 1er, par la loi du pays avec lequel il présente les liens les plus étroits. Le deuxième alinéa précise que ce pays est celui où la partie qui doit fournir la prestation caractéristique a sa résidence habituelle. Il ne serait pas logique que le juge, malgré cette localisation expresse, soumette le contrat, par le jeu du renvoi, à la loi d'un autre pays pour la seule raison que la règle de conflit du pays où le contrat a été localisé contient d'autres rattachements. Ceci vaut également lorsque le dernier alinéa de l'article 4 s'applique et que le juge a localisé le contrat à l'aide d'indices qui lui ont paru décisifs. En matière d'obligations extra-contractuelles l'exclusion du renvoi

---

[108] *Cf. Kegel,* IPR p. 161 ss.; *Batiffol/Lagarde* I p. 374; art. 2284 du projet français; art. 2 de la Convention sur la loi applicable aux ventes à caractère international d'objets mobiliers corporels.

a pu être proposée sans hésitation parce que la règle générale, consacrant l'applicabilité de la loi du pays où le fait dommageable s'est
produit, est accompagnée de la règle de l'alinéa 2. Cette dernière règle
reconnaît que la situation résultant d'un fait dommageable peut avoir
une connexion prépondérante avec un pays autre que celui où ce fait
s'est produit, par exemple si toutes les parties intéressées ont leur
domicile dans un pays et que le fait dommageable a eu lieu dans un
autre pays. Dans ce cas la loi du premier pays devra être appliquée.
L'article lui-même opère donc le renvoi qui pourrait découler de la
règle de conflit de la *lex loci delicti.* Que cette règle renvoie à une
autre loi est d'ailleurs difficile à concevoir.

Article 22 (Ordre public)

Cet article reprend pour la formulation de l'ordre public celle qui
est retenue depuis 1956 dans les conventions de la Conférence de La
Haye de droit international privé. A la différence de l'article 22 de la
loi uniforme Benelux, le présent article ne fait pas mention de la fraude
à la loi. Mais cela ne veut pas dire que la fraude à la loi ne pourrait
jamais jouer un rôle. Elle pourra être prise en considération lorsqu'elle
se traduit par une violation de l'ordre public.

La notion de l'incompatibilité manifeste avec l'ordre public oblige
le juge à motiver plus sérieusement l'existence de l'exception[109]. Il a
été par ailleurs admis au cours des discussions que l'ordre public ne
devrait pas être invoqué à l'encontre de lois étrangères dans le seul
but d'assurer *l'application* de dispositions internes contraires aux dispositions des Traités instituant les Communautés Européennes.

Article 23 (Clause générale d'application et d'interprétation)

1. Cet article s'inspire d'une formule élaborée par la Commission des
Nations pour le Droit Commercial International.

Le projet de révision de la loi uniforme sur la vente internationale
et l'avant-projet de convention sur la prescription et les délais dans
la vente internationale comportent en effet la disposition suivante:
«Dans l'interprétation et l'application de la présente Convention, il
sera tenu compte de son caractère international et de la nécessité d'en
promouvoir l'uniformité».

L'article 23 rappelle qu' en interprétant une convention internatio-

---

[109] *Cf.* Conférence de La Haye, Actes et documents de la Neuvième Session
III: Forme des testaments (1961) rapport explicatif p. 170.

nale il faut tenir compte de son caractère international et que, par
conséquent, le juge ne pourra assimiler les dispositions de la convention, quant à leur interprétation, à des dispositions de droit purement
internes. Il est apparu que l'un des avantages de cet article pourrait
être de permettre aux parties de se prévaloir en justice de décisions
rendues dans d'autres pays.

C'est dans l'esprit de cet article que doit être résolu le problème de
la *qualification,* sur lequel, à l'imitation de loi uniforme Benelux, du
projet français et de nombreuses conventions de La Haye, la Convention s'abstient de formuler une règle particulière.

Chapitre IV: Les dispositions finales

Article 24 (Caractère de la convention)

Dans les Etats contractants les dispositions des articles 1 à 23 seront
applicables même si la loi qu'elles désignent n'est pas celle d'un Etat
contractant. Elles s'appliquent donc *erga omnes* et indépendamment
de toute condition de réciprocité. Telle est la solution de la convention
de La Haye sur les conflits de lois en matière de forme des dispositions
testamentaires (article 6), de la convention de La Haye sur lo loi applicable en matière d'accidents de la circulation routière (article 11), et
de la convention de La Haye du 15 juin 1955 sur la loi applicable aux
ventes à caractère international d'objets mobiliers corporels (article 7).

Article 25 (Réserve du droit communautaire)

L'article 25 a pour objet d'éviter les conflits entre la présente Convention et les actes normatifs émanant des institutions communautaires
ainsi que le droit national harmonisé en exécution de ces actes, en
assurant la primauté des seconds sur la première. Cette disposition
n'a pas soulevé de difficultés particulières dès lors que (voir aussi la
déclaration annexée à la convention) les instruments visés à cet article
sont préparés en étroite coopération avec les experts des Etats membres qui participent à tous les stades à l'élaboration des textes.

Si les Etats contractants concluent, après l'entrée en vigueur de la
présente convention entre eux, des conventions qui y dérogent ces
conventions l'emporteront de toute façon.

Article 26 (Modification unilatérale de la convention)

Le système de cet article, qui peut être caractérisé comme un système de liberté surveillée, a été inspiré d'une part par le désir de ne pas figer le droit international privé et de laisser aux Etats la possibilité d'adapter leur législation aux évolutions futures et d'autre part par le souci que l'uniformité acquise ne soit pas abandonnée inconsidérément.

Si un Etat veut, dans une matière spéciale, déroger aux dispositions de la loi uniforme ou y apporter un complément en modifiant sa législation interne, cet Etat doit en prévenir les autres Etats contractants par l'intermédiaire du Secrétaire-Général du Conseil des Communautés Européennes. Celui-ci organisera alors à la demande de tout Etat membre des consultations entre les Etats contractants en vue d'arriver à un accord.

Si aucun Etat ne demande la consultation ou si dans un délai de deux ans, les consultations ne mènent pas un accord, l'Etat qui a l'intention de modifier sa législation pourra y procéder dans le sens qu'il avait indiqué.

Article 27 (Réserve des conventions antérieures)

En devenant partie à la présente convention les Etats n'entendent pas se soustraire aux obligations découlant pour eux des conventions entrées antérieurement en vigueur à leur égard. L'article 27 le confirme en disposant que les règles uniformes ne portent pas atteinte à l'application de ces conventions, qu'elles soient bilatérales ou multilatérales.

Articles 28 et 29 (Nouvelles conventions)

L'article 28 est le pendant de l'article 26. Il vise les conventions multilatérales ayant pour objet principal un règlement de droit international privé dans l'une des matières régies par les dispositions du titre 2. Puisque de telles conventions, qui pourraient être conclues dans un cadre plus large, par exemple dans celui de la Conférence de La Haye de droit international privé, du Conseil de l'Europe ou des Nations Unies, sont de nature à substituer à ces dispositions d'autres règles uniformes applicables *erga omnes* ou sur la base de la réciprocité, la procédure de consultation prévue par l'article 26 devra être suivie. Toutefois le délai de deux ans est ramené à un an. L'article 28 s'applique même si un Etat contractant désire dénoncer une telle convention. La dénonciation pourrait surprendre un autre Etat contractant en train de préparer son adhésion à la convention.

Mais l'article ne s'applique pas aux conventions multilatérales lorsque les règles de conflit de loi qu'elles contiennent n'en forment pas l'objet ou pas l'objet principal (traités d'établissement, conventions consulaires, traités de reconnaissance et d'exécution).

L'atteinte portée par ces conventions mixtes, ainsi que par des conventions bilatérales sera le plus souvent si légère que la liberté des Etats de conclure de telles conventions mérite d'être respectée. Si néanmoins l'uniformité risque d'être compromise par de tels accords recherchés systématiquement, l'application de l'article 29, prévoyant des consultations entre les Etats intéressés en vue de diminuer ce risque, pourra être demandée.

Enfin il est à signaler que les conventions n'ayant pour objet que des dispositions de droit matériel ne sont pas soumises à la procédure de consultation.

Article 30 (Révision de la convention)

Si les articles 26, 28 et 29 concernent la possibilité de déroger unilatéralement aux règles uniformes, l'article 30 prévoit la modification directe de ces règles par une conférence de révision convoquée, à la demande d'un Etat contractant, par le Président du Conseil des Communautés européennes.

Articles 31 à 36 (Clauses protocolaires usuelles)

Les articles 31 à 36 contiennent les clauses protocolaires usuelles. S'agissant d'une convention à vocation universelle, à la différence de ce qui est prévu par l'article 62 de la Convention concernant la compétence judiciaire et l'exécution des décisions en matière civile et commerciale, signée à Bruxelles le 27 septembre 1968, la présente convention entrera en vigueur le premier jour du troisième mois suivant le dépôt du *cinquième* instrument de ratification (article 33).

La convention ne contient aucune disposition transitoire. La réglementation de cette question – les nouvelles règles s'appliqueront-elles d'office aux procès déjà en cours au jour de l'entrée en vigueur de la convention? – est laissée au droit transitoire de chaque Etat.

ANNEXE

I. Liste des participants

Présents aux
réunions nos.:

Belgique

M. *P. Jenard* (Président du groupe), Directeur d'administration au Ministère des Affaires Etrangères et du Commerce extérieur — 1 à 11

Mme *A.-M. Delvaux*, Conseiller au Ministère de la Justice — 1 à 11

Mme *Oschinsky*, Directeur d'administration au Ministère de la Justice — 1, 2, 3, 4, 5, 6, 7 et 11

M. *R. Vander Elst*, Professeur à l'Université Libre de Bruxelles, Avocat près la Cour d'Appel — 1, 2, 3, 4, 5, 7, 8, 9, 10 et 11

M. *F. Rigaux*, Professeur à l'Université de Louvain — 1, 2, 3, 4 et 5

M. *G. Van Hecke*, Professeur à l'Université de Louvain — 1, 2, 3, 4

M. *Meersschant*, Directeur d'administration au Ministère de l'Emploi et du Travail — 9, 10 et 11

M. *A. Coppy*, Secrétaire d'Administration, Ministère de la Justice — 9, 10 et 11

M. *G. Denis*, Magistrat délégué au Ministère des Affaires Etrangères et du Commerce extérieur — 4

République Fédérale d'Allemagne

M. le Prof. *K. Arndt*, Professor an der Universität Münster; Oberlandesgerichtspräsident i. R. — 1 à 11

M. *B. Klingsporn*, Ministerialrat, Bundesministerium der Justiz — 1 à 11

M. *E. Rebmann*, Bundesministerium der Justiz — 2, 3, 4, 5, 6, 7, 8, 9 et 10

M. *Baron*, Bundesministerium für Wirtschaft und Finanzen — 4, 5, 6 et 9

M. W. *Pitzer*, Bundesministerium für Wirtschaft und   7, 10, 11
Finanzen

M. A. *Klein*, Bundesministerium für Arbeit   10

M. *Scheele*, Regierungsrat, Bundesministerium für Wirt-   1
schaft und Finanzen, Rechtsreferat

M. J. *Wolff*, Bundesministerium für Wirtschaft und   2, 3 et 8
Finanzen

France

M. H. *Batiffol*, Doyen Honoraire; Professeur à la Faculté   1, 2, 3, 4, 5, 6, 7, 9
de Droit de Paris   et 11

M. J. *Baudoin*, Président de Chambre à la Cour d'Appel   2
de Paris

M. P. *Grimaldi*, Magistrat au Ministère de la Justice   1, 2, 3, 4 et 5

M. P. *Lagarde*, Professeur à la Faculté de Droit de   1 à 11
Paris I

M. J. *Lemontey*, Chef du bureau Droit européen et   7 et 8
international, Ministère de la Justice

Italie

M. R. *Fulgenzi*, Magistrato di Tribunale addetto al Mini-   1 à 11
stero della Giustizia

M. M. *Giuliano*, Professore all'Università di Milano   1 à 11

M. R. *Miccio*, Consigliere di Corte di Cassazione; Mini-   1, 4 et 6
stero di Grazia e Giustizia

Luxembourg

M. A. *Huss*, Procureur Général d'Etat Honoraire   1, 2, 3, 4, 5, 6, 7, 10,
                                                             11

M. R. *Heiderscheid*, Président du tribunal d'arrondisse-   2, 4, 5, 6, 7 et 10
ment; Palais de Justice

M. C. *Wampach*, Substitut du Procureur d'Etat   2, 3, 5, 7, et 8

M. R. *Thiry*, Vice-Président du tribunal d'arrondisse-   2, 3, 4 et 8
ment; Palais de Justice

M. A. *Weitzel*, Premier-juge au Tribunal d'arrondisse-   9
ment

Pays-Bas

M. *L. I. de Winter*, Professeur aan de Universiteit van Amsterdam	1, 2, 3, 4, 5, 7, 8, 10 et 11
M. *Th. van Sasse van Ysselt*, Directeur, Ministerie van Justitie	1 à 11
M. *C. W. Dubbink*, Raadsheer bij de Hoge Raad	2, 3, 6, 7, 8, 9, 10, 11
M. *C. D. van Boeschoten*, Avocat près la Cour de Cassation des Pays-Bas; Directeur de l'Institut Juridique International de La Haye	5, 6, 7, 8 et 9

Observateurs

Conférence de La Haye de d. i. p.:

M. *M. H. van Hoogstraten*, Secrétaire Général	1 à 11

Commission Benelux pour l'unification du droit:

Mme *M. Weser*, Chargée de cours à l'Université Libre de Bruxelles; Avocat à la Cour d'Appel	1, 3, 4, 5, 7, 8, 9, 10 et 11

Commission des communautés européennes:

M. *W. Hauschild*, Chef de division

M. *T. Cathala*, Administrateur principal

M. *G. di Marco*, Administrateur

– *ont également participé à certaines réunions:*

M. *I. Schwartz*, Directeur à la D. G. XIV

M. *Maestripieri*, M. *Leleux*, M. *Telchini*, conseillers juridiques

Mme *Espion*, D. G. IV

M. *Geldens*, Chef de division à la D. G. V

M. *Brembati*, M. *H. J. Rimkus*, administrateurs principaux

II. Calendrier des réunions

Réunions préparatoires:

1. 26 au 28 février 1969
2. 20 au 22 octobre 1969
3. 2 et 3 février 1970

Réunions des rapporteurs:

1. 1 au 4 juin 1970
2. 27 et 28 septembre 1972

Réunions du groupe des experts:

1. 28 septembre au 2 octobre 1970
2. 16 au 20 novembre 1970
3. 15 au 19 février 1971
4. 15 au 19 mars 1971
5. 28 juin au 2 juillet 1971
6. 4 au 8 octobre 1971
7. 29 novembre au 3 décembre 1971
8. 31 janvier au 3 février 1971
9. 20 au 24 mars 1972
10. 29 au 31 mai 1972
11. 21 au 23 juin 1972

LIST OF PARTICIPANTS

[G] = Member of the EC Working Group of Experts. – The numbers on the right hand side refer to the participants' reports, to their contributions to the discussion, to the discussion of arguments raised by them with regard to the Draft Convention and to their participation in drafting the Convention.

[G] Mr. *J. van Rijn van Alkemade,*
Ministerie van Justitie,
's Gravenhage, Netherlands

[G] Professor Dr. *Karl Arndt,*   246, 247, 315
Oberlandesgerichtspräsident i. R.,
Bremen, Federal Republic of Germany

Professeur *Henri Batiffol,*   2, 4, 7, 10, 11, 14, 17, 20, 33,
Université de Droit, d'Economie et de Scien-   34, 35, 37, 38, 39, 40, 50, 51,
ces Sociales de Paris,   71, 76, 316
Paris, France

Departementsrådet *Birgitta Blom,*
Justitiedepartementet,
Stockholm, Sweden

[G] *C. D. van Boeschoten,*   317
Avocat,
's Gravenhage, Netherlands

Jur. cand. *Michal Bogdan,*
Universitet i Lund,
Lund, Sweden

Hovrättsfiskal *Pär Boqvist,*
Svea Hovrätt,
Stockholm, Sweden

[G] *Thierry Cathala,*   317
Juge au Tribunal de Grande Instance,
Versailles, France

Kontorchef *N. Christoffersen,*
Forsikringsrådet,
København, Denmark

Fuldmægtig *Jan Collin,*
Handelsministeriet,
København, Denmark

[G] Mme *Anne-Marie Delvaux,*   315
Conseiller juridique,
Ministère de la Justice,
Bruxelles, Belgium

Yves Derain,   20
Chambre de Commerce Internationale,
Paris, France

Direktor *D. Devine,*
Commission of the European Communities,
Bruxelles, Belgium

Professor Dr. *Ulrich Drobnig,*   8, 16, 18, 20, 30, 32, 34, 35,
Max-Planck-Institut für ausländisches und 36, 38, 40, 41, 46, 61, 64,
internationales Privatrecht,   67[115], 82–86
Hamburg, Federal Republic of Germany

Sektionsrat Dr. *Alfred Duchek,*   10
Bundesministerium für Justiz,
Wien, Austria

Marc Fallon,   48[26], 49[29], 50[32], 51[40], 52[43], 53,
La Hulpe, Belgium   54, 55, 60, 61, 73, 78, 87–98

[G] *Pierre Gothot,*   3, 14, 16, 17, 18, 35, 39
Chargé de cours à la Faculté de droit à
Liège,
Jupille sur Meuse, Belgium

Professor Dr. Dr. *Eugen Dietrich Graue,* 19 s., 32, 57[72], 99–104
Universität Kiel,
Kiel, Federal Republic of Germany

[G] *Eamonn Hanley,*
Legal Adviser,
EEC Division,
Dublin, Ireland

M. Hanotiau,
Secrétaire d'Administration,
Bruxelles, Belgium

Professor *Trevor C. Hartley,*   12, 15, 19, 26, 35, 39, 45, 55,
The London School of Economics & Polit-   57[72], 105–113
ical Science,
London, United Kingdom

[G] Dr. *Winfried Hauschild,*   317
Chef de Division,
Commission of the European Communities,
Bruxelles, Belgium

Professor *Lars Hjerner,*   10, 16 s., 23, 34, 35, 36, 38,
Institutet för Utlandsk Rätt AB,   39, 40, 49, 51, 71, 76
Stockholm, Sweden

Dr. *Bernd von Hoffmann,*   1–41, 42, 46[15], 54, 61, 70[129],
Max-Planck-Institut für ausländisches und   72, 75, 76
internationales Privatrecht
Hamburg, Federal Republic of Germany

R. *Holmes,*
Senior Legal Assistant,
Law Commission,
London, United Kingdom

[G] M. *H. van Hoogstraten,*   3, 7, 23, 33, 35, 37, 40, 49, 51,
Secrétaire Général de la Conférence de la   71, 76, 317
Haye de d. i. p.,
's Gravenhage, Netherlands

Univ.-Doz. Dr. *Hans Hoyer,*   2, 6, 24 s., 33, 36, 37, 41, 44[4],
Institut für Rechtsvergleichung,   59, 114–117
Wien, Austria

[G] *Alphonse Huss,*   316
Procureur général d'état hon.,
Luxembourg, Luxembourg

G. *Imbert,*   31
Chef de Division,
Commission of the European Communities,
Bruxelles, Belgium

[G] *P. Jenard,*   52, 65, 70, 71, 74, 76, 79, 245,
Directeur d'administration,   246, 315
Ministère des Affaires Etrangères et du
Commerce Extérieur,
Bruxelles, Belgium

Fuldmægtig R. *Johansen,*
Forsikringsrådet,
København, Denmark

Professor *Heikki Jokela,*   12, 34, 39, 118–120
Juridiska Fakulteten,
Universitetet,
Helsinki, Finland

Rättschefen *Anders Knutsson,*
Justitiedepartementet,
Stockholm, Sweden

Dr. *Gunther Kühne,* LL.M.,　　　　　　　21 s., 36, 40, 121–124
Oberregierungsrat,
Bundesministerium der Justiz,
Bonn, Federal Republic of Germany

[G] Professeur *Paul Lagarde,*　　　　　10, 11, 16, 17, 18, 33, 34, 35,
Boulogne s. Seine, France　　　　　　　38, 39, 40, 49, 52, 54, 71, 72,
　　　　　　　　　　　　　　　　　　　　76, 241, 246, 247, 300–309,
　　　　　　　　　　　　　　　　　　　　316

Professor dr. jur. *Ole Lando,*　　　　2, 3, 6, 8, 12, 13, 14, 15, 16,
Institut for Europæisk Markedsret,　　18, 20, 21, 22, 23, 24, 25, 26,
Handelshøjskolen,　　　　　　　　　　　27, 28, 29, 33, 34, 35, 36, 37,
København, Denmark　　　　　　　　　　38, 39, 40, 41, 44[4], 49, 51, 56,
　　　　　　　　　　　　　　　　　　　　115, 119, 125–154, 156, 161,
　　　　　　　　　　　　　　　　　　　　188, 194

[G] *Jacques Lemontey,*
Ministère de la Justice,
Paris, France

Mr. *Anthony McClellan,*
Barrister of the Legal Service of the Com-
mission of the EC,
Bruxelles, Belgium

Professor *Åke Malmström,*
Uppsala, Sweden

[G] *G. di Marco,*　　　　　　　　　　　317
Verwaltungsrat,
Commission of the European Communities,
Bruxelles, Belgium

[G] Herr *Ollenhauer,*
Commission of the European Communities,
Bruxelles, Belgium

Alfred E. von Overbeck,　　　　　　　9, 23, 32, 34, 35, 38, 40, 43,
Professeur à la Faculté de Droit,　　45, 48[27], 49[29], 50, 51, 52, 53[47],
Fribourg, Switzerland　　　　　　　　　54[52], 55[57], 59, 62[99], 64[106], 70,
　　　　　　　　　　　　　　　　　　　　75, 165–181, 191

Professor *Lennart Pålsson,*
Universitet i Lund,
Lund, Sweden

[G] Professor dr. jur. *Allan Philip,*
Hellerup, Denmark

Cand. jur. *Uffe Lind Rasmussen,*
Danmarks Rederiforening,
København, Denmark

[G] Mrs. *Jane Richardson,*
Legal Assistant,
Law Commission,
London, United Kingdom

Professor *J. W. C. van Rooyen,*
University of Pretoria,
Pretoria, Union of South Africa

Høyesterettsadvokat *Ole Torleif Røed,* Oslo, Norway	48^{23}, 53^{47}, 56, 57, 72, 77, 182 to 185
Professor *J. G. Sauveplanne,* Molengraaff Instituut voor Privaatrecht, Utrecht, Netherlands	12, 13 s., 25, 28, 32, 35, 36, 39, 41, 52, 53, 65^{111}, 186–194

Advokat *P. Scheel,*
Andelsudvalget,
København, Denmark

Karl-Heinz Schilz,
Hauptverwaltungsrat
auprès de la Direction Générale,
Bruxelles, Belgium

Herr *Schlude,*
Berater der Kommission der Europäischen
Gemeinschaften,
Generaldirektion Finanzen und Steuern,
Bruxelles, Belgium

Professor dr. jur. *Torben Svenné Schmidt,*
Institut for Privatret,
Århus Universitet,
Århus, Denmark

Univ.-Professor Dr. *Gerhard Schnorr,*
Innsbruck, Austria

[G] Professor *J. C. Schultsz,* Amsterdam, Netherlands	3, 11, 33, 37, 46, 54, 72, 76
Professor dr. jur. *Erling Chr. Selvig,* Nordisk Institutt for Sjørett, Universitetet i Oslo, Oslo, Norway	8, 10, 11, 16, 18, 19, 24, 29, 30 s., 34, 35, 36, 38, 39, 40, 41, 46, 47, 48, 54, 56, 57, 69, 71, 72, 75, 76, 77, 195–205

Dr. *Kurt Siehr,*   2, 8, 9^{30}, 24, 27, 32, 33, 34, 36,
Max-Planck-Institut für ausländisches und   37, 38, 41, 42–79
internationales Privatrecht,
Hamburg, Federal Republic of Germany

Professor dr. jur. *Erik Siesby,*   3, 5, 16, 19, 22, 33, 35, 37, 40,
Institutet for international ret og europaret,   54, 72, 76, 206–213
København, Denmark

Professor G. O. *Zacharias Sundström,*   55, 57, 58, 72, 77, 214–219
Turku, Finland

Lic. jur. *Paul Volken,*   11, 43, 45, 48^{27}, 49^{29}, 50, 52,
Ittigen, Switzerland 53^{47}, 54^{52}, 55^{57}, 59, 62^{99}, 64^{106},
                                                     70, 75, 165–181, 191

[G] *Brian Walsh,*
Justice of the Supreme Court of Ireland,
Dublin, Ireland

[G] Fuldmægtig *H. Wendler-Petersen,*
Justitsministeriet,
København, Denmark

TABLE OF LITERATURE

Batiffol, Les obligations contractuelles, in: Colloque sur les Conventions communautaires, Université Libre de Bruxelles, 13 et 14 décembre 1974, 9 p. (mimeographed paper).

Cavers, The Common Market's Draft Conflicts Convention on Obligations – Some Preventive Law Aspects: So.Cal.L.Rev. 48 (1974/75) 603–626.

Gamillscheg, Intereuropäisches Arbeitsrecht – Zu zwei Vorschlägen der EWG zum Internationalen Arbeitsrecht: RabelsZ 37 (1973) 284–316.

Haak/Jessurun d'Oliveira, Internationaal overeenkomstenrecht. Beschouwingen rondom en over het Voor-ontwerp E.E.G.-Verdrag nopens de wetten die van toepassing zijn op verbintenissen uit overeenkomsten en niet-contractuele verbintenissen (Mededelingen van de Nederlandse Vereniging voor Internationaal Recht). Deventer: Kluwer 1975, 136 p.

Kahn-Freund, La notion anglaise de la "proper law of the contract" devant les juges et devant les arbitres – Ses développements récents et ses affinités avec l'Avant-projet européen d'unification des règles de conflit en la matière: Rev. crit. 62 (1973) 607–627.

Lagarde, Examen de l'Avant-projet de convention CEE sur la loi applicable aux obligations contractuelles et non contractuelles: Trav. Com. fr. d. i. p. 1971–1973 (1974) 147–201.

Lando, The EC Draft Convention on the Law Applicable to Contractual and Non-Contractual Obligations: RabelsZ 38 (1974) 6–55.

D. Mayer, Comité français de droit international privé – Colloque du 24 mars 1973 sur l'Avant-projet de convention C.E.E. concernant la loi applicable aux obligations contractuelles et non contractuelles: Rev. crit. 62 (1973) 373–380.

Ortiz-Arce, Comunidad Económica Europea y Derecho Internacional Privado: Rev. de Instituciones Europeas 1 (1974) 1067–1118.

Von Overbeck/Volken, Das Internationale Deliktsrecht im Vorentwurf der EWG: RabelsZ 38 (1974) 56–78.

Philip, EF-kommissionens udkast til konvention om lovvalget med hensyn til forpligtelser i og uden for kontraktsforhold: Nord. T. Int. R. 42 (1972) 177–188.

Siehr, Zum Vorentwurf eines EWG-Übereinkommens über das Internationale Schuldrecht: AWD 1973, 569–587.

Vander Elst, L'Unification des règles de conflit de lois dans la C.E.E.: J. Trib. (Brux.) 1973, 249–254 = Foro It. 1973, V, 249–260.

id., Projet de Convention C.E.E. sur la loi applicable – Obligations non contractuelles, in: Colloque sur les Conventions communautaires, Université Libre de Bruxelles, 13 et 14 décembre 1974, 15 p. (mimeographed paper).

TABLE OF CONVENTIONS,
STATUTES AND OTHER INSTRUMENTS

I. EUROPEAN COMMUNITIES
CONVENTIONS AND INSTRUMENTS

The numbers in bold-face type refer to the French and English version of the
articles of the Draft Convention (p. 220–229 and 230–240) and to the principal
comments on them in the Rapport (p. 241–318).

II. OTHER CONVENTIONS AND DRAFTS

Benelux Project, Brussels, July 3,
1969
92, 93, 188, 242, 249, 312
Art. 2: 193, 310
Art. 13: 261
Art. 13 (1): 257 s., 258
Art. 13 (3): 259 s., 260, 270, 271[62]
Art. 13 (4): 270, 303[105]
Art. 14: 89 s., 96, 169[21], 190 s.
Art. 14 (1): 281 s.
Art. 14 (2): 190 s., 284
Art. 17: 192
Art. 19: 301[100], 303[103]
Art. 20 (2): 305[106]
Art. 20 (3): 305[107]
Art. 20 (4): 307
Art. 22: 311
Convention on the Law Applicable to
Traffic Accidents, The Hague, May
4, 1971
51, 92, 172, 292
Art. 3: 169[21], 284 s.
Art. 4: 285, 287
Art. 4 (a): 56, 174
Art. 6: 285
Art. 7: 60, 93, 174, 293
Art. 8: 56, 163, 176 s., 288 s., 290
(no. 5), 291 (no. 7)
Art. 9: 59
Art. 10: 64[107]
Art. 11: 66[112], 312
Art. 13: 64[106]

European Convention on State Im-
munity, Basle, May 16, 1972
179[34]
Convention on the Law Applicable
to Products Liability, The Hague,
October 2, 1973
50, 51, 68, 92, 97, 170[23], 172, 218
Art. 4: 169[21]
Art. 8: 56, 176
Art. 9: 60, 174
Art. 10: 64[107]
Art. 11: 66[112]
Art. 12: 64[106]
Convention on the Law Applicable
to Maintenance Obligations, The
Hague, October 2, 1973
69 s.[128]
Convention on the Limitation Period
in the International Sale of Goods,
New York, June 12, 1974
311
Draft European Convention on Prod-
ucts Liability in Regard to Person-
al Injury and Death, Strasbourg,
March 20, 1975
68, 74, 79
Draft Convention of UNCITRAL
Revising the Hague Convention
Relating to a Uniform Law on
International Sale of Goods
311

III. NATIONAL STATUTES

Austria

Allgemeines Bürgerliches Gesetzbuch
of 1811
Art. 866: 116
Entwurf eines Bundesgesetzes über

das internationale Privat- und Prozeßrecht (1971)
114 s.
§ 35: 9

Belgium

Code civil of 1804/1831
Art. 3: 248
3 (1): 277

Loi relative à la résiliation unilatérale des concessions de vente of
July 27, 1961
13, 142, 278

Czechoslovakia

Loi sur le droit international privé
et de procédure civile of December

4, 1963
Art. 10: 9

France

Code civil of 1804
   Art. 3: 248
      3 (1): 94 s., 277, 281
      3 (3): 153
   Art. 14: 101
   Art. 15: 101
   Art. 1251 no. 3: 300
   Art. 1325: 303 s.
   Art. 1341: 308

Draft of a Statute on P.I.L. (1967)
   249, 312
   Art. 2284: 310[108]
   Art. 2291: 310
   Art. 2312: 281
   Art. 2313: 256, 261
      2313 (2): 268
   Art. 2315: 302[101], 303[103]

Germany

Bürgerliches Gesetzbuch of August
18, 1896
   § 138: 130
   §§ 202–208: 176[33]
   § 242: 130
   § 276 (2): 99
   § 315: 130
   § 823: 99
   § 839: 179[35]
Einführungsgesetz zum Bürgerlichen
Gesetzbuche of August 18, 1896
256
   Art. 7: 248, 310
   Art. 11: 248, 301[100], 302[103]
   Art. 12: 169, 248, 281
   Art. 30: 248
Handelsgesetzbuch of May 10, 1897

   § 92 c (1): 100
   §§ 486 ss.: 202, 204
Verordnung über die Rechtsanwen-
dung bei Schädigungen deutscher
Staatsangehöriger außerhalb des
Reichsgebiets of December 7, 1942
163, 169, 248, 284
Grundgesetz of May 23, 1949
   Art. 20: 101
   Art. 34: 179[35]
Gesetz zur Änderung des Handels-
gesetzbuches und anderer Gesetze
(Seerechtsänderungsgesetz) of June
21, 1972
204[19]
   Art. 1: 202
   Art. 3: 202

Great Britain

Statute of Frauds 1677
149, 162
Law of Property Act 1925
   s. 40 (1): 162
Hire Purchase and Small Debt [Scot-
land] Act 1932
108 s.
   s. 1: 109
   s. 11: 109
Law Reform (Personal Injuries) Act
1948
64 s.[109]

Law Reform (Enforcement of Contracts) Act 1954
162
Hire – Purchase Acts 1964 and 1965
106 s.
Supply of Goods (Implied Terms) Act
1973
106, 109–111, 130
   s. 4: 110
   s. 7: 110
   s. 13: 110
Consumer Credit Bill (Draft)
   cl. 169 (1): 107

Italy

Codice di procedura civile of 1940
   Art. 2: 101

Disposizioni sulla legge in generale
of 1942

Switzerland

USA

INDEX

The numbers in bold-face type refer to the French and English version of the Draft Convention (p. 220–229 and 230–240) and to the Rapport (p. 241–318).